WITHDRAWN

DOGMATICS

HERMANN DIEM

DOGMATICS

Translated by
HAROLD KNIGHT

PHILADELPHIA
THE WESTMINSTER PRESS

230
D56d
56397
Dec. 1966

This is a translation of *Dogmatik: Ihr Weg zwischen Historismus und Existenzialismus*, published by Chr. Kaiser Verlag, Munich, in 1955, as Bd II of *Theologie als kirchliche Wissenschaft: Handreichung zur Einübung ihre Probleme*, by Hermann Diem.

Library of Congress Catalog Card No. 60-7630.

PRINTED IN GREAT BRITAIN

AUTHOR'S FOREWORD

ANYONE who is acquainted with the current debate in dogmatics knows how difficult it is for dogmatics to perform its true task while almost all the participants in the discussion either try to ignore the problematic character of their basic assumptions, or only concern themselves with the question whether dogmatics is still meaningful and necessary. Thus there is hardly any common ground on which the contestants can reach any understanding.

It has seemed to me that the only possible way of making a meaningful contribution to the debate is simply, first, to trace the problems which have been posed, secondly to take up my own position on them, and thirdly to debate my position, as comprehensively as possible, with those who are now in the front rank of the contestants.

The situation is most difficult for those who will not, or cannot, simply adhere to one of the major schools of theological thought and thereafter, as is unfortunately common today, subscribe like disciples to the teaching of one master and read nothing else. It is these people that I have tried to help. Of course I did not intend (nor would it have been possible) to discover a *via media* among all the various conflicting views. And since in order to clarify the problems in question I have had to cut right through all sorts of fixed positions, still less have I wished to create new antagonisms.

Judging by the good reception which my book has had in Germany, it seems that I have in some measure succeeded. And now in the fact that Presbyterian Scotland, alongside German Lutherans, is showing itself interested in the book, I may be permitted to see a sign that what I have envisaged as the task of theology and the Church in Germany, and what I have therefore undertaken, may over and above this have a meaning for the *Oikumene*.

HERMANN DIEM

TÜBINGEN,
Autumn 1958

Professor ordinaries publicus
of Systematic Theology,
Tübingen University.

CONTENTS

CONTENTS

CHAPTER I

THE CHALLENGE TO DOGMATIC THEOLOGY IN HISTORICAL CRITICISM AND EXISTENTIALISM

THE Athanasian Creed is the third ecumenical creed received even by the Churches of the Reformation, and stands not only among the confessional documents of the Lutheran Church, but is acknowledged also by the Evangelical Church in Germany in the preface to its foundation statutes of 13 July 1948.[1] It begins with the following words: "*Quicunque vult salvus esse, ante omnia opus est, ut teneat catholicam fidem, quam nisi quisque integram inviolatamque servaverit, absque dubio in aeternum peribit.* (Whosoever will be saved must above all things hold the Catholic faith. Whosoever does not keep the same pure and intact, will without doubt be eternally lost)." There follow [2] the individual propositions of the Creed, and in conclusion it is affirmed once more: "*Haec est fides catholica, quam nisi quisque fideliter firmiterque crediderit, salvus esse non poterit.* (This is the Catholic faith; whoever does not hold it firmly and faithfully cannot be eternally saved)."

Here faith is quite plainly understood to be a mental assent to the truth of propositions contained in a specific creed. Even though faith is not exhausted in this kind of assent, the latter, at all events, is regarded as an integral and essential part of faith. It is not merely in modern times that this understanding of faith has been disputed, but today it has once more been rejected with particular emphasis. The opposition it finds is directed not only to the presumption that one should subscribe to certain propositions as true and that such subscription is to be defined as faith. Rather, it is doubted whether such propositions have any validity today, and, further,

[1] Where it is quoted from *Bekenntnisschriften der evangelisch-lutherischen Kirche*, 1930, p. 28. [2] *Op. cit.*, p. 30.

whether, in any case, there are any criteria by which they can be demonstrated to be true. Thus dogmatic theology, which is concerned to acquire and apply such criteria, has probably today become the most questionable of all theological disciplines. The fact that dogmatic theologians, generally speaking, disregard this radical challenge to their work, or, if they do take account of it, dispose of it far too lightly, does not mend matters.

In what sense then as regards the teaching, the faith and the confession of the Church, can there be any question of systematic treatment? There are, as the whole history of philosophy and theology attests, endless ways of inculcating systems. All these systems have one thing in common, namely that they are intended to formulate *truth*, and therefore assert their doctrines to be *correct*, no matter what they understand at the time by the idea of truth, nor what methods and criteria they propose to apply for the verification of their formulae. In this most general sense, therefore, theology also, as a doctrine of God, can be nothing other than a system of truth. In that case, dogmatics, as a special discipline of theology, would have the specific task of verifying this teaching about God. If we regard theology as, in this most general sense, a system of knowledge about God, the task of dogmatics offers no special or fundamental difficulties; for "dogma" would then seem to be no different from any other principle by means of which truth is discoverable, and "dogmatics" becomes a system of principles not essentially distinct from corresponding efforts in the broad field of intellectual disciplines. If this be so, then it is clear that, in order not to arouse false expectations (or false suspicions), the term "dogmatics" should as far as possible be avoided; and that, in order to emphasise this common ground, some such phrase as "philosophy of religion" (or "teachings of the faith") should be preferred, as has in fact become the general practice since the nineteenth century.

Unlike the philosophy of religion, theology, however, in so far as it is true to itself, is not concerned with the knowledge of God in this broad sense.[3] Theology occupies itself not with the being of God in Himself, but only with the reflexion of

[3] Cf. Diem, *Theologie als kirchliche Wissenschaft*, BD. I (*Exegese und Historie*), Munich 1952 (henceforth cited as *Theol.*, BD. I), p. 282.

that being in the divine self-revelation attested in the Old and the New Testament. It is only secondarily that it is concerned with the essential being of this self-revealed God. All the pronouncements that theology makes about God presuppose, therefore, a specific historical event. All theological doctrines accordingly are only *a posteriori* judgments about this event in its actuality and significance.

The verification of these doctrines is the special task of dogmatics within the broad framework of theology. But what exactly does such verification imply? It might be considered that the question of truth with which dogmatics was faced was both a question of historical actuality and also of meaning. But essentially every scholar who has to make valid pronouncements about any historical phenomenon whatsoever is faced by the same dual problem. Thus the historian can never be merely concerned with the question of historical fact, for, in imposing a pattern on the facts and seeking to explain their sequences, he is also concerned with the question of their deeper meaning. Even the philosopher, however abstractly he conducts his enquiry into truth, cannot avoid either the desire or the possibility of occupying himself with the history of philosophy, of discovering and explaining historical contexts within which the question of truth was posed and answered. This applies in particular also to the philosopher of religion, for, even when (like Kant) he is writing of "religion within the bounds of pure reason," he must also concern himself with the historical religions, and especially with Christianity, and must strive to determine the relation between the religion of nature and reason and the religion which presupposes a background of positive historical events.

When the science of historical criticism had been applied to its subject matter, theology, too, was finally obliged to treat the question of truth with which it was faced as a question of historical fact and meaning. Yet there did not arise any new conception of the special task of dogmatics or of the status of dogmatic pronouncements and judgments. What happened was rather the reverse: for when, with Ernst Troeltsch, this new development had been for the time being completed, dogmatics seemed to have been dissolved without remainder into the history, the psychology, the sociology, and the philosophy of religion. Consistently applying the method of historical criticism to Christianity itself, Troeltsch tried to show that even the Christian revelation, with which theology is concerned, is subject to the principle of uninterrupted continuity which moulds the whole process of history. Hence the idea of the "dogmatic" could henceforward only be applied in a disparaging sense: the suggestion was that anyone who thought dogmatically was failing to appreciate the fact that all truth is historically conditioned. Thus not merely was the old orthodox system of dogma condemned, but Troeltsch fought against the last traces of dogmatic thinking even in those who, while accepting the historical approach, did not, so he thought, consistently adhere to it.

(a) The end of dogmatics in the work of Ernst Troeltsch

Troeltsch's point of departure is the hypothesis which in his opinion is the only possible one, namely that Christianity "is a religious idea or principle." If this is so, "then there is no need for any historical work of salvation"; [4] or, specifically in relation to the meaning of Jesus, "there is no inner necessity for an historical event, and from the outset there is no real need for the historical personality of Jesus and the saving work He accomplished." [5] This inner transformation of Christianity, as a result of which "its connexion with the old faith in a historical redemption was severed," [6] has evolved through many stages since the mystics of the time of the reformation. First the historical element was still necessary in order to affirm the truth of Christianity. Finally it was "no more than the means of introducing the Christian idea into history. But, once introduced, that idea was to depend on its intrinsic resources and maintain itself by them alone, for it corresponded to the clear requirements of the moral consciousness, and after its necessary simplification to a theism which inspired the power of doing good, it was neither capable of, nor needed, any further scientific proof. Thus thought Lessing and Kant as

[4] *Die Bedeutung der Geschichtlichkeit Jesu für den Glauben*, Tübingen 1911 (henceforth cited as *Bed.*), p. 6.
[5] *Bed.*, p. 7.   [6] *Bed.*, p. 8.

the leaders of German culture, and of those idealists who ethically and religiously aimed at a conservative type of progress. The historical facts 'served for illustrative rather than demonstrative purposes,' and would, on that understanding, be given over to scientific criticism. This type of thought naturally attained its sharpest expression in the school of Hegel, which, with its thoroughly historical outlook, defined it as at once a necessity of thought and of a correct understanding of history that while religious faith grows out of history, in its inner truth and validity it is not dependent on history." [7] David Friedrich Strauss carried this view further with his distinction between a principle of Christianity and the person of Jesus as the historical starting-point for the rise and growth of this principle. This statement of the problem was "then put forward with the utmost clarity by Biedermann, the Tübingen school, and Pfleiderer." [8] This was the line of development which Troeltsch proposed to carry through to its logical conclusion. In so doing, he dissociates himself from "those hybrid forms in which the distinction between person and principle, person and idea, is not so rigidly maintained, but is expressed with a moderation which asserts at least a relative, subjective necessity for the historical person and for a personal relation to him if the Christian faith in divine redemption is to remain alive. . . . This is the point of view taken by the later, churchly Schleiermacher, and which today has been set forth most emphatically by Ritschl and Herrmann." [9] For Schleiermacher it is the suggestive power of the personality of Jesus which makes the mere idea an efficacious vital force. For Ritschl the emphasis falls rather on the authority of Jesus, which effects the forgiveness of sins and thereby participation in the kingdom of God as the sphere of "a God-fearing conscientiousness in life's practices." For Herrmann "the mortifying and uplifting fact of the personality of Christ is an historical reality, which only the evil and impenitent will can deny, just as it is only the trustful, God-aspiring will distressed by sin that can apprehend it." [10] For Troeltsch this whole type of mediation is insecure against historical criticism. This was already shown by Strauss in his critique of Schleiermacher's *Life* of Jesus, and

[7] *Bed.*, pp. 9 f.   [8] *Bed.*, p. 10.   [9] *Bed.*, p. 11.   [10] *Bed.*, p. 12.

became perfectly plain from the development of the Ritschlian school, "for it was just out of the latter that the so-called discipline of the history of religions sprang, which is especially to be explained by the harsh contrast existing between Ritschl's portrait of Christ and the findings of historical criticism, which he himself nevertheless accepted. It is the natural reaction to Ritschl's violently arbitrary attitude. And even Herrmann's talk about the 'fact of Christ,' which cannot be established like other facts, but only apprehended by faith, is an obscurely mystical expression of the same temper, and almost unintelligible for any one who thinks critically and historically." [11]

A man like Troeltsch could hardly have been expected to understand the inner necessities of this type of mediation, or to appreciate its painstaking endeavours to remain open to the formulations of historical criticism, while at the same time preserving its dogmatic heritage by increasing precision in definitions. He has only a sharp eye for the failures and inconsistencies of its attempts at a solution, and handles the whole history of the problem according to his principle that "to define being means to shape being." [12] Hence he sees only the direction in which the problems themselves press on to, and demand, their solution. This he sees in a radical deliverance of Christianity from the incubus of dogma, and in commenting on the line of development which proceeds from Scleiermacher to Herrmann he says: "The whole position is impossible to maintain in the face of the pressure of historical criticism, and accordingly it has taken almost no part in the development of Biblical criticism and research. On the contrary it has reserved itself for dogmatic thinking. But dogmatics is a discipline which exists today only in the narrowest of theological circles, and even there it languishes." [13]

In his essay on the dogmatics of the history-of-religion school,[14] Troeltsch says: "Such dogmatics presupposes scientific knowledge and methods, but is not in itself a science. It is a confession and an analysis of the creed of the Church for the purpose of guiding the Church's preaching and teaching, which are based on the creeds but need detailed clarification

---

[11] *Bed.*, p. 20.
[12] *Gesammelte Schriften* (cited below as *Ges. Schr.*), BD. II (1913), p. 431.
    [13] *Bed.*, pp. 20 ff.   [14] *Ges. Schr.*, BD. II, pp. 500 ff.

and guidance.[15] It may be said that there is no dogmatics here, no development of firmly-established, unchangeable truth. This being so, the term 'dogmatics' may be dropped, as Schleiermacher proposed. Instead of 'dogmatics,' he might say 'the teaching of the faith,' thus indicating the subjective and confessional character of this study. It is merely a question of terminology, the word 'dogmatics' having certain linguistic advantages and being supported by tradition. But as far as the thing itself is concerned, the general opinion is that in fact there is no such firm unchangeable truth. Not only would such truth be beyond the reach of man's insight; it is precluded by the process of becoming in which the world is involved—a process which excludes any ready-made system which has merely to be carried out, and makes possible only the ever new and vital appreciation of the movement of world being in its constant self-initiated development. But this kind of dogmatics is not pure subjectivism, if only for the reason that it emerges from the great self-revealing movement of history, and is conscious of working in the direction of an absolute end." [16]

And in what direction does Troeltsch himself wish (while avoiding the mixed type represented by Schleiermacher, Ritschl, and Herrmann) to extend the line of development which runs from Lessing through Kant, Hegel, Biedermann and the Tübingen school? His firm principle is that "the historical serves only to illustrate, not to prove, the faith." From this point of view the historical is of significance in that "the person of Jesus is essential socially and psychologically for the purposes of cult, the vital power and the propagation of the faith, and this is enough to justify and maintain the historical connexion." [17] And "so long as there exists in any sense at all such a thing as Christianity, it will necessarily place the Christ right at the centre of the cult, or it will cease to be." [18] But this is no longer a dogmatic affirmation, "it rests on social psychological laws, which have produced exactly the same phenomenon in other religions, are still, on a small scale and in manifold ways, producing the same effects today, and render quite utopian the whole notion of a piety which springs

[15] *Ges. Schr.*, BD. II, p. 514. [16] *Ges. Schr.*, BD. II, p. 516.
[17] *Bed.*, p. 30. [18] *Bed.*, p. 29.

merely from the inner life of the individual, is always the same, needs no reciprocal stimuli, and yet is powerfully alive." [19]

If in this way the significance of Jesus for the faith as a necessary cultic symbol is not based upon any dogmatic soteriological considerations but purely upon social psychological ones, yet the symbolic figure itself "needs to be rooted in historical fact. . . .[20] This is the justification for Herrmann's talk about the fact of Christ. . . .[21] It is a question not of details but of the historicity of the whole phenomenon of Jesus, and of the basic features of His preaching and religious personality. If the symbolic figure of Christ is to be firmly and essentially based on fact, then it must be possible to establish, by historico-critical methods, the historical reality of His person and teaching. . . .[22] The struggle must be fought out, and were it to end unfavourably to the historicity of Jesus, or to suggest that the historical Jesus can no longer be recovered and known, that in fact would mean the beginning of the end of the Christ as a valid symbol for cultured people. And from thence doubt and decay would soon percolate to the lower classes of the people, in so far as the seeds of them are not already sown among the latter by their desire for social reform and general anti-clerical tendencies. It is merely a phrase to say that one desires to hold fast to the Christian principle and leave historical questions alone." [23]

When we read these words today we ask ourselves, with astonishment, whence Troeltsch derived the optimism or the desperate courage to build absolutely everything on the possibility of recovering the knowable reality of Jesus by historical critical methods. When he wrote, the first edition of Albert Schweitzer's *Quest of the Historical Jesus* [24] had already been published. But clearly it had not yet been appreciated that this piece of research spelt the end of endeavours to establish the life of Jesus on a historico-critical basis. The radical dissolution of dogmatics resulting from the challenge to theology represented by historical method was taken to its

---

[19] *Bed.*, pp. 29 ff.   [20] *Bed.*, p. 31.   [21] *Bed.*, p. 32.
[22] *Bed.*, p. 33.   [23] *Bed.*, p. 34.
[24] *Geschichte der Leben-Jesu-Forschung: Von Reimarus zu Wrede*, Tübingen 1906. Eng. trans., *The Quest of the Historical Jesus*, by W. Montgomery, 1911. 3rd edn., London 1954.

extreme conclusion by Troeltsch at the very moment when historical criticism itself was prepared to declare the bankruptcy of its own attempt to establish the historical reality of Jesus. Hence it is not astonishing that Troeltsch marked a terminal point in the history of theology from which there could be no further progress in the same line of development. It is equally clear that the questions which Troeltsch had thought out so radically and thoroughly were by no means settled, and must be taken up again somehow or other. Theology tried to escape from Troeltsch's *impasse* largely by going backwards, and by re-adopting solutions which had not passed through the fire of historical criticism: but such a strategy was hardly likely to succeed.

(b) Lessing's question and Kierkegaard's answer

Behind this whole line of development terminating in Troeltsch stands the ancient question with which Lessing's thesis had challenged theology: "Incidental truths of history can never furnish the proof of truths of reason" [concerning the validity of reason and virtue]. When the theologians at last realised that, so far from effecting a solution of the problem, Troeltsch's historical approach had only made it more desperate, they remembered that Søren Kierkegaard, the great outsider in theology, had long ago come far more radically to grips with Lessing's question than school theology had ever done. In his *Philosophical Fragment*,[25] and in his *Unscientific Postscript*,[26] he formulates it in the following terms: "Can there be an historical point of departure for a consciousness that is eternal in quality? How can such a point of departure be more than of historical interest? Can eternal salvation be built on historical knowledge?" The question, therefore, is (1) How can an historical event have decisive significance for faith, and (2) how can the gulf of time be overcome, so that this event affects me not merely as a datum of history but also as a factor in my contemporary situation? Kierkegaard's attempt to solve these problems consisted in confronting his contemporaries so sharply with the scandal of the Christian message that in

---

[25] *Philosophische Brocken*, 1844, in *Gesammelte Werke*, Jena (Gottsched & Schrempf: henceforth cited as *Ges. Werke*), VOL. VI.

[26] *Unwissenschaftlichen Nachschrift*, 1846, in *Ges. Werke*, VOL. VII.

deciding whether to believe or be scandalised they were made contemporary with the first eyewitnesses. Thus both questions are answered simultaneously.

We must concern ourselves somewhat more closely with this attempted solution of Kierkegaard's, because on the one hand it signifies the end of the historical method, and on the other (whether intentionally or not may for the moment remain undecided) it introduces existentialism into theology. For this reason, it has come to bulk largely in contemporary theological discussion.

Under the famous pseudonym of John Climacus, Kierkegaard occupies himself at first with the traditional method of posing the question whether Christianity is objectively true. Anyone who adopts this procedure will of course admit that there must also be a subjective relation to the truth thus objectively established. But first the truth must be so established, then it is to be presumed that the subjective relation will naturally follow. At the outset, the question is whether Christianity is historically true. This is to be ascertained by a critical examination of the various sources of information, and not on different lines from the establishment of historical certainty in other spheres. At the outset, Climacus does, however, say "that the problem does not emerge decisively in this way, since it lies precisely in the matter of decision." [27] But since the scholarly mind does in fact enquire about the objective historical truth of Christianity, such attempts must be examined. This historical approach is concerned primarily with the Bible as an official document. But for Climacus the difficulty lies in the following points: if, on the basis of the Bible, I attempt to establish critically (1) that Christ actually lived, and (2) that He was also the being whom the testimony of Scripture claims Him to have been, then I can never attain anything but approximative results, which can never be of decisive importance, for or against, in connexion with the decision which is here in question. "What a piece of luck it is," says Climacus, "that this desirable hypothesis, the dazzling dream of critical theology (namely by means of historical science to guarantee that Christianity is true) turns out to be an impossibility, since even the fullest realisation of it can be

[27] *Ges. Werke*, VOL. VI, p. 118.

no more than an approximation. And again what luck for the men of scholarship that this is by no means their fault! If all the angels united their efforts, they could only bring about an approximative knowledge, since here historical knowledge amounts to no more than an approximative certainty, and it is far too slight a basis on which to build eternal blessedness." [28] Faced by this difficulty, we can have recourse to dogmatics, which by the doctrine of inspiration vouches for the truth of the canonical Holy Scriptures. But "the disagreement between inspiration and critical research is similar to that between eternal salvation and historical science, for the idea of inspiration can only be an object of faith." [29] Hence we can neither guarantee the conclusions of research by means of the doctrine of inspiration, nor can we support this doctrine itself by means of higher criticism. We are faced by the dilemma of a comic self-contradiction, of which Climacus says: "When faith begins to cease to be faith, then proof becomes necessary, so that in adopting a sceptical attitude we do not cease to be respectable in the eyes of the bourgeois. Let us not speak of the rhetorical stupidities perpetrated by clerical speakers owing to the confusion of categories in this matter." [30] Since the Bible is exposed to historical criticism, an attempt has been made to fall back on the Church as the guarantor of the historical truth of Christianity. Here Kierkegaard is thinking especially of the Danish theologian Grundtvig, but in fact what he says is relevant to a theology that is still widespread today, when Climacus comments: "As formerly the Bible was supposed to decide objectively what was or was not Christianity, now the Church is said to be our secure objective basis. In more detail, it is the living voice of the Church, the confession of faith, and the Word in the sacraments." [31] The difficulty with regard to Scripture was that the latter was an historical document of the past, and hence there could be no relation to it of immediate certainty. In the bosom of the Church, as shown by its confession of faith, I am confronted by a living present reality. It needs no proof of itself other than the fact of its present life and actuality. But it goes further and claims that it is identical with the

---

[28] *Ges. Werke*, VOL. VI, p. 125.   [29] *Ibid.*

[30] *Ges. Werke*, VOL. VI, p. 126.   [31] *Ges. Werke*, VOL. VI, p. 132.

Apostolic Church, with the Church of the Apostles commissioned by Jesus Christ. Hence it becomes itself an historical phenomenon, and needs to demonstrate the identity it claims. If it tries to do so by pointing to its historical continuity and proving the Apostolic origin of its creed, we are in exactly the same situation as we were in regard to Biblicism, for again some introductory knowledge is necessary which can only lead to approximative results.

Even if it could be proved that the Bible, the creed, and the Church are an historical sequence flowing from the fact of revelation, yet it must be recognised that that fact is a paradox, and hence all these historical phenomena are the result of a paradox, and thus are themselves paradoxical. Even they cannot change the uncertainty of a faith, which must decide against the scandal of the Gospel, into a state of immediate certainty. Just as the fact of revelation itself becomes dialectical as soon as I am to appropriate it myself, so it is with the Bible, the creed, and the Church. It would be useless to invoke the Church's authority in order to prevent this lapse into dialectics. Nor would it be of any avail to replace the one authority by the other, to base the credibility of the Bible on the authority of the Church, its creed, or its preaching ministry. This would in no way put an end to dialectics, for in that case the dialectical enquirer would still address those who regarded the Church as authoritative and ask them why they did so. In so doing he would not deny that these historical phenomena have a great significance for faith. But he would never agree that one should believe *in* them, *in* the Bible, *in* the confessions of faith, *in* the Church. It criticises such a one "not for the faith which he has through his confidence in these institutions, but for the faith which he has *in* them." [32]

All this shows that the question of the historical objective truth of Christianity can only be answered approximately, which is an insufficient basis for eternal salvation. But, secondly, it may be asked whether Christianity is philosophically true. "Then we are concerned about the relation of the doctrine historically given and received to eternal truth." [33] The speculative approach to Christianity attempts to answer this question, for it endeavours so to rationalise Christianity

[32] *Ges. Werke*, VOL. VI, p. 120, n. 1.   [33] *Ges. Werke*, VOL. VI, p. 118.

as an historical phenomenon that at last it emerges as eternal thought. As we have seen in the case of Troeltsch, this attempt had a great influence on those nineteenth-century theologians who were influenced by Hegel. Why Kierkegaard so passionately fought against this attempt can only be understood when we have appreciated the magnificent audacity of Hegel's plan. In this connexion, we should read the section on Hegel in Karl Barth's *Die protestantische Theologie im 19. Jahrhundert*,[34] from which we can attain a better understanding of Hegel than from Kierkegaard's necessarily one-sided polemic. It will then be seen that in his polemic Kierkegaard came to grips with the core of the danger to which nineteenth-century theology—perhaps even Kierkegaard himself—so extensively succumbed. This may be confirmed by a few quotations from Barth's chapter on Hegel: "It is not only, but it is pre-eminently, philosophy which is now essentially orthodox, for it maintains and preserves the principles which have ever been received as valid, and all the foundation truths of Christianity." [35] "In philosophy far more dogma is preserved than in dogmatics itself or theology as such." For the fact is that "the content, the need, and the interests of philosophy are utterly at one with those of religion; its object is eternal truth—that is to say, nothing other than God and an understanding of Him. In interpreting religion, philosophy is interpreting only itself, and *vice versa* . . . thus philosophy and religion coincide . . . philosophy is in fact the worship of God." On this Barth comments: "Could theology want more than this affirmation of solidarity and identity with its old enemy? And the really fascinating thing about this declaration is that in the last resort it does not imply what the rationalisation of theology meant for the Enlightenment, and even for Kant: no jettisoning of history, no surrender of the concretely unique in favour of the timelessly rational; it meant in fact that the historical element in Christianity was not merely placed in a decent and suitable relation to the rational, but was exalted to the position of the decisive factor, and that the universal and rational themselves were in this outlook understood in thoroughly historical terms. In this view, Herder's special concern

[34] 1947 (henceforth cited as *Prot. Theol.*), pp. 343-78.
[35] Quoted from Hegel in Barth, *Prot. Theol.*, p. 367.

was, and is, taken deeply into account. Anybody who thinks
he can help theology by organically connecting together
revelation, faith, and history, should clearly realise that in
this respect Hegel has helped it long since. And along with
history, dogma and all the inmost mysteries of Christianity—
especially its deepest and most irrational doctrines—were
dazzlingly rehabilitated by Hegel's philosophy of religion,
defended against the attacks of philosophy and the faint-
hearted theologians themselves, and brought to honour." [36]
Kierkegaard rightly saw that with Hegel methodology is
everything, and assailed him in this regard by trying to show
that his dialectics cannot be brought into operation. He
persistently asks how the subject of pure thought is related to
the empirical ego of the thinker, or how this empirical ego is
concerned in the dialectical self-initiated movement of pure
thought. He finds no answer to this question in Hegel.[37]
The same objection is raised by John Climacus against the
speculative answer to the question whether Christianity is
objectively true. He says he is not concerned with speculation,
for the latter cannot doubt everything, overcome doubt, and
believe on behalf of the individual engaged in existence.
Instead, he concerns himself with the subject of all this
speculation, and hence with the speculator himself, to whom
he addresses his question: "So, my dear man, my esteemed
thinker, may I be allowed to approach you with a personal
question? My dear fellow, how do *you* regard Christianity?
Are *you* a Christian or not?" And why does he proceed thus?
This is what he sees. "The thinker is proposing to examine
Christianity. It is a matter of indifference to him whether
anyone accepts it or not. Such cares we leave to seminarists
and laymen—and of course to real Christians to whom it is
by no means a matter of indifference whether they are
Christians or not. He looks at Christianity in order to
penetrate its essence with his genuinely speculative thought.
But suppose this whole procedure were chimerical; suppose
that it could not be done; suppose Christianity were precisely
the same as subjectivity, inwardness; suppose therefore that

---

[36] *Prot. Theol.*, p. 367.

[37] Cp. Diem, *Die Existenzdialektik von Sören Kierkegaard*, 1950 (henceforth
cited as *Existenzdialektik von S.K.*, § 4 ("*Logik und Ontologie*"), pp. 13 ff.

only two classes of men could ever know anything about it—those who with endless passionate concern for their eternal salvation build in faith on their believing relation to Christianity, and those who with equal but opposed passion reject it—i.e. the fortunate and the unfortunate amateurs; suppose, in other words, that the attitude of objective indifference could never know anything whatever about it." [38] From this point of view it remains to be discovered and established in detail what errors speculation commits, of what surreptitious gains it is guilty, for, says Climacus, "Christianity cannot be examined objectively, because its aim is to pierce the depths of the subjective; when the subjective is thus brought into operation, it cannot rest its eternal salvation on speculation." [39] Speculation does not allow the real problem to emerge. Consequently its whole answer is a mystification.

Climacus now poses the subjective question, namely, "How is the subject to come into a personal relation to Christian truth?" or, simply, "How is a man to become a Christian?" First of all, he expresses his gratitude to Lessing, in whose writings we never know really whether he is defending or opposing Christianity, because he concentrates our attention always on the difficulties which stand in the way of one who wants to become a Christian and is helped neither by views of world history nor speculative considerations. Lessing said: "Incidental historical facts can never furnish the proof of eternal truths of reason, and the transition by which you pass from an historical record to the edifice of eternal salvation is a leap." [40] Lessing boggles at this leap because he supposes he can no longer trust his old legs and his heavy head to make it. But it is just this leap which is the meaning of becoming a Christian, for only by accomplishing it can we appropriate Christianity. It is just this act of appropriation which is in question, for as Climacus says, "Take away this subjective side, and what is Luther's merit? But open his works and feel in every line the strong heart-beat of subjective appropriation, feel it in the vibrating onward dash of the style, which has as it were always behind it that tempest of terror which slew Alexius and created Luther. Had not the Papacy enough

[38] *Ges. Werke*, VOL. VI, pp. 145 ff.   [39] *Ges. Werke*, VOL. VI, p. 150.
[40] *Ges. Werke*, VOL. VI, p. 179.

and to spare of objectivity, and objective considerations, the objective, always the objective? What did it lack? Personal appropriation! Inwardness!" [41]

But the special characteristic of Kierkegaard's thought is that he does not *begin* by making sure, either historically or philosophically, that Christianity is objectively true, before going on to ask how its objectively valid truth can be subjectively appropriated. His position is rather that from the standpoint of an objective thinker the question whether Christianity is true cannot even arise, unless it can, in its bearing on the thinker's own eternal salvation, be seen to be, equally, a question of poignantly subjective judgment. Hence the question whether Christianity is true must be asked and answered at one and the same time, both objectively and subjectively. Methodologically, it is clear this is a far more difficult undertaking than Hegel's whole dialectic.[42]

If God becomes a specific historical man, this means that He becomes an historical datum, with which I have to deal as with any other historical datum. It can be directly appreciated either by direct perception as an eyewitness, or on the basis of the testimony recorded by contemporaries. But what is thus directly perceived is not the historical. Such direct perception applies only to a natural event which either simply is or has happened, so that the question whether it has thus happened necessarily or by free self-determination does not arise. But if I am considering an historical datum as an event of history, I reflect at the same time on its becoming, and cannot be content to accept its having become in such and such a way, because it might possibly have come to be in a different way. If the historian supposes that what he directly perceives is the effect of a certain cause, and hence might have come to be in a different way, then he is drawing a conclusion against which doubt is possible. In order to preclude such doubt, his statement must not simply assume the form of an inference, it must be a resolve. And this act of resolution Kierkegaard equates with faith as the general instrument whereby we apprehend the historical, though without at this juncture implying anything with regard to the specifically Christian.

[41] *Ges. Werke*, VOL. VII, pp. 61 ff.
[42] On what follows, cp. Diem, *Existenzdialektik von S.K.*, esp. pp. 11-13.

By interpreting faith as the instrument by which we apprehend the historical, Kierkegaard intends simultaneously to
solve two problems which are normally treated separately:
(1) the question of the historical actuality of events, and
(2) the question of my personal relation to them. The
historical is a reality alien to the individual, towards which
he must adopt a position. So long as he does so aesthetically
or intellectually, he remains indifferent to that reality. But
it is otherwise when man is concerned about this reality from
a moral standpoint, for he then enquires about it in order to
assimilate it to the reality of his own life. But man has no
faculty whereby to grasp an alien reality as reality directly.
In order to do so he must first transpose it back into the reality
of its becoming, in order to appropriate and fulfil it as a
possibility in his own life of decisive becoming. "The historical
is ever only so much raw material, which only he who appropriates it to himself can reduce to its *posse* in order then to
assimilate it in its *esse*." [43] Thus from an ethical standpoint
any mere examination of the historical is excluded, because
the historical always implies a reality that has been pur-
chased by thought and is vitally related to my own personal
reality in that it summons *me* to realise its possibilities. In
this connexion the question of the actuality of an event is of
minor importance, for it contributes nothing to the understanding of the historical. By hiding the essential beneath
inessentials, it may even prove an obstacle to such an understanding and in the mere effort to reconstruct historical facts
Kierkegaard can see an inducement to an unintelligent
attitude. "Intelligence is to enquire about two things:
(1) Is what is said at all possible; and (2) can I do it? But it is
unintelligent to ask: (1) Is this real, and (2) has my neighbour
Christophersen really done this thing?" [44]

This, then, is the situation when we are dealing with any
historical fact you like to take. Now when God reveals
Himself as man, that is in the first place an historical fact like
any other: the God-man as man. In this regard all the
traditional detail about the "historical Jesus," his teachings
and deeds, has its place, for fundamentally it classifies him with
other historical happenings as a man among men, compara-

[43] *Ges. Werke*, VOL. IV., p. 405.   [44] *Ges. Werke*, VOL. IV., p. 407.

tively within a big historical process. And the instrument by
which we enter into relation with this Jesus is faith, in the
broad sense in which it permits us to enter into relation with all
other historical facts. Hence both his contemporaries and
those of later times stand merely in a Socratic relation to the
God-man as man.

From this appearance of the God-man as man, whereby he
becomes a general historical fact (or, as Climacus says, the
historical as a primary historical potency) we must be careful
to distinguish revelation as an eternal fact, or the God-man as
God (the historical in its secondary potency). When faith
as the instrument by which we apprehend the historical enters
into relation with this historical fact of secondary potency,
its potentialities, too, are modified. As Climacus says, "here
faith is to be understood in a wholly pre-eminent sense—a
sense which can only apply in one connexion, and though oft
repeated has but one unique significance." [45] The reason for
this lies in the object of this faith, namely revelation, which is
not a simple historical fact. Inasmuch as it declares that God
has become man, it is saying something self-contradictory, for
it is affirming of God an act of historical becoming, although
the very nature of God is to be eternal and not to be involved
in becoming. By this self-contradiction the absolute Christian
paradox becomes repulsive not merely by virtue of the objective
uncertainty which clings to it, but by virtue of its absurdity.
And in grappling with this absolute paradox, faith has to
overcome, not only the objective uncertainty, but also this
very absurdity. How is that possible?

First of all, it must be observed that there is no essential
distinction between eyewitnesses and later Christians, or (as
Climacus puts it) between the pupils at first and second hand.
The fact of revelation has in general "no immediate contemporaries in so far as it is historical in primary potency (faith in
the general sense). But neither has it any immediate contemporaries in its secondary potency, where it implies
a self-contradiction (faith in the pre-eminent sense)." [46]
Hence nearness or distance in time from the event is a matter
of complete indifference. There can be no *immediate* knowledge or appreciation which eyewitnesses could communicate

to their successors; for that the fact itself is what it purports
to be is something which even the eyewitnesses themselves
can only *believe*. They can only report: "I believe and have
believed that this has come to pass, even though it is folly to
the reason and a scandal to the human heart." [47] Thus the
eyewitness has no advantage over his successors; but neither
have the latter any advantage over the eyewitness. Those
consequences of the fact which he sees before him—the
Church, the Bible, the creeds, etc.—are the consequences of a
paradox and hence equally paradoxical. They can only
arouse his attention as they did with the eyewitnesses, and
cannot bring him one whit nearer to an understanding of the
fact or an acceptance of it. Thus revelation is equally near to
all times. Faith in the Christian sense arises only in the
situation of metaphysical contemporaneity which is independent of historical nearness or distance. By these considerations the whole pursuit of historical enquiry is closed for
Climacus, and he can propound that famous (or infamous)
dictum: "Had the contemporary generation left behind them
nothing but these words: 'We have believed that in such and
such years God showed Himself to us in the humble form of a
servant, lived and taught among us and then died,' it would
be more than enough." [48]

We shall see what significance these thoughts of Kierkegaard's
have for present theological debate. His impressive attempt
to answer at one and the same time the questions of historical
and philosophical truth, or as Troeltsch would say, the
question of the essence of Christianity and that of the historical
person of Jesus, and to do so not by means of any systematic
theory, but by an existential act which both objectively and
subjectively solves the problem, is something so novel and far-
reaching that it might well appear as a great emancipation to
a theology which seemed, after Troeltsch, to have absolutely
nothing more to say. It was only gradually (and even today
it has by no means been generally) recognised that the methodological peculiarity of Kierkegaard's work makes it unacceptable
to the theologian either as a whole or in detail. It is even
truer of him than of his great opponent Hegel—with whom

[47] *Ges. Werke*, VOL. VI, p. 93.
[48] *Ges. Werke*, VOL. VI, p. 94.

alone he is strictly comparable—that method means everything in his work. If Hegel's dialectical method was intended
to secure the objective truth of Christianity by illuminating
it as a moment in the self-development of mind, Kierkegaard's
existential dialectic was, in extreme contrast, designed to
achieve true subjectivity by determining man to live as a
Christian. But this implies no renunciation of the objective
validity of Christianity, of the fact of the Christian revelation.
Rather he simply presupposed the truth of the latter and took
it straight from Church dogmatics. He can even say:
"Doctrine, as usually expounded, is on the whole correct. I
am not disputing about that. My sole concern is how far it
can be effective." [49] He did not himself do any work in
dogmatics because he felt that his task consisted not in showing
what Christianity is, but how one becomes a Christian. This
end was served by his whole enormous apparatus of a two-
edged oblique method of communication by means of
pseudonyms, intended as a discipline in Christian existence.
But he is thoroughly clear about the fact that this type of
oblique communication is only possible in constant dialectical
relation to the direct authoritative communication implied
in the preaching office of the Church which is being fulfilled
at the same time, and that by Christianity he simply means
putting into practice the dogmatic teaching of the Church.
Thus he says of the "experiment in thought"—which means
the *Philosophical Fragments* and is to be understood simply as a
parody on Hegel's synthesis of philosophy and Christianity—
"that great efforts were made as if something quite extraordinary and indeed new were being achieved, while at the
same time the everyday orthodoxy of the Church is being
taught in all due strictness." [50] In all this he proposed to be
merely a corrective to existing Christianity, merely a touch of
cinnamon to the food of normal Christian doctrine. But
Kierkegaard was also aware that in this undertaking he could
have no successor, not merely because his pseudonymous
method of working could hardly be imitated, but because he
had quickened and set aflame his oblique approach by the
drive and force of his own personality.

[49] *Sören Kierkegaards Papirer*, Copenhagen 1909, Pap. X, 635.
[50] *Ges. Werke*, VOL. VI, p. 346 n.

(c) The repercussions of Kierkegaard's work in theology

When Kierkegaard was rediscovered about the turn of the century, and began to acquire, especially after 1918, an increasing influence on philosophical and theological thought, all this was at first completely overlooked. It was thought that this existential dialectic could be taken over by itself, without regard to the fact that it was only possible and intelligible as a corrective to the doctrine and teaching of the Church. His own warning that to take the corrective as the whole must inevitably lead to a lapse into something onesided passed unheeded. This unavoidable lapse was not long in taking place. The Danish philosopher Harald Höffding said, for example, that Kierkegaard had sought truth at the subjective psychological pole, and had made it the object of personal feeling.[51] As a result, Kierkegaard influenced philosophy, fruitfully indeed, in the direction of an increased delicacy and depth of psychological structural analysis, but with the effect also of relativising all objective statements of truth. Those who were interested in his work chiefly as Christians interpreted his subjectivity largely as pietistic inwardness in personal religion. In theology the effect of this misunderstanding was that the theologian was required to think existentially, i.e. the theologian's own existential concern in his dogmatic statements was required as at least a supplementary criterion of the truth of what he had to say. The result was to provide a new modern version of the old efforts to secure a *theologia regenitorum* which applied very well to the nineteenth-century movement that reduced dogmatics to a mere explanation of Christian consciousness and thus gave a strong impulse to the development of an anthropological theology.[52] It was only slowly understood that the subjective thinker Kierkegaard was aiming at something quite other than resigning all objectively valid thought; that rather, with the keenest passion and earnestness, he was concerned to find objectivity in the subjective so as to realise universally valid objective truth in the subjective existence of an individual man. Of the thinkers who occupied themselves with Kierke-

[51] *Kierkegaard als Philosoph*, 1922, pp. 74 ff.
[52] Diem, *Theol.*, BD. I (*Exegese und Historie*), pp. 39 ff.

gaard's work, Martin Heidegger was the first who—turning to existence itself on these lines—once more sought the objective in the subjective. He did so, of course, freely and independently as a philosopher, without regard to the fact that Kierkegaard believed objective truth to be anchored in the dogma of the Church. Rather he sought objectivity through an illumination of the existential structure of the individual life. This effort is connected with Kierkegaard's work only in so far as it provided him with an abundance of ontical material for the discovery of ontological structural relationships. What Heidegger makes of this is however his own responsibility and he says himself that while Kierkegaard vividly understood and thought about life as existential "the problematics of the existential" were foreign to him, and that (apart from the "concept of dread") we can therefore learn more of philosophical interest from his edificatory writings than from his theoretical ones.[53]   Hence Heidegger sees quite rightly that his own philosophical aim of finding objectivity in the subjective was far removed from the Kierkegaard mentality. In fact, on the basis of his own presuppositions, Kierkegaard would surely have seen that same *hybris* against which he himself had striven so fiercely now, in Heidegger's existentialist ontology, undertaking the impossible task of constructing a "system of existence." Hence the difference between them is that whereas Kierkegaard saw the problem as an existential task, a summons to the existence and life-situation of the thinker, Heidegger is concerned to clarify the existential structure of an existence which, as such, has not yet anything to do with the thinker's own existential attitude. To this there corresponds the equally essential difference in their formulation of the problem of truth: in the old subject-object pattern of transcendental idealism, Kierkegaard wants to find a basis of unity between thought and being, and finds it in the concrete existential act of the thinker who lives his life in responsibility and so exists as both individual and universal man. It is in this deepest sense that he declares that "truth is subjective," and, on the other hand, that "subjectivity is truth."

Heidegger on the contrary does not enquire how a thinking

[53] *Sein und Zeit*, 1927, p. 235, n. 1.

subject can reach and grasp its object and become one with it. His question is: "What makes it possible from an ontological point of view that entities can encounter us within the world and that in consequence of this encounter they can be objectified?" [54] Thus the question of truth takes the form of discovering the latent or concealed being of entities, of analysing the existentiality of existence, in which connexion "the entity which we have to analyse is always ourselves." [55] But this exposure of the existential structure of an existence tells us nothing about the existential behaviour of the one who is thus interpreting the existence. "Nevertheless—as Heidegger himself says in regard to the interpretation of conscience for example—the existentially more original interpretation also discloses possibilities of an original existential understanding, provided that the ontological conception is not arbitrarily divorced from the ontical experience." [56]

This fundamental difference between Kierkegaard and Heidegger makes their respective insights really incommensurable, but has not in fact prevented their being linked together again and again, nor has it been able to prevent Kierkegaard from being widely understood today, especially in the school of Bultmann, in the sense of Heidegger's existential philosophy. This distortion has taken place with a quite particular motive which has both a philosophical and theological bearing. Especially characteristic in this respect is, for instance, the work of the Dane K. E. Lögstrup. [57] Although Lögstrup is very well aware of the difference between their respective points of view and alludes to it in certain details, yet in regard to the question how philosophy is related to preaching, he refuses to discriminate between them. He does this in the following formulation of the problem: "Philosophy in the name of existence makes a certain demand on preaching, namely that its affirmations should reflect the structure of human existence." This means "that the analysis of existence

[54] *Sein und Zeit*, p. 366.   [55] *Sein und Zeit*, p. 41.

[56] *Sein und Zeit*, p. 295. [For the translation of these quotations from Heidegger, I am indebted to Mr. John Macquarrie, who is, with Professor Edward Robinson, engaged in translating Heidegger's *Sein und Zeit*.—Tr.]

[57] See K. E. Lögstrup, *Kierkegaards und Heideggers Existenzanalyse und ihr Verhältnis zur Verkündigung*, Berlin 1950, cited below as Lögstrup.

furnishes a touchstone for every proclamation of a message and makes quite specific demands on it." [58] In this connexion preaching or proclamation is understood in the broadest sense as "a declaration about existence that is determined by the content of human experience," and the contrast between preaching and philosophy is described as that between "an exposition of human life which is filled with a rich subjective content and one which is formal and empty." [59] This content is not yielded by an analysis of the structure of human life but "from the standpoint of philosophy preaching consists of mere assertions." [60] These assertions must, however, reflect the structure of human existence, because otherwise "the difference between preaching and benighted superstition" would cease to exist and there would be no further possibility of "distinguishing between faith and coercion." [61] But does not this mean that there is applied to preaching (by which we now mean in particular Christian preaching) a criterion that is alien to its nature? About this Lögstrup says: "From a purely historical point of view, the situation is that it was only with the help of the Christian message that philosophy considered as the analysis of existence . . . became aware of the decisive factors in the structure of human existence. If we view the matter rightly, we see that Christian preaching is tested and criticised by the Christian gospel, even though this takes place in the form of a philosophical critique, and by the aid of purely formal concepts. This of course becomes quite clear when philosophy in its exposition of the purely formal structure of existence is animated by a Christian inspiration." [62] Neither does Lögstrup want "theology to accept philosophy uncritically and to regard its analysis of existence as authoritative. The point is rather that a debate between them should arise and not be precluded from the outset by prejudices. In the last resort it is in spite of everything the same human existence with which both philosophy and theology are concerned. This concern which they have in common should itself make a fruitful interchange of views between them appear quite natural." [63]

[58] Lögstrup, p. 110.   [59] Lögstrup, pp. 107 f.
[60] Lögstrup, p. 108.   [61] Lögstrup, pp. 108 ff.
[62] Lögstrup, pp. 116 f.   [63] Lögstrup, p. 117.

What the philosopher here affirms is gladly repeated by the theologians of the school of Bultmann. For them this reciprocal influence consists in the fact that the understanding of existence which the exegete brings to the text both elicits the truth of the text and at the same time is itself constantly criticised and called in question by this self-interpreting text and the message it conveys. From such reciprocal influence, as long as it is allowed free play and is not disturbed by any sort of prejudice containing the compulsion to believe, there then spontaneously arises a genuine criterion which must ceaselessly bring out "the difference between preaching and benighted superstition." From this point of view the dogmatist must appear as some one whose vocation it is to hand on these prejudices and who therefore cannot be trusted any longer to move with the necessary impartiality in this interplay of influences. Hence, according to this outlook, the decisive theological work falls no more to the dogmatist but to the exegete of Scripture who consciously practises this hermeneutical method. In his authentic and free fulfilment of this mutual relationship it must in the last analysis be of no importance to him whether he carries on his work as a theologian or as a philosopher.

(d) The hermeneutics of dogma in Hans Jonas

The inevitable consequences of all this for dogmatics are shown in quite a classical fashion by the work of Hans Jonas.[64] The very formulation of the problem which he takes as his point of departure significantly reveals his approach to the phenomenon of dogmatic elaboration: "What significance attaches to the dogmatic elaboration of religious experience, which deals with elements of fundamental importance in human existence or with such as are existentially and vitally related to it by the insights of faith?" This approach implies the view "that . . . there lies at the basis of even the most remote and metaphysical dogmatic hypostatisations some concrete and original structure of experience in which are primarily realised certain basic motifs and aspects of life demanding such dogmatic hypostatisation, and that in consequence these hypostatisations are in

[64] See H. Jonas, "Die hermeneutische Struktur des Dogmas," in *Augustin und das paulinische Freiheitsproblem*, Göttingen 1930, cited below as Jonas.

C

fact the translation of something, of that which is demonstrably intrinsic to the depths of existence itself." The way in which —as Jonas himself says—such experience is related to dogma is "a philosophical problem in itself" which he does not further discuss. But he points out that it is by no means a question of temporal successiveness, "so that we might distinguish a primary phase in which the phenomena were immediately palpable in their pure form" from a later one in which they were subjected to hypostatisation.[65] With regard to the hypostatical aspect Jonas asks what is formally implied in the fact of dogmatic elaboration. According to their outward form dogmas are formulae which have objectified the substance of their statements by a process of consistent logical thought. These statements which deal in tangible factors and events have a symbolic representative character and thus reflect original subjective and existential phenomena "which as a result are metaphorically expressed in the mode of things, facts and events." Hence "the fundamental activity which makes possible and sustains dogmatic constructions is an objectification of inner subjective phenomena striving to express themselves in speech, or a basic self-objectification of existence oppressed by its inner secrets and desirious of interpreting itself." In every early creative period of the interpretation of existence this process of self-objectification " strives to achieve transcendence by means of the metaphysical or mythological, i.e. reaches out after a symbology transcending subjective existence, and going beyond what is expressible and demonstrable on a subjective plane from which nevertheless it springs." The decisive factor in this process of transcending and symbolising is a "fundamental ontological transformation of phenomena, a translation into another mode of being which affects the deepest elements of subjective existence: their hypostatisation so that from being merely existential quantities they become quasi-observable realities analogous to the phenomena of the external world." [66] Coupled with this process is the rationalisation of such pictorial symbols, as a result of which the underlying subjective phenomena become capable of theoretic discussion—i.e. in so far as these pictorial symbols pass over into the free movement of ideas.[67]

[65] Jonas, p. 66.   [66] Jonas, p. 67.   [67] Jonas, p. 68.

The whole of this process has its roots in an "inescapably basic characteristic of the human mind itself, i.e. in the fact that it tends to explain itself by means of objective forms and symbols . . . in order to realise the nature of its own consciousness." "In the last analysis dogmas are therefore human self-objectification." [68] In this special case, however, apart from the general ontological conditioning of the possibility, "dogmas serve to satisfy specific theoretical interests . . . by subjecting the problematical factor in human existence to the already constructed objectified system of the metaphysic of being. In this constructive role . . . dogma is in many ways a ready answer to torturing rationalistic antinomies which paradoxically enough have themselves arisen from the attempt to construct a systematic metaphysic. . . ." [69]

What then does all this amount to for the understanding and interpretation of dogmas in detail? The rationalistic character of dogmas might mislead us in such a way as to make us overlook their existential basis. In this case we should be ascribing to dogmas a structure of meaning which they do not intrinsically possess. We should be subjecting their pronouncements to the laws of logic which would lead to insoluble contradictions. Among the outward signs of this approach to dogmas is for example the emergence of the question of compatibility: "For instance, how is human freedom compatible with divine omnipotence and prescience? How is predestination compatible with human responsibility?—and so forth? The emergence of this viewpoint is however 'an unmistakable sign that we are viewing the phenomena in question in a non-intrinsic way. For the very logical structure of thought in consequence of which the alternative arises . . . presupposes a specific ontological interpretation of the theme which is essentially inappropriate to its existential character.' In the sphere of existence 'contradiction' means something essentially other than what it means in the rational and objective sphere. Whereas in the latter the *principium contradictionis* means that only the one or the other of the alternatives can be true . . . existence is the living unified fulfilment of irreconcilables . . .; only because and in so far as it is essentially free can it be predetermined; and only in so far as it lives out

[68] *Ibid.*   [69] Jonas, pp. 68 f.

this essential predetermination can it be free. . . . But this living concrete 'both-and' inevitably becomes petrified in the expounded objectifications of dogma, it is broken up and hypostatised in the fictitiously objective sphere of dogma as individualised quantities which are bound to conflict with each other and lead to a logical impasse." [70]   Hence, just as "on the one hand the objectified rationalistic structure of dogma in general and in particular the logical terms in which the question of compatibility is couched, show that we are here faced by an ontological misunderstanding, so also on the other hand the essential insolubility of the antinomies thus suggested is an indication of a genuine dialectic in the underlying existential foundation which has simply been inappropriately expressed by the rationalistic antinomy and its conceptual form." From this point of view it becomes clear what the essential task of interpreting dogma consists in: namely in the dissolution of its pronouncements to their existential basis and meaning. Jonas shows the implications of this by two examples, the dogmas of original sin and pre-destination. The existential phenomena which lie at the root of these dogmas are, in the case of the former, "the phenomenon of human insufficiency in the face of God," [71] and in the case of the latter, "the awareness that the funda-mental meaning of human existence has always already been decided." [72]

The dissertation of Jonas is guided in its study of the formal characteristic of the construction of dogmas by his interest in discovering a formal criterion for the right interpretation of dogma generally. Hence the question as to the genesis of those basic experiences which Jonas thinks underlie dogma is never discussed by him. He is interested only in the phenom-enon of the structure and formation of dogma as such. For this reason too he does not feel any need to speak theologically of the fact of revelation which in regard to the development of Christian dogma must be understood as the originating cause of those experiences which lie behind and determine the forma-tion of individual dogmas. Furthermore, as far as Jonas is concerned, the question remains open whether all dogmatic development does not spell a process of corruption, as a result

[70] Jonas, pp. 69 f.   [71] Jonas, p. 72.   [72] Jonas, p. 75.

of which essence forfeits the element of existence. He has told us that the evolution of dogma has its origin in an inescapably basic characteristic of the human mind as such, namely that it comes to self-awareness by interpreting itself in terms of objectified forms and symbols. But this same mind must also dissolve its own self-objectifications in order to discover anew the spirit that is thus expressing itself inappropriately. It is in any case not possible for any one on the basis of these pre-suppositions to produce dogmatic structures. Only sub-sequently, after the unfortunate (may one really say so?) process of dogmatic elaboration has set in, can we attempt to render dogma intelligible and once again destroy the result of our own work.

(e) The dissolution of dogmatics in existential dialectics

Further, Jonas clearly supposes that in the trend of his thinking he is treading the same path as Kierkegaard, for he incidentally remarks that the dogma of original sin had to traverse a long process of development before reaching the Kierkegaardian stage. Now it could easily be shown that Kierkegaard by no means dissolves the dogma of original sin in order to discover the "phenomenon of human insufficiency before God" which underlies it. In the short sketch of doctrine with which he prefaces his *Begriff der Angst*, he shows that sin as a universal factor in human life cannot be explained as a "phenomenon of existence," but is only to be explained by means of the dogma of original sin. But original sin itself "is not to be explained by reference to dogmatics; it can only be presupposed like that vortex of which Greek nature speculation had much to say as a motivating something which no system of knowledge can grasp." [73] In his *Krankheit zum Tode*, he lays the decisive stress on the dogmatic point that sin is a positive and not a negative, and says: "Orthodoxy has constantly contended for this and has consistently rejected as pantheistic every definition of sin which made it into something merely negative, such as weakness, sensuality, finiteness, ignorance, and so on. Orthodoxy quite correctly realised that battle must be joined at this point, that here the line had to be drawn and resistance offered. It also realised, and again with justice, that the whole

[73] *Ges. Werke*, VOL. X, p. 13.

Christian position becomes insecure once sin is described in negative terms. Accordingly orthodoxy insists that a divine revelation must teach fallen man what sin is and that such teaching must be believed as a systematic whole and as dogma. And it can be easily understood that paradox, faith, and dogma, these three terms, form an alliance which provides the surest ground and the firmest bulwark against all heathen wisdom." [74] But this appeal to Kierkegaard himself does not settle the matter. Even if we are right in thinking that, as far as Kierkegaard himself is concerned, a dissociation of his existential dialectics from its dogmatic basis is unthinkable and would be senseless, the question still remains whether in this respect Kierkegaard has correctly understood himself and whether his existential dialectics, in spite of himself, does not demand those consequences which have been drawn from it. This is how Wilhelm Anz, for example, sees the matter.[75] He considers this whole development, which under the leadership of Kierkegaard has decisively affected theology, to be completely mistaken and he tries to show that the original source of the error lies in Kierkegaard himself. He thinks that Kierkegaard attempts to understand even dogmas as categories of existence and asks "whether in thus narrowing down dogmas to their existential bearing we are enquiring into their truth in accordance with their proper presuppositions, or whether in the last resort we are not as it were annexing them to existence." [76] For, as far as Kierkegaard himself is concerned, dogmas are "correct in so far as they cause or occasion the decisive acts of Christian existence. He leaves entirely out of account, for instance, the question of their teaching about the world as a whole, its origin and end, and the course and character of time." In so far as dogmas express saving facts, they fall within the sphere of dialectics. "Faith is the sole,

[74] *Ges. Werke*, VOL. VIII, p. 91; cp. Diem, "Dogmatik und Existenz-dialektik bei Sören Kierkegaard," in *Symposion Kierdegaardianum*, Copenhagen 1955.
[75] See Wilhelm Anz, "Fragen der Kierkegaardinterpretation, I," in *Theologische Rundschau* (cited below as *Th. R.*), 1952, pp. 27 ff.; "Philosophie und glaube bei Sören Kierkegaard: über die Bedeutung der Existenz-dialektik für die Theologie," in *Zeitschrift für Theologie und Kirche* (henceforth cited as *Z. Th. K.*), 1954, pp. 50 ff.
[76] *Th. R.*, 1952, p. 55.

exclusive and unsurpassable mode of access, enabling us to understand and personally to appropriate the fact in its significance." [77] All this suggests "an over-emphasis on faith which is understandable as a reaction against pure speculation and which makes faith appear not only as the legitimate mode of approach, but as exercising a critical function with regard to its content. Faith not only confronts the existential subject with the necessity of decision, but it also decides about its own content and presumes to say whether this is qualified to be an appropriate faith-content, i.e. to become the occasion of true existential fulfilment." In certain formulations this goes so far "that the content of faith is defined with reference to the act of faith." [78] As a result "the object of faith is in fact defined by the manner of faith. We can leave undecided the question whether faith itself is aware of its critical function and its part in creating significance. It is enough to note that for the thinker concerned with dialectics it has acquired this role. In this respect dogma has in fact become a category of existence, not otherwise than the Socratic paradox." [79] In his second essay Anz draws out still wider implications and comes to the conclusion that Kierkegaard with his idea of appropriation has introduced into the classical Christian faith all the ambiguities of modern subjectivity. Nothing remains of dogma in consequence except its existential purpose. There is no longer a *fides quae creditur* in some sense presupposed as the basis of belief. "Hence revelation is no longer objectively true, but rather the act of faith gives to the object of faith the possibility of proving itself to be true: but does this mean that the dogmatic tradition of the Church is in fact being reproduced in a new and (where possible) more inward way?" [80]

The result is that the inner subjective life of the believer takes precedence over the content of his faith, by which, however, the act of believing should be determined.[81] Hence Kierkegaard does not content himself with the "indisputable truth that the knowledge of God is not an objective possession guaranteeing the Christian life, but risks the converse implication that the erroneous and false knowledge of God, if seized upon with subjective and passionate conviction, will lead man

---

[77] *Th. R.*, 1952, p. 56. [78] *Th. R.*, 1952, p. 57. [79] *Ibid.*
[80] *Z. Th. K.*, 1954, p. 102. [81] *Ibid.*

to true existence. This is as much as to say that in these
matters there is no longer any question of dogma but only of
the ideas by which faith lives. Decisive reality can be ascribed
only to the decisions of faith." [82] "Theology, understood in
the sense of existential dialectics, becomes exclusively the
explication of the decisions of faith." [83]   Whether Anz is
right or not, the fact remains that in contemporary theology
all these inferences have indeed been drawn, with or without
reference to Kierkegaard himself, and even though for the
most part they are not admitted so plainly and their full
import has not been realised. In any event, so much should
be clear, namely that Kierkegaard's existential dialectics
offer us no help towards a recreation of dogmatics after its
dissolution by historicism. Kierkegaard has provided no
means of escape from the *impasse* to which dogmatics
succumbed as a result of historicism. But even if there is
hardly any theologian who would be prepared to adopt the
masterly conception in consequence of which Kierkegaard
answers the theological question of truth both as regards
objective history and subjective meaning by reference to the
thinker's existential situation and to his personal involvement
in the issue, yet in modern theological discussion the opinion
prevails that in this respect Kierkegaard so radicalised the
problems by which we are confronted that it is no longer
possible to go back to previous attempts at a solution. But
above all we must trace Kierkegaard's persistent influence in
the attitude of strong suspicion aroused by all supposed
objectively valid dogmatic pronouncements which do not
immediately disclose their life-situation, i.e. their relation to a
corresponding existential position. Here and there we see
emerging the danger which already threatened with Kierkegaard himself, namely that in this way the act of faith
could determine the content of faith, though it is felt that the
danger is countered by the development of Kierkegaard's existential dialectics into Heidegger's philosophical existentialism.
Friedrich Gogarten, for example, expects nothing but good
from this change, as a result of which philosophy has turned
away from the old idealistic subject-object pattern to a
phenomenological structural analysis of existence itself. He

[82] *Z. Th. K.*, 1954, pp. 102 ff.   [83] *Z. Th. K.*, 1954, p. 103.

expects from it not only a new and fruitful reciprocal influence of theology and philosophy as Lögstrup did, but also the possibility of a new setting of theological problems. So far hardly any attempt has yet been made to discover from this point of view a new basis for dogmatics, but so far, as we saw to be the case with Jonas, the efforts to find the right hermeneutical method have resulted only in a new interpretation of the character of dogma. The question whether by this means we may and should proceed further to develop a real dogmatics is still an open one, in so far as it has not been decided negatively, as, for example, in the work of Bultmann and Gogarten.

Further, this outlook has produced a new attempt to solve the problems raised by historicism. Here again the question of hermeneutical method tends to occupy the foreground. It is very striking that the question of historical truth recedes behind that of the significance of historical events, and here again we must see the legacy of Kierkegaard. The tendency at present is to refer the whole question of theological truth to the question of hermeneutics, and generally speaking no longer to pose it in dogmatic terms but rather with reference to methods of Scriptural exposition. In regard to the latter it is hoped to find objectively valid criteria through the existential structural analysis of existence. Thus there seems no longer to be either any necessity or any possibility for the independent existence of dogmatics, poised as it is between historicism and existentialism. More and more, exegesis seems to be replacing it and making it superfluous.

(f) The protestations of the Lutherans

But this development in contemporary theology did not take place without causing violent opposition, as was to be expected. Here we shall leave Barth out of account and merely mention the fact that, unlike almost all his fellow combatants in theology who were working in this period of flux and change, he resolutely disregarded Kierkegaard in proceeding to write his *Kirchliche Dogmatik*. We must, on the other hand, mention above all those German Lutherans who tried to rescue dogmatics from Bultmann's programme of "demythologisation." Their first big attempt to make a stand is seen in the

Wort lutherischer Theologen zur Entmythologisierung, published by
Ernst Kinder.[84]   In the form of warnings, desiderata, and
postulates, they were concerned to point out that the truths of
revelation enshrined in theological formulae must not be
allowed to become merely the contents of subjective consciousness, but their argument was not based on any dogmatic
conception which might be capable of taking into account
the challenge with which dogmatics was inescapably faced.
Hence Friedrich Gogarten in his work *Entmythologisierung und
Kirche* [85] found it only too easy to set aside their doubts by
asserting that the authors either had ignored or had not
understood the overcoming of the subject-object scheme in
philosophical thought.   The same contradiction was again
indicated in the periodical entitled *Kerygma und Dogma*
published by Wilfried Joest and a number of mainly Lutheran
theologians.   In the first volume [86] it is surprising to see to
what an extent these writers welcome from their own point of
view the challenge to theology arising from Kierkegaard and
existentialist philosophy.[87]   In studying Luther's theses for
the Heidelburg disputation, Edmund Schlink comes to the
conclusion: "The new and striking thing about Luther's
theses is that he did not objectify the experience of justification,
nor did he try to make it cohere with a given ontological
pattern of thought, but remained content with the faith-
experience itself and the human answer to God's address
which it yielded, expounding this answer as if it were in the
truest sense an exact theological statement." [88]   The result is
that "in Luther's *Paradoxon* we find an attack on the ontological foundations of Aristotelian thought.   Thus historically
and existentially determined thought was here breaking down
the scaffolding of Aristotelian-scholastic forms of thought."
Schlink then goes on to show how Luther's attack on Aristotelianism could not succeed, and how, under the influence of
Melanchthon and the universities, "metaphysics as ontology"
again come to prevail.[89]   It was only with the rise of the modern

---

[84] Munich 1952.   [85] Stuttgart 1953.   [86] Göttingen 1955.
[87] On the following, cp. Diem, "Dogmatik zwischen Ontologie und
Personalismus oder das 'Theologische Klima' heute," in *Evangelische
Theologie* (henceforth cited as *Ev. Th.*), 1955.
[88] Schlink, *Weisheit und Torheit,* p. 6.   [89] *Op. cit.,* p. 7.

natural sciences that the latter was effectively broken up. What Melanchthon and, under his influence, scholastic Protestantism wished to hinder did now in fact take place. "The unity of knowledge, as regards method, concepts, and results, was now shattered. . . ."[90] Modern man stands estranged from himself and solitary in the midst of a surrounding hostile nature and history"; and Schlink counts it as a merit in existentialist philosophy that "it has clearly brought out the characteristic consciousness of our time, namely the consciousness of being enclasped by nothingness." [91]

But how does Schlink from this point of view come to construct dogmatic statements? The break-up of the ontology of scholastic Aristotelianism by an historically and existentially determined type of thought is today being continued by "actualistic personalism." The latter can indeed make statements about the action of God in history, but with its anti-ontological tendencies does not succeed in making explicit what is implied by the answer of faith in regard to the being of God. Hence the two aspects, the personal and the ontological must be combined constructively, and Schlink finds the basis and possibility of such a combination in doxology: "In the praise of God, in the glorification of His faithfulness shown in His government of the world from its beginning to its end, there arise necessarily constructive statements about the divine being. Hence it is no accident that while Luther in his anthropology shattered the ontological conceptualism which he had inherited, he remained faithful to it in his doctrine of God." [92]

In all this we see a further characteristic of the present-day situation in theology, which is that for its personalistic type of thought it appeals not only to Kierkegaard but also to Luther, and indeed to the Luther of the "*pro me*" as he is known to us particularly from his explanations of the creed in his catechism. Nor does Schlink seem to have been able to escape this tendency of the times. He proposes to counter the danger to which dogmatics is thereby exposed by distinguishing two aspects in Luther, namely the Luther who in his anthropology thinks personalistically and the Luther who in his doctrine of God thinks ontologically, and to fuse the two by means of doxology.

[90] *Op. cit.*, p. 10.   [91] *Op. cit.*, p. 11.   [92] *Op. cit.*, p. 13.

This new impetus is carried further by Gerhard Gloege,[93] who emphasises even more strongly than Schlink: "We cannot, we will not, and we must not, retreat from theological personalism. This does not mean that we should embrace any particular brand of personalism, but that in general we should feel obliged to think personalistically." [94] Nevertheless he too is afraid that the existential interpretation of Bultmann's hermeneutics may not only fail to do justice to the ontological problems raised by specific Scriptural statements, but may also have dangerous consequences for dogmatics: "If the category and principle of personalism were worked out systematically and consistently . . . it would mean the dissolution of all dogmatic thinking. . . ."[95] "In any case, viewing the matter as a whole, it has meant the transubstantiation of dogma into sheer *kerygma*." [96] In order to meet this danger, Gloege demands, after his confession of personalism: "Let us go back to the problematics of ontology which has been far too much neglected!" This raises the question how in a system of dogmatic statements ontological and personalistic thought are related to each other. "The essential answer must be sought in the following point of view: Ontological and personalistic thought are categorically and intrinsically distinct from each other and therefore must be distinguished; but on the other hand they are thematically and materially always bound up with each other and hence must be vitally related into a coherent whole." [97] The conclusion is that ontology must be orientated towards personalism, and, conversely, personalistic thinking presupposes ontological foundations. This Gloege thinks to be true of all the great personalistic thinkers of Christianity: Paul, Luther, Pascal, Kierkegaard, and even Gogarten. In this connexion we would like to ask of course whether we are to see in the work of Paul, Luther and Kierkegaard the dialectic of ontology and personalism, and especially whether it was by means of this dialectic that they evolved their dogmatic structures. Gloege at any rate considers this possible and conceives such a dialectic in the following way:

[93] See G. Gloege, "Der theologische Personalismus als dogmatisches Problem," in *Ev. Th.*, 1955, pp. 23 ff.

[94] Gloege, *op. cit.*, p. 34.   [95] *Op. cit.*, p. 37.

[96] *Op. cit.*, p. 38.   [97] *Ibid.*

"Ontology is dissolved by personalistic thinking. The latter represents a crisis for ontological modes of thought and expression." [98]   And consistently with this view he must say, like Bultmann, Gogarten, etc.: "The usefulness of a dogmatic statement is to be tested by the extent to which it can be recast in terms of personalistic thought."   But this "dissolution" is meant only in a dialectic sense: the *conservare* corresponds to the *tollere*, for "ontology is conserved by personalism. Personalistic thinking lays the foundations of ontological formulations and retains them in its service.   The life situation of the ontological synthesis is found in doxology."   Here Gloege is adopting and interpreting the suggestion of Schlink: "Doxology, however, is a mode of personal existence.   The fact is that the personal experience of salvation demands a super-personal ontological statement transcending that experience itself."

Let us compare with this the remark of Hans Jonas already quoted,[99] to the effect that dogmas represent "a fundamental ontological transformation of phenomena, a translation into another mode of being which affects the deepest elements of subjective existence: their hypostatisation so that from being merely existential quantities they become quasi-observable realities analogous to the phenomena of the external world," which incidentally Gogarten quotes with approval.[100]   But Jonas and Gloege draw opposite conclusions from this precisely similar explanation of the character of dogma.   For Jonas the task of interpreting dogma lies in the dissolution of its formulations into their existential basis, and with Bultmann and Gogarten this attitude leads to the disintegration of dogma itself, while Gloege, on the other hand, uses the "personal experience of salvation" as a means of laying the foundation of the ontological content of dogma and thus giving a solid scientific basis to dogmatics.   But what does this difference of intention amount to in the end?   Both thinkers find themselves faced with the same dialectic of "ontology" and "personalism," only they for the moment take opposite sides and have contrasting purposes: it is of no use to Gloege that he simply attempts to retreat to an earlier stage in the dialectical process

---

[98] *Op. cit.*, p. 40.   [99] Above, p. 26.
[100] *Die Verkündigung Jesu Christi*, 1948, p. 474.

by which dogma is ultimately disintegrated. This whole process can have no other end but the dissolution of dogmatics and the triumph of consistent personalism; and this development cannot be held up or reversed by postulates and desiderata.

In this way the radical threat to dogmatics is only unintentionally confirmed by those Lutherans who intervened to rescue the latter. From the Lutheran standpoint, some quite different possibilities are suggested by, for example, the work of H. J. Iwand.[101] He tries to show "the meaning and the part played by the *pro me* within Protestant theology before and after Kant" and to compare the two stages. He is concerned to "point out that a fundamental change took place in the theological significance and the scholarly use of the *pro me*." He thinks that "the Reformers' *pro me* had in the main an intrinsic significance and was an integral part of the Gospel of Jesus Christ 'who was put to death for our trespasses and raised for our justification' (Rom. IV. 25); later, however, it acquires a formal significance and denotes a methodological distinction between two modes of knowledge, and although one of these does not concern me as a person and is therefore called objective or metaphysical knowledge, the other is of vital import to my existence as man and confronts me as subject with the question of God, challenging me to decide whether or not I shall accept the existence of a supreme being as a religious unity transcending the law of nature and the law of ethics. In this formal or even existential sense the *pro me* has been made a methodological principle by which is decided, in the sphere of revelation, between two methods of knowledge, the objectified and the non-objectified, the objective and the subjective, the impersonal and the personal." [102] Hence the author is concerned to forbid here that very distinction between formal and intrinsic on which Gloege builds everything. "Perhaps we might say that at least from A. Ritschl through the line of W. Hermann up to R. Bultmann and F. Gogarten this methodological use of the

[101] "Wider den Missbrauch des '*pro me*' als methodische Prinzip in der Theologie," *Theologische Literaturzeitung* (henceforth cited as *Th. Lit.-Z.*), 1954, pp. 453 ff. (also in *Ev. Th.*, 1954, pp. 120 ff.).
[102] Iwand, *op. cit.*, pp. 453 ff.

pro me is practised as something typically Protestant and that its use results in the equation 'dogmatic statements = metaphysical statements,' which stands like an impassable barrier before the free development and formation of theological ideas. I am concerned to consider whether this barrier is of such a nature that it indicates a divinely-ordained limit and can be ignored only by the theologian who is actuated by the interests of arbitrary speculation, or whether it is only an apparent barrier which it must be the task of a theology of revelation to overcome or transfer. I may add that I am of the latter opinion, which if followed would open up to us a broad and long neglected field of dogmatic insights and judgments. For it is not without necessity and not merely for the sake of breaking with established practice that we feel compelled to produce this theory which shatters a significant tradition of Protestantism." [103]

In order to complete our study of the present situation in dogmatic theology we must point out that voices such as these are raised. But they are hardly heard, still less have they been able to check the critical challenge to dogmatics. The actual situation is as Ernst Käsemann no doubt rightly describes it: "Not without reason has W. Janasch [104] spoken of a 'harmful cleavage between critical exposition and systematic tendencies,' and of the fatal impression one has 'that dogmatic theologians and New Testament critics have two quite different New Testaments before them.' He then continues: 'This impression suggests, in my judgment, one of the severest disabilities weighing upon our younger theologians, who go about their work either rejecting all dogmatics and armed merely with a more or less one-sided and critical exegesis, or on the other hand they regulate their exegesis by the principles of dogmatics.' This brings out a characteristic feature of the situation: consistently as New Testament scholarship has turned away from a merely historical point of view and has come to envisage wider theological implications, it has done so in full continuity with its own previous history, and this in fact means in continuity with historical criticism. The degree of consistency with which this has been done varies in detail, but not really the line of approach as such. On the other hand, the

[103] *Op. cit.*, pp. 454 ff.   [104] In *Th. Lit.-Z.*, 1951, p. 5.

tendency of modern systematic theology in general has been to feel little need to engage in a serious consideration of the questions, the insights, and above all the methods of exegesis. It exploits or it attacks the conclusions of the latter, according as it finds them agreeable or not, yet for the most part it passes right over the deep problems of historical criticism with a curious unconcern or perhaps embarrassment, and not seldom constructs its own theses as though the last two centuries of theological development had not taken place or had really been satisfactorily terminated. As a result exegesis on its part has been compelled to ask questions or to make formulations which ignore the dogmatic efforts of our time with equal detachment and aloofness. Open discussion between these two disciplines has in fact been abruptly suspended and all possibility of understanding has become extremely difficult. The consequences of all this firstly for students and secondly for the Church are immediately plain; theological activity is now being carried on quite insufferably on two separate lines. Exegesis has become visibly aggressive while dogmatics is above all concerned to preserve and protect Church tradition." [105]

[105] Käsemann, "Probleme der Neutestamentlichen Arbeit in Deutschland," in *Die Freiheit des Evangeliums und die Ordnung der Gesellschaft*, Beiträge zur *Evangelische Theologie*, BD. XV, 1952, p. 138.

CHAPTER II

DOGMATIC AND BIBLICAL THEOLOGY

As an introduction to the debate between dogmatic and Biblical theology we shall refer chiefly to the work of Karl Barth and Rudolf Bultmann as the exponents of the two types of thought which most strongly conflict in this matter. But we would like first to deal with the Roman Catholic position, since not only does it form historically the background to Evangelical theology, but also as the limiting conception always belongs to the discussion.

(a) *Roman Catholicism and Heinrich Schlier*

The division between dogmatic and Biblical theology, and hence the discrepancy between dogmatics and exegesis, is unknown to the doctrine of the Roman Catholic Church. The Vatican Council decreed: *"Porro fide divina et catholica ea omnia credenda sunt, quae in verbo Dei scripto vel tradito continentur, et ab Ecclesia sive solemni iudicio sive ordinario et universali magisterio, tamquam divinitus revelata credenda proponuntur."* [1] Here no distinction is admitted between historical and dogmatic truth, since dogmatic statements which are described as *veritates revelatae* concern a historical event, the self-revealing action of God. But this revealing event is regarded as the norm for dogma not merely in one specific period, i.e. the earthly life of Jesus, or the period in which the canon of Holy Scripture evolves through the tradition of the Church. Rather the period of revelation is extended to cover the history of the Church, so that neither the life of Jesus nor the canon of Scripture is considered as a piece of Church tradition qualitatively distinct from the later tradition of the Church, and neither can nor must be fixed as a norm to check the latter. The tradition of the Church receives from the mediation of

[1] H. Denzinger, *Enchiridion definitionum*, (henceforth cited as Denz.), No. 1792

D

Holy Scripture and the *regula fidei* of the creed (which at least in its earliest forms goes back to the Apostles) its historical continuity with the life of Jesus, and hence the process of revelation continuing in the history of the Church gains a historical basis. But this historical basis does not have to verify the dogmatic formulae; rather it is the opposite: the decisions of the teaching office of the Church legitimate the results of historical development, inasmuch as, from time to time, they exalt to the status of *dogma fidei* what previously was believed in the Church only implicitly or virtually.[2]

In this way a dogmatic formula can never be challenged by historical criticism, no matter whether it is a question of lending dogmatic authority to a particular event (e.g. the resurrection of Jesus or the bodily assumption of the Virgin Mary), or of expressing in dogmatic form the interpretation of such an event. The idea of the *veritas revelata* embraces truth in both senses. But on the other hand all desirable freedom is given to critical investigation of Scripture and the history of the Church. The one result of such research which the Catholic Church would have to fear would be the disproof of its hypothesis of historical continuity between the Church and the life and work of Jesus. But it is impossible to prove in any general sense the lack of such continuity, and further in the special sense in which the Church lays emphasis on this continuity, namely the Apostolical succession of its episcopate; no positive counter-arguments can be adduced owing to the lack of uninterrupted sources. But the Church not only need not fear the results of historical research, it can positively avail itself of the latter in order to make intelligible its dogmatic decisions. Although the conclusions of historical research do not have to bear the weight of any burden of proof, nevertheless the Church is interested in them, for at least it is concerned to push the basis of the presuppositions and principles behind its dogmatic decisions as far back into history as possible and so to escape the difficulty, ever more advertised by Evangelical theology, that between the formation of Scripture and the beginning of the history of dogma there lies a gulf which can scarcely be bridged. The fusion, so characteristic of Catholic theology, between historical and dogmatic judgments, brings

[2] Cp. Diem, *Theol.*, VOL. I.

with it of course the danger to which Catholic historical research constantly succumbs, that a later stage of development is projected back into an earlier time, and that the earlier stages are interpreted in the light of the later. But even if they were in any degree capable of proof, the historically mistaken judgments which arise in this manner become irrelevant by reason of dogmatic presuppositions.

A quite remarkable example of this is the work of Heinrich Schlier.[3] Here, not only has the work been done with all the resources of modern New Testament scholarship—Schlier is a pupil of Bultmann—but also the great change in philosophy from the idealistic subject-object pattern to phenomenological ontology has been accomplished. Schlier, who became converted to Rome in 1953, wrote this dissertation as an Evangelical theologian, but hardly any better New Testament basis for Catholic dogma can be discovered than what he attempts to furnish here. He treats, according to 1 Cor. Paul's debate with Greek Christianity under the heading of *kerygma* and *sophia, faith* and *gnosis.* Paul has to contend against the misunderstanding that in the Gospel it is principally a question of something like a philosophical *logos*, and that the Gospel is a degenerate variety of the Greek *sophia* or philosophy.[4]

This would destroy the whole saving effect of the Cross of Christ, which depends on the way in which the Gospel is presented, whether with "the wisdom of words" or with "the foolishness of preaching" (1 Cor. 1. 21).[5] Both the *sophia* which is here being attacked and the *logos* in which it is appropriately expressed are qualified firstly by the word συζητεῖν (1 Cor. 1. 20)—"in the vocabulary of the New Testament a word denoting disputation by Jews and heretics." [6] Secondly, by the word ἀποδεῖξις (1 Cor. 11. 4)—which means "demonstration by argument and conclusion. The *logos* in wisdom of this kind persuades or convinces by putting forward

[3] See H. Schlier, "*Kerygma* und *Sophia*, zur neutestamentlichen Grundlegung des Dogmas," henceforth cited as Schlier, in *Ev. Th.*, 1950-1, pp. 481 ff.

[4] Schlier, pp. 481 ff.   [5] Schlier, p. 482.

[6] Schlier, p. 483 (but cp. Mk. 1. 21, IX. 10, XII. 28; Lk. XXII. 23, XXIV. 15; Acts VI. 9, IX. 29—where the disciples, Jesus Himself, and Paul do this same thing, and where the word in no way suggests an attitude typical of the σοφία τοῦ κοσμοῦ).

cogent intelligible grounds." Thirdly, by dependence on a human tradition, "which in the last resort springs from the elements of this world." Fourthly, by the fact that the exponents of the wisdom of the *logos* claim for themselves the possession of *gnosis*. "Hence in the enquiring argumentative *sophia* Paul sees something which Jews, Greeks, and Corinthian gnostics have in common—at any rate by comparison and contrast with the *kerygma* which is contrasted with all such wisdom. . . . This wisdom is always and from the start the result of the way man and the world are experienced and interpreted by a self." [7]

How does it come about that Paul describes this wisdom as ματαιότης? By the sending of the *kerygma* God has put all such wisdom "out of currency" and "passed it over as a way to true knowledge," and that because this wisdom has missed the "opportunity of enlightenment that was originally open to it, and thus has already proved itself to be folly." [8] This original possibility of enlightenment lies in the fact "that God so created the world by His wisdom that the reflexion of the divine wisdom within it pointed to its Creator." Or, in other words: "To know is here nothing else than a mystical awareness of God through the illumination of that which has come to be in the divine light of being itself. . . . But, the Apostle thinks, the situation of man and the world, as history reveals it, is as follows: at present man, in the knowledge which he gains through the creation, is no longer referred back to God the Creator, his knowledge now refers him back only to himself the creature. As shown by Rom. 1. 21, his understanding no longer leads him to the recognition of God as Creator. . . . Since he refuses to acknowledge his debt to God and fixes his attention solely upon the creature, the knowledge he gains from the created world takes him no farther than the latter itself. . . . Involved as he is in self-deception through his own perverse ingratitude, man distorts even the truth of his own being, i.e. his own palpable created reality. Therewith he falsifies such knowledge as he has attained." [9] Of course among the various philosophers there are degrees of approximation to naked and original truth and reality; thus, for example, Plato and the pre-Socratics are to be preferred to

[7] Schlier, p. 484.   [8] Schlier, p. 485.   [9] Schlier, pp. 485 f.

the moralistic Stoicism of the first century A.D.; but here too
the reflective observer must note that "being itself withdraws
when it is reflected in that which has come to be. Thus being,
when it illuminates the creature, infects it with error." [10] From
this point of view, even Paul admits at least a relative correctness of understanding on the part of the creature, when in
Rom. II he says that the Gentiles have some intimation of the
good, and even fulfil it in sporadic and fragmentary good
deeds, which express their search for goodness itself.[11]

First we note here with a question mark the statement that
not only as a preacher, but even, before that, as a reflective
philosopher, Paul is aware of the tragic destiny of man and his
wisdom in history, and we enquire further what, in contrast
to the *sophia* which Paul rejects, is that *kerygma* which is the
appropriate and true expression of the Gospel. As "the word
of the Cross" it too is plainly a *logos*. It is to be understood
as the "authentic public preaching of a message, it concerns
all men, can readily be crystallised into a formula," and its
content is the event of the person of Jesus, acknowledged as
the Lord and the Christ. "Accordingly, the *kerygma* is the
proclamation of the events of the death and resurrection of
Jesus Christ, which have already taken place and are at work
with saving effect. It is the public proclamation by the
Apostles of Jesus Christ as the Lord, couched in the clear
terms of a formula, and of the events of His cross and rising
again from the dead, which demonstrate Him to be such." [12]
This significance of the *kerygma* is exemplified in the dogmatic
phrases of I Cor. xv. 1-11, where we see in the resurrection of
Jesus Christ from the dead "the full and unique revelation of
that truth which has been concealed in and by history," and
which is now enshrined in "the exclusive word of Apostolic
witnesses, a word dictated by the events themselves." [13] In this
testimony the revelation of the truth was handed on in the form
of human words.[14] This word of revelation is marked by a
tendency to unified expression in the testimony of all the
witnesses to it, and thus becomes "normative for the Gospel
and its preaching, normative also for faith which is essentially

[10] M. Heidegger, *Holzwege*, 1949, p. 310.
[11] Schlier, p. 488. [12] Schlier, p. 490.
[13] Schlier, pp. 490 ff. [14] Schlier, p. 491.

bound up with this epitomising formula." [15]   Paul refers the
Corinthians to the crystallised tradition, and "this *paradosis*
is, properly speaking, the Gospel itself.   For it is the essential
core of the Gospel.   And not only that—it is the norm of the
Gospel also."   The "symbol" which thus emerges is therefore
not something secondary and derivative from Gospel or
Scripture, but rather "it is itself the source of the Gospel,
which as preaching develops the *kerygma* and the word of
revelation it contains.   The *kerygma* as the normative Apostolic
paradosis precedes both in time and, in the last analysis, in
substance also, the Gospel considered as preaching." [16]   Only
in this way can the real sharpness of the contrast between
sophia and *kerygma* be appreciated.

The decisive link in this argument is the weight of significance
assigned to the so-called pre-symbols, i.e. the formal statements
of belief contained here and there in the New Testament
writings.   Schlier thinks that these credal formulae are not
simply to be understood, as they commonly are, as confessions
of faith, but that "these pre-symbols and the credal formulae
in general are, in accordance with their origin, the self-revelation of the Risen Saviour reflected in the words of the Apostolic
witness," and "in a literal sense were the outcome of the self-
attestation of the Risen Lord in the presence of witnesses." [17]
This testimony of witnesses is taken up by the Church through
the agency of the Holy Ghost, elaborated and repeated.   Here
we are in the presence of, firstly, "an extension of the revelation
of the Risen Lord in a continuously resounding Apostolic
word;   and, secondly, of an inspired confession of the Church
adopting this word as the very mark of its life. . . .   Thus the
credal formulae have, in accordance with their origin, the
dignity of revelational statements grasped, crystallised, and
formulated by the general consensus of the Church under the
inspiration of the Holy Spirit."

At this point we must note that the temporal and intrinsic
priority of the *kerygma* in the shape of the pre-symbol, as the
very essence and norm of the Gospel itself, will have decisive
consequences for the relationship of Scripture and dogma.
By identifying the *kerygma* with the credal symbol which is
engendered by a literal formulation of the content of revelation,

[15] *Ibid.*   [16] Schlier, pp. 491 f.   [17] Schlier, p. 492, n. 17.

Schlier has reached the earliest possible historical locus for the genesis of dogma, and has placed this prior to the Scriptural crystallisation of the Gospel tradition. At the same time, dogma as the norm of Scripture is made intrinsically superior to the latter. Dogma is nothing other than *kerygma* in its later form. No doubt for the further development of dogma in the history of the Church, Scripture, growing up around the *kerygma* as its nucleus and as the historically oldest part of tradition, has an important part to play. But it can never acquire a normative significance for the development of dogma. Rather the relationship is the reverse; and the elaboration of the *regula fidei*, proceeding in parallelism with the formation of the canon of Scripture, is by no means intended merely as a summary of the content of Scripture for pedagogic, missionary, and liturgical purposes, but rather provides an authoritative norm for the interpretation of Scripture itself.

The proclamation of the resurrection of Christ means in fact "the proclamation of the foundation and beginning of a new aeon, of that aeon which lives in the strength of the destruction of death through Jesus Christ, and in which therefore is known the resurrection of the dead." [18] This tradition fashioned by the *kerygma*, and implying the new world with its future to be revealed by God, "is utterly groundless and undemonstrable from the point of view of the old world and its traditions . . .,[19] is indeed " unthinkable and inexpressible," [20] and so as regards the *kerygma* there can be but unproven faith in the proclamation, and there is no possibility of demonstrative argument. "This crystallised *kerygma* remains outside of and prior to all human seeking and enquiry." [21] It lies "so authoritatively beyond all human arrangement and control that even the Apostle can be but its poor human tool." Faith in this *kerygma* "consists in the acceptance of the validity of a presupposition, the presupposition namely that in the resurrection of Jesus Christ through the power of God is contained the authentic disclosure of ultimate reality."

We note that this unprovableness, permitting of no discussion, but only believing acceptance of the proclamation, applies not only to the preaching of the revelatory events but also to

[18] Schlier, p. 493.   [19] *Ibid.*   [20] Schlier, p. 494.   [21] *Ibid.*

the *kerygma* in which the revelation is enshrined. Schlier's
disinclination towards the συζητεῖν, and his one-sided emphasis
on this idea in a bad sense, is here once more corroborated by
reference to the Pastoral Epistles, with their warning against
λογομαχεῖν (II Tim. II. 14), μωρὰς ζητήσεις (Tit. III. 9), etc.,
and their injunction to preserve the deposit, the Apostolic
inheritance ἐκτρεπόμενος τὰς βεβήλους κενοφωνίας καὶ ἀντιθέσεις
τῆς ψευδωνύμου γνώσεως (I Tim. VI. 20; cp. II Tim. II. 2-16).
This does not exclude, it includes, the development of the deposit
in various ways in teaching, persuasion, explanation. . . .
This doctrine is essentially (i.e. by reason of its origin) no
ζήτησις but an interpretation and explication of the Apostolic
paradosis.[22]   Among the texts quoted by Schlier stands
II Tim. III. 14, but noticeably not v. 15 ff.—just as in dealing
with the formula of I Cor. xv he ignores the repeated κατὰ τας
γραφάς (v. 3 ff.).   Hence the extremely important question
how the Apostolic deposit is related to the γραφή remains open.
Perhaps Schlier does not go into this question because for him
it goes without saying that the formulated *kerygma*, thanks to
the newly-founded tradition, becomes the norm *even of the Old
Testament*, although it is not the historical kernel of the Old
Testament as it is of the New.   In that case, the relation
between dogma and Scripture would be the same for the Old
as for the New Testament except that in the domain of the
New Testament the attempt to provide an historic basis for the
dogmatic structure would be lacking.   Or it may be that
Schlier after all understands by the ἱερὰ γράμματα (II Tim.
III. 15) and the γραφὴ θεόπνευστος (v. 16), not at all the
Scripture of the Old Testament but the crystallised pre-
symbol. This, too, would be possible and even historically
justifiable, if Walter Bauer is right [23] in maintaining (a) that
it is most improbable that the Old Testament was regularly
and thoroughly read by the earliest Christian communities,
but (b) that it is highly probable that there arose very early a
written formulation of the most important Christian doctrines,
even if this early fragmentary literature [24] certainly did not
merely contain the pre-symbols, but already included all

[22] Schlier, p. 494, n. 20.
[23] *Der Wortgottesdienst der ältesten Christen*, 1930.
[24] Bauer, *op. cit.*, pp. 47 ff.

sorts of narrative material too. It would fit in very well with Schlier's outlook as a whole to describe this type of tradition as γραφὴ θεόπνευστος. But the supposition would be contradicted by the fact that among the Greek-speaking Jews ἱερὰ γράμματα is the name for the Scriptures of the Old Testament, as Martin Dibelius [25] shows by quotations from Philo and Josephus. But however Schlier may conceive the relation of the deposit to the Old Testament the normative status of formulated doctrine excluding all ζήτησις is for him the decisive factor. Here we see an anticipation of the characteristic Catholic relationship between Church doctrine and theology, according to which in all theological questions the decisions of the Church's teaching office are final, and though theological disputation may explain, comment on, and draw out the consequences of these decisions, it remains itself, in the last resort, of no binding force.

What, now, does it mean for man when he "is turned away from *sophia* and directed towards the *kerygma*"? [26] To those who are called by the Gospel, *kerygma* serves among other things for true wisdom and understanding. "To understand in this sense is a means to personal fulfilment through enlightenment." [27] The wisdom mediated by the *kerygma* frees man from his self-concern, his self-security, his self-edification. "This applies of course only to that faith which is a concrete acceptance of the proferred *kerygma*, not to that—for in truth it is no faith at all—which means man's decision to accept his personal being and freedom" (here Schlier is no doubt attacking Bultmann). This self-committal to the *kerygma* which is effected through the death of man and gives him a new and quite different *sophia*, is "alien only to his historical and not to his true and original being, for which rather it frees him by means of his mortification." [28] Thereby man renounces all the superiority which he gains from the *logos* of the *sophia*. Belief in the *kerygma* and the wisdom which it brings implies therefore "the surrender of all other knowledge for the sake of the sole knowledge of Christ and Him crucified. And, secondly, it means the decision to dare to be inferior in the world of reason." [29] But "through the submission of the

[25] *Handbuch zum Neuen Testament, s.v.* [26] Schlier, p. 495.
[27] Schlier, p. 496. [28] Schlier, p. 498. [29] Schlier, p. 499.

intellect to the irrational *kerygma* a new knowledge is attained and also an insight, which are gifts of God, and as such impart to the believer a new and real superiority in wisdom and understanding." [30]   God has superseded the σοφία τοῦ κόσμου so characteristic of historical man, and by the gift of His wisdom in Jesus Christ and His self-revelation in the *kerygma* has shown it to be "ignorance and folly." "To Jesus Christ, and so to the wisdom of God, there is no longer any access by enquiry and argument, by the advancing of reasons, but only by obedient acceptance in faith. In the decline of the process of history, wisdom is only to be found in obedient assent to the self-revelation of God in the concrete declarations of the *kerygma*." [31]   But the supremely important question is whether Christ is wisdom for the believer in such a way that the latter is wise only in the moment of religious faith, and so only as a believer. Or does divine wisdom work in such a way that *kerygma* and faith free the believer to move in the direction of their own wisdom—in such a way that Christ is wisdom in the sense that He opens up to the believer, through the *kerygma*, a new wisdom that is manifested in his way of life and speech? According to Paul there is no doubt about this.[32] As a charismatic gift this wisdom is a real capacity, at the basis of which some natural capacity may well lie, "such as the faculty of perception, judgment, reflexion, speech, etc." [33] But in obedience to the *kerygma* there comes into existence an intellectual impartiality conducive to the discovery of truth, which is "essentially the grace of the wisdom of love"; and hence follows "a newly awakened wisdom of the creation." [34] This wisdom is a different thing from the doctrine engendered by the *kerygma*. "As a gift it is legitimate in the mouth of every Christian, whereas in principle the *kerygma* and the doctrine which flows from it presuppose mission and hence authority." [35] . . . "Thus this wisdom says nothing other than the *kerygma*, but it dwells more with the man and his world that are saved by Christ than with Christ and the event of salvation." [36]

We note "that *kerygma* and *sophia* are intrinsically not

---

[30] Schlier, p. 500.   [31] *Ibid.*   [32] Schlier, p. 501.
[33] Schlier, p. 502.   [34] Schlier, p. 503.
[35] Schlier, p. 504.   [36] *Ibid.*

divorced in the Christian manner of life, but yet are distinct and separable." [37] This suggests that the doctrine containing the *kerygma* is strictly related to the events of revelation, though at the same time it gives birth to a wisdom which searches and illuminates the whole field of human existence and experience. The revelation recorded in the *kerygma* is the basis of this wisdom. "In the *kerygma*, wisdom is once more disclosed as a foundation principle of life." [38]

The determinative presupposition behind all these inferences is Schlier's distinction between original and historical man. "Knowledge of the truth belongs to man's original being. But this being is no longer apparent in the actual life of humanity." [39] Because man refuses to recognise his debt to God, he understands the ultimate ground of creation only in the light of the creation itself. But being itself, the naked truth of things, is not therefore cancelled, it "constantly presses for recognition, and despite his ever-present distortions man has some intimation of it." The *kerygma* opens up once more the possibility of enlightenment, but this arises not from search and enquiry within the human situation, but from a direct revelation of the truth itself. Now there are not only "records of man's own interpretation of his experience in the world, but records of God's own interpretation of life, summed up in the *kerygma*." [40] The *kerygma* "offers us essentially what in later theology is called '*dogmata fidei*,' or more briefly 'dogma'. For the two essential phases of dogma—the *veritates a Deo revelatae et ab ecclesia propositae* with all that they include—constitute also the essence of the *kerygma*." [41]

In the new world situation thus opened up man can once more be wise. "This applies to all wisdom, which of course is one in essence. The spirit of wisdom as aroused by dogma implies a fundamental fusion of natural and supernatural wisdom, the former being the now emancipated wisdom of the creature, the latter the proffered wisdom of the Redeemer. The separation of wisdom in philosophy and theology, if intended as an essential distinction, is an abstraction, which, as we have seen, the Apostle does not recognise, because it does not correspond to the reality of the knowing mind." [42]

[37] *Ibid.*   [38] Schlier, p. 505.   [39] *Ibid.*
[40] *Ibid.*   [41] Schlier, p. 506.   [42] Schlier, pp. 506 f.

The positive conclusion is that, "thanks to the advent of dogma, knowledge of the truth once more exists in this world. That such knowledge is possible again is a sign of the grace under which this aeon stands: the grace of salvation. The fact that *kerygma* and dogma, which have superseded all self-centred thinking, stand in the midst of all human wisdom, to give it back to man in a higher form—that is essentially a fact of eschatology." [43]

(b) Karl Barth

Barth begins with the thesis: "Dogmatics as a theological discipline is the scientific self-examination of the Church with regard to the content of its characteristic message concerning God." [44] The "question of truth" thus raised is expressed in the following terms: "The question of the agreement of this characteristic message about God with the essential being of the Church." [45] Thus the criterion of truth is the "essential being of the Church," i.e., however, as Barth adds in elucidation, "Jesus Christ = God in His gracious self-revealing and redemptive action directed towards man." This criterion is to be applied to the theological problem of truth in a threefold way: "Does the Christian message *flow from* this divine source? Does it *lead to it*? Does it *reflect it*? None of these questions may be asked without raising the others, but each must be put independently with all due weight." [46] There follows from this a distribution of theological work into three disciplines: "*Biblical* theology is an enquiry into the source, *practical* theology is an enquiry into the end, *dogmatic* theology is an enquiry into the content of the Church's characteristic message." [47]

With reference to these definitions, let us consider first the relation of *Biblical* to *dogmatic* theology. The duty of Biblical theology is to enquire into the basis of what the Church says about God's turning to man in Jesus Christ, in the sense that it must decide whether the message of the Church flows from God. How is this to be understood? Here it is clearly pre-

---

[43] Schlier, p. 507.

[44] *Kirchliche Dogmatik*, (henceforth cited as *K. D.*), vol. i. 1, p. 1. (Eng. trans., *Church Dogmatics*, tr. G. T. Thomson, Edinburgh 1935).

[45] *K. D.*, vol. i. 1, p. 2.   [46] *Op. cit.*, p. 3.   [47] *Ibid.*

supposed that theology is primarily concerned not with a truth but with a happening, with the revealing Word of God, and with what the Church declares about it. Again, it should be noted that this Word is not the communication of a truth about God, but an action in which God at every stage is the subject of the revealing action. It is from this point of view that we must understand the enquiry of Biblical theology into the basis of the Word, and the question whether this really flows from God. Thus there can be no question of proving that the Word, which lies behind the Church's message, is possible and has actually taken place. So much is simply assumed, or rather is founded *a posteriori* on the existence of the Church, and on the fact that the Church speaks about this Word of God. The question of proof can therefore only be put in regard to the question of the identity and continuity between this Word of God and the Church's message. This is what is meant by asking whether the Church's message really flows from a divine source. The enquiry is essentially the task of Biblical theology, because the Church knows of this Word of God only through the message of the Bible and on that basis.

But does not this mean that the enquiry is an *historical* one, i.e. an enquiry about the origins and understanding of this Biblical message, and further about the history of its interpretation in the message and life of the Church? Should not Biblical theology accordingly hand over its task to historical theology, or at least share it with the latter? This is denied by that sentence of Barth's which has become so famous, and which has caused so much head-shaking among historians of theology: "So-called Church history can answer no question that may be independently raised about the Christian message of God, and so may not be conceived as an independent theological discipline. It is an indispensable ancillary science for exegetical, dogmatic, and practical theology." [48] In saying this, Barth can hardly wish to dispute that the being of the Church in all its forms and at every stage of its teaching is an historical phenomenon, so that it must be, all along the line, a subject of historical research. So we must ask how he proposes to make use of historical science as an ancillary to theological study. For if we define the task of theology as

[48] *Ibid.*

Barth does, historical research can neither ask nor answer theological questions; neither can it do so if, like Troeltsch, we define it as that of examining and interpreting historical phenomena in forms of the causal continuity and interlocking of all events. If, in treating of the Church, its Scripture, and its preaching as historical phenomena, historical science (thus understood) were to discuss it with reference to the Christian message about God, it would in fact be unable to give a theological answer. For a theological approach to this question would imply that the being of the Church is regarded, not only as an historical phenomenon, but as an event, as to which we must ask whether it is continuous and identical with the self-revealing Word of God. But historical science as such has no means and no criterion for this task.

When, with reference to the questions that both have to answer, Barth says that each question must be put separately, and with all due weight, he expressly emphasises that the tasks of Biblical and dogmatic theology must be kept apart from one another.[49] Thus he rejects the fairly widespread practice of confirming the Church's present doctrinal pronouncements by an equally dogmatic and prejudiced exegesis of Scripture. Such a fusion of Biblical and dogmatic questions and methods would ensure that Scripture itself became, as in the Roman Church, part of the Church's doctrinal tradition, and would no longer be able to act as a check on it. But how can Barth himself avoid this danger? In his scheme of division, Biblical theology has the task of clarifying the Word of God in its original form as contained in Scripture. Dogmatic theology is required to test the soundness of the Church's later doctrine, by measuring it against this original form of the Word of God. But how, in fact, can this come about? Obviously it is not simply a question of systematising the Biblical texts as recovered by Biblical theology, and then passing off a summary of them as dogmatics. Dogmatic theology must pursue its enquiry independently, must ask whether the Church's message is consonant with the truth of God—that is, with the Church's essential being, Jesus Christ Himself. It cannot resign this enquiry to the hands of Biblical theology, because the Biblical affirmations themselves are not *veritates revelatae,*

[49] *K. D.,* VOL. I. I, p. 3.

are not truths of revelation. "A truth of revelation is the free initiative of God Himself and that alone. . . ."[50] Hence dogmatics enquires not what the Apostles and Prophets have said, but what we ourselves are to say on the foundation of the Apostles and Prophets. We cannot leave this task to the investigators of the Scriptural basis whose work must precede it." Thus Barth repudiates the Roman Catholic conception of dogmatics, according to which the truths of revelation deposited in the Biblical texts and in oral Apostolic tradition have only to be further unfolded by the living teaching ministry of the Church. "But neither in dogmatics can it be a question of merely repeating in more systematic and precise form the content of Biblical doctrine." This again repudiates the conception of dogmatics which prevailed in some older Protestant schools in connexion with the later editions of Melanchthon's *Loci communes*.

This Catholic and old Protestant method is impossible, because the Church's being (which is the abiding criterion of all its utterance) *is* the person of Jesus Christ—i.e. "an *action* of God's towards man, an action in contradistinction to which human interpretation of it, however expressed, and especially the dogma believed by the Church, however worthy of attention, simply are not infallible and not removed from continuing criticism as to their soundness." [51] Thus dogmatic formulae are not to be equated with the truth of revelation itself, though they aspire towards it inasmuch as they criticise that equation of God's word with man's which is assumed in the teaching and preaching of the Church. "The essence of all such formulations, that which all dogmas aiming at revealed truth wish to say, is dogma itself; and *that* is the subject of dogmatic enquiry. In describing it as the essence of all such formulations we imply that it is not itself a formulation, and was never proclaimed by any Church. It is what is intended by all such formulae—the dogma for the sake of which the Church proclaims its dogmas. Dogma means the reality whose appearances must take the form of dogmas, and conclusions of dogmatic thought, and by whose authority real dogmas and dogmatic conclusions can come to be, when

[50] *Op. cit.*, p. 15.
[51] *Op. cit.*, p. 14.

they are moulded by it." [52] In this sense Barth could describe dogma as an "eschatological idea" in order to ward off all the illusions and anticipations with which a *theologia gloriae* claims to possess the secret of dogma. But since the term "eschatology" has come to be used in so many different ways it seems no longer advisable to employ this particular expression for Barth's meaning. Otherwise an idealist might suppose that dogma is related to dogmatics in the same way as the thing in itself to the appearance, and thus would imply something transcendental. From this an existentialist would infer that dogma as an eschatological idea suggests in general a fundamental challenge to every possible human statement about God. Thus it will be better if we call dogma, as Barth does, "a concept of relationship." The point is that in dogmatic formulae there should be a connexion with the Word of God. And dogma not only asks dogmatic theology the question whether this is indeed the case, but also lays upon it the task of concerning itself about such a relationship, and that not only in a formal but also in a substantial sense. How can such a relationship be discovered?

Here we must consider the significance of Biblical theology for dogmatics, or more precisely the significance of the Word of God as enshrined in Scripture for the preaching of the Church. "The Bible is not in itself the act of divine revelation." But it *is* "the concrete means by which the Church is reminded of God's self-revelation, is summoned to expect future revelations, and thus invited, strengthened, and guided in its work of preaching." [53] And "only by using this means is the Church able to become aware of the Word of God as a quantity distinct from its own preaching." [54] Thus the task of dogmatics is to test the preaching of the Church as a "primary form" by the "secondary form of the Word of God in Scripture, in so far as the latter again is a witness to its third and original form, viz. revelation itself." Hence the idea of dogma as an idea of relationship may be more closely defined as "the preaching of the Church in so far as it is truly consonant with the Bible as the Word of God." [55]

We might well ask here whether Barth has overcome all

[52] *K. D.*, vol. I. 1, p. 283.   [53] *Op. cit.*, p. 114.
[54] *Op. cit.*, p. 280.   [55] *Op. cit.*, p. 283.

the difficulties to which dogmatics succumbed after the entrance of historical science into the sphere of theology, and in particular whether his point of view permits us to overcome that divorce between exegesis and dogmatics noted by Käsemann. If we start from Troeltsch's outlook we shall hardly understand Barth's point of departure, much less be able to consider it a possible means of solving the problems with which we are faced. He puts the theological problem in a way which could never be accepted by historical science. And so we must ask whether, on the other hand, Barth has thought out the difficulties with which theology was confronted by history, or whether he has simply overleapt them. What, for example, does he make of Lessing's question?

As we have seen, the question is (1) how a specific historical event can have decisive significance for faith, and (2) how the historical gulf is to be overcome so that this event can affect us now. For Barth the first question seems far more interesting and urgent than the second, which he feels to be merely a "subterfuge," the outcome of a covert attempt to hide behind "the problem of the distance between the there-and-then of Jesus and our here-and-now," [56] thus obscuring that quite different and far more genuine difficulty which lies in Peter's exclamation (Lk. v. 8), "'Depart from me, for I am a sinful man, O Lord.' Does not this mean: 'How do you come into my environment and what can become of me in yours? How can you and I exist in the same space and time?' That is the voice of an eyewitness who did not regard the problem of distance as one that really concerns us, and found no difficulty in accepting the testimony supplied by others, and by his own senses. So much the more was it concerned about quite another problem of distance." [57] Lessing's question about the problem of historical distance is thus overshadowed by a far bigger problem, namely what becomes of the man to whom Jesus Christ has already become contemporaneous through the Holy Spirit in the word of the preacher. Lessing's problem becomes for Barth the problem of Peter.

Even so, an historical problem remains when Barth distinguishes the three forms of the Word of God as follows: (1) the present preaching of the Church as related to the word

[56] *K. D.*, VOL. IV. 1, pp. 320 ff.   [57] *Op. cit.*, p. 319.

E

of Scripture and referred to it as a norm; (2) the witness of
Apostles and Prophets as contained in the canon of Scripture;
and (3) the Word of God itself as revelation. Here at any rate
the distinction of time implies an historical problem. Barth
however treats the question not as an historical but as a dogmatic
problem, when he says that his Word of God in all its three
forms concerns an action of God's, and therefore is "contingently
contemporary, thus emphasising the character of this contemporaneity as action and event." [58] Hence the distinction
of time becomes quite different from that which characterises
other historical events. The difference here is conditioned
"by the different attitude of God towards men." [59] In His
unity with God Jesus Christ stands in a different relation to
men from that of the Biblical witnesses, who as religious men
are not essentially different from the later teachers of the
Church or of other religions, though in their capacity as
witnesses they have over against all others a unique and
characteristic position. Again, our own situation in the
Church, by reason of our connexion with Scripture and
thereby with revelation, and also because of the Church
experience which lies between the Apostles and our own
time, constitutes a third and special position. "It is these
differences of before and after, above and below, which
constitute the time differences of the Word of God" [60]—a
fact which does not apply to other time differences. These
time differences subsisting within the potential simultaneity
of the Word of God may be "resolved, of course, by over-
looking the distinction of these times in the order of God, by
regarding them not as time distinctions in the Word of God,
but as something immanent, i.e. by interpreting them and
appraising them according to their actual human contents.
In that case the appraisal of these distinctions not only need
not hinder a direct appreciation of the continuity and unity
underlying them—the appreciation of our contemporaneity
with Christ and all His saints—but rather is a view which
alone makes possible and gives a basis for such an appreciation,
in that it teaches us to regard and understand the man of
the past, whether he is called Jeremiah or Jesus or Paul or
Luther, as our fellow man, to be criticised, of course, but

[58] *K. D.*, VOL. I. 1, p. 154.   [59] *Op. cit.*, p. 150.   [60] *Ibid.*

also to be venerated and loved, in brief to be lived with as a contemporary." [61]

Barth thinks that in connexion with the formulation of the problem in Lessing and his successors, from Herder and Schleiermacher up to Troeltsch and Harnack, we are faced with such a reduction of the time distinctions in the Word of God to a mere difference of human historical periods, and hence with a reduction of the Word of God to a general revelation of God in history. It was perfectly possible for Lessing to neutralise an historical gulf so understood, together with the nasty time-span yawning between the Bible and ourselves, and the historians who followed him could teach us to do so ever more skilfully. Even the contrast between the incidental truths of history and the necessary truths of reason was likewise surmountable for Lessing by such considerations as the following: "Religion is not true because the Evangelists and Apostles taught it, but the fact is that they taught it because it is true. The traditions of Scripture are to be explained on the basis of their intrinsic truth, and they cannot make it true if it is not so." [62] And, clearly, by virtue of his own insight and experience, Lessing can be the judge of this intrinsic truth. "It was, as he quite rightly saw, the insurmountable difference between Christ and the Apostles, on the one hand, and ourselves, on the other, that disturbed him, and he purposely neglected it in favour of an immanent difference which could then be immanently surmounted. Thenceforward all the more progressive minds, unlike the Enlightenment and Kant, no longer found it difficult and scandalous to interpret revelation as history and history as revelation." [63] But this means that the idea of the Word of God in the strict sense, and to a great extent indeed all that Barth understands by theology and especially by dogmatic theology, is simply lost.

Once again it becomes plain from a different angle why Barth can admit history to be only of subordinate importance within theology, and cannot grant it the capacity for independent theological enquiry. If the time difference in the various forms of the Word of God is made simply a problem of general historical understanding, then that difference can

[61] *K. D.*, VOL. I. I, p. 151.
[62] Lessing, quoted in Barth, *K. D.*, VOL. I. I, p. 151. [63] *Op. cit.*, p. 152.

no longer be viewed within a transcendent potential contemporaneity, and the true theological problems are lost sight
of.　We might ask what significance history has for the
theology of Barth in this subordinate capacity.　For even when
it is seen in the light of potential contemporaneity, the time
difference does after all entail real historical intervals, and
becomes a problem for historical understanding.　This applies
both to the difference between the words of Jesus and the
Scriptures, as also to that between Scripture itself and the
present-day utterance of the Church.　In this matter Barth
would certainly grant that both the preacher and the theologian
should use all the resources of historical science at their
disposal in order to gain an accurate understanding of the
Biblical text.　But he would be concerned to ask whether the
"time for more or less arbitrarily chosen themes of study is
not past, whether the exegesis of the canonical Scriptures as
such, the interconnected exegesis of Genesis, Isaiah, Matthew,
etc., in their unity and consistency, is not the only possible
goal of Biblical scholarship, and whether it should not be
recognised as such and taken in hand with new energy.　This
unique task has been neglected long enough, and as material
for it, the conclusions of higher criticism, which so far has been
practised on different presuppositions, must not and may not
be neglected.　Thus it cannot be by any means a question of
eliminating, and in future leaving out of account, that critical
point of view which has been the hallmark of Biblical research.
The relevant historical questions must be asked of the Biblical
texts, which in their very essence are witnesses, and the
historical distinctions resulting from the answers can only be of
real use when this kind of criticism is made definitely subservient
to the task defined above, and no longer serves the absurd
purpose of trying to recover an historical truth lying behind the
texts.　The historical truth, which Biblical science has to
ascertain in its own way, lies in the true meaning and continuity
of the Biblical texts themselves.　Thus it is not distinct from
the Biblical truth which has to be sought.　Once this is understood and the foolish chase after an historical truth *super
scripturam* is given up in favour of the enquiry, which can be
made with every resource, into the *veritas scripturae ipsius*, then
free and full scope can and must be given to the critical

questions and answers which are demanded by the character of the Biblical testimony as a human document, and therefore an historical quantity. Such questions and answers can and will then simply express the fact that Scripture is being taken seriously in its true character. And this critical approach will then serve to remove Bible-reading and Scriptural exegesis from the arbitrary treatment by which they were constantly threatened in the days prior to criticism, and also to direct and keep on specific lines the question about its objective content, the revelation of God. Thus what is required is not to annul the results of the Biblical research undertaken in recent centuries, not to break off and neglect the enquiries pursued along these lines, but radically to reorientate the *aim* of such research, by recognising that the Biblical texts must be investigated *for their own sake* because the revelation to which they bear witness stands, takes place, and is to be sought, not behind or above them, but in them." [64]

From this point of view it is possible to answer the question how Barth tries to overcome the divorce between exegesis and dogmatics. The first essential for the understanding of scripture is *explicatio*, and its "most important stage is obviously literary-historical examination." [65] Here the most important point is not to be prejudiced by any preconception of what may actually have taken place behind the Scriptural report, and so not to obscure one's approach to the text. For the correct procedure here no special Biblical hermeneutics is required, but the principles of general hermeneutics must be applied to the Biblical text.[66] "The second clearly distinguishable stage in the interpretation of Scripture is the act of *reflexion* about what has been told us in Scripture." In this *we* are "just midway between *sensus* and *usus*, *explicatio* and *applicatio*," [67] and in regard to which it is also to be noted that this act of reflexion guides the examination of the text. For such reflexion we always use a specific scheme of thought or philosophy; we must be aware of this and its dangers, and must be prepared to abandon the scheme of thought whenever our study of the text itself so requires. Thus we must always

[64] *K. D.*, vol. i. 2, pp. 547 f.   [65] *Op. cit.*, p. 810.
[66] Cp. Diem, *Theol.*, vol. i, pp. 102 ff.
[67] Barth, *K. D.*, vol. i. 2, p. 815.

be ready to correct our scheme of thought in the light of Scripture. Precisely the same applies if we proceed, not with philosophical, but with certain theological categories. Here we must be as wary, as we are open to all the possibilities of human thought. In this process of reflexion consists the task of dogmatic theology, as that of Biblical theology consists in *explicatio*. If both take place rightly, by listening to the word of the text, then there can be no real divorce between them; but since this reflexion is a free act of man which he has to accomplish in faith and personal responsibility, there can on the other hand be no guarantee that it will be correctly accomplished and the divorce avoided.

At this juncture we take note of certain queries which have been addressed to Barth, and to which we shall later have to return: is it that on the part of New Testament scholars the impression has arisen that Barth has by no means overcome the divorce between dogmatics and exegesis, even though he has given full scope to critical research and appraised its results positively? This also and especially applies to those New Testament scholars who agree with Barth in refusing to allow that it is permissible to seek behind the texts the figure of the "historical Jesus." Hence it cannot be simply answered that such New Testament critics are still entangled in an historical type of thought and repudiate Barth's dogmatic position. What makes their acceptance of his position so difficult seems rather to be that Barth sets to work only after the conclusion of the canon, and assumes the latter to be a unified and closed dogmatic whole, which has its basis in a special moment of the Word of God, and thus stands outside the factual estimates of historical criticism. As we have seen, the only work left for historical criticism to do is to study the meaning and the context of the individual Biblical writings. In this way, for Barth, historical and Biblical truth coincides. But when the New Testament critics do precisely this, and on the basis of their research come to the conclusion that the individual New Testament writings conflict on decisive questions, as for example has been shown by Philipp Vielhauer in regard to Luke's Acts and the letters of Paul,[68] and by

[68] See P. Vielhauer, "Zum 'Paulinismus' der Apostelgeschichte," in *Ev. Th.*, 1950-1, pp. 1 ff.

Ernst Käsemann for the Second Epistle of Peter,[69] then they cannot avoid asking, with Käsemann, "What are we to think of the canon in which II Pet. has its place as the clearest witness to early Catholicism?"[70] On this we may compare the controversy between Wilhelm Andersen,[71] Götz Harbsmaier,[72] and Philipp Vielhauer, where in the last resort it is a question of whether the theological differences between Paul and Luke concern the "how" but not the "what" of the preacher's message—Andersen affirming this and Vielhauer denying it. He asks: "Are such studies to be allowed only a relative freedom because their inconvenient results disturb our quiet prejudices?"[73] The question is not whether Vielhauer with his more radical conclusions is right as against Andersen, but the more radical one whether the theologian can grant the historian only a restricted liberty for his research, as Andersen suggests [74]—to which the historian must answer with resignation: "The course of the controversy so far, as is seen for example in regard to the discussion about de-mythologising, shows that there can scarcely be any hope that profitable results can be attained from the co-operation of theologians and exegetes."[75] We would prefer not to rest content with this divorce and the resignation to which it must give rise, and would like to ask whether and to what extent it can be resolved in terms of the Barthian position. Up to now he seems not to have succeeded in persuading New Testament scholars that he can resolve it.

(c) Rudolf Bultmann

In considering the theology of Rudolf Bultmann also from the point of view of the relation between dogmatic and Biblical theology, our procedure might be considered doubtful in so far as it is questionable whether and in what sense his theology

[69] See E. Käsemann, "Eine Apologie der urchristlichen Eschatologie,' in *Z. Th. K.*, 1952, pp. 272 ff.

[70] Käsemann, *op. cit.*, p. 296.

[71] See W. Andersen, "Die Autorität der apostolischen Zeugnisse," in *Ev. Th.*, 1953, pp. 467 ff.

[72] See G. Harbsmaier, "Unsere Predigt im Spiegel der Apostelgeschichte," in *Ev. Th.*, 1950-1, pp. 352 ff.

[73] Vielhauer, "Zu W. Andersen," in *Ev. Th.*, 1953, p. 484.

[74] Andersen, *op. cit.*, in *Ev. Th.*, 1953, p. 471.

[75] Vielhauer, *op. cit.*, in *Ev. Th.*, 1953, p. 484.

gives rise to any dogmatic conclusions at all. But behind the exegesis of Bultmann there stands in any event—let us say it without prejudice—a systematic conception. His intention is, just as much as Barth's, to provide, through his exegesis, an answer to the questions which have arisen in theology since the challenge it has received from historical science. Let us then consider how he tries to deal with the questions which have agitated theology from Lessing to Troeltsch.

It goes without saying that the Biblical authors do not pose the question of truth in regard to the events they report in the same sense as that in which such questions occur to the modern historical thinker. Hence they did not distinguish two aspects of this matter of truth: on the one hand, the question of historical fact; on the other, that of meaning. But according to Christian Hartlich and Walter Sachs,[76] whose introduction to the problem of demythologisation Bultmann himself, to our surprise, has described [77] as the best treatise that has been written on this theme, Bultmann thinks "he has proved that at least in the case of Biblical theologians like Paul and John the use of their ideas about the outward events of salvation is conditional upon and determined by the existential content of the *kerygma* and its existential appropriation, by faith towards which the fundamental purpose of both is demonstrably directed. It was Bultmann's intention to prove, in his life's work of exegesis, the essential character of the existential motive and the merely accidental character of the New Testament mythology of salvation considered at the time as real." [78] Once we admit that, Bultmann has succeeded in exegetically proving his thesis. Bultmann's thesis is, of course, that the existential interpretation of the mythology of salvation presented in the New Testament as factual reflects the intention of the New Testament authors themselves; and once he has succeeded in proving this thesis exegetically, there results a surprisingly simple solution to the question of historical fact that has kept theology so breathless since the time of Lessing: namely that the questions (*a*) of the historical truth

---

[76] See C. Hartlich and W. Sachs, "Einführung in das Problem der Entmythologisierung," in *Für Arbeit und Besinnung* 1950-2.

[77] *Kerygma und Mythos*, VOL. II, p. 179.

[78] Hartlich and Sachs, *op. cit.*, 1952, p. 53.

of saving events and (*b*) of their meaning no longer have any-thing to do with each other. On this point we may once more quote Hartlich and Sachs: "If in the mind of the New Testa-ment authors faith as the means of assimilating salvation is of *existential* character, and if, as such, it is shaped by the *message* preached, inasmuch as the latter has existential significance, i.e. brings about a new life in virtue of its content; if, further, the existential understanding, both of faith and of the Word is shown to be the *unconditionally* guiding and basic motive of these New Testament authors, then it follows that the assertions contained in their writings with regard to the factuality of certain saving events is *fundamentally* separable from the existential significance of the latter." [79] But, "as a consequence of a changed historical intellectual situation, it may come about that these two phases still held inseparable in the statements of the New Testament come into conflict, and the belief that certain saving events, also interpretable as mythical, are factual becomes an obstacle to the existential appropriation of the saving message. Then, says Bultmann (with exegetical justification and in conformity with the sense of the New Testament itself), the question must be answered to the effect that, in accordance with this basic *existential* motive, the need to believe that these events are factual can be justly eliminated in favour of the existential character of the message and of the faith which appropriates it—even although such a possibility of conflict was not and could not be present to the minds of the authors themselves." [80]

Leaving aside the question whether this takes place with exegetical justification, we now ask why the two aspects which for the New Testament belong together must today be in conflict. A twofold answer is given. It is said (1) that the actuality of these events cannot be verified by the methods of modern scientific thinking. Here Hartlich and Sachs in-defatigably insist that those who today try to maintain the actuality of these events are failing to think responsibly and strictly,[81] "either by self-deception or untruthfulness or con-scious sacrifice of responsible thinking and judging," [82] are un-

---

[79] *Op. cit.*, 1951, p. 337.   [80] *Op. cit.*, p. 338.
[81] In opposition to Barth; Hartlich and Sachs, *op. cit.*, 1951, p. 340.
[82] *Op. cit.*, pp. 341 ff.

aware of the "moral bearing" of their procedure, and make a
sacrificium intellectus, because in spite of Kant they have not yet
understood that "*a posse ad esse non valet consequentia.*" [83] But
(2) a second answer is given, which has nothing to do with the
difficulty of verifying the truth of these statements, but bases
the incompatibility referred to on a certain conception of
faith: "Bultmann means, in fact, that faith, in the sense of
accepting it as true that certain mythical saving events said
to have occurred in space and time did actually happen, is
incompatible with faith in the sense of existentially appropriat-
ing salvation." [84] But it is not contradictory to combine these
two reasons, of which the one argues that the verification in
question cannot succeed by modern standards, and the other
that in the interest of a certain conception of faith not only
does it not need to succeed, but must not succeed.

Perhaps it is because these interpreters of Bultmann are so
prosaic in their procedure that the contradiction seems so
harsh, even though it appears to be explicable in terms of
Bultmann's own understanding of faith. As an example of the
difficulties of interpretation we might consider F. Gogarten,[85]
who criticises the Lutheran theologians whom he is attacking
on the ground that in their almost pathetic, self-assured
ignorance they completely misunderstand Bultmann's use of
the concepts of "meaning" and "meaningfulness," because
they take them in the usual sense—in exactly the same way as
Hartlich and Sachs, the interpreters praised by Bultmann
himself, do. "For they make no effort to understand this idea,
not even the slightest. It would probably be wrong to suppose
that the temptation to take this idea in the customary sense
was too great for them to be able to resist it. For if we suppose
Bultmann to employ it normally, then everything that he says
is false, and nothing is easier than to refute him. But in their
naïve straightforwardness these theologians inevitably think
in the subject-object pattern of modern philosophy, and that
no doubt is why they take this term, uncritically, almost
unconsciously, in its current subjective sense." [86] "A little
reflexion will enable us to recall that now and then the idea is

---

[83] *Op. cit.,* p. 343.   [84] *Op. cit.,* p. 338.
[85] See F. Gogarten, *Entmythologisierung und Kirche,* 1953, p. 83.
[86] Gogarten, *op. cit.,* p. 84.

used in a sense other than the current one, namely in the sense:
'He pointed out to me,' which is more than 'he said to me,'
and means rather 'He made to me an important explanation.'
It would then be understandable that Bultmann can say:
'The meaning of the history lies in what God wants to convey
to me thereby.' And it is also at once clear what Bultmann
means by the event of salvation which constitutes the meaningfulness of the history of Jesus: in this history it happens that
God tells me something—'that and how Christ is the Saviour
of the world'." [87] But no matter who may in this regard be
interpreting Bultmann correctly, there are, for Bultmann
himself, no historical events in whose real happening he could
or should be interested. The only reality in which he is
interested is the actual existence of the believer. This is
engendered by the fact that "God meets us in His Word." [88]
This takes place in our encounter with the *kerygma* of the New
Testament, where man is affected by the latter as a *verbum
externum*. Such a confrontation produces faith as a new and
existential understanding of the self, in which man is both
pardoned and judged in the concrete actuality of his present
existence. History, which is historically provable neither as
such, nor in its single moments, can take place as true history
only in this process of concrete actual living. We cannot speak
of "the living God" except in terms of this actual concrete
process. [89]

It would be wrong to impute to Bultmann the idea that this
interpretation of the historicity of existence implies only a
philosophical approach to the problem of human existence.
The theme of philosophy, he says, "is not, strictly speaking,
existence itself, but the potentiality of existence; not facts,
but the possibility of facts; it examines existence in the light
of potentiality, but it does not address itself to the urgencies
of actual living." [90] But the encounter of man with the *kerygma*
is relevant to the latter. "It may therefore be said, even at
this point, that theology (unlike philosophy) as a positive

[87] *Op. cit.*, pp. 83 ff.

[88] Bultmann, *Kerygma und Mythos*, VOL. II, p. 202.

[89] Bultmann, *op. cit.*, p. 204.

[90] Bultmann, "Die Geschichtlichkeit des Daseins und der Glaube," in
Z. Th. K., 1930, p. 342.

science is essentially historical, since it speaks of a definite event in the process of actual existence." [91] But—and this is of decisive importance—the ultimate historical fact still accessible to this science is the New Testament *kerygma* concerning the events of salvation, and not these events themselves.

It may be asked whether this definition of theology in contrast to philosophy as a positive science, i.e. as a science which presupposes historical events, is adequate. Clearly its meaning is different from what was implied in our description of theology as an *a posteriori* type of knowledge. But we must notice Bultmann's attempt to distinguish theology not only from philosophy but also from the science of history— even when he himself makes this difficult for us. Hence, in the first place, his view ought not to be interpreted in terms of his novel solution of, and concern with, the question of historical fact, but of his understanding of the New Testament as a proclamation of the Gospel. Here we would allude to Hellmut Traub: [92] "It is the great merit especially of R. Bultmann, in conjunction with M. Dibelius and K. L. Schmidt, to have worked this out and appreciated it anew. This new understanding on the part of Reformed scholars brings an end to centuries of dangerous deviation. These dangers consisted either—in the orthodox form— of misunderstanding dogmatic truth as a question of historical, controllable and guaranteeing fact, as a result of the simple equation 'The Bible is the Word of God' (thus especially in the distortions of fundamentalism, 'everything is in fact exactly as it is stated in the Bible to be'), or in the liberal form which seeks by critical means to separate out from the Gospel genuine history, what really happened, what was factual. In this case a criticism working with its best available resources would have to provide a preliminary guarantee of something which in the first place demands our faith and is in fact only accessible to our faith. In both cases faith is exchanged for an idolatry of the letter or for a reliance on critical scholarship. Dogma or scholarship thus make faith impossible by the security (of

[91] Bultmann, *op. cit.*, p. 343.

[92] See H. Traub, *Anmerkungen und Fragen zur neutestamentlichen Hermeneutik und zum Problem der Entmythologisierung*, 1952.

course an imaginary one) which they demand. Hence it must be pointed out in reply to any criticism of Bultmann which supposes that we are to seek behind the Gospel a solid basis for faith, that all such criticism has understood neither the meaning of Gospel nor that of faith and is not a legitimate criticism." [93]

If, then, we agree with Bultmann that we may not seek behind the *kerygma* of the Gospel a basis for faith, the fact, nevertheless, may not be overlooked that the occurrence of certain specific saving events is precisely what the *kerygma* proclaims. Although, on the one hand, these events may not be historically provable, and may, on the other, require faith as an existential attitude of man, yet the *kerygma* itself and faith in it depend utterly on the supposition that such events did actually happen. Is it legitimate therefore so simply to dissociate the question of the reality of these events from the question of their existential meaning as Bultmann does? At one decisive point Bultmann himself makes an exception to his rule. Although the New Testament assertions have, in detail, a meaning for salvation that is separable from the question of the truth of the events which they report, yet, as a whole, its *kerygma* (for Bultmann) is not to be dissociated from the history of Jesus. Because they are connected with the text as an historical document which reports the history of the crucified and risen Christ, the *kerygma* and faith too are bound up with this history. Thus the further question arises whether Bultmann thinks that between the *kerygma* of the history of Jesus and this history itself there is such a nexus as to imply a real dependence of the *kerygma* and its exegesis on this history. On this point Günter Bornkamm [94] says: "The insistence on the meaning of the saving events is unquestionably with him the one factor which prevents a transmutation of theology into anthropology, a dissolution of the Christian message into an enlightening truth. . . . But the events of salvation are for him reducible to the brute fact, the bare, completely inaccessible fact, which in its unprovableness requires the utmost submission of faith—the fact *that* in Jesus Christ the revelation of God took place and God acted for our redemption. Jesus

[93] Traub, *op. cit.*, p. 7.
[94] See G. Bornkamm, "Mythos und Evangelium," in *Theologische Existenz heute*, n.s., XXVI (1951).

Christ has become a mere saving fact and has ceased to be a person. He Himself has no longer any history. . . . Everything which goes beyond this brute fact, one might almost say, this grammatical 'that' of the saving fact, is either past history or mythology which anthropologically (or, better, existentially) can no longer be elucidated." [95]

The problem whether and to what extent the question of the reality of these saving events is separable from their significance thus recurs and reaches a decisive point in the question how the proclamation *about* Jesus Christ is related to the proclamation made by the historical Jesus Himself. Here it becomes manifest how old problems return even under the guise of the new formulation by which it was hoped to solve them, whenever it was the case that they were simply disguised and never found any real solution. We saw this in the case of Troeltsch, who in spite of his repugnance to the mediating theology of Wilhelm Herrmann was forced to see in the "fact of Christ," which the latter so emphasised, a justified concern. Hence it is by no means an accident that with Bultmann, who wishes to bring to an end the line of development of the older liberal and "History of Religion" school, the old question recurs as the decisive problem, in spite of the fact that his own new approach seemed to have solved it. The great discovery in which all are at one from Barth to Bultmann, that behind the text one neither can nor should look for the historical Jesus, has obviously not eliminated the problem which to modern theological thought wears so liberal an appearance. And it seems altogether questionable whether Kierkegaard's solution, which is palpable behind Bultmann's "brute fact," really provides a way out of the difficulty. Here we simply allude to the problem, which we shall have to treat in detail later, and now proceed to ask further about the relation of dogmatic and Biblical theology in Bultmann.

Bultmann's concern lies especially in distinguishing theology from philosophy, on the ground that it is a positive discipline having to do with the contingent realisation of God's self-revelation. But he does not, like Barth, divide this discipline into Biblical, dogmatic, and practical theology, nor, on the other hand, does he differentiate it from the task of the

[95] Bornkamm, *op. cit.*, p. 18.

historian. Perhaps, for the expediency of the scholar, he makes such distinctions in practice, but all these activities have the same end: to isolate the *kerygma* from the Scriptures and so to interpret it that it becomes a challenge to the hearer to decide to live towards self-fulfilment. In this setting of the goal all the tasks of theology converge: whether exegesis, dogmatics, preaching or historical research. All are in the same way concerned with the Biblical text. From this point of view there can no longer be any distinction between Biblical and dogmatic theology, because there is no real occasion for such a distinction. By dogmatics Bultmann can obviously mean nothing other than the attempt "to present the theological ideas of the New Testament as a coherent whole—to compose, as it were, a New Testament dogmatics." [96] The alternative to this that he himself prefers consists in presenting the ideas of the New Testament "in their diversity as dictated by the individual writings or groups of writings, with the result that these individual members can be seen as component parts of one historical process." No objection can be made to this, since on these lines the individual authors can be illuminated in their concrete physiognomy. But Bultmann links this up with his rejection of dogmatics when he continues: "The second method would in any case clearly express the fact that there cannot be a normal Christian dogmatics, because it is not possible to furnish a definitive solution to the task confronting the theologian, namely that of developing and systematising the understanding of God (and thus of man and the world) which arises from faith. A task of this kind permits only ever-repeated efforts at a solution in the face of the developing situations of history." Thus by dogmatics he understands a systematised Biblical theology which expounds in normative and final fashion the Biblical understanding of God, the world and man.

One might ask whether Bultmann is not here tilting at windmills. Certainly there may be, even today, dogmatic theologians who have such a primitive conception of their task. But in any case what he says does not apply to the dogmatics of Barth with its specific distinction between

[96] Bultmann, *Theologie des Neuen Testamentes*, henceforth cited as *Theol. des N.T.*, 1953, p. 577.

Biblical and dogmatic theology, each with its own task; at most, it reflects on those essays of Roman Catholic, and partly also the older Protestant dogmatics, which, as we saw, were expressly rejected by Barth himself. But in this matter Barth and Bultmann can be contrasted all the same, inasmuch as, for Bultmann, unlike Barth, it is doubtful whether there is room for an independent dogmatics alongside Biblical theology. In this connexion we must note what he understands by a dogmatic statement: "It is of the highest importance that theological ideas should be understood and explained as concepts proper to faith, i.e. as concepts in which the believer's awareness of God, the world, and man, is unfolded; hence not as the product of free speculation or the scholar's handling of the problems concerned by means of objectivising thought. Theological principles, even those of the New Testament, can never become the object of faith, but only the explanation of the outlook implicit in faith." [97] The *kerygma* itself is the sole object of faith, and everything depends on keeping clear the distinction between the *kerygma* and theological principles.

The idea of the *kerygma* has, in Bultmann's theological outlook, a similar significance to that of dogma as an idea of relation in the world of Barth. Bultmann opposes every attempt to view theological statements as a mode of thought dissociated from living action and thus objectivising. "Such an outlook leads to the misconception that the object of faith is theology as the correct doctrine, whereas the *kerygma* alone can be described as the correct doctrine which is the object of faith. Whereas the statements of philosophy, in so far as they contain truth, are correct teaching, the statements of the theologian are never in themselves correct teaching; but, in so far as they contain truth, they point the way to the correct doctrine, which is not discoverable by the critic but is given in the *kerygma*. Yet the *kerygma* itself can never be grasped in its ultimate reality, but only as something conceptually understood, i.e. as something which has already become the subject of theological exposition." [98] Thus the theologian seeks to discover the *kerygma*, even though he can grasp it only in a provisional form, by setting it free from the theological formulae in which we always find it fettered, so

[97] Bultmann, *Theol. des N.T.*, p. 578.   [98] *Theol. des N.T.*, p.580.

that it "may be understood as a possibility of man's deeper
self-understanding and thus express a challenge to decision." [99]
In contrast to Barth, with his distinction between the three
forms of the Word of God—the word of revelation itself, the
testimony of Scripture and the preaching of the Church—
theological thought is here concerned only with the two last
of these forms, since revelation itself has penetrated the *kerygma*
and the only question with regard to it can be that of how the
kerygma has come to pass. This again is why Barth enquires
about dogma and Bultmann about the *kerygma*. Neither
dogma nor the *kerygma* is identical with the Word of God,
since neither is recoverable in definitive shape, but in seeking
them the theologian is seeking the Word of God. Barth does
so with the help of dogmatics in order to appraise the teaching
of the Church "by the second form of the Word, i.e. Holy
Scripture, in so far as the latter is a witness to the third and
original form of the Word, i.e. revelation itself." [100] In this
connexion dogma as an idea of relationship or an eschatological
idea is defined as "the preaching of the Church, in so far as it
really agrees with the Bible considered as the Word of God." [101]
Bultmann does the same with his theological discipline in that
he measures the Scripture, the preaching and the doctrine of
the Church by the criterion of the *kerygma* extracted from
Scripture as the latter's immanent critical norm. Here
kerygma might be defined as the challenging word of Scripture,
inasmuch as it becomes for me a call to decision, and thus is
equivalent to the Word of God. Bultmann performs this work
as an historian whose task it is "to interpret the phenomena
of past history in the light of man's understanding of his
existence and so to make us aware of it as furnishing a basis for
our present self-understanding. His duty is, by making the
past live again to bring home to us the truth: '*Tua res agitur.*'
It concerns you yourself." [102] He does so as an exegete by
applying these principles of historical interpretation to the
contingent events of salvation, as they are reported in the
kerygma of Scripture. He does so as a preacher in presenting
the New Testament *kerygma* as a call to present decision. He
does so as a philosopher by seeking so to clarify man's under-

[99] *Theol. des N.T.*, p. 581. [100] Barth, *K. D.*, VOL. I. 1, p. 280.
[101] Barth, *op. cit.*, p. 283. [102] Bultmann, *Das Urchristentum*, 1949, p. 8.

F

standing of his life and its special quality as, in the light of it, to make the appeal of the *kerygma* intelligible.

But what could the *dogmatic* theologian have to do in addition? Of course Bultmann is aware also of the phenomenon of doctrine, not merely in the present teaching of the Church, but also in the New Testament itself. In Paul, for example, it is seen in the necessity he feels to explain the insights of faith in polemic against Judaism and gnosticism. Hence with him "the *kerygma* as a direct address and theology as an indirect address are clearly distinct.[103] Since "the *kerygma* of Paul announces a fact—Jesus Christ whom God sent forth, when the time was fulfilled, who dies and is risen again, because of our trespasses, etc.—the doctrine of the *kerygma* is primarily the communication of a fact. It is not a new conception of God that is proclaimed—as, for instance, that really God is gracious and not angry—it is an act of God. . . . Corresponding to that, faith ($\pi\iota\sigma\tau\iota\varsigma$) is not a human disposition or attitude, e.g. trust in God and so on, but faith is conceived strictly with reference to its end, it is faith in something, i.e. in the act of salvation, just as it is obedience." [104] By this obedience the hearer of the *kerygma* learns how to understand himself anew. Hence the revelation is "primarily an event, not a communication of knowledge; but it is the basis of a new knowledge and doctrine in so far as it makes possible a new understanding of oneself." [105] "The *kerygma* or summons is hence a doctrine in so far as it implies a certain new understanding. It informs us of a fact which may not be viewed like any other fact of world history. . . .[106] Of course it cannot be said in general terms to what extent the understanding of the hearer must be explained from time to time in order to find expression in the confession of the faith and the propagation of the appeal. . . . The conceptual explanation of believing insight can be consciously and intentionally undertaken as a duty. But if such theological theoretical work is not to go astray, if it is to remain an indirect summons and the obedience of faith is to be expressed in it, then the task will be undertaken only from a sense of duty, not

[103] Bultmann, "Kirche und Lehre im Neuen Testamentes," in *Glaube und Verstehen*, 1933, p. 176.
[104] *Ibid.*   [105] *Op. cit.*, p. 178.   [106] *Op. cit.*, p. 180.

from the motives of scholarship, to which presumably theology also belongs." [107]

Bultmann shows this, for instance, by considering the debate of Paul with the Gnostics. The Gnostics fail to appreciate "the historical ground of Christian knowledge, i.e. that it is self-understanding through the obedience of faith, and that thus one never has wisdom as a possession, and can never have mastered it. The Gnostics boast that they can do this and thus as it were constitute the divine wisdom through their own." [108] Hence they commit the primal sin against the Word of the Cross, which requires the surrender of all human claims and all self-praise, in order to be realised as the power and wisdom of God (1 Cor. 1. 14). On the other hand, Christian wisdom— "for there is such also"—implies "that one stands in faith and is no longer a babe and carnal (1 Cor. iii. 1-3). Hence it can be but the interpretation of faith itself, which subsists and renews itself in wisdom. Once wisdom as speculation gets torn asunder from this root, it has become folly. *Gnosis*, which exalts itself to an independent status and which is lacking in obedience, consequently sees its true object in the character of that which exists." [109] But the believer looks not at the things which are seen (τὰ βλεπόμενα) but at the things which are unseen (τὰ μή βλεπόμενα, ii Cor. iv. 18); he leads his life not in sight (διὰ εἴδους) not in the perception of that which exists in this world, but in faith (διὰ πίστεως, ii Cor. v. 7) [110]

In theology "*kerygma* is present in the form of debated doctrine. Hence it is clear that this theology itself is subject, at times, to criticism, though naturally only to a criticism which is rooted in obedience; otherwise it is true that 'the spiritual man judges all things but is himself judged of no man' (1 Cor. ii. 15). But the *kerygma* is subject to no criticism, for as a summons requiring obedience it cannot be judged from any independent point of view, but requires the surrender of private judgment." [111] In practice, *kerygma* and theology are not plainly distinguishable, for the *kerygma* "always expresses itself in the form of human thought. . . . But this is only correctly understood when it is realised that it can only be

---

[107] *Op. cit.*, p. 181.   [108] *Op. cit.*, p. 183.   [109] *Op. cit.*, p. 104.
[110] *Op. cit.*, pp. 185 ff.   [111] *Op. cit.*, p. 186.

truly understood in obedience and must therefore ever be understood afresh. And in this is rooted the necessity of theology as the conscious interpretation of the understanding of the believer." [112]

This theological activity is carried out within the framework of a tradition. But this, again, must ever be subjected to critical polemic reactions. For "the continuity of theology through the ages consists not in the rigid adherence to fixed principles but in continuous living awareness by which faith, in the strength of its source, masters by its insights ever new historical situations." [113] An interesting example of such a critical interpretation of dogmatic formulae is provided by Bultmann in his essay [114] on the Christological confession of the World Council of Churches. He was asked to examine the Confession of Amsterdam, which states that "The World Council of Churches is composed of churches which recognise Jesus Christ as God and Saviour," and to answer the question "whether this formula is consonant with the New Testament." [115] His answer is: "I do not know! And for the reason that this formula is by no means unequivocal." He goes on: "Are we to understand by the description of Christ as God a reference to His nature, His metaphysical being, or His significance? Has the statement a soteriological or a cosmological implication, or both?" [116] An examination of the titles of Christ in the New Testament suggests that the decisive question is "whether and how far they aim at describing the nature of Jesus, or whether objectively they propose to describe Him as He is in Himself, or whether they are concerned to suggest His significance for man and faith. Do they speak, in other words, of the φύσις of Christ, or do they speak of Christ *pro me*? How far is a Christological definition something which has a bearing on my life?" [117] In the early Church, of course, in accordance with the tradition of Greek thought, the minds of men were turned towards the φύσις, the nature, of Christ, but "it may be said that in the New Testament, at any rate *a parte potiori*, the statements about the divinity or Godhead of Jesus in fact are statements designed to express

[112] *Ibid.*
[114] In *Ev. Th.*, 1951, pp. 1 ff.
[116] *Op. cit.*, p. 2.

[113] Bultmann, *Theol. des N.T.*, p. 578.
[115] *Op. cit.*, p. 1.
[117] *Op. cit.*, pp. 5 f.

His significance for the world. . . . Hence I would say that in so far as such statements are distorted into objectifying formulae, they must be approached critically." [118] Bultmann then shows in a few examples how such objectifications arise— for instance how the originally undogmatic character of the consciousness of Christ as the world's judge and the sense of responsibility towards Him is hardened into the dogmatic statement later enshrined in the *Symbolum Romanum*: "From thence He shall come to judge the quick and the dead" [119]; or how the early Church, while no doubt realising the problem raised by the definition "true God and true man," sought inadequately to solve it by means of objectifying Greek thought, a solution which found in the Chalcedonian symbol terms quite unacceptable to modern thought," and which in the Amsterdam formulation was summarily suppressed.[120] Our task now is so to interpret the message of Jesus Christ "that He is seen as the eschatological event, which can never be objectified as an event of the past nor as an event in any human sphere, and which on the contrary is refractory to any attempt at objectification." [121] In this sense, it *can* be said that God confronts us in Christ. But "the formula 'Christ is God' is false in any sense in which God is understood as an objectifiable factor, whether it be understood in an Arian or a Nicean, an orthodox or a liberal sense. It is correct if God is understood as the event in which God acts. But I would ask: should we not on account of possible misunderstanding preferably avoid such formulae and content ourselves with saying that Christ is the Word of God?" [122]

This example strikingly illustrates the fact that with a massive alternative, a relentless *either/or*—e.g. "*either* nature of Christ" or "Christ *pro me*," *either* "metaphysical being" or "significance for the world," *either* "objectification in a past event" *or* "actualisation in the present event of preaching"—all those theological differences which have agitated the Church throughout the formation of its doctrine can, as it were, be flattened out and the totality of dogmatic statements be relegated to the sphere of metaphysics, as if in the case of each of these stark alternatives there might not also be, starting

[118] *Op. cit.*, p. 6.   [119] *Op. cit.*, p. 7.   [120] *Op. cit.*, p. 10.
[121] *Ibid.*   [122] *Ibid.*

from the New Testament period itself, a *both/and*. Hans Jonas [123] (from whom Bultmann seems to have learnt something with regard to the hermeneutics of dogma) is capable of expressing all this with finer shades of difference and in, for example, his interpretation of the doctrine of original sin, allows himself every opportunity of choosing between Augustine and Pelagius. Should not something of this kind also be possible in the case of Christological dogma, once one is committed to it? Or must the postulate "no objectification" lead in all circumstances to this hopeless levelling-out of dogmatic problems? We could see our way more clearly in this maze if, with his own critical reactions to dogma, Bultmann would also give us a positive example of a doctrinal statement which from his own point of view is valid. His formula that Christ is the Word of God can hardly be regarded as such an unexceptionable doctrinal statement, for—at least to the same extent as the formula which he opposes—it, too, is liable to misunderstanding, quite apart from the fact that it deals with the problematics of "true man and true God" just as little as the Amsterdam Confession which he criticises for not doing so. On his own doctrinal premises, Bultmann—in critical and polemical situations at any rate—ought to give such an answer, and the fact that he does not is probably no accident. The retort that he is a New Testament scholar, not a dogmatist, and therefore is not obliged to make such dogmatic statements, is an objection that we could not accept, in the light of his conception of the aims of the various theological disciplines and in consideration of his powerful interest in the critical interpretation of dogma.

(d) Result

In conclusion we may sum up Bultmann's outlook under two headings. First, doctrine has the task of explaining the believer's insight, in the special sense of unfolding the implications of the Christian understanding of life. In this latter sense it is distinguishable from mere speculation, and only so can it be an indirect summons and address through which the obedience of faith is expressed.

Secondly, this task of moulding theological doctrine should

[123] See above, p. 27.

only be undertaken where it becomes a duty as a result of some special occasion. "Thus if theology is to be valid it will always have to be critical and polemical in character." [124]

On comparing all this with Barth's dogmatics, we find that the latter would not measure up to these requirements.

With regard to the view that doctrine has the task of explaining the implications of the Christian understanding of life, Barth asks, on the contrary, whether it is true that we can only describe a theological statement as valid when it can be shown to be a genuine part of the Christian understanding of *human existence*. He answers: "The main articles of the Christian confession do not fulfil this postulate. No doubt they are all related to human life. They make possible and furnish the basis for a Christian understanding of it, and thus they then become—in a different form—motivating forces in human existence. But they are not originally such." [125] Nor, for the same reason, can Barth admit that doctrinal statements are an indirect mode of appeal. They may well merge into preaching itself—in the same way as (for example) confessional formulae were taken over into the liturgy—yet essentially it is not the task of dogmatics to preach, but to examine the intrinsic appropriateness of preaching. Hence Barth could not, in the last analysis, say that the obedience of faith finds expression in doctrine. To be sure, it is the *fides quaerens intellectum* which enquires into doctrine, but theology has no control over the faith of the theologian and therefore its statements cannot be based on the latter nor measured by it. Similarly with regard to the view that theology is necessarily critical and polemical. The task of theological thinking is not for Barth something which becomes a duty solely as a result of some polemical occasion, but is an activity which should be regularly pursued, because its purpose is to test the Church's preaching, which is always going on. Barth, too, emphasises that its function is always a critical one. But for him this arises from the fact that dogmatics must examine the present utterance of the Church in the light of Scripture, and, through the latter, in the light of the word of revelation itself. Bultmann considers this ultimate form of the Word of God to be identical with the

---

[124] Bultmann, " Kirche und Lehre im N.T." (above, n. 103), pp. 181 ff.
[125] Barth, *K. D.*, VOL. III. 2, p. 534.

second, the *kerygma* of Scripture. Thus for him the critical function of theology lies between the *kerygma* of Scripture as the norm of present-day preaching and the hearer's own insight into life.

This difference between Barth and Bultmann is by no means limited to their conception of dogmatics relatively to Biblical theology: it extends to the ultimate presuppositions of theological work as a whole. Hence it would seem no longer possible to find a common basis of discussion between them. Likewise the possibility of confronting them, not only with each other, but also with the theology of the Roman Catholic Church, is completely excluded. It is consequently understandable that today a mood of resignation prevails among theologians, who see no further possibility of fruitful discussion, with the inevitable result that each pursues his lonely way through the problems at issue and contents himself with defining his thought in contrast with that of others. Since it is difficult to rest content with this state of things, there is a growing inclination to recover the lost unity of theology by adopting inquisitorial methods. This is of course the most desperate of all attempts to find a way out. If the situation really is that no common ground subsists with regard to the ultimate presuppositions of theology, then the discrimination between orthodoxy and heresy is the very last thing of which we might be capable.

Our opinion is that no matter how inevitable it may appear to be in view of the present theological situation we must not in any event allow ourselves to adopt this attitude of resignation. Otherwise it is no longer possible to do the work of a theologian at all. And whether our comparison of Schlier, Barth, and Bultmann reveals any possibility of involving them in debate with one another will not depend on whether we can reduce their positions to one common denominator. For this seems in fact no longer possible. Here the only possible method of procedure is to think out further for ourselves the problems which they have defined and treated. If, considered as a theologian, each of them is, though admittedly in his own way, a master of the subject—and we have no right to doubt it—then, in any event, they must meet in regard to those problems which are the concern of us all, however much

they may differ in their solutions.   To this end we isolate one
problem which in fact is central to all three theologians and
which seemed to us in need of further discussion, namely the
question of the meaning of the historical Jesus for the preaching
and doctrine of the Church.   At the same time this will keep
us on the axis of our subject, for the question is not only of
basic importance for the right relationship of dogmatics and
exegesis, but also for the understanding of the essential task of
dogmatics itself.

CHAPTER III

THE MEANING OF THE HISTORICAL JESUS FOR THE PREACHING, DOCTRINE AND FAITH OF THE CHURCH

(a) *The exchange of roles between liberals and orthodox*

ERNST KÄSEMANN in his report on the problems of New Testament scholarship in Germany [1] points out a remarkable exchange of roles in the history of New Testament research: "This began about two hundred years ago with the intention of freeing the historical Jesus from the fetters of dogmatics. Now this attempt ends with the confession, made by its most radical representatives, that the Easter faith is the Church's foundation and the sole means of access to the historical Jesus Himself. In order that this spectacle, so interesting to those who understand, should not be altogether lacking in human comedy, a new orthodoxy (or what is considered such) is, at the same time, endeavouring to show that, both as regards method and intrinsic necessity, the only way out of the difficulty is to recover the life of the historical Jesus, and out of the Gospels is accordingly making factual reports. The critics have become dogmatic and the orthodox liberal. Now the fight is being waged the other way round. It is clear from this development (if anywhere at all) that the time of the historical approach is past—a fact which has escaped the attention only of the guardians of tradition, who now in reality are fighting a rearguard action. Nevertheless a very difficult problem remains open here and it is right that conservative critics should insist on the fact." [2] The problem

---

[1] See E. Käsemann, "Probleme der Neutestamentlichen Arbeit in Deutschland," cited below as "Prob.," in *Die Freiheit des Evangeliums und die Ordnung der Gesellschaft*, Beiträge zur *Evangelische Theologie*, BD. XV, 1952, p. 138.　　　[2] Käsemann, "Prob.," p. 149.

is in what relation the faith, doctrine and preaching of the Church stand to the historical Jesus.

In going into this problem, we shall not further concern ourselves with the orthodox (who have, as Käsemann says, turned liberal), and that for two reasons. First, they are not theologically interesting, because they are afflicted with the same disease as their liberal partners, whom they have begun to fight. Whereas it appeared necessary, to incipient liberalism, to detach the fundamental propositions of faith from all those parts of the Bible that could not withstand historical criticism, orthodoxy attempted, on the other hand, to establish all those propositions of faith which must, it felt, be maintained in face of this criticism. In so doing the orthodox have fallen victims to the same error as their partners of the left, that of identifying the Word of God with an historical report, or, as would now be said, supposing it to be discoverable in historical fact. In this matter we agree with Karl Barth's judgment: "This liberalism and this orthodoxy are both children of the same weak spirit, and it is not worth while to follow them further." [3] But, secondly, we do not pursue it because form-criticism of the New Testament, with its elucidation of the declaratory character of the Gospel, has shown that we simply have no means of reaching an historical Jesus behind the Gospels themselves.

This liberalising orthodoxy is exemplified by Ethelbert Stauffer in his book *Die Theologie des Neuen Testaments*,[4] and especially his lecture on demythologisation and realistic theology.[5] We should *not* wish simply to include in this category W. Manson's *Jesus the Messiah*.[6] In his discussion of form-criticism Manson tries to show how its methods transgress their due limits when the critics wish to decide, purely on grounds of form, which elements of the tradition are historically genuine. Form-criticism supposes that in the primitive Christian communities there were typical situations and movements which to some extent constituted the matrix for

---

[3] Barth, *K. D.*, VOL. III. 1, p. 89.   [4] 3rd edn., 1947.

[5] "Entmythologisierung oder Realtheologie?" Programmatischer Vortrag vor dem Deutschen Pfarrverein. See Bultmann, *Kerygma und Mythos*, VOL. II, p. 13 ff.; cp. also Diem, *Theol.*, VOL. I, p. 64.

[6] *Jesus the Messiah: The Witness of the first three Gospels to the Revelation of God in Christ, with reference to Form Criticism*, 1943.

the form of the various individual elements in the tradition.[7] Surely it is better here to give up all *a priori* ideas and to concentrate our whole attention on the material before us, which gives us information about the growth of the tradition, in this case about stages of development which stand out clearly in the literary redaction of the Gospels. [8] Thus he finds considerably more passages of the Synoptics which are to be claimed as historically genuine than, for example, Bultmann. This should provide a warning to New Testament scholars against too confident a reliance on the infallibility of the methods of form-criticism. But the decisive question will not be whether they think they can find more or less genuinely historical passages, but what consequences may be drawn from this for the foundation of the faith. Manson considers that the transformation of Jewish Messianic ideas in primitive Christianity is inexplicable unless we suppose that its basis lies, not first in the thinking of the Church after the death of Jesus, but already in the Messianic consciousness of Jesus Himself. This is only a minimal supposition, which, however, must not be undervalued, for here lies the essential basis for the development of the whole of Christian theology and its historical starting-point. [9] We might agree, and yet ask, with the form critics, whether this historical starting-point is the basis for an historical account of Jesus, or not rather for preaching about Him. If, with the form critics, we accept the latter hypothesis, then the life and teaching of the historical Jesus are merely reflected in the post-Resurrection *kerygma* and are so deeply embedded within it that it is impossible subsequently to reconstruct the historical facts about Jesus. The Synoptics obviously believed that they were reporting historical facts, even if, as measured by our modern sense of history, they did so in a naïvely uncritical way. But their account of the facts is intended solely to serve the *kerygma*, which is concentrated on the Cross and Resurrection. If an historical account as such, alongside the *kerygma*, had had an independent meaning for faith, then it would be difficult to understand why most of the New Testament writings mention, from the life of Jesus, only the facts of His death and resurrection. Further—and

[7] Cp. M. Dibelius, *Die Formgeschichte des Evangeliums*, 2nd edn., 1933.
[8] Cp. Manson, *Jesus the Messiah*, p. 22.   [9] Cp. Manson, *op. cit.*, p. 11.

this seems to us of special importance—it must in that case
have been absolutely necessary, at the time of the composition
or, at latest, at the time of the canonisation of the Gospels, to
harmonise these historical reports. That the need to do so
was felt later is shown for example by the *Diatessaron* of Tatian,
which significantly, however, was not admitted into the canon.
On this point Käsemann says: "The justification of our faith
in the Christ can by no means be derived from the history of
Jesus, in such wise that the historical basis guaranteed the
truth of the faith. This is impossible—even though such a
view at times finds expression in the New Testament itself,
for example in Luke. Only the Resurrection demonstrates,
by the word of Christian preaching, the justification and
necessity of our faith." [10]

But, again, this cannot mean that according to the New
Testament the history of Jesus had no significance for faith.
Thus Käsemann continues: "On the contrary, the whole of
the New Testament asserts that at Easter the disciples do not
recognise a heavenly being, much less an abstraction such as
dogma, but Jesus Himself. The Christ believed in and
proclaimed from Easter onwards is continuous with the so-
called historical Jesus, and apart from such continuity faith
and preaching would in the opinion of the early Christians be
meaningless. To be assured of this continuity is an inescapable
theological necessity. A theology which wished, as a result of
eccentric dogmatics, to give it up, would not deserve its
name." [11] The type of theology thus alluded to reminds us
inevitably of Bultmann's, when Käsemann says that "for
theological reasons it forbids us to go behind the event of
Easter," and then continues critically: "All too easily it
makes a virtue of necessity, so that we cannot be content with
it. Can the Church be summoned from scepticism to faith,
and on the other hand can New Testament scholarship and
theology be required arbitrarily to abandon their enquiries
at some given point? Surely this cannot be the case, for then
faith would not be genuine, nor scholarship authentic. Nor
can it really be the case that each should form his own private
opinion of the historical Jesus, on the assumption that it is of

[10] Käsemann, "Prob.," pp. 150 ff.
[11] *Op. cit.*, p. 151.

no relevance for the faith and message of the Church, for we live and must live in the light of the Christ that is preached." [12]

(b) The preaching of Jesus and the preaching about Jesus, according to Rudolf Bultmann

Perhaps this criticism does not wholly apply to Bultmann in so far as he does not refuse to take his enquiries further than the proclamation of the Christ, but behind the Easter event studies the preaching of the historical Jesus Himself. But the question is what theological relevance he admits the preaching of Jesus to have for the proclamation of Jesus as the Christ. In his *Theologie des Neuen Testaments*,[13] his answer is that the preaching of Jesus, while forming the background to the theology of the New Testament, is not an integral part of that theology. "Christian faith first arises from the existence of the Christian *kerygma*, which declares Jesus Christ to be the eschatological saving work of God—i.e. Jesus Christ as the crucified and risen one. But this takes place only in the *kerygma* of the primitive Church, not already in the preaching of the historical Jesus, although the community has woven into its account of Jesus many of the motives of its own *kerygma*! . . . Thus the theology, strictly so called, of the New Testament begins only with the *kerygma* of the primitive Church. The appearance and the preaching of Jesus belong no doubt to its historical background, and in this sense the preaching of Jesus Himself must be taken account of in the presentation of New Testament theology." [14] But the result of an historical study of the preaching of Jesus remains irrelevant for theological questions, which arise only from the *kerygma* of the primitive Church, and that not merely because of the trifling and uncertain conclusions that such a study would yield, but because they could not have any essential bearing on faith. This Bultmann shows in considering the question whether Jesus held Himself to be the Messiah (which he denies): "the possible establishment of the fact that Jesus knew Himself to be the Messiah or the Son of Man would be," he adds, "an historical conclusion, but could not prove any declaration of faith. Rather the recognition of Jesus as Him in whom we

---

[12] Käsemann, "Prob.," p. 150.   [13] Above, p. 71, n. 96.
[14] Bultmann, *Theol. des N.T.*, pp. 1 f.

decisively encounter the Word of God, whether we call Him Messiah or Son of Man or Lord, is a sheer act of faith independent of the answer to the historical question whether Jesus considered Himself to be the Messiah. This question can only be answered by the historian, in so far as it is in any sense answerable; and faith as personal decision cannot be dependent on the historian's work." [15] The question of faith only arises in reference to the *kerygma* of the primitive Church which is the starting point for the theology of the New Testament proper. In so far as it can be elucidated, the earlier history can only have the historical significance of showing how the preaching of Jesus was changed when it passed over into the *kerygma* of the Church. Bultmann thinks this change consisted in the following: "As the Synoptic tradition shows, the primitive Church took over the message of Jesus and proclaimed it more widely. And in so far as it did so, Jesus was for it a teacher and prophet. But He was, at the same time, more than that, namely the Messiah; and the decisive point is that it proclaims Him as such. He who was formerly the bearer of the message has now been made a part of the message, and has become its essential content. The announcer has become the subject of the announcement: but in what sense? That is decisive." [16] We should assume that the sense in question would necessarily coincide with the message announced by the historical Jesus. In any case we should assume that the Church lived in the conviction that such was the case. Bultmann thinks that the Church may have supposed this, though in reality it was far from being true. The Church indeed declared Jesus to be a prophet and teacher, and, further, it invested him, the concrete man, with " the vague, mythical shape of the Messiah," though " for Paul and John the teaching of the historical Jesus is of little or no significance," [17] just as for the New Testament in general the personality of Jesus has no significance.[18] But how did the preaching of Jesus become transformed into the *kerygma* of the primitive Church? "In consequence of the crucifixion of Jesus, the decision that the disciples had already made about His mission by following Him had to be made anew and more radically. In a sense,

[15] *Op. cit.*, p. 26. [16] *Op. cit.*, p. 34.
[17] *Op. cit.*, p. 35. [18] *Op. cit.*, p. 36.

the Cross posed the decisive question all over again; for as
little as it could call in question the content of his preaching,
so greatly did it cast doubt on his authority, and on the assertion
that he was the messenger of God bearing the final and decisive
word.   The Church had to resolve the scandal of the Cross,
and did so by its Easter faith." [19]   Thus since the rise of the
Easter faith in the resurrection of Jesus and in consequence
of that faith, all that had gone before appears "in a new light.
If, now, the person and work of Jesus is irradiated by the light
of the Easter faith, it means that His significance lies neither
in His teaching nor in any modification of the Messianic idea.
Rather the point is that the very fact of Jesus having come is
the decisive event by which God summoned His Church, and
is itself eschatological." [20]   The question how the transition
from the preaching of Jesus to the *kerygma* of the primitive
Church occurred must now be asked as follows: "How did it
become the Easter faith of the disciples?"   Bultmann's answer
is: "How this decisive event came to pass in detail, how the
Easter faith arose among the individual disciples, has been
obscured by legendary elements in the tradition and is of no
significance." [21]

It is indisputable that the tradition about the rise of the
Easter faith has been obscured by legend.   It would be absurd
to attempt to verify the Resurrection as an historical event.
This is not only impossible on account of the legendary form
of the tradition, but is also impossible intrinsically.   It is
hopeless to want to prove by means of historical science an
event which according to the presuppositions of that science is
impossible.   But what does Bultmann mean by suggesting
that it is of no material importance how the Easter faith of the
disciples arose?   He says: "The true content of the Easter
faith is the fact that God made the prophet and teacher
Jesus of Nazareth Messiah," [22] and indeed, one must add, by
the clear witness of the New Testament, in raising Him from
the dead.   *How* this happened may be of no material importance, but not *that* it happened.   But what really happened
here?   Bultmann says: "According to 1 Cor. xv. 5-8, where
Paul recounts the appearances of the risen Lord as the *paradosis*

[19] *Op. cit.*, pp. 45 ff.   [20] *Op. cit.*, pp. 43 f.
[21] *Op. cit.*, p. 41.   [22] *Op. cit.*, p. 44.

presents them, the Resurrection means also an exaltation, only later was it interpreted as a temporary return to earthly life, and as a result the story of the ascension arose (Lk. xxiv. 51-3; Acts i. 3-10)." [23] Thus he thinks that he can distinguish historically an earlier stage, in which the resurrection of Jesus was understood as an exaltation without any return to earthly life, from a later stage, in which we have such a return and the consequent story of the Ascension. But again it is of no material importance, for whether the one or the other interpretation is true is historically unverifiable, since neither possibility is capable of proof, and even if one or the other could be proved, it would remain of no consequence for faith, for faith cannot mean an assent to the reality of any historical event.

But what precisely, in this connexion, is "of material importance"? Bultmann would have to reply: "Nothing other than the Easter faith of the disciples and the *kerygma* to which it gives birth as a challenge to our own faith." But what is the "matter" that is "material" here? We cannot simply reply "faith," but must say more precisely "*that* in which this faith believes." Now we have been told that this faith believes that the crucified Jesus was the Messiah. But it believes this just because it has first believed that God raised this Jesus from the dead. Hence the question is whether, in believing Jesus to be the Messiah, the disciples decided in favour of a possible new interpretation of the Cross which seemed to them a suitable means of overcoming its scandal, or whether they so decided because of a new and no less scandalous happening, namely that God had raised this Jesus from the dead. We think there is no doubt that at any rate the New Testament itself understands the Easter faith in this second sense. But then, even in regard to the Easter faith and the transition to the Church *kerygma* which it produced, everything depends on the factuality of the resurrection, and just here, at the centre of the New Testament, as little as elsewhere, can the question of the factuality of a saving event be dissociated from that of its significance.

For Bultmann, however, everything depends on this possibility of dissociation. But then the text is no longer asked

[23] *Op. cit.*, p. 46.

to yield the secret of the event it proclaims, but a certain idea of what constitutes history is applied to it as a criterion, although it must be admitted that this idea along with other sources is derived from a partial aspect of Scripture. Yet in all this what task has the historical and critical investigation of Scripture to perform? Above [24] we said it was Bultmann's merit, pointed out by Hellmut Traub, that his understanding of the Gospel in its declaratory character had led us to realise the mistake of seeking history behind the Gospel. Now, however, that appears to be true only in a qualified sense. He tries persistently to get behind the *kerygma* of the text by critical methods, in order to establish what in fact happened, and he does so with the same resources (although sharpened by the methods of form criticism) as the whole of historical-critical research before him. But he does not do so—and here is the decisive difference—in order to base faith on the historical conclusions attained, but, on the contrary, in order to make impossible any such basis for faith, and thus he has greater scope for the most radical results than any of his predecessors. Always, for him, faith must be made insecure and all historical foundations withdrawn from it. That historical criticism (at any rate in regard to the history of Jesus) might have another, positive significance, is not apparent. Hence one cannot quite see why the frantic energies of the researcher should be used for precisely this end. It is well known that the school of Bultmann refers to Luther in regard to this insecurity of faith and has brought critical research into line with the Reformation understanding of faith. Thus Gerhard Ebeling has said: "As is the case throughout Reformed theology, so here, too, in regard to the question of historical basis, the welcome given to insecurity is only the reverse side of the assurance of salvation *sola fide*." [25] To which Erwin Reisner has replied,[26] suggesting that one might say just this to Bultmann: "Since the world began and

---

[24] See above p. 68.

[25] See G. Ebeling, "Die Bedeutung der historisch-kritischen Methode für die protestantische Theologie und Kirche," in *Z. Th. K.*, 1950, VOL. I, p. 42.

[26] See E. Reisner, "Hermeneutik und historische Vernunft," in *Z. Th. K.*, 1952.

certainly since Adam ate of the Tree of Knowledge, it has never yet occurred to anyone to investigate in order to become uncertain. As in all other cases of research work, without exception, so still more understandably in regard to the criticism of the Scriptures, the aim is to be certain and nothing else. Or should the security of profane knowledge be, indeed, the reverse side of the insecurity of faith? By his scholarly work, which *as such* is directed towards certainty, does Ebeling really intend to attain nothing else than the insecurity of his faith? This would be hyperparadoxical. For the rest, it must not be denied that the assurance of faith and theoretical evidence are mutually exclusive; on the contrary. I must simply dispute energetically the proposition that one aims at the insecurity of faith while, at the same time, and in the same act, eagerly seeking scientific certainty." [27]

At most one might ask whether we have here one and the same act and not rather two distinct dialectically related acts, as a result of which, naturally, the danger of a divorce between thought and existence would only be greater. What then is Bultmann's position with regard to the reverse side of insecurity —the assurance of salvation *sola fide*, for which historical criticism is to clear the way? To what does this faith cling, or what does it believe after every kind of historical basis is withdrawn from it? It believes in the *kerygma* which it encounters in the Gospel, or, more exactly, in its confrontation by the *kerygma*, and in view of the absolute unprovability of the latter, it overcomes the scandal by a decision for faith, which stamps life with a new quality. In order that faith may arise, the *kerygma* must authenticate itself. Hence the *sola fide* seems to be in the strictest sense preserved; faith deprived of all security and support becomes certain of itself in the very act of believing. But does not this simply mean that faith shatters its own self-despair by trusting in its own power of belief? Bultmann would say emphatically in reply that this is excluded because the *kerygma* impinged on me as a *verbum externum*, and that not only in the sense that it tells me something which I could not otherwise have known and could not have

[27] Reisner, *op. cit.*, p. 233. That we take up this question of Reisner's does not mean that we adopt his position. Cp. E. Fuchs, "Gesetz, Vernunft und Geschichte: Antwort an Erwin Reisner," in *Z. Th. K.*, 1954, p. 251 ff.

told myself. The proclamation of the Word of God in the *kerygma* of Scripture is rather a contingent event in which the Word meets me from without and thus constantly calls in question even my own power of belief. In this event of proclamation through which the Word by the Spirit creates belief, there is thus, in Bultmann's opinion, a constant movement from the Word to faith, and this movement, on which he thinks everything depends, appears sufficiently assured in its irreversibility. This makes clear why, in its understanding of faith, Bultmann's theology is so strongly reminiscent of Luther; for it seems impossible to bring out more clearly the *sola fide* in its relation to the *sola scriptura*.

But how far, in truth, can we be assured of that irreversible movement by which the Word initiates faith?   Here, in contrast to the dubious foundations of faith—and particularly when these are given up—there must be real security. The whole interest of Reformed theology is concentrated at this point after its surrender of all other bases of security; for if this certainty is destroyed then we may still think that we have the *sola fide*, but the *solus Christus* and the *sola scriptura* are finished and we can no longer be delivered from the situation in which preaching becomes a conversation of the Church with itself and the believer now only believes in his powers of belief. How does this foundation stand in Bultmann's theology?

It would have to lie in the *kerygma*. But the question is whether in Bultmann's outlook there is not a mere relation of interchangeability between (on the one side) the *kerygma*, which calls forth faith and a new understanding of life, and (on the other) man's own insight, which causes him to hear in the *kerygma* the call to decide for its existential fulfilment and thus to recognise the *kerygma* as *kerygma*. The *kerygma* as the action of God can proclaim nothing other than what corresponds to man's prior understanding of historical possibilities and can be interpreted as effecting a new insight into the self, and so as *kerygma*, only in so far as it helps a man's vision of life to find existential fulfilment. In reply to all such objections Bultmann usually stresses the fact that this prior understanding must not be regarded as a criterion applied to the preaching of the Word, but rather as something which must be challenged and corrected by the *kerygma* if human existence is to find fulfilment through the Word. But all such assertions cannot change the fact that *kerygma* and faith, as such, and in their detailed content, here stand in a relation of interchangeability, which allows no preponderance to the *kerygma*.

Bultmann would probably admit this, but would say that the preponderance of the *kerygma* can only and must only be shown in the event of preaching and its awakening of faith, whereby the purity of the *sola fide* is maintained. Further, the movement from the Word to faith is maintained in its irreversibility by the fact that the existential fulfilment of self-understanding cannot happen apart from the *kerygma*. Yet the latter is not a mere function of self-understanding, because it has its real and objective ground in the historical fact of the crucified Jesus of Narareth, though in this connexion it must be remembered that this historical fact has no saving significance as such but is endowed with saving efficacy only through the *kerygma*. For, so runs the much debated sentence which Barth once wished so much to interpret truly: "not because it is the Cross of Christ is it the saving event, but because it is the saving event it is the Cross of Christ." [28] This however brings us back once more to interchangeability rather than preponderance.

It is clear that at this point we can get no further with our question as to the security of the movement from the Word to faith because Bultmann's argument moves in a circle: the *kerygma* cannot be a mere function of man's self-understanding because it has its origin and motive power in the historical fact of the crucified Jesus of Nazareth. But as a mere historical fact this is not only irrelevant for faith, neither can it be the object of the *kerygma*—rather it becomes such only through the *kerygma*, since the latter declares its meaning and thus confers upon it its value as a saving event—but here again we do not emerge from the interchangeability of Word and faith.

Again and again we come up against this twofold hypothesis

[28] See Bultmann, *Kerygma und Mythos*, VOL. I, p. 5; cp. also Barth, "Rudolf Bultmann, ein Versuch ihn zu verstehen," in *Theologische Studien*, XXXIV (1952), p. 21.

of Bultmann's with regard to the history and preaching of Jesus on the one hand and the *kerygma* of Jesus Christ on the other. The historical background concerning Jesus is, in its sheer factuality, the presupposition of the *kerygma*, in the sense that it has occasioned the birth of the *kerygma*. But this historical cause in its mere actuality amounts to nothing as regards the meaning of the *kerygma* so pregnant with consequences for existence. For the *kerygma* acquires this meaning and hence its theological relevance solely as a result of the fact that it becomes a call to decision when it is preached and by its preaching awakens a new self-understanding. But we cannot and must not go beyond this interpretation of the *kerygma* to enquire into the Christ-event itself which the *kerygma* announces; we must be concerned only about the event of the *kerygma*. The continuity between the historical Jesus and the Christ that is preached, which Bultmann in his own fashion tries to preserve, is not grounded in the preaching of Jesus Himself, but in the fact that subsequently the first Church invested Him with the royal mantle that lay ready to hand,[29] although He Himself, according to historical conclusions, never thought of claiming this dignity. Bultmann reaches this conclusion by his dualistic approach, firstly investigating the historical facts about Jesus, and then—unconnected therewith or connected only by historical sequence—investigating the *kerygma* of Jesus. The first time the texts are studied from the point of view of historical enquiry, an enquiry which leads to the establishment as a historical fact of the truth that Christ died on the Cross. The second time the texts are searched for the *kerygma* which they contain, and then the enquiry is directed no longer to the saving event itself announced in the *kerygma* but to the actualisation of the *kerygma* as it affects the historical existence of the believer. The first time it is a question of historically ascertainable history and the second time of history in the sense of the historical action whereby I apprehend the potential meaning of my own existence through the appropriation of the fullness of meaning contained in the Cross of Christ. It is impossible to resolve this dualism in which Bultmann on the one hand searches behind the text for the historical Jesus and on the

[29] Cp. W. Manson, *Jesus the Messiah*, p. 5.

other hand remains stuck and does not succeed in piercing the reality which the text implies.

(c) *The problem of the historical Jesus in Karl Barth*

More consistently than Bultmann, Barth seems to adhere to the purely declaratory character of the Biblical texts. As we saw, he insists that the question of the truth of the event attested in the Bible should be framed in such wise that the enquiry is directed to the real meaning and continuity of the texts. By this means the question of historical truth is asked in the only sense appropriate to the matter in hand, because the event here attested, the self-revealing action of God towards mankind, does not lie behind the text as if it were a series of events discoverable through the texts but dissociable from them and independently to be established. The history takes place rather in the witness of the text itself and hence can only be found within that witness. The elucidation of the happening through the study of the Biblical witness is thus both a theological and historical task. Unlike Bultmann, who approaches the object of the text with two different ideas of history, Barth works with only one: The history in question is the history attested by the texts as having really taken place and as taking place anew through this witness: it is the history of the dealings of God with man. In this connexion there is an interweaving of "historical" and "unhistorical" elements, i.e. of the history that can be established as true by the ordinary methods of historical enquiry, and of such as cannot be so established.[30] Barth however insists that this idea of history be applied not only to the history attested by the Bible but to history as a whole: "History as a whole is always partly unhistorical, history as a whole can only be described as unhistorical, inasmuch as God's creative action is always at work in the whole process of history, and history as a whole, in all its movements, relations and forms, always has an aspect by which it is immediately related to God and is of immediate divine ordinance. And how can we overlook the fact that in the last resort all history is truly important and significant only in so far as it has this element, in so far as it is not merely historical but also unhistorical? How could we forget that all

[30] Cp. Diem, *Theol.*, VOL. I, pp. 107 ff.

historical writing must be unreasonable and profitless to the
extent that it proposes to speak only in historical terms and
not also unhistorically?" [31]

It is illuminating to note that when Barth applies this idea
of history to the happenings attested in the Bible or, conversely,
when he receives it from thence to judge the rest of history—
he can pose the question of historical truth only in the sense of
discovering the true meaning and interconnexion of the Biblical
texts, and sees no further possibility, nor indeed any occasion,
to pose the question of historical fact. Hence the problem
with which we are concerned about the relation of the preaching of Jesus to the proclamation of the Christ has no meaning
for him. It is solely a question of defining the meaning of
the happenings attested in Scripture, by the statements of the
witnesses, and these happenings of course embrace, as one
continuous process, both the preaching of Jesus and the proclamation of the Christ. What could be problematical here?
Barth presupposes that the events attested in the Bible, the
revealing action of God, are exceptional events forming the
real foundation on the basis of which all history is to be interpreted. He presupposes further that the canon of Holy Scripture contains exceptional literary documents, which because
of the exceptional history to which they bear witness demand
a specific hermeneutic procedure, which supplies the basic
principles for general hermeneutics applicable to other texts. [32]

The exceptional character of the events here exceptionally
attested is inferred primarily not from the exegesis of Scripture
but from the "being of the Church." In this connexion we
should not primarily think of the historical being of the Church,
but also of that being of the Church, not historically
demonstrable, which is identical with Jesus Christ Himself.
Jesus Christ as thus identical with the being of the Church is
attested by Scripture and by the preaching by which the
Church extends its witness. Through these two witnesses the
being of Jesus Christ is incarnate historically. As we have
seen, the task of theology, and especially of dogmatics, is to
consider the agreement of these two witnesses and also their
agreement with the event of revelation itself in Jesus Christ.

[31] Barth, *K. D.*, vol. iii. i, pp. 84 f.
[32] Cp. Diem, *Theol.*, vol. i, pp. 98 ff.

The event of revelation is not to be grasped as an historical fact, but is accessible to us only in the historical witness of Scripture. This would be the point at which to ask our question about the relation of the historical Jesus as the primary event of revelation to the secondary event of the proclamation of Jesus as the Christ. But Barth does not pose this question, and does not need to pose it, because he sees the secondary witness of Scripture not only as an historical derivative of the primary event of revelation but as a new and second form of God's dealings and conversation with men, or, as he says, as a new phase of "the times of the Word of God." By means of a dogmatic presupposition—namely the different time phases of the Word of God—Barth transcends and eliminates the historical question concerning the development and transmutation of the witnesses to revelation; and this is probably the decisive point in his approach. Certainly these various times—the action of God in Jesus Christ, in the witness of Apostles and Prophets in Scripture, and in the witness of preaching based on Scripture—have a historical continuity even in earthly history. But again they receive their material identity from a dogmatic presupposition, namely their potential contemporaneity as the speech and action of God. This cannot, however, be demonstrated by their historical continuity but, on the contrary, gives that continuity its basis. From this point of view it is sufficient for Barth to find the actual occurrence of the revelation of God (which is potentially contemporaneous in all its stages) as an historically apprehensible event in only one of its two past phases, namely in the speech and action of God reflected in the witness of Scripture. On the basis of his dogmatic presupposition, the primary event of revelation itself, both in its "that" and in its "what," may then be inferred from that testimony.

At this point it should be noted that these dogmatic presuppositions of Barth's are in no sense merely speculative, and may not be considered to be ideas of time and history derived from speculative thought. Rather we can precisely define what he means by a dogmatic statement: it is always a statement about an event which, because of the agreement of the testimony of Scripture and the preaching of the Church about this testimony, makes the claim to be a moment in the process

of divine self-revelation itself. As a result Barth claims that
all his dogmatic opinions are derived from Scripture itself,
and is prepared to prove this exegetically in each individual
case. Hence if we accept his presuppositions it is hardly
possible to raise any serious objection to him. Thus an
objection resting on the idea that any dogmatic opinion is
from the start to be rejected as mythological or metaphysical
would be completely wide of the mark and rightly could make
no impression on him.

But even if we accept his dogmatic presuppositions there
are still a few questions to be asked. His dogma of the three
potentially contemporaneous time-phases of the Word of God
makes God's revelatory action primarily apprehensible as an
historic event in the witness of Scripture only, and the problem,
both historical and theological, then is to discover the true
meaning and coherence of the various Biblical texts. In this connexion we must further assume that this testimony of Scripture
has a basic unity. But in what does this unity consist? Barth
would have to reply that it consists in the fact that all these
texts bear witness to the one Christ, though he would certainly
not disagree that they do so in different ways. We should
then have to ask more precisely whether this unity consists
only in the words and acts of Jesus Himself, or also in the
witness of the New Testament authors—a witness that is
moulded by their personality, their views and the sources at
their disposal. In the light of Barth's assumptions, the answer
would be that the illuminating unity of the witness to Christ
must be presupposed despite the obvious diversity of the
witnesses, but that it cannot be demonstrated by the method
of historical comparison, since, on the contrary, this alleged
unity alone makes possible and checks the comparison. But
when the historical comparison leads to such different conclusions as, for example, we have seen in the case of Vielhauer
and Käsemann,[33] how can this dogmatically assumed unity
act concretely as a norm? Barth refuses to extricate himself,
as Andersen attempts to do, by conceding only a limited
freedom to this comparative historical study, and admitting
possible differences only in the "how" but not in the "what"
of the Gospel preaching. This would be inconsistent with

[33] Cp. above, pp. 62, n. 68; 63, n. 69.

his own equation of the question of historical truth with that of the true meaning and continuity of the Biblical texts, in connexion with which he is thinking primarily of each individual author, but cannot well exclude their being compared with one other. Thus even as regards the comparison of the texts it must be true that historical truth is also theological truth, and conversely. He would then say, and in fact would have to say, not that historical study in this sense *must* not challenge this alleged unity, but that, if done well, it cannot do so. To this such New Testament scholars as Käsemann and Vielhauer—we allude to them only as an example—would have to reply that they would like Barth to show them in what way they were misguided when their historical study led them to see these divergences, or, if that is not possible, to show them how such divergences are compatible with the supposed unity.

We do not know what Barth would say to this, and so will endeavour to think out the question further for ourselves. It seems to us of great importance, not only because at this point New Testament theologians and historians can today no longer come to an understanding with each other, but also because we see, in the question of those New Testament critics who ask by what criterion the theological assertions of Scripture should be examined with regard to their unity, a query concerning the authority of dogmatic statements generally— a query which Barth does not yet seem to have answered in any way convincing to New Testament scholars.

It cannot be Barth's opinion that such normative authority would simply flow from a concordance of Biblical texts, since this could only mean a levelling out of their concrete individuality, on the elucidation of which through Biblical theology Barth places such emphasis. But if Barth avoids this method, must he not have some other norm by which he appraises the values of individual Scriptural texts? But this attempt to find a canon within the canon he also rejects, even if it were derived from the canon itself—as for example, the doctrine of justification—because this would mean fettering the *facultas semetipsi interpretandi* of Scripture.[34] Nor could he consider as such a possible norm the preaching of the historical

[34] Cp. Diem, *Theol.*, VOL. I, pp. 93 ff.

Jesus, since this is accessible to us only in Scripture, which we must not seek to get behind. But in this circular argument—which states that dogmatics must test present-day preaching as regards its accordance (*a*) with the word of Scripture, and (*b*) with revelation, which is apprehensible only in Scripture—how can we find a norm for dogmatics? In this matter is there any other possible resource but that of critically ordering and interpreting in detail the Biblical texts from some systematic point of view derived from the Bible itself? Barth of course repudiates this method also. But is he doing anything else than applying this method when, in the first chapter of his *Dogmatics* he expounds "the Word of God as the criterion of dogmatics," and, in the second, in considering the doctrine of the Trinity, substantially applies the same principle?

We come up against the same insurmountable difficulty in Barth when, from a different point of view, and instead of enquiring about the norm for dogmatics, we enquire about the relation which he considers to exist between the word of revelation and preaching. This is the same question as we asked of Bultmann; and in his case it took the form of asking whether the relation between the *kerygma* and faith, and hence doctrine, as the interpretation of the believer's insights, was an assuredly one-way relation, so that faith does not simply become a matter of believing in its own powers of belief. Bultmann gave us no satisfactory reply to this question, because his argument was circular and did not overcome the merely interchangeable relationship between the Word and faith. With Barth the question assumes another form, namely the relation of the canonical word of Scripture to present preaching and so to faith. Here irreversibility seems absolutely assured by the dogmatic assumption of the different times of the Word of God, as a result of which, historically and theologically, the Word always remains prior to faith. But it is a question of interpreting the Word of God embodied in the word of Scripture, by means of Biblical theology, and, further, of dogmatic theology's concern about the consonance of the word of present preaching with the word of Scripture, and so with the word of revelation. What seems to be lacking here is an assurance of the priority of the word of revelation itself to the word of Scripture, as something both historically and theologically based. The question is whether Barth does not overlook this: historically, because we no longer can nor must ask about the events which took place between the event of revelation itself and the canonisation of Scripture, about the relation between the history of Jesus Himself and of Scripture's witness to Him; and hence also theologically, because in this way the priority of the Word of God to the word of Scripture is no longer substantially based—rather, the relation between the two becomes an intra-Biblical dialectic which can indeed be unfolded by a Biblical theology, but which makes question-able Barth's purpose of basing the approach of dogmatics independently of Biblical theology.

With these questions we are not telling Barth anything new; he is already discussing them in his *Prolegomena zur christlichen Dogmatik*, for which he later substituted the first volume of his *Kirkliche Dogmatik*.[35] Here he attempts to distinguish his definition of the Word of God as the formal principle of dogmatics from a *material Biblicism*, and says: "Dogmatic affirmations must have a *Biblical attitude*."[36] By this he means "the mode of thinking characteristic of Prophets and Apostles. It is the attitude not of observers, reporters or philosophers, but of witnesses, of men who, whatever they say, originate from the reality of the Word of the Lord, as of something absolutely given, and speak with the impetuous power of a torrent rushing down the mountainside."[37] Here we are faced by "a form of thought, to think in which the dogmatist must learn to practice, as anything else is learnt. But, what is more, a form of thought which does not appear in other connexions, and in which we cannot learn to think except in the school of witnessing Apostles and Prophets."[38] The Biblical attitude is something "to which we can grow accus-tomed only by the exegesis of Scripture itself, just as a new-born child accustoms itself to breathe and drink."[39] But this Biblical attitude as the determining factor in dogmatics cannot spell a material Biblicism: "At its climax, where exegesis must pass into original thought, a dogmatics which limits itself to being merely a Biblical exegesis, inevitably becomes

[35] Cp. ch. 24: Die dogmatische Norm, pp. 429 ff.
[36] Barth, *Die christliche Dogmatik*, 1927, VOL. I. 1, p. 435.
[37] *Op. cit.*, p. 436.   [38] *Op. cit.*, p. 437.   [39] *Op. cit.*, p. 438.

the pious word of the man of today, to qualify which is, however, its very business. All too often, material Biblicism has in
fact made an arbitrary '*Sic volo, sic jubeo,*' the first and last
word of the dogmatist who adheres strictly to the Biblical
text, and has caused historical, psychological and speculative
thought to reign unhindered as though dogmatics were non-
Biblical; and dogmatics, *qua* critical discipline, has thus
neglected its very task. It should not be forgotten that whereas
material Biblicism is quite a modern phenomenon, only too
closely related to the psychology of religion, the Biblicism of
Reformed dogmatics, for example Calvin's, is clearly distinguished from mere exegesis, and in distinction from preaching *and* exegesis invites us to a Scriptural attitude of thought
which is formal Biblicism." [40] In order to avoid misunderstandings it should be noted that Barth is here using the terms
"formal" and "material" Biblicism in a sense different from
what is normal. "Formal Biblicism" usually means the rigid
adherence to a Biblical vocabulary, the attitude which
Marcellus of Ancyra repudiated as ὁμοούσιος. But Barth
calls this "material Biblicism." For him "formal Biblicism"
means "*consentire cum prophetis et apostolis,*" while the Biblical
attitude means "*consentire,*" not with the words and idea of the
Biblical testimony, but with the thing to which the Bible
testifies.

Probably the question whether a dogmatics expresses a
material or only a formal Biblicism will be decided not by its
formal governing principle but by its actual content. And
what Balthasar [41] says with special reference to Barth's
handling of the problem of analogy is true of his dogmatics
as a whole: "A final agreement about it can hardly be expected
to arise from its purely formal basis, if the whole breadth of
its content is not kept constantly in view. The discussion can
only move forward if there is a reciprocal movement between
theological *a priori* and *a posteriori* judgments." [42] He means
that after completing his *Prolegomena* Barth turned his back on
the whole formal question in order to occupy himself only

[40] *Op. cit.*, p. 439.

[41] See H. U. von Balthasar, *Karl Barth, Darstellung und Deutung seiner
Theologie*, 1951, cited below as Balthasar.

[42] Balthasar, p. 57.

with the content of dogmatics; and he says this with reference
to his own efforts to show that his dogmatics has a far stronger
affinity with Catholicism than would appear possible from its
formal basis.   Though we do not think that Balthasar was
successful in this attempt, we essentially agree with his observation: "If the question of formal principle is justified in
dogmatics, then that is only so with regard to its prelimin-
aries. It would thus be wrong to carry on the discussion about
Barth's later dogmatic developments by constant reference to
his formal principles.   The discussion would then be wide of
the mark.   The essential point is Jesus Christ.   In what sense
Jesus Christ can be the *concrete* form of Christianity, and also
of dogmatics, without the latter merging in Biblical positivism,
but rather, in virtue of its source, having its own validity as
a unique discipline—in the last resort that can be shown only
by the fulfilled existence both of Christianity and within it of
dogmatics." [43]

Hence it will hardly do for us to try to answer the question
about the ground of assurance, historically and theologically,
in Barth's dogmatics by referring only to his formal principle,
and suggesting that in the light of it such assurance *cannot* exist.
Not only could this not be done in view of the general considerations we have been urging, but it is forbidden, when we look
at the content of the dogmatics, by the meaning which Barth
assigns to the forty days after the resurrection of Jesus.   Here is
the point where for him the factual reality of the history of Jesus
gains decisive significance for dogmatics.[44]   The controversy in
which at this point Barth engages with Bultmann concerning
his demythologisation of the Easter event is a striking example
of the way in which he in practice applies his formal principle.
He does *not* argue on the basis of his presupposition about the
canon of Scripture, but says that "for good or ill the acceptance
or non-acceptance of the Gospel, at any rate in the sense in
which the New Testament understands itself, will be identical
with the acceptance or rejection of the '*evangelium quadraginta
dierum.*'   In the New Testament sense either one believes in the
risen Jesus Christ, or one does not.   That is a point on which
both believers and non-believers, simply by looking at the

[43] Balthasar, p. 63.
[44] Cp. Barth, *K. D.*, vol. iii. 2, pp. 524 ff. (527 f.).

sources, should agree." [45]   But the application of the New
Testament writings as sources proceeds differently in Barth
and Bultmann.   With regard to the Resurrection event Barth
infers from them that the actuality of this event, as attested by
the New Testament documents, is of integral significance
for the content of the Easter message, which otherwise would
be a pure speculation, "without any foundation in the Word
and revelation of God." [46]   On the basis of these pronouncements by witnesses, he then develops his dogmatic teaching of
"Jesus as the Lord of time," in connexion with his anthropological doctrine of "man in his time."   But the factuality of
the resurrection is not deduced *a posteriori* from the doctrine as
its supporting basis (as in the detailed argument might
occasionally appear to be the case), but is stated *a priori* by
acceptance of the New Testament witnesses who alone are in
a position to assert it, "because they exist by reason of the
resurrection of Jesus from the dead." [47]   Thus the witnesses
belong to the history not only by *what* they report of it, but by
reason of the fact *that* they report it and that it is *they* who
report it.   What Barth says in general about the history of
Jesus applies also to the post-Easter events, and conspicuously
so on account of their central significance, namely: "Simply
everything as regards the eternal salvation of all men depends
on the fact that one can *narrate* this history in the terms 'it
happened once', " [48] and, we may add, on the fact *that* it is
narrated by the Apostles.   Thus the *argument* here is not based
on the dogmatic presupposition of the exceptional importance
of the speech of the Apostles, but that presupposition arises
subsequently by inference.   Thus we see that Barth's use here
of the New Testament writings as sources shows the theological
movement between the *a priori* and the *a posteriori* which Urs
von Balthasar described.

But now Bultmann, who reads the New Testament writings
as a collection of historic sources like any other, comes to the
conclusion that the factuality of the Resurrection in the sense
which Barth means is not relevant for the Easter faith.   In
view of Barth's statement, quoted above, about the common
interest of both believers and unbelievers in the discoveries

[45] *Op. cit.*, p. 531.   [46] *Op. cit.*, p. 557.
[47] *Op. cit.*, p. 558.   [48] *Op. cit.*, p. 529.

resulting from an investigation of the sources (and since it is a question only of freedom from presupposition, we might say historians and dogmatists), he would have to reply that as an historian Bultmann has clearly not mastered his material, i.e. has not read the text as it should be read, and therefore has interpreted it inappropriately. Barth does say this implicitly and occasionally even explicitly. But in this way we simply cannot get further, as the previous discussion about the theology of Bultmann has shown. For just as Bultmann reproaches Barth with the circularity of his argument in dogmatics, so, too, Barth reproaches Bultmann because his exegesis moves on the basis of a hermeneutics which rests on systematic pre-suppositions, and hence they can no longer meet on the ground of exegesis, where alone the rights and wrongs of this argument could be thrashed out. In this regard it is not merely a question of Barth and Bultmann, but, as we have seen, of the cleavage between dogmatics and historical exegesis in the whole area of present-day theological discussion.

To this Barth might reply that, in his theology, this cleavage does not exist, and that the reason for it lies in the inappropriate procedure of the historians. And if we have rightly understood Barth, his dogmatic presupposition itself gives him the right to argue with the historian on his own ground, and without needing to rest his argument on this presupposition itself, as we saw in his treatment of the Resurrection story. But just on account of this we would like to ask Barth: If it is the case that as far as Scripture is concerned the historical and theological approach to truth are one, then it is not clear why only the theological aspect of the matter can be grasped, while the historical approach is excluded through a dogmatic presupposition. On the contrary, must it not be true that it is through the historical approach that we reach the theological aspect, or, at the very least, that the historian and the theologian come to pose the same question? Of course this must not be taken to mean that in this way the Resurrection can be verified as an "historical fact," which Barth would agree to as little as Bultmann. But we are of course asking whether this would not be a possible way by which dogmatists and historians might reach an understanding as to the relation between historical and unhistorical elements on the basis of the New

H

Testament itself. For example, Barth agrees with Bultmann when the latter says of the Church: "It is not an historical phenomenon in the sense in which we normally understand that phrase: but it *is* an historical phenomenon in the sense that its life is embodied within history"; [49] and he comments: "Just this is pre-eminently true of the resurrection of Jesus." [50] If it is possible for them to come to an understanding about the meaning of "unhistorical" and "historical" in regard to the Church, why can they not agree about the phenomenon of Scripture and on that basis about individual historical and theological problems?

In asking Barth whether in this way he could not come to an understanding with the historian and even for once proceed to work from history towards dogmatics, it is not our concern to mediate between Barth and Bultmann. In any case we could not in this way reach a *via media* between the two. Nor do we mean that at this point Barth should make a single concession to the historian but rather that he should consider the question whether to adopt this method might not to some extent secure him against certain dangers attendant on his dogmatic work. Above [51] we enquired about the secure basis for the irreversibility of the relation between the Word and faith, and we found that Bultmann offered no such security. We have asked the same question of Barth, and now we can make it more concrete and particular by asking whether his formal Biblicism is secure against a deterioration into a material Biblicism. Perhaps there can be no absolute security in this connexion; but if material Biblicism is considered to be as dangerous as Barth considers it, when he sees that in its wake "historical, psychological and speculative thought reign unhindered as though dogmatics were non-Biblical, and thus dogmatics *qua* critical discipline has neglected its very task," [52] then in any case we must strive to find any possible guarantee against such dangers.

From the questions we have addressed to Barth there springs positively the task of exploring, historically and theologically, within Scripture itself, the relation between the Word of God

[49] Bultmann, *Offenbarung und Heilsgeschehen*, 1941, p. 68.
[50] Barth, *K. D.*, VOL. III. 2, p. 535.
[51] See above p. 93.   [52] See above, p. 102.

and preaching, rather than allowing ourselves, as dogmatists, to be hypnotised by the closed canon of Scripture, and, as historians, to seek only what lies behind it. And from our questions addressed to Bultmann, who seeks to grasp that relation within the canon itself, it would follow that we must not do this (as he does) by using a dual conception of history, nor in such a way as to make this irreversible relation an interchangeable one. But before turning to this task, we address the same questions to the Roman Catholic position of Schlier.

(d) *The relation of the revelation of the historical Jesus to the kerygma and dogma of the Church in Heinrich Schlier*

Heinrich Schlier would seem fully to meet the requirements implied in the questions we have addressed to Barth and Bultmann. The secure relationship we are seeking exists in his work, both historically and theologically, through the process by which revelation is extended in kerygma and dogma; moreover any danger of the relation becoming an interchangeable one is there excluded. The process in question involves a *procedere* in the literal sense, a movement by which God steps forth out of His hiddenness disclosing Himself in the life, words, and works of Jesus, whose authority is then extended by the committal of the deposit of revelation to the Apostles, by the genesis of Scripture crystallising around the symbol, and further by the whole tradition of the Church. From this point of view the whole history of the Church, and world history, too, is to be understood as the history of the proclamation of the Word of God, and the historical continuity and material identity of this continuous proclamation is absolutely assured. And the faith to which this proclamation appeals becomes the *fides quaerens intellectum*, the faith to which wisdom as a gift of God falls, in so far as it adheres to the revealed doctrine, to the *kerygma* as a fundamental principle of such wisdom.[53]

From this point of view the Word of God becomes a new philosophy of being, an ontology which makes it possible for man once more to grasp the truth and life of being, after falling away from being through the fall and original sin. But

[53] See above, p. 49

truth and life are by no means as a result accessible to the philosophical insights of the natural man, they are mediated only by the fact that the obedient believer places himself within the process of the history and proclamation of salvation. But how is such mediation of ontological truth effected by the *kerygma*? What in this connexion is declared to man? What has he to hear and believe? The continuation of revelation into the formation of dogma and thence into ontology which Schlier somewhat summarily assumes gives us no precise answer to these questions.

Hence for the sake of clarity we must complete one or two gaps in the sequence of Schlier's argument. What for example does Schlier mean precisely when he says that the story of the Cross and Resurrection as Paul proclaims it in 1 Cor. xv offers us a fundamental principle which makes possible a new understanding of the being of man in history? The statement (vss. 3 ff.) about the death, burial, and resurrection of Christ seems to be primarily a historical report. The added comment (vs. 3) that it happened for our sins aims at giving this historical account a teleological interpretation; and the enumeration of the witnesses (vss. 5 ff.) is intended to vouch for its factual happening. But what does Paul want to teach or "preach" by this account? Wherein does the *kerygma* consist in the pre-symbol here quoted? Does the *kerygma* in fact consist, as Schlier contends, in the truth of a principle? But this is exactly how the message of the Resurrection was understood by the people whom Paul is here attacking. They did not dispute the historical truth of the resurrection of Jesus but only our own resurrection from the dead (vs. 12). From their point of view the resurrection of Jesus was by no means meaningless. On the contrary, it was for them the exemplifica-tion of a principle that in modern idealistic terms we might call the principle of "Die to live." The significance of the resurrection of Jesus lay for them in the fact that basically it made possible a new life and by the application of a principle opened up the path to victory over sin. But Paul attacked this point of view with the argument that if they derived *only* this principle from the Easter message and did not hear or believe the message of their own resurrection from the dead, then all is vain. If it is merely the *principle* which is true, then Christ is not risen and they are yet in their sins (vss. 16 ff.), i.e. the historical truth of the resurrection of Jesus is meaningless. In contradiction to this, Paul is obviously concerned to emphasise that Jesus did not rise for the illustration of a principle or basic truth which in its significance for human life might be separable from the factuality of the resurrection of Jesus and our own resurrection. Hence from vs. 20 he abandons the dialectical argument *e concessis* and returns to his starting point: "But in fact Christ has been raised from the dead, the first fruits of those who have fallen asleep," that in the kerygma He may confront them as the ever-living one.

But how does Schlier conceive the relation of his principle to the historical truth of the resurrection of Jesus? We have seen how by means of phenomenological ontology Schlier gives a new and broader basis to that commonplace principle of idealism and conceives it as the restoration to man of access to unveiled being which belongs to the essence of archetypal man, and also shows how man in history has lost this access through sin, i.e. his refusal to give God thanks. He confronts man in history with archetypal man and brings them into connexion with each other by means of a doctrine of *analogia entis* to which his phenomenological ontology gives new foundations. The question whether he has thus in fact overcome the idealism of Catholic anthropology or has only added to it an interesting modern variant, we can here leave open. We are here only concerned with the principle as such and the question arises as to what connexion there exists between the truth of this principle and its declaration through a revelatory event. Such a connexion exists for Schlier because for him *kerygma* and dogma in the last resort are one. Hence the simple conclusion: the truth of the dogma and of the ontology derived as a principle from it lies in the actualisation of the *kerygma* as event, and on the other hand the reality of the event attested in the *kerygma* is grounded in the truth of the dogma. Within this circular argument by means of which Schlier projects Roman Catholic dogma back into the New Testament, he is unassailable by any historical or dogmatic question.

It is not possible to say that Christ has thus become a mere principle, as happened among the Corinthians whom Paul is attacking, nor, in modern terms, that He has risen only in a new ontology. This is precluded by the fact that faith "is the concrete assent to the *kerygma*, not . . . a mere decision of man to accept himself and his own freedom." [54]   Faith spells the entrance into a new reality placed before it, into the process of the preaching of salvation, in which Jesus Christ means absolutely everything—the historical beginning and the living continuance and the guarantee of the new reality, while being at the same time the foundation of the truth which it discloses. But in regard to this process of the preaching of salvation, in what precisely does the *preaching* consist? This is the decisive question which must be put to Schlier's Roman Catholic theory. If we allow him to give us the answer himself, we are of course caught up again in his circular argument: *kerygma* is both the preaching performed by the historical Jesus and also the preaching of the Christ by the primitive Church, crystallised into the pattern of the apostolic pre-symbols; and also the witness of Scripture, standardised by the *regula fidei* as its nucleus; and also the *propositio ecclesiae*, or the preaching of the *dogmata fidei* by the Church's teaching office; and also the regular proclamation of doctrine by the bishops; and finally the catechetical and liturgical practice of the Church supervised by the bishops. Even from the point of view of this understanding of the *kerygma* a few critical questions might be asked, as for example: Has the concrete preaching at the lowest stage of this hierarchy, within the life of the Church, only to echo the official declarations of Church teaching, or has it to announce the witness of Scripture? If it did the latter, the possibility would arise that it might challenge official Church teaching and shatter the identity of *kerygma* and dogma. Here we touch on one of the sorest points not only in the theology, but also in the cultic practice, of the Roman Church, which knows very well what it is doing when it regards preaching as unessential to the life of Church worship. We might then go on to ask whether Jesus Christ is the real *subject* of the *kerygma* after His imprisonment in the ecclesiastical objectivised form of it, and consequently can only speak through the *kerygma* of the Church but no longer constitute its critical touchstone. We merely suggest by these questions how equivocal is Schlier's use of the idea of the *kerygma* which

[54] Schlier (above, p. 83, n. 3), p. 498.

at any moment can be objectivised as dogma.   But since such possibilities are considered and rejected in Schlier's system, they can form no decisive objection to his position.

Thus it will be good if we ask what is understood by "preaching" in the New Testament itself and thence seek a solution of the historical and dogmatic problems which we have come up against and this in contradistinction to the compact position of Schlier as also to the essentially more differentiated dogmatic position of Barth and to the emphatically undogmatic position of Bultmann.

CHAPTER IV

THE HISTORY OF JESUS CHRIST
WHO IN HIS PREACHING REVEALS AND
AUTHENTICATES HIMSELF

"To preach" has, in the New Testament, a quite specific sense. It means the form of verbal communication in which the Gospel of Jesus Christ entered the world and was proclaimed. This applies both to the preaching of Jesus Himself and to the subsequent proclamation of Him as the Christ. If we begin our study with the Synoptic Gospels and first with the preaching of Jesus Himself, we become aware that this preaching is given to us only in the form in which the primitive Church understood it and handed it down. Whether it was right in assuming that its own preaching was identical with that of Jesus Himself is a question which we will leave aside for the present, because it seems to us arbitrary and wrong for the historian, above all, to dispute this identity from the start. His first task in handling the texts must be to establish from them how they understood the preaching of the Gospel and in what they thought the identity to consist. Only after this has been done can further critical tasks arise.

(a) The idea of preaching in the Gospels

We begin, therefore, with our question about the essential content of preaching in the Synoptic Gospels.[1] The fundamental meaning of κηρύσσειν, which Luther translates as "to preach," is to proclaim an event and is best translated "to *proclaim*," if by "proclamation" it is understood that what is proclaimed thereby gains current reality or validity exactly

[1] On the following, cp. G. Friedrich, *s.v.* κῆρυξ, in G. Kittel's *Theologisches Wörterbuch zum N.T.* (henceforth cited as Kittel), VOL. III, pp. 682 ff.; cp., too, H. Traub, "Zur Verkündigung von dem verkündigenden Jesus," cited below as "2. Verkündigung," in *Ecclesia semper reformanda*, Munich 1952, pp. 121 ff.

as a law becomes operative through its proclamation. This can be most clearly illustrated by the scene in the synagogue of Nazareth (Lk. IV. 18 ff.), where Jesus declares the Messianic age foretold by the Prophets to be now a present living reality and says (vs. 21): "Today this scripture has been fulfilled in your hearing." He Himself describes the preaching of these tidings as His own special task for which He has been sent into the world by the Father (Mk. I. 38; Lk. IV. 43). And what has He to preach? The central point in the content of His preaching as applies also to the preaching of John the Baptist is the sovereignty of God (Mt. III. 1, IV. 17 [par. Mk. I. 14 ff.], IV. 23, IX. 35 [par. Lk. VIII. 1], X. 7 [par. Lk. IX. 2], XXIV. 14). "The other specific features of the message are to be understood in the light of the βασιλεία τοῦ Θεοῦ;[2] the requirement of repentance (Mt. III. 1 ff., IV. 17; taken up in the preaching of the disciples Mt. X. 7; Lk. IX. 2), and in fact repentance unto the remission of sins (Mk. I. 4, cp. Lk. III. 3; Lk. XXIV. 47). All this is comprised in the preaching of the Gospel (Mt. XXVI. 13), more precisely defined as the Gospel of God (Mk. I. 14), or the Gospel of the βασιλεία (Mt. IX. 35, XXIV. 14). The noun κήρυγμα is found in the Synoptics only in Mt. XII. 41 (par. Lk. II. 32) to indicate the preaching of Jonah in the sense of preaching of repentance. The absence of the noun is not accidental, for "stress is not laid on the κήρυγμα itself as though Christianity had brought into the world something decisively new as regards content and meaning: a new doctrine, a new vision of God, a new cult, or something of that kind. Rather the decisive thing is the action, the event of the preaching itself; for the latter marks the inauguration of the age for which the Prophets had waited. By means of the preaching of the Kingdom itself God breaks forth into the world with power. It is therefore the act of preaching the Gospel which is new. By that preaching the βασιλεία τοῦ Θεοῦ comes." [3]

It should be noted that in several texts the verb κηρύσσειν is also used absolutely, without any qualification as to the content of the preaching (Mt. XI. 1; Mk. I. 38 f., III. 14; Lk. IV. 44; and with reference to the disciples, Mk. III. 14, XVI. 20). The fact that this absolute use is possible shows, as Hellmut Traub points out, "that quite definitely and characteristically and

[2] Friedrich, *op. cit.*, p. 710.   [3] Friedrich, *op. cit.*, p. 702.

from the first the content of the message itself may be regarded as identical with the act of its proclamation." [4]   Traub connects this with the further observation that the preaching is bound up with the coming of Jesus and that this is quite definitely stressed (e.g. Mt. IV. 17, 23, IX. 35, XI. 1; Mk. I. 14, 39; Lk. IV. 44, VIII. 1). This close connexion of the Advent of Jesus with the preaching of Jesus, which, moreover, is found also in regard to the διδάσκειν of Jesus,[5] has no parallel in the prophets.[6]   It not only emphasises once more that the content of the preaching is identical with the act of preaching, but at the same time binds the preaching to the event of the coming of Jesus as the authoritative preacher.   The exclusive sense in which the coming of Jesus is understood to have as its aim the preaching of the Gospel, and in which He understands Himself simply as the proclaimer of the good news, is shown especially plainly in, for instance, Mk. I. 38 f.: "Let us go on to the next towns, ἵνα κἀκεῖ κηρύξω· εἰς τοῦτο γὰρ ἐξῆλθον. καὶ ἦλθε κηρύσσων εἰς τὰς συναγωγὰς κτλ." In the parallel Lk. IV. 43, Jesus adds: ὅτι ἐπὶ τοῦτο ἀπεστάλην. From these two texts we can illustrate the thesis which Traub establishes on a broad basis: "The divine initiative expressed in the 'coming' bears an absolute character, that of revelation." [7] And since this coming is adequately fulfilled in κηρύσσων we must add: "In His preaching revelation is fulfilled."

If the content of the preaching, the breaking-forth of the eschatological reign of God, thus coincides with the event of proclamation, and this event is grounded in the divinely appointed coming of Jesus to proclaim the Kingdom, then we can summarily assert that Jesus proclaims the rule of God in that He declares Himself to be the one who ushers in that rule.[8] We are chiefly concerned about this formula denoting Jesus as Him who proclaims Himself, because whereas the answer to the much-debated question about the Messianic self-consciousness of Jesus, is normally felt to depend on the

[4] Traub, " 2. Verkündigung," p. 126.   [5] Traub, op. cit., p. 122, n. 6.

[6] Cp. Bultmann, Das Evangelium des Johannes, 1941, p. 30, n. 3.

[7] Traub, op. cit., p. 124.

[8] In this connexion, cp. K. L. Schmidt's allusion to the concept of αὐτοβασιλεία used by Origen as the appropriate term to denote the relation between the Kingdom of God and Jesus Christ Himself (Kittel, VOL. I, p. 591).

question of the relation of the preaching of the first Christians to that of Jesus Himself, we consider that the question itself should really be seen in connexion with the implications of His preaching as a whole and answered only in the light of them. In this connexion we agree with Friedrich Gogarten, who says: "The question of the Word of God leads us to the person of Jesus, who not only, according to the doctrine of the Apostles, forms the true content of the preaching, but whose own preaching most paradoxically consists in the proclamation of Himself. The problem thus implied should not be simplified and misrepresented by attempting to solve it through an exegetical clarification of the Messianic titles applied to Jesus. This method would entangle us in the contemporary (whether Palestinian or Hellenistic) idea of the Messiah or Saviour, and it would not be understood that, assuming Jesus applied these titles to Himself, He profoundly transformed their meaning. Hence what these Messianic titles imply in their application to Him cannot be appreciated from the titles themselves, but only from Jesus Himself. But who He was and whom He knew Himself to be can be appreciated solely from a study of His preaching as a whole, and, above all, from the fact that as a whole this preaching, whatever its theme in detail, refers basically to Himself. By this we mean Himself in His relation to God, or more accurately in the relation of God to Him." [9] Certainly the question of the meaning of the titles of dignity which He claimed or which were applied to Him and their interpretation in the preaching of the primitive Church, has its part to play. But materially, and—at any rate in the presentation of the Synoptics—historically, the primary datum to which we must in this matter adhere is the preaching of the Jesus who in so doing proclaims Himself.

Let us now cast a glance at St John's Gospel. Although κηρύσσειν is not used here, we find the same situation expressed in other terms. To the Synoptic view of the divinely appointed coming of Jesus into the world, there corresponds the emphatic Johannine use of ἔρχεσθαι implying that Jesus has been sent by God (Jn. I. 11, III. 2, 31, V. 43, VI. 14, VII. 28, IX. 39, etc.; and in this respect cp. Bultmann on Jn. VII. 28). "The revealer Himself bases His claim simply on the fact that He

[9] F. Gogarten, *Der Mensch zwischen Gott und Welt*, 1952, pp. 263 ff.

knows God: ἐγὼ οἶδα αὐτόν. And again His knowledge of
God consists not in any mythological or speculative theology,
but purely in the consciousness of His mission: ὅτι παρ' αὐτοῦ
εἰμι κἀκεῖνός με ἀπέστειλεν. He does not claim any metaphysical
qualities of any sort and does not appeal to any bar of judgment
which might also be recognised by the Jews, but only to His
awareness of having been sent. Only as one who has been
sent does He come before His hearers with His claim, and only
when He is recognised as the authentic ambassador of God is
it known who He is and whence He comes." [10] All this may
not simply be equated with our formulation of the Jesus who
proclaims Himself. The Johannine circle of ideas involving
the use of μαρτυρεῖν instead of κηρύσσειν does not permit such
an equation; for at most it is only possible to say that Jesus
"has borne witness to Himself," as in Jn. v. 31 ff., viii. 18,
where the witness of Jesus to Himself is only true self-witness
when supported by the Father's witness to Him. But since
in the Synoptics He proclaims Himself only, as we saw, in
connexion with "the relation of God to Him," materially it is
exactly the same when, using the μαρτυρεῖν formula, He here
(v. 32) says: "There is another who bears witness to me; and I
know that the testimony which he bears to me is true." Here too
the content of the μαρτυρία coincides with the act of μαρτυρεῖν,
and in fact the identity once more consists only in the fact
that it is He to whom witness is borne. Thus, more directly,
the Johannine formula of revelation Ἐγώ εἰμι expresses the
self-proclamation of Jesus.[11]

(b) The development of Gospel preaching and the historical reports of it

According to the Gospels, this preaching of Jesus has a history
which begins with the first public appearance of Jesus and ends
with His crucifixion, resurrection and ascension. But in their
system the Passion is not a fortuitous ending of the story, in
which case the preaching might have had another final result.

[10] Bultmann, *Das Evangelium des Johannes*, p. 225; cp. also pp. 224, n. 4,
and 286, n. 3.

[11] Cp. Bultmann, *op. cit.*, pp. 142 (on Jn. iv. 26), 167, n. 1, and 168 n. 3
("The Ἐγώ εἰμι formula must not be understood as an expression of
metaphysical truth, i.e. it does not describe the being of Jesus in itself,
but points rather to the event of revelation").

This issue is not simply a divine δεῖ (Mk. VIII. 31, etc.), as the predictions of the Passion suggest, and towards which, from the start, Jesus moves obediently: it is no longer on the plane of speech, but on that of action, it is a suffering which constitutes the central and decisive element in the revelatory event of the Gospel preaching, and as a consequence of it the Kingdom of God attains present reality and power. This is not inferred merely from the content of the Gospels themselves, but is also reflected in their literary pattern and the history of their formation. "The nucleus [of the Gospels in their literary form] is the *kerygma* of the death and resurrection of Jesus, so that it has been justly said [12] that the Gospels are stories of the Passion furnished with a detailed introduction." [13]   Moreover, the preaching of the Gospel itself confronts the hearer with the necessity of suffering and resurrection for discipleship (Mk. VIII. 34, X. 45, etc.).   Only in the light of this central event and not, for instance, as so many precepts bearing on religious and ethical conduct, is the rest of the preaching of Jesus to be understood.   Thus the history of Jesus is the history of His self-proclamation which culminates in the Cross and Resurrection.

In saying this we have represented the history of Jesus as it is reported to us by the Evangelists themselves.   The latter clearly start from the presupposition that Jesus from the very beginning was the Christ, hence that He did not become so after the Resurrection only, nor did He become so merely as a result of the Easter faith of the disciples.   The Evangelists make this clear not only by ascribing to Him Messianic titles and dignity, but primarily by representing Him as the one Who in His preaching proclaims Himself.   Here, of course, there arises for the historian the urgent critical question whether the Gospels are historically reliable sources, and whether, therefore, this representation of the preaching and message of Jesus corresponds with the real history of Jesus. But in this regard he must be careful not to bring to his text a critical criterion which is not consistent with its intrinsic nature.   Hence he must first ask in what sense the text itself understands itself to be an historical report.

[12] M. Kähler, *Der sogennante historische Jesus und der geschichtliche biblische Christus*, 1896, p. 80.   [13] Bultmann, *Theol. des N.T.*, p. 85.

Two of the Evangelists tell us themselves something relevant to this issue: at the close of St John's Gospel (XXI. 24) we read: "This is the disciple who is bearing witness to these things, and who has written these things; and we know that his testimony is true." In the language of John, where, as we have seen, κηρύσσειν is replaced by μαρτυρεῖν this means that he wishes by this writing to continue the witness of Jesus, or, in other words, to continue the preaching of Jesus by proclaiming Him as Messiah. The idea that he wishes to do so by giving an historical report is by no means appropriate, although it goes without saying that in accordance with ὁ λόγος σὰρξ ἐγένετο (I. 14) he is attesting from the beginning to the end of his account a history upon whose actual happening everything depends, in spite of all the freedom which he, above all, allows himself in the use of his sources. Strathmann points out [14] that in profane Greek μαρτυρεῖν already had a dual meaning in the sense of witness to facts and the declaration of opinions or truths—a dual meaning which is continued in the New Testament use of the word. If, therefore, in XXI. 24 the Evangelist describes his whole book as a μαρτυρία he understands that "not only, and not even primarily, in the sense of witness to external historical facts, but in the sense of bearing witness to what faith in Jesus has permitted believers to apprehend." [15] True, "the author of the Fourth Gospel and the First Epistle of John claims, indeed, to be a witness in the historical sense also, an eyewitness. But in view of his conception of testimony this is not important in the same sense in which it is important for Luke, namely as a means of proving the historical truth of certain events, but in a far deeper sense, i.e. that he has been vouchsafed the favour of a direct impression of the δόξα of Jesus ὡς μονογενοῦς παρὰ πατρός, πλήρης χάριτος καὶ ἀληθείας, and he can do no other than bear witness to us of this impression. He who is only an eyewitness in the historical sense sees simply nothing of this δόξα. It discloses itself only to the believer (I. Jn. v. 9 f.)." [16]

The sense is somewhat different when, in the introduction to his Gospel, Luke states that after many others have under-

---

[14] In Kittel, VOL. IV, pp. 477 ff.   [15] Strathmann, op. cit., p. 505.
[16] Strathmann, op. cit., pp. 503 f.

taken to report, according to the tradition of eyewitnesses and ministers of the word, those matters which have been fulfilled among us, "it seemed good to me also, having followed all things closely for some time past, to write an orderly account for you, most excellent Theophilus, that you may know the truth concerning the things of which you have been informed" (I. I-4). It is clear that Luke is very concerned about the factual happening of the events which he reports and aims at giving as reliable an account of them as possible. This is not surprising. For if the history he is reporting did in fact happen in this world—and for him everything depends on this—why should it not have left its historical precipitate, and why should he not investigate this as far as possible with all available means of historical enquiry as it was then understood? We must not apply to his work our own modern criteria, which in every report of facts see at once the possible danger of a mere *fides historica*. "It would be a superficial judgment," says Strathmann,[17] and with justice, "in the words of the prologue and other chronological notices (e.g. II. I ff., III. 2) to see only the joy of the historian in establishing exact dates. The real operative motive here is the same as that which has brought the name of Pontius Pilate into the Apostles' Creed." On this point Eduard Lohse also [18] draws attention to the remarkable expression according to which (I. I) it has been reported of matters "which have been accomplished among us." But this implies something other and more than a mere historical factual report. "The sonorous perfect passive participle indicates that God has brought to pass the fulfilment of certain things whose significance has meaning for the present, and is fundamental to the life of the Church. This motive of realised fulfilment sounds repeatedly in the historical work of Luke.[19] Hence the point of vantage from which Luke develops his historical perspective is the Church which believes in Jesus Christ." [20] From that point of view he reports the individual facts (πράγματα) which have found fulfilment. In the light of this perspective it also becomes

---

[17] Strathmann, *op. cit.*, p. 496, n. 53.

[18] See E. Lohse, "Lukas als Theologe der Heilsgeschichte," in *Ev. Th.*, 1954, pp. 256 ff.

[19] Lohse, *op. cit.*, p. 261.   [20] Lohse, *op. cit.*, p. 266.

clear what Luke means by what he has to say about the
hoped-for effect of the reading of his work: Theophilus is to
realise the reliability (ἀσφάλεια) of the words in which he was
instructed (1. 4). By this he cannot mean the mere historical
reliability of the reported facts, for the facts in themselves
would not illuminate what matters have been fulfilled, but the
truth vouched for by many eyewitnesses and—a by no means
meaningless addition—ministers of the Word consists in the
fact that in the fulfilment which Jesus accomplishes the age of
salvation has dawned. "In that Luke bears witness to the
Church about the present fulfilment of saving history, inaugurated by Jesus Christ, his report makes vividly present
for the Church this actual fulfilment." [21]   And when at the
close of his Gospel (xxiv. 48), and in Acts 1, Luke uses the
term μάρτυς in relation to the disciples whose mission it is to
propagate the preaching of Jesus, we must see in the term the
twofold meaning of the Johannine μαρτυρία; for, as Strathmann says, "the uniqueness of the object with which this
witnessing is concerned implies therefore that the witness
includes both the attestation of definite facts and the believing,
confessing and proselytising proclamation of their meaning.
The witness to the facts and the witness to the truth here
coincide, which is the inevitable consequence of the fact that
in the Gospel we have to do with revelation in history." [22]

Hence the question is whether there is any *independent*
interest in the historical truth of what is reported. But this is
excluded by the fact that the Gospels serve the purpose of
preaching. By this we do not mean only their use in Christian
worship, but above all the fact that they preach Jesus Christ
who in His preaching proclaims Himself and they do so with
the object of awakening faith and the spirit of discipleship.
The words (Lk. x. 16) "He who hears you hears me" apply
also to the preaching of the Evangelists, even when this is
not *verbis expressis*, or at least in effect said (cp. Jn. xxi. 24),
in as much as it may be inferred from the content of the Gospel
that is preached. This is still more decisively shown by the
use of the idea κηρύσσειν outside the Synoptics. The post-
Resurrection preaching of the Church not only has the story
of the life and ministry of Jesus Christ as its theme, but Jesus

[21] Lohse, *op. cit.*, pp. 270 f.   [22] Kittel, VOL. IV, pp. 495 f.

Christ is Himself the subject of its own preaching. Thus in Rom. x. 17 we read: "So faith comes from what is heard, and what is heard comes by the preaching of Christ." Or again consider II Cor. i. 19, "Jesus Christ whom we preached among you," and v. 20, "We are ambassadors for Christ." According to the words of Jesus in Lk. xxiv. 46 f., this preaching belongs to the process of revelation just as much as the suffering and resurrection of Christ. When, however, Jesus Christ is the subject of the preaching, it is no longer possible to distinguish between the earthly Christ and the exalted Lord, but the preaching is self-identical both as regards subject and content: it is always the history of the Jesus Christ self-proclaiming from His earthly life onward to the presence of the exalted Lord in the proclamation of the Apostles. When in Rom. xvi. 25 Paul speaks of τὸ εὐαγγέλιόν μου καὶ τὸ κήρυγμα Ἰησοῦ Χριστοῦ he does not mean to add together his gospel and the preaching of the ascended Lord, "but he is rather stressing the agreement between his preaching and that of the earthly Jesus. Hence τὸ κήρυγμα Ἰησοῦ Χριστοῦ can only mean the message which Jesus Christ announced." [23] Hence, though we must speak of the preaching of Jesus Himself as that which has happened, we cannot speak of it as past history. Hence the preaching of Christ is "not simply historical instruction about the words and deeds of Jesus. However edifying, all stories about Jesus are empty (I Cor. xv. 14); they are old stories which are not real, and are more or less useless for the present, if they are not understood from the standpoint of faith in the risen Lord. The reality of the Resurrection constitutes the fullness and potency of the early Christian *kerygma*. The former is a fact which cannot be apprehended as a fact, like any other historical event . . . it is a saving fact which requires to be preached and the preaching of it is part of the process of saving events." [24]

But is it only true of the fact of the Resurrection, or is it not equally true of all the other facts in the history of Jesus, that they cannot be apprehended simply as historical facts?

That the answer to this question can have important consequences is seen in the case of Bultmann, who in this connexion distinguishes between the Cross and the Resurrection. The

[23] Kittel, VOL. III, p. 716, n. 16.   [24] Kittel, VOL. III, pp. 710 ff.

I

cross of *Jesus* is for him an historical fact which, just like other
historical facts, can be demonstrated and taken note of—but as
a saving event—the Cross of *Christ*—it can only be preached
and believed. On the other hand, the Resurrection of Jesus is
not an historical fact, it can only be the theme of the *kerygma*.
As far as Christian preaching is concerned, this distinction
means that while the historical truth of the Cross is essential,
that of the Resurrection is irrelevant. Hellmut Traub says, on
the contrary: "The death of Jesus Christ is attested as an event
just as well or ill, which means: it is attested only in the
preaching of the early Christian community, just as the
resurrection of Jesus Christ is so attested. In view of this it is
surely arbitrary to attribute to the former event historical
truth, and to decree that the latter is not an historical event,
but a pure myth which is intended to bring out the meaning of the former. This is sheer arbitrary interpretation." [25]
Although Traub's denial of the consequences which Bultmann
draws from this distinction may be justified, we cannot agree
that in this way one may casually dismiss the historian by
emphasising the evangelistic character of the text. It can
hardly be disputed that in regard to Biblical events there is
a greater or lesser degree of approximation to what we call
an historical fact, and that from this point of view there is a
real difference between, for example, the Cross and the Resurrection of Jesus. Hence the evangelistic character of the text
must not be stressed in such a way as to banish the historian
to a realm of darkness where all cats are grey. This radical
verdict of Traub's affects not only Bultmann but the New
Testament authors themselves, in that it faces them with the
stark alternative of either an evangelistic text or an historical
report—a situation which was remote from their thinking.
Hence this approach will not do. There can be no question
that in their preaching the New Testament authors thought
that they were also reporting historical facts. The question
can only be whether they had any interest in the historical
fact as such, and apart from its proclamation as an element of
the Gospel story.

In any case it might generally be agreed that the New
Testament authors are nowhere and in no sense interested in

[25] H. Traub, *Anmerkungen und Fragen*, p. 26.

a reconstruction of historical facts which are demonstrable like other historical facts, and capable of being known as such. On the one hand, the Synoptics, with their interest in the historicity of the life of Jesus are, as Ernst Käsemann [26] puts it, concerned to "present as the presupposition of faith the *extra nos* aspect of our salvation. Their faithful adherence to history is a way in which this *extra nos* of salvation finds expression." [27] On the other hand, it is true of them, as of the whole of early Christianity: "It interprets what has become historical for it in the light of its own experience, and for this purpose uses the medium of preaching. Just in this way it delivers past facts from the possibility of being regarded as mere curiosities and miracles. By this means it declares that Jesus is not for it just a wonder-worker; but much rather the *Kyrios*, by whom man knows himself to have been pardoned and to be under an absolute obligation to God. Expressed in paradoxical terms, it maintains historical continuity with Him who once walked this earth by the very fact that it allows the historical events of the earthly life of Jesus to fall to a great extent into oblivion, in order to replace them by its evangelical appeal." [28]

The same is true of Paul, who says (II Cor. v. 16): "even though we once regarded Christ from a human point of view, we regard him thus no longer." By this, of course, Paul does not mean that the truth of the earthly history of Christ is a matter of indifference, but that this history now concerns us only in the evangelical preaching of it, i.e. in the διακονία τῆς καταλλαγῆς (v. 19) given to the Church, or in the λόγος τῆς καταλλαγῆς (v. 20). In this connexion the Apostle is not primarily concerned about the knowability, historical or otherwise, of the history of Jesus Christ, but about our own share in it, i.e. his concern is that "those who live might live no longer for themselves, but for him who for their sake died and was raised " (v. 15). To know one who so lives means to know him not κατὰ σάρκα, i.e. no longer as the person he would be apart from this history. For participation in this saving history it is of no importance whether we have known

[26] E. Käsemann, "Das Problem des historischen Jesus," in *Z. Th. K.*, 1954, pp. 125 ff.
[27] Käsemann, *op. cit.*, p. 141.   [28] Käsemann, *op. cit.*, p. 129.

Christ after the flesh or—thus we must logically continue—
we project ourselves back into the situation of the eyewitnesses
in an attempt to reconstruct the history of Jesus. The important thing is rather that through faith in the Christ who
meets us in the Gospel preaching, we become contemporaneous
with Him. On this point Otto Michel,[29] following Adolf
Schlatter, emphasises the polemical character of the text.
Ernst Fuchs[30] quotes the text as illustrating that "actual
experiences within the world are of no importance when it is a
question of the revelation of God in Christ," [31] but sees the
possible misunderstanding that facts about the historical Jesus
are of no consequence corrected by St John's Gospel, for John
realised that "theology may not eliminate the real historicity
of Jesus (the Pauline formula in II Cor. v. 16 is one-sided), but
that theology must be developed from the gulf which exists
between faith and the historical Jesus." [32] The same point is
at issue when in I Cor. I. 18 it is not the Cross—as an historical
event—but the λόγος τοῦ σταυροῦ which effects discrimination
between souls, and in fact ἵνα μὴ κενωθῇ ὁ σταυρὸς τοῦ Χριστοῦ.
Hence here it is not a case of making a virtue of necessity, as
though the reconstruction of the historical facts were no longer
possible. This is in harmony also with I Cor. xv, although
at first sight this chapter seems to show just the opposite.
Paul is here plainly attempting to authenticate the Gospel
statement and the article of faith which he quotes—ὅτι
ἐγήγερται τῇ ἡμέρᾳ τῇ τρίτῃ κατὰ τὰς γραφάς (xv. 3)—by
reference to the statements of eye-witnesses, hence to affirm it
as an historical fact. But why should he not do so, since the
Resurrection, if it really happened, had eyewitnesses too?
Here again we must keep at arm's length that modern purism,
which out of sheer anxiety to avoid a mere *fides historica*, feels
compelled to ignore the historical contours of revelatory
events. Hence it appears to us both impossible and unnecessary
when Barth denies that Paul here intended to adduce an
historical proof,[33] and when Bultmann, on the contrary,
stresses that Paul in fact did just that, but thereby fell into

---

[29] "Erkennen nach dem Fleisch," *Ev. Theol.*, 1954, pp. 22 ff.
[30] See E. Fuchs, *Hermeneutik*, 1954.
[31] *Op. cit.*, p. 127.   [32] *Op. cit.*, p. 242.
[33] Barth, *Auferstehung der Toten*, 1954, pp. 74 ff.

self-contradiction.[34]   In our view one should accept Paul's argument as it stands, but notice at the same time what use Paul makes of his argument from history in what follows. What he is anxious to maintain is that the Gospel of the resurrection of Jesus Christ from the dead implies our own resurrection from the dead (xv. 12).   His opponents certainly disputed the latter;   whether they also disputed the former is doubtful.   But the whole point is that both belong together. In order to show this, Paul argues, in the succeeding verses, *e concessis*, and says not only that in this case the whole historical factuality of the resurrection of Christ is useless to them, but that, if indeed his opponents are right, it cannot have happened at all (xv. 16).   The merely incidental nature of this whole historical method of demonstration cannot be more strongly brought out than Paul does in this instance.

There should further be agreement about the fact that the New Testament authors, in spite of their lack of interest in the historical issue as we have formulated it, are in the highest degree concerned about the actual happening of the history of Jesus which they proclaim.   For our historical approach, this may seem contradictory, but in any case it was not felt to be such by the New Testament writers themselves in so far as they were not—as the Synoptics certainly were—conscious of "presenting in good faith authentic traditions about Jesus." [35]   But the question is whether they did not feel this contradiction only because they had not such a highly developed historical sense as we ourselves.   In that case we would have perhaps the right and also the scholarly duty to investigate this contradiction with our available means of historical research.   But clearly there is an intrinsic reason for their not perceiving any contradiction here.   What they preach is a history which by its very essence does not permit a mere scientific apprehension.   Of course it is a history which runs its course in this world and therefore at every stage includes facts which essentially are more or less capable of being historically established also.   But such mere historical-scientific appreciation would in any case fail to do justice to the essential import of this history.   For this history requires from the

---

[34] Bultmann, *Glaube und Verstehen*, VOL. I, 1933, pp. 54 ff.
[35] Käsemann, in *Z. Th. K.*, 1954, p. 131.

hearer of its evangelical presentation, instead of the mere apprehension of facts, not only, as we like to say since Kierke-gaard, a personal decision between scandalisation and faith (for this would not get to grips with the essential point), but rather it requires from the hearer faith that *in this history* a decision has been made affecting himself personally and his whole personal destiny. To believe in the message it announces means to become a disciple of Christ, which means that we live by the faith that we too are crucified and risen again with Christ. To miss the import of the history of Jesus Christ, means therefore to miss also one's whole personal significance and destiny. We may fail to appreciate this history by not believing in the evangelical message it affords, for the history cannot make its impact on us except through the preaching of this Jesus who discloses and authenticates Himself in the gospel He declares. And, on the other hand, we must say: the guarantee that in this history it is a question of real events which, only because they have once happened, happen still again and again, lies purely in the event of the preaching itself. For intrinsic reasons there cannot be any other guarantee of the historicity of this history apart from the preaching of it.

The failure to apprehend this history through unbelief can take various forms. One of them would be the attempt to withdraw from the impact of the preaching of it and thus to place oneself in a position of detachment from it, by seeking to base its reality on purely historical grounds. In this connexion it is of no fundamental importance from what motive this is done—whether it be to establish its truth on a secure historical basis, or on the other hand to call it in ques-tion, or even only to make it eventually so clear and transparent that it can also be apprehended without the medium of preaching and faith—nor does it matter what result is attained. We would not in any case be interested in this result, of whatever import.

(*c*) *The cleavage between the historical and theological approach to the question in Bultmann, and the attempt to overcome that cleavage by means of the kerygma.*

Naturally the historian cannot be forbidden to search behind the text for the historical facts underlying this history; for he would plead that it would be an offence against his conscience as a scholar were he arbitrarily to pause in his questioning at some particular stage. The reply to that objection would of course be that it is not something arbitrary, but the intrinsic nature of the text itself, which warns him against failing to apprehend the history it proclaims by his critical historical approach. If he does not heed this warning, then the onus is on him to see how subsequently he may render the results of his historical research compatible with the evangelical character of the text. An interesting example of how one can be aware of this intrinsic nature of the text and nevertheless approach it with the attitude of the critical historian lies in the work of Bultmann—which also and not least shows how difficult it is subsequently to bring the two things into accord. His *Theologie des Neuen Testamentes* reminds us that "the coming of Jesus was itself the decisive event by which God summoned His people, that it was in fact already an eschatological event." [36] This could be interpreted consistently with our view of the Jesus who in His preaching reveals Himself. Bultmann says, however, that this view arose only with the post-Resurrection experience of the Church and by no means accords with the pre-Resurrection preaching of Jesus Himself. But how can we have access to the pre-Resurrection history of Jesus so as to be able to compare it with the post-Resurrection preaching of Him? This can be done by an investigation of the history of the Synoptic tradition such as has been carried out recently especially by the form critics, who attempt to disentangle its historically oldest parts and thus to pierce to the oral tradition underlying it, so as thus to separate the pre-Resurrection history of Jesus from its post-Resurrection interpretation. [37] On these lines Bultmann has reached the conclusion that what we have regarded as the development of the message and preaching of Jesus according to the Synoptics is simply the result of the post-Resurrection recasting of the sources and is not the same thing as the preaching of the historical Jesus.

[36] Bultmann, *Theol. des N.T.*, pp. 43 ff.

[37] On the method by which this palaeontology of the Gospels (for so it was described as a result of K. L. Schmidt's *Overbeck*) is carried on, cp. K. L. Schmidt, "Formgeschichte," in *Religion in Geschichte und Gegenwart*, 2nd edn., VOL. II, pp. 638 ff.

Let us grant that by this palaeontological approach it is possible to identify, among the small literary units of which the Gospels are composed, the oldest elements; that, further, certain firm conclusions can be drawn as to the previous oral tradition, and even in this way probably authentic words of Jesus discovered. Let us take as an example the first two such texts that Bultmann [38] instances: Lk. x. 23-4 and vi. 20-1. These intend to say: "The preaching of Jesus is an eschatological message, i.e. a message that the fulfilment of the promise is now at hand, that the Kingdom of God is dawning." [39] Why may this not be understood in the sense of the Synoptic redactors, as meaning that Jesus is here referring to and proclaiming Himself? The text not only permits this but makes it an obvious exegesis, and the same is true also in regard to Mt. ii. 5; Mk. iii. 27; Lk. x. 18-19, xi. 20, xxii. 15-8. At least the texts themselves leave us the choice either of understanding them in the sense meant by the Synoptic Evangelists, or, with Bultmann, in the sense that they proclaim a Messiah who is yet to come and who is not Jesus Himself. Do we not see here the influence of a prejudice unworthy of the historian above all, to the effect that the Synoptic presentation must be a subsequent distortion of the preaching of Jesus —a distortion made necessary by the death of Jesus on the Cross and possible by the Resurrection? To counter this objection it might be pointed out that there are certain historically authentic texts which plainly understand the preaching of Jesus as Bultmann understands it, and where Synoptic distortions can be detected. This seems to be the case with Lk. xii. 8-9, the next quotation: "Every one who acknowledges me before man, the Son of man also will acknowledge before the angels of God. . . ." [40] Let us assume it to be correct that these verses represent the oldest version, then Bultmann explains the change in the parallel passages as follows: "It is characteristic that for the later Evangelists the original meaning of the title has become lost and the phrase 'Son of Man' has become so familiar as the self-description of Jesus that Matthew can just as easily replace a traditional 'Son of Man' by an 'I' (Mt. x. 32 f. [par. Lk. xii. 8 f., Mk. viii. 38];

[38] Bultmann, *Jesus*, 1926.   [39] *Op. cit.*, p. 28.
[40] *Op. cit.*, p. 31.

XVI. 21 [par. Mk. IX. 31], v. 11 [par. Lk. VI. 22]) as, on the other hand, an 'I' by a 'Son of Man' (XVI. 13; Mk. VIII. 27)." [41] But we are unable to see why this interchangeable use of "I" and "Son of Man" was possible only to the Evangelist and not already to the earliest tradition of Lk. XII. 8. In this case the passage would be useless as a proof of Bultmann's theory. We do not of course know what words Jesus Himself uttered, nor whether He attributed to Himself the title of the "Son of Man," and on this point the earliest source can tell us nothing for certain. Hence all that we can infer is merely the possibility that according to the earliest form of the *logion* Jesus made a distinction between Himself and the coming Son of Man. But it is also just as possible that this earliest tradition of the *logion* used the title as much as the later Evangelists—unless again we make the presupposition that this simply cannot have happened before the rise of the Easter faith. Thus Lk. XII. 8 seems to us too narrow a basis for the burden of proof which it is used to bear. Of course, however, it is only a single stone in the whole edifice of Bultmann's argument. In addition there are the predictions of the Passion, of which he asks: "How can there be any doubt that these are all *vaticinia ex eventu?*" [42]; the contradictions in the statements about the *parousia*; the theory of the Messianic secret, with which, especially in Mark, the disparity between traditional material and evangelical report is smoothed over [43]; and so forth. About this last point we should, moreover, bear it in mind that the question to what extent Jesus was recognisable as the Christ before the Resurrection or was so recognised is a special problem of its own which should not be confused with the problem of the identity of the announcements of Jesus and the preaching of Him as the Christ, as has for a long time been too readily done in New Testament criticism and especially since William Wrede. [44]

All these points certainly involve very difficult problems for the exegete. But the question here again will be whether we ought not to attempt to explain these contradictions in the

[41] Bultmann, *Theol. des N.T.*, p. 31. [42] *Theol. des N.T.*, p. 30.
[43] *Theol. des N.T.*, p. 32.
[44] See W. Wrede, *Das Messiasgeheimnis in dem Evangelium, zugleich ein Beitrag zum Verständnis des Markusevangeliums*, 1901.

sense of the Evangelists themselves first of all, who no doubt did not leave them in their versions out of pure inattention, before solving them by reconstructing from them a history of Jesus which stands in contrast to the post-Resurrection faith of the Evangelists. Here we have gone into only a few of the texts quoted by Bultmann in order to indicate the problems which they raise.

But Bultmann himself is remarkably uninterested in the conclusions of his historical research into the preaching of Jesus. In any case for the positive interpretation of the faith of the New Testament they have no significance or at most the negative significance that the latter cannot appeal to historical facts. In his *Theologie des Neuen Testamentes* he seems to start all over again after his research into the preaching of Jesus and says: "Thus only with the *kerygma* of the primitive Church does theological thinking begin, and the theology of the New Testament proper.[45] It is no longer of any importance that the primitive Church preaches Jesus as the Christ, which according to the conclusions of historical research he was not, and did not intend to be." Why then did he institute his enquiry? If he was driven to do so by his conscience as an historical scholar, why is it a simple matter for him to expound later, as a theologian, a gospel whose historical basis he has himself demonstrated to be false? We have from the outset declared ourselves to be uninterested in this historical reconstruction of the teaching of the original Jesus. But Bultmann's lack of interest has quite other reasons than our own, which seem to us to be also those of the New Testament. He is concerned about the meaning of the New Testament, which is detachable from the factuality of the story which it proclaims, and hence historical facts discernible in that story have no part to play either for or against. The justification of the *kerygma* can, so to speak, be derived only from a forward view, from the fact that it becomes to the hearer a challenge and a call to decision. But the faith with which the hearer decides in favour of the truth of the *kerygma* is not (as we have defined faith) the decision to share in the history of the Christ who discloses and authenticates Himself but the decision to accept the historical reality of one's own existence. The message of

[45] Bultmann, *Theol. des N.T.*, p. 2.

the *kerygma* is not, as we conceive it, that the full dimension of the hearer's existence is already decided by the fact of his participation in the cross and resurrection of Christ, but that the hearer has to make his own decision about the full import and reality of his existence. Even with Bultmann this decision is to some extent connected with the history of Jesus, inasmuch as it is the advent of the latter alone which makes possible such a decision. But in this respect the history of Jesus is reduced to the mere fact of His having come, and for the establishment of this fact Bultmann uses quite a different concept of history from that which he uses when he talks about the historicity of existence. As a result of this dual conception of history which we are always encountering in Bultmann, the "historical fact" of Jesus and the preaching about Him become completely disparate.

In the last resort all this depends on the peculiar use which Bultmann makes of what is for him the central idea of the *kerygma*. He regards as *kerygma* not the Scriptures as a whole, but only the challenging word of Scripture which finds the hearer and calls him to a decision and thus becomes for him the Word of God. This *kerygma* is never to be found in a pure state in the Scriptures, where it always faces us in the guise of its theological elaboration. It must be disentangled from the latter so that "it may be understood as furnishing the possibility of man's self-understanding and so mediating a call to decision." [46] Thus at every point he must analyse out "kerygmatic" elements, which means that he must try to interpret texts "kerygmatically." An instructive example of this is the way in which he interprets kerygmatically the thought of reward in the preaching of Jesus, which would not at first seem to fit in with his own understanding of the *kerygma*. Thus he shows that "the motive of reward is only the primitive expression of the idea that what is at stake in the conduct of man is his own true being—i.e. his very self which he is not yet but has still to become." Thus instead of the non-kerygmatic thought of retribution with its allusion to heavenly reward and its threat of the fire of hell, he adopts the paradoxical truth of the kerygmatic word: "Whoever seeks to gain his life will lose it, but whoever loses his life will preserve

[46] Bultmann, *Theol. des N.T.*, p. 581.

it" (Lk. XVII. 33).[47]   None of those parts of Scripture which
are not capable of being interpreted kerygmatically in this
sense, and especially the historical statements or expressions of
pure doctrine, can mediate a call to decision; thus no such part
of Scripture can be a divine address to man, i.e. a word of God.
But the idea of the *kerygma* is *never* used in the New Testament
in the sense which Bultmann gives to it!   In the few texts
where the noun κήρυγμα, from the verb κηρύσσειν, is used
(Rom. XVI. 15; I Cor. I. 21, II. 4, XV. 14; II Tim. IV. 17;
Tit. I. 3) it means either the act of preaching or the content of
the message, though the two senses may merge into each other.
But nowhere has it the precise meaning of a specific call to
decision in contradistinction from other words which merely
report events or make statements about doctrine.   The verb
κηρύσσειν, too, is in no sense used only for such specifically
kerygmatic statements as Bultmann understands the term,
and this is suggested by the mere fact of its frequent juxtaposition with διδάσκειν.   The material reason for this is that the
whole content of the Gospel message and proclamation flows
from the real history of Jesus Christ and the hearer is invited
by this proclamation to appropriate the decision thus made
about his own personal destiny and not purely by his own
decision to attain for the first time the full historical dimension
of his existence.   Unlike Bultmann, in our own use and
interpretation of the idea of Gospel proclamation we have
adhered to the New Testament, and therefore cannot accept
his distinction between the specifically kerygmatic and other
texts, nor, like Bultmann, see the theologian's essential task
in the isolation of the former.   In this connexion it is clear
how his whole conception of the essence of theology depends
on his understanding (in our opinion, incompatibly with the
New Testament) of the *kerygma* and why the object of this
theology cannot ultimately be the history of Jesus Christ, but
only the self-understanding of the believer who no longer has
any relation to the truth of this history.

We do not of course propose to play off against Bultmann a
New Testament historian like William Manson,[48] who with
the same historical critical methods of research arrives at

---

[47] Bultmann, *Theol. des N.T.*, p. 14.
[48] *Jesus the Messiah*, 1952.

just the opposite conclusions and declares that before going
to the cross, Jesus, somewhere and somehow, must openly
appear before His disciples as the Messiah.[49]   He could
have established his thesis more cogently and luminously than
Bultmann did his.   But essentially he misses the point of the
history of Jesus just as much in saying, with reference to the
Messianic self-consciousness of Jesus which is demonstrable
as an historical fact, that "here lies the essential basis for the
development of the whole of Christian theology, and indeed
its historical locus." [50]   This basis is assuredly not the historically demonstrable self-confession of the historical Jesus but
the self-proclamation of Jesus in the Gospel.   If Manson had
said that, we would have been in complete agreement with the
last sentence.   It is just here, in fact, that the starting-point
for the whole of Christian theology is to be found, and this
indeed is its historical locus, for in this connexion arise both
the theological and genuinely historical problems with which
the Gospel confronts us.

(d)   The controversy about the historical Jesus between
Ernst Käsemann and Rudolf Bultmann

The problem is viewed in quite a different light by Ernst
Käsemann.   We have already seen [51] that he insists on penetrating to the history behind the event of Easter.   "The Christ
believed in and proclaimed after the Resurrection is thus
continuous with the so-called historical Jesus, without which
continuity faith and preaching would in the opinion of primitive Christianity be meaningless. . . . In view of this we are
required, even, and especially, as historians, to go back behind
the Resurrection event." [52]

He has addressed himself to this task in his dissertation
Das Problem des historischen Jesus.[53]   His objection to Bultmann's
thesis is that "here the Christian faith is understood as faith
in the exalted Lord, for which the historical Jesus as such no
longer has constitutive significance." [54]   But what primitive
Christianity intended to propagate, if not as historical tradition,

[49] Cp. Manson, p. 11.   [50] Ibid.   [51] Ibid.
[52] E. Käsemann, "Prob." p. 151.
[53] Above, p. 123 n. 26.
[54] Käsemann, Das Problem des historischen Jesus, p. 126.

then in the form of the *kerygma*, was in its own opinion always something grounded in history, though the relation of the individual writings to the history of Jesus shows considerable differences. But, for us, in any case, they are all of essentially the same import in that "we have access to this Jesus only through the medium of the early Christian message, and instead of facilitating such access this message in fact blocks it. It is not the historical Jesus whom we find in the New Testament—the only real authentic document giving us information about Him—it is not Jesus as He was in and for Himself, but the Lord of the believing community. Only in so far as from the first He was and could be the Lord does His story play any part in our Gospels. What He was in other respects is completely blurred, so that we are no longer in a position to establish, even with *some* degree of accuracy and adequacy, His personality and the actual course of His historical development, and in this matter we are compelled for the most part to grope blindly." [55]   In spite of this the decision of early Christianity "should not cause us to stifle the question of the earthly Jesus in spite of the dubiety which clings to it, when it is isolated and emphasised, and in spite of the difficulty of answering it." [56]   For, however sharply the outlook of early Christianity may differ from the history of Jesus Himself, and "however much the real story of Jesus be concealed beneath Church proclamation, it is purely to the interest taken in this history that we owe the genesis of those literary documents which stand out so vividly against the background of the rest of the New Testament and contemporary literature generally." In this regard let us remember especially that Käsemann sees himself required, as an historian, to pierce beyond the *kerygma* of the primitive Church to the historical facts. It will have to be shown to what an extent he *can* do so as an historian and how far he *must* do so as a theologian. To be sure, "the Gospels are concerned to bring out the contingency with which the eschatological event is linked to this Nazarene, to the arena of Palestine, and to this concrete period of history with its special circumstances." [57]   But this "contingency of revelation manifest in the connexion with a

---

[55] Käsemann, *Das Problem des historischen Jesus*, p. 132.   [56] *Op. cit.*, p. 133.
[57] *Op. cit.*, p. 138.

concrete period of history " [58] seems to us even for Käsemann
to be at bottom historically interesting not as *this* particular
contingency, but only in so far as it becomes known "in its
connexion with *one* concrete phase of history." Käsemann
says, indeed, that this contingency produces "the *kairos*
which is according to circumstances one of grace or of guilt."
But again the question arises whether the *kairos* in question
essentially presupposes as such some *one* historical situation,
or whether, because it is *this* specific *kairos*, it needs *this* specific
historical situation. If we are determined to use the idea of
the *kairos*, then we shall have to accept the latter interpretation.
Otherwise the historical character of the *kairos* inevitably
vanishes: i.e. inevitably the *kairos* will be understood merely
in the sense that it is not a question of decision in regard to
some universal truth, but in regard to a truth which at some
time or other has emerged historically. But this is not a
genuine antithesis, for even universal truths are accustomed to
appear for the first time in history somewhere and some when
—only to be severed eventually from their historical origin.
In the former case on the other hand the separation from the
historical locus will not be possible, because it is not the
general truth which constitutes the *kairos* but the fact of its
emergence and the how, when, and where. But only in this
latter case has the historical character and uniqueness of the
contingent event a really decisive significance.

It is not really clear whether Käsemann understands
"contingence" and "*kairos*" in the first or the second sense,
and whether he has in fact at all noticed this vital distinction.
No doubt it is for this reason that his further considerations
are so obscure. We realise, of course, that his ambiguity can
find confirmation in St John's Gospel; and, describing its
double meaning as "the reverse side of the divine condescension," he himself adds that "the Evangelist [John] brings
this out in narrating the history of the exalted Lord as that of
the one who was mortified and abased." [59] And with regard
to Johannine symbolism he says that the effect of this "is
utterly to remove from what had previously happened any
sort of historical uniqueness and to represent it basically as

[58] *Op. cit.*, p. 139.
[59] *Op. cit.*, p. 140.

only a mirror of present experience. Even the events of Good Friday, Easter, and the Ascension are no longer sharply distinguished. It must be said that nowhere else in the New Testament is history so undermined as here where it seems to be almost a projection back of the present into the past." [60] Here in any event it would almost certainly be a question of contingence in the second sense, whilst of the Synoptics Käsemann says that "they do not yet give scope to that kind of symbolism." [61]

"The disadvantage of the historico-critical method with regard to our problem" lies in the fact that its application has become too radical among us: "For our Evangelists still believed that they possessed largely reliable tradition concerning the Lord. Historical criticism has shattered for us this good faith," [62] and indeed to such an extent that "we have to show today not the right of criticism but its limitations." But these limitations are difficult to determine since, after all, "apart from the material of the parables, we have simply no formal criteria for the disentanglement of authentic material about Jesus." [63] At this point form-criticism leaves us completely in the lurch, "since its main concern is to establish the life-situation of the various types of story, but not to discover what one might call historical individuality. It is of use only in so far as it excludes as unauthentic what the life-situation shows to be plainly such." Here Käsemann enumerates a "whole series of conundrums" which are left in complete obscurity by precisely the same "oldest stratum" about which it may be said that everything depended on bringing it into relief against the tradition of Jesus. "We have *comparatively* firm ground under our feet only in one single instance, i.e. when, for whatever reasons, the tradition can neither be derived from Judaism nor imputed to primitive Christianity, especially in those cases where Judaic Christianity has toned down or glossed over as too audacious what was handed down to it." [64] From this point of view Käsemann tries to establish what separated Jesus both from friends and enemies, in order thus to infer the special characteristic of His mission.

"Exegesis as a whole is in agreement on the point that there

[60] *Op. cit.*, pp. 149 f.   [61] *Op. cit.*, p. 140.   [62] *Op. cit.*, p. 142.
[63] *Op. cit.*, p. 143.   [64] *Op. cit.*, p. 144.

can be no doubt about the authenticity of the first, second, and fourth antitheses in the Sermon on the Mount." On the basis of this assumption Käsemann concludes that "the only category which does justice to His claim, quite regardless of whether He Himself used or demanded it, is the one which His disciples did in fact proceed to attribute to Him, namely that of the Messiah" [65]—though we would ask whether, in connexion with the claim bound up with this category, it is at all legitimate to disregard the question whether Jesus did or did not raise that claim. Käsemann then goes on to show that these texts from the Sermon on the Mount do not stand in isolation, in the Synoptic Gospels, but are materially in correspondence with the attitude of Jesus about the Torah in the matter of Sabbath-breaking and ritual cleanliness, though "in this regard it is very doubtful whether Jesus has already claimed for Himself the title of the Son of Man." [66] Käsemann then concludes: "With unheard-of authority Jesus can supersede the literal application of the Torah and the authority of Moses. This sovereignty not only shakes the foundations of late Judaism, and becomes, therefore, a decisive cause of His death, but also, moreover, unhinges antiquity's whole world-view, with its antithesis between the cultic and the profane, and its demonology." [67] In doing this Jesus must have understood Himself to be inspired, i.e. "to be an instrument of the living Spirit of God which Judaism expected to be the mark of the latter days"; accordingly Jesus "thought that with His words the *basileia* came upon His hearers." [68] This inevitably raises the question so fiercely debated in New Testament criticism: "Did He regard Himself as Messiah?" Käsemann is extremely cautious in answering it. Though he is "convinced that there is absolutely no possibility of proving an affirmative answer," [69] he also thinks that "Jesus did not count on a Son of Man other than Himself, as Bultmann supposes"—though, in his opinion, if "Jesus never made any express claim to Messiahship, that would be extremely characteristic. By this reticence He would differ both from late Jewish expectations and from the Gospel preached by His own Church. He did not sketch out any picture of the future, but did what was

[65] *Op. cit.*, p. 145.   [66] *Ibid.*   [67] *Op. cit.*, pp. 146 f.
    [68] *Op. cit.*, pp. 148 f.   [69] *Op. cit.*, p. 150.

K

necessary to be done in the present, and placed at the focal point of His message not His person but His mission. But His Church showed itself to have understood the uniqueness of His mission precisely by answering His call and proclamation through its own confession of Him as Messiah and Son of God." If we understand Käsemann rightly, the Church did exactly what, according to Matthew (XVI. 16), Peter did in his confession at Caesarea Philippi, and in this connexion it will not have been of small importance, at any rate for the Evangelists, that Jesus expressly authorised this confession.

As the result of his historical criticism Käsemann concludes that "the characteristic feature of the earthly Jesus is to be found in His preaching." How this conclusion bears on our thesis of the Jesus Christ who in His preaching proclaims Himself will have to be shown by reference to the content of this preaching. Since Käsemann leaves open at least the question whether Jesus understood Himself to be the Messiah, it is possible that he would not agree with our contention, which rests upon the assumption that the faith of the primitive Church depends for its validity on the identity of the Lord it proclaims with the earthly Jesus. Käsemann characterises the content of the preaching thus: "Jesus did not come in order to proclaim general religious or moral truths, but to say what was implied in the *basileia* which was breaking forth into the world, namely that God has drawn nigh to man in gracious freedom. Jesus brought to mankind and Himself lived the freedom of the children of God, who remain children and free only so long as they find their Lord in the Father." [70] But does not this amount simply to the proclamation of "general religious or moral truths" about "the freedom of the children of God"? At this point we are once more faced with the question which we have already posed about Käsemann's use of the concepts of contingence and *kairos*; and in the course of Käsemann's further considerations it seems to us to become ever clearer that in his discussion of the matter he has disregarded the distinction to which we have drawn attention. We might concede that in pursuance of his historian's task he has succeeded in showing "that out of the darkness which enshrouds the history of Jesus certain specific features of

[70] *Op. cit.*, p. 151.

His preaching stand out relatively sharply, and that primitive Christianity included them in its Gospel." [71] But Bultmann has already said essentially the same thing, though in detail for different reasons. In face of this, it seems to us comparatively unimportant that Bultmann considered that Jesus distinguished the coming Son of Man from Himself, whereas Käsemann rejects this supposition, and leaves the question of the Messianic self-consciousness of Jesus in the main open. Of course, an essential difference between them consists in the fact that for Bultmann the historical Jesus is a teacher of law, whereas for Käsemann He corresponds, in spite of everything, to the Gospel which the primitive Church preached about Him. But this difference in the conclusions of the historical critics— and though it is considerable, it is debatable—seems to us to provide no better ground for the theological approach. We feel, rather, that Käsemann, with his attempt, clearly directed against Bultmann, to probe, in his capacity as an historian, behind the *kerygma* of primitive Christianity and discover the historical Jesus, has made no more progress than Bultmann himself; for the latter might just as well say: "The question of the historical Jesus, rightly regarded, is the question of the continuity of the Gospel through the discontinuity of periods and the changing forms of the *kerygma*." [72] All historians at least since the time of Albert Schweitzer have been brought up against this *question*. But the point is whether as historians they can give an *answer* to it.

Käsemann does not give an answer any more than any one else when he says that in the last analysis Jesus "cannot be classified either with reference to the category of the history of religions, or that of psychology, or that of history. If it is valid in any connexion, the idea of historical contingence is valid for Him." [73] For, he continues, "the problem of the historical Jesus is to this extent not our own invention, but the riddle which He sets us. The historian may note the riddle, but is unable to solve it." Far be it from us to reproach Käsemann with the disappointingly negative result of his historical research. We measure the result rather against his own declared intentions. For if even the eyewitness of the life of Jesus, in so far as he was not a believer, could make

[71] *Op. cit.*, p. 152.   [72] *Ibid.*   [73] *Ibid.*

no valid pronouncement as to whether the preaching of Jesus Himself was what it was later declared to be in the *kerygma* of primitive Christianity, how can today's historian do so? But it seems to us that ultimately Käsemann steps outside the category of the historian when he continues: "This riddle can be solved only by those who confess Him, since the Cross and the Resurrection, to be the one whom during the course of His earthly life He did not claim to be and yet was already becoming, namely their Lord and the bringer of the freedom of the sons of God, which is correlative to the Kingdom of God." [74] If the historian cannot solve the conundrum and can make no positive suggestions for its solution, how can he make the negative assertion that Jesus "did not claim to be the Messiah"? And how are we to understand the idea that He was in the process of becoming such? Käsemann can only mean that He became such through the belief of primitive Christianity, and, further, that He becomes such ever afresh through the belief of later Christianity. "For there corresponds to His contingency the contingency of faith, for which the history of Jesus is re-enacted, now as the history of the exalted one who is proclaimed as Lord, yet still, as formerly, an earthly history where the appeal and the claim of the Gospel are at one." Here again we should note the use of the idea of contingency: to the contingent event of the history of Jesus there corresponds the contingent event of faith. But in what does this correspondence consist? No doubt it is intended to mean that to the historical contingency of Jesus there corresponds the historical event of the faith, by which alone man can become related to that history. And this correspondence is more closely described in detail as the correlation of the freedom of the sons of God to the Kingdom of God which is proclaimed. But again what exactly is the meaning of this correlation? Does the reign of God mean that He proclaims Himself as its bringer with His appeal and His claim, thus demanding faith in Himself as Him who effects the freedom of the sons of God, or does it merely mean that His preaching imparts this freedom which brings about a new attitude to God, namely the faith which goes back to Him as its historical initiator, so that those who have seized this possibility in faith

[74] *Op. cit.*, pp. 152 ff.

confess Him as Lord for the sake of the high significance of His preaching? In the latter case, it would not be He Himself, but simply the *kerygma* of early Christianity, which makes that appeal and claim. We can put the question thus in summary and simple terms: Was He in reality the one whom the *kerygma* proclaimed Him to be, or was it only the *kerygma* which invested Him with such claims? Obviously the latter, and thus in spite of all differences between Käsemann and Bultmann, in this last decisive question, we find that we have reached once again Bultmann's exact position.

(*e*) *The historical and theological approach to the story of Jesus Christ who is self-disclosed in His preaching*

The story of Jesus Christ who is self-disclosed in His preaching comes before us in the Gospel message of the New Testament both as a complex of historical facts, in so far as this history that is preached runs its course within the general history of civilisation; and also as a theological situation, inasmuch as this preaching voices the claim to declare to man the Word of God. For the historian, of course, the complex of facts may be of a very peculiar kind, such as he has nowhere else encountered; but he will not be able to avoid facing it if he proposes to direct his attention to the New Testament. But what questions and problems remain for the historian to deal with if we set aside the possibility of penetrating behind the preaching, in opposition to the self-understanding of the text, in an attempt to discover the historical Jesus, and if we exclude such an attempt on the grounds that it is inappropriate and misplaced in view of the special nature of the historical facts? He must first enquire, as we have already done, how the proclamation of the Gospel story views itself. He will presumably find himself here faced with a situation where his normal historical categories break down. In the texts he finds proclaimed a history which just at its climaxes—we are thinking for example of the Resurrection narrative—is historically apprehensible only at its extreme edges. We recollect further that the crucified and risen Christ is regarded not only as the *object* but at the same time as the *subject* of this Gospel proclamation according to its own self-understanding. The historian can have before him only the alternative, either of insisting that only such history is real as is demonstrably true according to accepted historical criteria, and can be known in the same way as other historical events, or else of questioning his presuppositions at least in respect of this particular history. If he adopts the former of these alternatives, there remains nothing else for him to do but once again to become side-tracked in the pursuit of the historical Jesus whose figure lies concealed behind Gospel proclamation. But in so doing he fails as an historian competent to deal with the Jesus Christ who in His preaching proclaims Himself, and can therefore be neglected. If he adopts the latter alternative, then quite specific questions and problems are put before him as a result of the peculiar situation that we find the history of Jesus Christ only in the history of Gospel proclamation and that it is historically apprehensible only in the latter form. His object can therefore be only the history of Gospel proclamation as it lies before us in the texts. But in what exactly consists the question of historical truth with which he must examine the texts? The latter are historical documents relating to the situation that in the preaching of the Church the history of the self-revealing Jesus is proclaimed as a history that has taken place in the past, but is not simply past, since it is a history that is being re-embodied ever afresh. This situation implies the problem that Jesus Christ is indeed the subject of this Gospel proclamation, but the latter takes place only through the agency of men. Or the same problem may be expressed in other terms as follows: to the history of Jesus Christ Himself there corresponds a history of the Gospel preaching about Him, which in these texts becomes also a human history of trans-mission. Hence arises the problem of what criteria for the appraisal of this history of proclamation and transmission result from the fact that this history conceives itself and will be conceived as corresponding with that of the preaching of Jesus Himself. Speaking in general terms, the question of the historical truth in relation to the New Testament texts can only be the question what criteria are suitable for testing this correspondence. But this is also the question of theological truth which must be posed in face of the texts. Hence a separation between the work of the historian and that of the theologian is no longer possible. If the historian proceeds by appropriate methods, i.e. as required by the nature of this special object, he will come up against precisely the same question as the theologian.

We have now to explain further what is implied in this correspondence. In this regard our point of departure must be that the uniqueness of the preaching of Jesus Himself demands a correspondingly special form of transmission and clearly has also found such—a form to which Hellmut Traub repeatedly draws our attention. That preaching cannot be handed on by mere reporters of history, for the latter cannot see the decisive factor, viz. that this Jesus discloses and authenticates Himself as the Christ; and what they can see— the rabbi and the exorcist whose work, moreover, failed— they will hardly consider worth reporting, in so far as they themselves are not vitally affected by His preaching and the desire to hand it on. In point of fact the very oldest strata of the Synoptic Gospels contain no mere historical reports. Rather they reproduce the message and proclamation of Jesus Himself in the form of new preaching.

(f) The history of Gospel preaching as a problem for historico-critical research

If thus the whole history of Gospel proclamation is to be understood as an evangelistic transmission of the preaching of Jesus, to the end that He should be believed in as the Christ, then it is quite easy to see why this tradition shows such considerable differences. The proclamation takes place in ever new and varying situations. Hence the narratives and sayings handed on are submitted to a constant process of transformation and amplification to which contributes not only the ever changing Gospel situation, but also, and not least, the person of the proclaimer of the Gospel in his human character. If the Gospels are thus interpreted as a tradition of preaching, then the differences between them are not surprising—naturally this would apply too to the differences between the other New Testament authors—but from this point of view one can also understand why, on the other hand, a harmonisation of the Gospels such as would have facilitated later research into the life of Jesus not only did not take place, but simply could not possibly have taken place. This consideration provides the right answer to Bultmann's question "How did it come about that four Gospels were received into the canon, and that the attempt to reduce them to a unity either by the recognition of one alone (Luke's by Marcion, Matthew's by the Ebionites), or by the production of a harmony embracing them all (Tatian), never triumphed?" [75] But it also becomes clear from this point of view what immense positive significance critical research can have for the clarification of the history of Gospel transmission in that it makes us acquainted with the individual witnesses in their particular historical concrete circumstances.   Hence the task of such criticism would be, not to penetrate behind the text to the historical facts which it is purporting to record, but rather to enquire into the history of texts themselves.   The history of the proclamation is mirrored in the formation of the text, for the history of the text is the one historically apprehensible piece of this history of preaching.

    This summary affirmation of the significance of historico-critical research in its application to Biblical exposition will not find general acceptance as long as such disagreement prevails about the criteria to be employed in the matter. Today we find ourselves constrained to explain in detail and in various ways what Barth said in 1938: "The real decision as to whether in this field we are really making progress will depend on how far . . . the *exegesis* of canonical Scripture as such, the continuous exegesis of for instance Genesis, Isaiah, the Gospel of St Matthew, in their present form, will again be regarded as the ultimately *sole* possible aim of Biblical scholarship and will come to be pursued once more." [76] "Historical truth, which in its own way Biblical science too has to mediate, is to be found in the true meaning and continuity of the Biblical texts as such.   Hence it is not different from Biblical truth, which it is also a question of discovering.   Once that is clearly understood and the foolish chase after an historical truth lying *supra scripturam* is stopped in favour of a renewed comprehensive study of the *veritas scripturae ipsius*, then the fullest scope can and must be allowed to critical questioning and answering such as is required by the character of the Biblical

[75] Bultmann, *Theol. des N.T.*, pp. 485 f.
[76] Barth, *K. D.*, VOL. I. 2, p. 547.

witness as a human document and hence as an historical factor." [77]

But has the foolish chase after an historical truth *super scripturam* really been stopped with the ending of the liberal epoch of research into the life of Jesus? The hopes of Barth can hardly have been fulfilled by the re-discovery (which he hailed) of the objective concrete environment of the New Testament and Biblical witness generally through the methods of form criticism as applied by M. Dibelius, R. Bultmann, K. L. Schmidt, nor by "the fresh consideration of the *form* of the testimony reflecting this objective environment," [78] such as is seen in the collaborative work of theological dictionaries. In any case, the discovery of the proclamatory character of the Biblical texts, from which so much was expected, has not, on the one hand, hindered the search for the history of Jesus behind the texts, nor, on the other, has it altogether been conducive to a fresh consideration of the significance of the texts in their present form, since the text was not taken seriously in its canonical wholeness, but rather its theological relevance was reduced to the specifically kerygmatic parts. From the few examples quoted by us it can be seen how today all questions about problems and methods in regard to the critical approach to the Biblical witness are once again open.

If the history of the revelatory process confronts us only in the history of proclamation, and the latter is, in the main, a question of the history of the Biblical text—by which we do not mean the critical study of manuscripts in the usual sense— then we cannot be content to regard the Biblical books in their canonical wholeness, but will always have to make enquiries in a certain sense into the background of the canonical text. If we grant Barth's thesis that the "historical truth" which the aim is to mediate and which coincides with Biblical truth, "constitutes the true sense and consistency of the Biblical texts as such," then the enquiry into this sense and consistency must not be limited to the text in its present closed form, but if we are to understand the matter aright will have to be extended to the history of the genesis of the text. This will not of course happen in the way which today is still widely considered to be the only possible way consistent with exact

[77] *K. D.*, VOL. I. 2, p. 548. [78] *K. D.*, VOL. I. 2, p. 547.

scholarship, i.e. by feeling it necessary not only to eliminate the opinion of the editor or redactor but to be fundamentally critical towards it—as indeed must be done if we regard the texts merely as a collection of sources in face of which the historian cannot be sufficiently critical. Nor can we allow ourselves to be content with investigating and separating the sources underlying the individual writings, or with isolating the various doctrinal opinions of the different authors, but shall have to concern ourselves with establishing an appropriate criterion for the critical appraisement of the history of the text. But how can such a criterion be discovered?

In this connexion we must not *begin* with a literary-critical destruction of the present form of the text, but, on the contrary, shall have to take as our point of departure the canonical text itself and its self-understanding as an instrument of proclamation. Here it seems to us that Ernst Fuchs, for example, is on the right track in allowing scientific considerations only to follow, not to precede, exegesis, and in warning us against a "disparagement of the verbal text." [79] If the aim of the text is to proclaim Jesus Christ, or rather (as we have suggested) more precisely, to allow Jesus Christ to proclaim Himself through the manifold richness of the textual material, then only that method of exegesis can be right which does not thwart this process by arbitrary and extrinsic questions, but fits in with the process itself. This means that it reads the text as the result of a previous history of Gospel proclamation and expounds it in view of further proclamation of this kind—though in this connexion exposition and proclamation may remain two quite distinct tasks. Then the New Testament historian is engaged in nothing other than Church history, as Barth has defined it: "The history of the government of the Church by the Word of God; the history of that exposition of Scripture in the Church which is carried out by Scripture, i.e. by Jesus Christ. *Scriptura scripturae interpres.*" [80] From this point of view we can establish a critical method for the appreciation of the history of the text, by investigating whether and in what

---

[79] Fuchs, *Hermeneutik* (above, p. 124, n. 30), p. 150; cp. also p. 177.

[80] Barth, *Gotteserkenntnis und Gottesdienst nach reformatorischer Lehre*, 1938, p. 177; cp. also G. Ebeling, *Kirchengeschichte als Geschichte der Auslegung der Heiligen Schrift*, 1947.

various ways the individual writings attest the history of the Christ who in His preaching proclaims Himself, what factors have influenced the process by helping or hindering, to what extent the Biblical authors themselves eventually were diverted from their central purpose, and how in this way the single testimonies assumed their present canonical form and are to be understood. This is the method which we ourselves have adopted in our research into the story of the Christ whose proclamation testifies to Himself.

Our next task results from the fact that this history is not an absolutely new beginning, but takes its place in the history of proclamation which is attested in the Old Testament. Thus it is itself a history of the exposition of the Scriptures of the Old Testament, and we must enquire to what extent Jesus is the Christ of the Old Testament itself.

CHAPTER V

JESUS THE CHRIST OF THE
OLD TESTAMENT

WHEN in II Cor. v Paul says that God set up among us the λόγος τῆς καταλλαγῆς (vs. 19) and that God intreats "by us" (vs. 20), he is indicating that the Church is the sphere and the bearer of proclamation. In both these senses the Church is a constituent factor in the history of the message of salvation. In the body of the Church Jesus Christ becomes effectively present through preaching, and this makes it clear that preaching is not primarily the exposition of the truth of salvation but is itself an event in the process of salvation. Thus the Church is not only the bearer of Gospel proclamation and faith, but also and at the same time the latter's object. This again coheres with the fact that in spite of its initiating character the coming of Christ is no absolutely new beginning, but the fulfilment of the process of proclamation in the Old Testament. Thus by implication the latter is characterised as the preparation for the revelation actualised in Christ. As Christ died on the Cross with the word τετέλεσται (Jn. XIX. 30) on His lips, so the Church He founded is the Church of the latter age, in which all the promises given to Israel find fulfilment. As witnesses to the true Israel the Twelve represent the Church *in nuce* and authorise its *kerygma*.

(a) *The Church of the New Testament as a factor of
significance for the exposition of the Old Testament*

The connexion between proclamation and Church on the one hand, and between the Churches of the Old and the New Testaments on the other, is shown especially plainly in the First Epistle of Peter, for here the connexion is brought out in the course of anti-Jewish polemic. In this epistle the Church is called to a right understanding of its life in opposition to the misunderstandings arising from its environment. In this sequence of thought the central idea is that of the βασίλειον ἱεράτευμα (II. 9), which like all other descriptions goes back to the predicates applied to Israel in the LXX version of Ex. XIX. 5 ff. Like Is. LXI. 6 and II Macc. II. 17, the Hebrew text, which may be translated as "kingdom of priests" does not point to a hieratic kingdom represented by its priesthood, but implies that all the members of the people are priests. This is amplified in I Pet. II. 5 by the image of the "spiritual house" and the "living stones." The predicates of the saving grace and the dignity of Israel are given to the Christian community: a peculiar people, a priesthood with its spiritual sacrifices, a temple, etc. But they suffer a change corresponding to the changed situation resulting from the coming of Jesus: the οἶκος πνευματικός, the spiritual edifice of the temple, is the Church built up on the chief cornerstone Jesus Christ which springs up into a ἱεράτευμα ἅγιον, a holy priesthood created by the living God. This figure of the house and stones is an essential component of the original Christian proof from Scripture, and the use which is made of it shows that it is not really a question of a "proof," but rather of an evangelistic renewal of the Old Testament proclamation by means of a Christological interpretation of certain leading statements such as Ps. CXVIII. 22.

This οἶκος, on account of its derivation from the temple, is not here mythological, nor is it primarily to be understood as a building. It is rather an image expressing something collective and conveying the idea of communion in its aspect of holiness. Hence the image of the house may merge into that of the priestly corporation, the ἱεράτευμα. The essence of the metaphor is the coherence of the stones with Christ as the "chief corner-stone laid in Zion" (Is. XXVIII. 16; Ps. CXVIII. 22), and this brings the house into relation with the Temple at Jerusalem. The holy place, like the qahal, the people of God, is superseded by the Church, which embodies in its new life those old factors. But, says Vielhauer,[1] with justice: "More important than the opposition to Judaism and its temple—to amplify which Barnabas . . . sincerely toiled—is the positive importance which the author attaches to the word 'spiritual': the οἶκος is

[1] See P. Vielhauer, Oikodome, 1939.

the work and property of the Spirit of God which controls and administers it; the house belongs not to this world but to the world beyond, and its very existence is a miracle. Hence its attribute, too, is that of holiness, it is a temple, as is clear from the following words ('holy priesthood'). By the conjunction of the many living stones with the one living stone is the house built. According to 1 Pet. II. 6 ff., Christ is not the final stone added but the foundation stone on which the other stones are raised. In vs. 7, οἰκοδομεῖσθε antithetic to οἰκοδομοῦντες is probably not an imperative but an indicative, not middle but passive. It denotes how the growth of the Church is brought about, and suggests that it is an event which is accomplished on mankind but does not proceed from them. They are of service to the construction only as living stones, whose life flows from Christ. Just as little as in Ephesians is the coming of Christ separated here from the coming to the community, the people of God, but by coming to Christ one is integrated into the structure of the Church; οἰκοδομεῖσθαι is the consequence of προσέρχεσθαι. The two are possible only in conjunction with each other. . . . Christians as living stones, and in their collective aspect as a spiritual house represent the temple of God which belongs to God and in which God is present for men. This positive implies also a negative: the suspension of the Jewish cultus." [2]

If in this matter we wish to talk about a spiritualisation of the promise given to the Old Testament people of God, it is legitimate to do so only if by *spiritus* we mean the Holy Spirit. For the fulfilment spiritualises the promise only in so far as it no longer binds the activity of the Spirit of God to physical descent from Israel. But if such ideas as γένος and λαός are used for the new fellowship, it is intended thereby to preclude any sort of false spiritualisation and to say that since it represents the miracle of creation by the Spirit of God the γεννᾶν which is in question here has nothing at all to do with the human succession of generations; and the λαός which arises in this way is not marked by any of the normal characteristics of ethnic formation. It is this miracle of its divine origin which makes this community recognisable for what it is only to faith. But the ἀρεταί of God (vs. 9) can only be believed in and

[2] Vielhauer, *Oikodome*, pp. 148 f.

known within the life of this community *sui generis*, in which the fellowship of members with their Lord and each other takes place in the οἰκοδομεῖσθαι effected by the preaching of the ῥῆμα Κυρίου (I. 25).

Thus the evangelistic presentation of the Jesus Christ who in His preaching discloses Himself enters into the continuity of Old Testament proclamation and continues it. Hence what is proclaimed is not the historical Jesus but Jesus as the Christ of the Scriptures. This does not simply mean that as a basis for the proclamation proof from Scripture has taken the place of the historical facts of the life of Jesus. It is rather the case that the historical facts as such prove nothing but that the meaning ascribed to them in the proclamation is justified solely by the demonstration that they have so taken place κατὰ τὰς γραφάς. So long as we can ask whether this proof from Scripture amounts to nothing more than a mere *vaticinium ex eventu* we have misunderstood the essence of it. We are regarding it as something which is intended to take the place of an historical basis that is lacking, and have not yet understood that and why such a basis is not provided for in the scheme of Gospel proclamation. Hence it would be better not to speak of a proof from Scripture. If we do so, however, then we should bear in mind that the Scripture quotations are not in the strict sense used for the purposes of argument, but are exploited because they form part of traditional Biblical proclamation. This happens, above all, in argument with the Jews, who are thus referred to the tradition of proclamation in which they themselves already stand. Within this framework of proclamation argument then proceeds in so far as the legitimate use of Scripture is denied to the Jews and claimed as the right of the Christian community. This argumentation may be carried on at times with all the resources of Rabbinic dialectics and hermeneutics as used by the opposing side, and in this case long passages of detailed argument may conceal the fact that it is still basically a question of Gospel proclamation. But in such argument the issue cannot be settled *disputando*, it is rather that the disputation always implies the already-declared decision of Christ for the Church and against the synagogue. Its *ultima ratio* is therefore not an argument, but the very fact of the existence of the Christian community, which attests the risen Christ as its Lord. But this fact itself in its true essence can only ever again be proclaimed and believed.

Thus we have shown by a sample case (very variable in its detailed application) how the Old Testament is used in New Testament Gospel proclamation. Thus, for example, in Lk. xxiv. 25 ff., 44 ff., we are told how Jesus opened the mind of His disciples that they might understand the Scriptures (vs. 45), and in ii Cor. iii. 13 ff. we read that He removed Moses's veil from the Old Testament. The revelation promised in the Old Testament and fulfilled in the coming of Jesus are one and the same according to New Testament preaching. The opening of the Epistle to the Hebrews states plainly that the speaking of God in which this identity is grounded takes place within a stream of history which includes differences as regards time and manner of speech. But after the abrogation of this diversity of time and mode through Ἰησοῦς Χριστὸς ἐχθὲς καὶ σήμερον ὁ αὐτός, καὶ εἰς τοὺς αἰῶνας (xiii. 8) every single σήμερον of the Old Testament process of proclamation has become present also in the σήμερον of present preaching (iii. 13 and Ps. xcv. 7-11; Heb. iii. 7-19, iv. 6 ff.). Thus the Gospel message of the New Testament claims for itself the whole of Old Testament Scriptures, and tries to show in its debate with the Synagogue that the proclamation of Scripture as a whole is only rightly to be understood as the promise and expectation of this fulfilment. And, on the other hand, the revelatory events of the New Testament are authorised in their special significance if seen as the fulfilment of the Old Testament promise and expectation. The whole use of the Old Testament in the New moves within this circle.

But, as we have seen, no argument can show the rightness of this circular inference and convince the Synagogue that it *must* read the Old Testament in the way advocated by the Church. It is clear that in fact it does not so read the Old Testament. But *could* it have read it in this way? According to St John's Gospel it would seem to have been possible: "If you believed Moses, you would believe me, for he wrote of me. But if you do not believe his writings (γράμμασιν), how will you believe my words (ῥήμασιν)?" (v. 46-7). But this possibility is frustrated by the fact that even in the Old Testa-

ment period, those γράμματα had already produced hardness
of heart rather than faith, as Jesus says in Jn. XII. 35 ff., with
reference to Is. LIII. 1 and VI. 9 ff. The fact that Isaiah "saw
His (Jesus's) glory and spoke of Him" (Jn. XII. 41) helped them
just as little at that time as it helped the Jews to see Jesus in
the flesh. The same question is in St. Paul's mind in II Cor. III,
where he says (vs. 6), "The written code kills, but the Spirit
gives life," and (vss. 7-8) opposes the διακονία τοῦ πνεύματος to
the διακονία τοῦ θανάτου ἐν γράμμασιν—the latter being practised
by Moses and the former by Christ, who is the Spirit (vs. 17).
Here again it is noted that in the Synagogue the Old Testament is read according to the letter and not according to the
Spirit, and hence provokes impenitence rather than faith,
"for to this day, when they read the old covenant, that same
veil remains unlifted, because only through Christ is it taken
away. Yes, to this day, whenever Moses is read a veil lies
over their minds" (vss. 15 ff.). It is not right in this matter
simply to equate the contrast of letter and Spirit with that of
Law and Gospel, as is often done, with the result that the
relation of the Old Testament and the New is schematised by
the dialectic of Law and Gospel. Even Ehrhard Kamlah [3]
comes to the following conclusion: "In my judgment, the
Apostle's distinction between γράμμα and πνεῦμα is typified
and systematised in the Lutheran antithesis of Law and
Gospel." [4] Nevertheless Kamlah has no doubt rightly understood that with his antithesis γράμμα — πνεῦμα Paul is attacking
Rabbinic Judaism, for which the will of God is so unequivocally
drawn up in the words of the Torah that God Himself is
fettered by it and has no further possibility of speech. But
the real question is whether γράμμα assumes a negative significance only under the stress of this polemic aim, or whether as
the inner principle of the Old Covenant it should in general
be appraised as negatively as "the book of the Law, with its
commands and prohibitions," [5] though, in spite of all, to its
ministry has been ascribed δόξα (II Cor. III. 7 ff.). If we
interpret the "inner principle of the Old Covenant," as
Kamlah does, then we must distribute Law and Gospel
between the Old and New Testaments respectively, and in so

[3] See E. Kamlah, "Buchstabe und Geist," in Ev. Th., 1954, pp. 276 ff.
[4] Kamlah, op. cit., p. 282.   [5] Op. cit., p. 278.

L

doing we shall hardly be able to avoid the danger of tearing them asunder. For this reason we would prefer to read no more out of II Cor. III than the fact that the Jews understood the Old Testament as the written code which kills and so understand it up to the present day. The question whether before Christ they *might* have been able to understand it otherwise, i.e. as the Spirit which gives life, is not asked and would be meaningless, since in the Gospel of Jesus Christ they are in fact confronted with the evangelical understanding of Old Testament Law. The same is true of the question whether before Christ they must have known themselves to be accused by Moses. The urgent point is that now when they are faced by the true understanding of the Law, and in proportion as that happens, "it is Moses who accuses you, on whom you set your hope" (Jn. v. 45; cp. Acts VII. 51 ff.), and that as a result they should allow themselves to be turned from the false understanding of the Old Testament which prevails in the Synagogue to the right understanding of it which is the mark of the Church.

(b) The relation of Jesus to Jewish tradition

In connexion with this we must now see how Jesus, as portrayed in the Synoptics, regards the Old Testament and the tradition of Judaism in general.[6] First we must enquire what kind of understanding of tradition Jesus finds in contemporary Rabbinic opinions. The fundamental basis of the tradition is the Torah, the Book of the Covenant (Ex. XXIV. 7; II Kings XXIII. 1 ff.; Neh. x. 29 f.), which is not limited to the Pentateuch, but which may include the canon as a whole, at least the Law and the Prophets. In addition there is oral tradition which likewise forms part of the Torah, and in conjunction with the written tradition constitutes the full revelation of God. It is assumed that every valid principle of law can be shown to be part of the revelation at Sinai and to have been handed down thence. But "also every principle of doctrine accepted

---

[6] On the following, cp. W. G. Kümmel, "Jesus und der jüdische Traditionsgedanke," in *Zeitschrift für die Neutestamentliche Wissenschaft*, 1933, pp. 105 ff. F. Büchsel's article *s.v.* παραδίδωμι, παράδοσις, in Kittel, VOL. II, pp. 171 ff., unfortunately makes no very significant contribution to the subject.

by tradition is indicated in the Torah." [7] In this matter, however, the Scribes if need be can abrogate old teaching and institute a new principle for "the Scribes have now taken the place of the Prophets; they too stand in the stream of tradition, and are thus authorised to declare what is the will of God for the present." [8] This belief in and acceptance of tradition is what determines at the time of Jesus both Rabbinical practice and Pharisaic piety, though no real dogma of tradition had yet been evolved. If we want to draw a comparison from the history of the Christian Church, the situation here is similar to that governing the relation of Scripture and tradition in the Roman Church in the period before the Council of Trent, and before the promulgation of the dogma of tradition. The Sadducees on the contrary "rejected, like everything new, the revolutionary idea of a progressive development of oral tradition and refused to grant the validity of this extension of the Torah beyond the bounds of the written law." [9] But neither had their traditions any divine justification, and it was therefore impossible for them to derive from the Torah any valid indications for present circumstances. "Hence Judaism with its faith in revelation felt compelled to repudiate the doctrine of the Sadducees and the people never had any love of them. Only the Pharisaic belief in tradition guaranteed the continued vitality of the once-for-all revelation and could disclose the present bearing of the will of God revealed to the Fathers." [10]

Jesus grew up in this faith in the tradition of Sinai, and recognised its validity by His attitude. Thus, like the Scribes, He quotes alongside the Pentateuch other books of Scripture, refers in a general way to the Scriptures, and also quotes oral tradition with approval. How, in spite of all this, He comes into conflict with the Pharisees is shown particularly clearly in Mk. VII. 1-23, where He opposes to the παράδοσις τῶν πρεσβυτέρων (vss. 3-6), τῶν ἀνθρώπων (vs. 8), ὑμῶν (vs. 9), the ἐντολὴ Θεοῦ (vss. 8 ff.) or the λόγος Θεοῦ (vs. 13), and in so doing makes emphatic reference to Scripture. In this respect Jesus by no means rejected the *paradosis* as such, but applied to it a critical norm as follows: where the Law as the content of

<hr>

[7] Kümmel, *op. cit.*, p. 114.   [8] Kümmel, *op. cit.*, p. 117.
[9] Kümmel, *op. cit.*, p. 118.   [10] *Ibid.*

the *paradosis* is no longer understood to be the present concrete requirement of God, demanding the self-surrender of man, but rather serves as a form of human righteousness which can be manipulated by man himself in the interests of his own self-justification, then the law in question is to be rejected. A further example of this is the Sabbath conflict in Mk. II. 23-8, III. 1-5, where we read: "The Sabbath was made for man and not man for the Sabbath" (II. 27). Is the purpose of the Law to convey to man that divine command by the fulfilment of which he can count on God's sanction of his life? In that case it will be inevitable that man should analyse the Law and reduce it to convenient detailed indications in order that by the utmost degree of compliance he may secure the divine approval and favour as much as possible. Or is the Law given for the sake of man to make available to him life in harmony with God and in accordance with God's plan in creation? Then from God's Law, man will, in the first instance, have to derive help in the living of a good life, and not the command to prove his rectitude of life by his conduct in detailed acts.

The same problem recurs when instead of the merely formal *paradosis* we turn our attention to its content, the διδασκαλία.[11] The idea of διδασκαλία in the New Testament cannot be explained on the basis of secular linguistic usage, where διδάσκειν is equivalent to δεικνύναι, for in this case the teacher addresses himself to the intellect and will. His teaching is truth considered as the correct understanding of the matter and requiring to be reflected in conduct. His teaching consists in argument with the object of persuasion. The sole authority—if, in this connexion, the word can be used at all —is the evidence of the truth itself compelling recognition. All these characteristics are lacking in the teaching of Jesus. From the point of view of history and tradition he cannot be classed with Greek or Hellenistic philosophy, but only with that of Rabbinical teaching: the rabbi as teacher has the task of interpreting the Law as the summary of the revealed will of God. For him "teaching" means the handing on of the Law itself and its explication in concrete directions for the details of life, hence its casuistical application and the giving of

[11] On the following, cp. K. H. Rengstorf's article *s.v.* διδάσκω, etc., in Kittel, VOL. II, pp. 138 ff.

authoritative decisions necessary for this task. In all this there can be no question of "teaching" in the sense which attaches to the word in secular use. If the term διδασκαλία is used—as happens occasionally already in the LXX—then it is a matter of concession to this linguistic usage, when the essence of the thing would be better expressed by the term νόμος. Jesus forms part of this teaching tradition of the Rabbis in which διδάσκειν and διδασκαλία are used absolutely, since there is no question of any other kind of teaching except the exposition of the Law, and he belongs to it in regard to the manner (Synagogic), the form (Rabbinic) and the material (exposition of the Law) of his teaching.

But at the same time He breaks with this tradition at the decisive point: He opposes the tendency to establish the Law as an absolute by putting forward the point of view that the Law exists for the sake of man and not man for the sake of the Law. By this means He refers us back from the Law to the Lawgiver, and thus changes as radically as possible the meaning of the Law itself by restoring its original connexion with the divine Covenant. The Rabbis have forgotten the consolation and the promise of the Law and no longer envisage the Scriptures as a whole, as the Book of the Covenant, the document which bears witness to the Covenant grace of God. They know Scripture only in the sense of the Law requiring absolutely to be fulfilled. To this end it must be analysed into single detailed commands that can be discussed and manipulated, and the function of teaching reduces itself ever more and more to such analysis. The eschatological proclamation of the Prophets concerning the salvation that is to come has no more place in this Rabbinic teaching—and even in the LXX the idea is never used in this sense—or in any event such proclamation in so far as it lives on in a depraved form in the apocalyptic of Judaism has no vital connexion with teaching. The two aspects once more come together in the work of the Synoptic Jesus, because in Him the promise of the Law is fulfilled. His teaching goes hand in hand with His Gospel and His proclamation of the dawning Kingdom of God. If he uses διδάσκειν and διδάσκαλος in an absolute sense just as much as the Rabbis then it is because He is the διδάσκαλος (Mt. xxviii. 16) in whom even Moses sees himself fulfilled.

Thus we see His connexion with the Rabbinic tradition of teaching and at the same time the source of His conflict with it. He does not violate the authority of the Scribes and Pharisees who sit in the seat of Moses (Mt. XXIII. 2 f.), just as no iota of the Law will be allowed to perish until all things be accomplished (Mt. v. 18). There is absolutely no reason to dispute, with Kümmel, the genuineness of these two texts and to consider them as a secondary Jewish-Christian development.[12] In that case Kümmel must doubt also the genuineness of Mt. XXIII. 23: "These you ought to have done, without neglecting the others," [13] whereas we ourselves think we see in this word the very key to the solution of the apparent contradiction in the attitude of Jesus towards the tradition of teaching. Jesus reproaches His adversaries with the fact that they correctly fulfil the law of tithe to the point of caricature, whereas they neglect judgment and mercy and faith (Mt. XXIII. 23). No objection can be raised to the carefulness of their proceeding. It cannot be a question of watering down to suit the needs of average humanity that requirement in which the Law as the holy will of God confronts them, or of leaving it to the free estimation of the individual according to his own spontaneous insights, as, for instance, Bultmann suggests in his comment on Mk. x. 2-9: "Hence it is clear that man is not bound by formal authority, but if he is able to make such discriminations in regard to Scripture, then obviously he is himself credited with the insight to become aware of what God really requires." [14] Or, more plainly still: "Radical obedience is only possible where man understands the command and spontaneously assents to it. And only of such obedience is it meaningful to say that in the fulfilment of the Moral Law he is fulfilling the command of God; for God requires radical obedience." [15] Jesus, however, by no means sees the mistake of Rabbinism in the fact that obedience " is understood as a purely formal thing . . . an obedience to the Law simply because it is commanded." On the contrary, just in regard to this "formal authority" of the Law, He is at one with the Rabbis, and hence the attempts to extend this authority

---

[12] Kümmel (above, p. 154, n. 6), pp. 127 f.
[13] Kümmel, *op. cit.*, p. 128, n. 85.   [14] Bultmann, *Jesus*, p. 71.
[15] Bultmann, *Theol. des N.T.*, p. 11.

of the Law to all, even the remotest regions of practical conduct,
are countenanced by Jesus. Adolf Schlatter agrees also [16]:
"In Mt. xxiii. 23 it is expressly said that the first point is not
a cause of reproach; here too the ground of reproach lies
only in the contradiction implied in the conjunction of the two
things." [17] The casuistical analysis and application of the
Law serves the cause of their perfectionism by facilitating self-
justification. As by this means they themselves seek to escape
the judgment of God, and to do without His mercy, so they
can only be unmerciful judges towards others, and "can offer
no solution to the problem of guilt." [18] The πίστις which they
lack is no doubt not only loyalty to our neighbour, who needs
our kindness, but also trust in God. But Pharisaism "has no
understanding of man's attitude of trust in God and dependence on His grace." [19] This means again that the Pharisee
tears asunder the Law and the Covenant of God, and conceals
from himself the fact by unloading the burden of the Law on
to others rather than bearing it himself to his own eventual
ruin (Mt. xxiii. 4)—for it is indeed a law whose precepts grow
with irresistible momentum and necessity because there is no
situation which does not involve the obligation of doing the
will of God and no action which can be deemed right except by
its strict accordance with the divine law. In contrast it
becomes clear to the disciples of Jesus that "He bound the
great burden not on to the backs of others but bore it Himself,
and that this was a fundamentally different attitude from that
of the Pharisees." [20]

With regard to the antitheses of the Sermon on the Mount
(Mt. v. 21 ff., 27 ff., 33 ff.), in which Jesus turns specifically
against the tradition of the fathers, Kümmel says: "This
insight of Jesus implies essentially a far more radical view of
the will of God, a return to the divine will in all its depth and
endless scope." [21] The idea of a radical view, which Bultmann
also uses,[22] would only be appropriate in this connexion if it

[16] See A. Schlatter, *Der Evangelist Matthäus*, 1929.
[17] Schlatter, *op. cit.*, p. 678. [18] Schlatter, *op. cit.*, p. 667.
[19] Schlatter, *op. cit.*, p. 680.
[20] Schlatter, *op. cit.*, p. 668; cp. Ernst Haenchen, "Matthäus 23," in
Z. Th. K., 1951, pp. 38 ff.
[21] Kümmel, *op. cit.* (above, p. 154, n. 6), p. 126.
[22] In *Theol. des N.T.*

denoted a return to the real root, if, therefore, it was meant to suggest that Jesus wished to turn Jewish legalistic piety away from faith in the abstract Law and back towards faith in the Lawgiver, who gave the Law as a confirmation of His gift of the covenantal bond.   But Kümmel intends to say exactly the opposite, namely that Jesus dared "to cut off Jewish belief in the Law at its root . . .[23]   This 'I say unto you' at one stroke sweeps aside the whole theory of tradition so characteristic of Judaism." [24]   Hence Kümmel is compelled to consider such texts as Mt. v. 18, xviii. 23, as spurious and to interpret the πληροῦν which stands in opposition to the ἀναλύειν in v. 17 as meaning that He "fulfils the Law through teaching . . . [25] He did not wish to abolish the Torah, but to explain it *rightly* according to the will of God and in utter disregard of the letter of human traditions, thus giving it its true meaning." [26] For "in Scripture, as in tradition, the will of God is to be found only in human form; hence the question is to extract the will of God from this husk." [27]   And this He could do, since "He knew the will of God apart from the Law," [28] and behind His whole attitude to the Law "we see at work His consciousness of being sent by God, of being appointed God's Messiah in the Kingdom." [29]

We cannot agree with all this.   Kümmel replaces the Pauline dialectic of letter and *Spirit* in ii Cor. iii by a quite different dialectic of letter and *meaning*, as a result of which he loses sight of what is for Jesus the decisive point, the re-orientation of the Law by referring it back to the God of the Covenant as Lawgiver.   His "Messiah" is not, as with Paul, "born under the law, to redeem those who were under the law" (Gal. iv. 4 ff.), but as a heavenly being He promulgates with immediate knowledge the will of God, and at the same time destroys the force of the whole history of the Covenant while unfolding its true "meaning."   This is no longer the Jesus of the New Testament, but rather the Jesus of Lessing's *Erziehung des Menschengeschlechts* who concerns himself with the history of the Old Testament Covenant only to cancel it and dissolve it into a mere example for the instruction of mankind as a

[23] Kümmel, *op. cit.*, pp. 126, 130.   [24] Kümmel, *op. cit.*, p. 126.
[25] Kümmel, *op. cit.*, p. 129.   [26] *Ibid.*   [27] Kümmel, *op. cit.*, p. 127.
[28] Kümmel, *op. cit.*, p. 129.   [29] Kümmel, *op. cit.*, pp. 126 f.

whole. This is something very different from what is implied in the Pauline statement, ὅτε δὲ ἦλθεν τὸ πλήρωμα τοῦ χρόνου (Gal. IV. 4) in which the πληροῦν of that which God has promised and commanded is realised. Instead of this, God has inaugurated for humanity through Jesus a new stage of maturity, which is no longer bound up with the history of Israel or of the New Testament Church, but which is attainable by whomsoever "assents in faith to this claim of Jesus" and "thus in faith trust himself to the guidance of Jesus." [30]

According to Ernst Käsemann,[31] again, the whole situation is to be pictured differently. Far more strongly than Kümmel did, he sets Jesus in sharp contrast to the Jewish tradition. For him the peculiarity of the message of Jesus is connected precisely with the fact that Jesus openly breaks with the authority of Moses and the Torah and by this attitude proves Himself to be the Messiah even though He has not yet claimed to be so Himself. For our question about Jesus as the Christ of the Old Testament this is not of decisive importance in that we see the continuity of the history of proclamation in the Old and the New Testaments grounded primarily in the contingent fact of the New Testament Church, which believes the promises to Israel to have been fulfilled in itself, and hence claims for itself the Old Testament predicates describing the dignity and unique significance of Israel. In any case, in this matter we must see the historical Jesus in the light in which the primitive Christian Church saw Him and believed on Him. This Church was created and is maintained by proclaiming the Gospel in which Jesus proclaimed and revealed Himself and it is at one and the same time the sphere, the bearer, and the object of this proclamation. The material identity underlying the continuity between the Old and the New Testaments lies in the speech of God which is self-identical in both dispensations despite all differences of time and mode. This speech of God confronts us in the Old Testament Scriptures. Jesus is preached as the Christ of the Old Testament. Hence the primary and basic critical norm of the Gospel preached is that the pattern of events which form its theme must be κατὰ τὰς γραφάς.

[30] Kümmel, op. cit., p. 130.
[31] See E. Käsemann, Das Problem des historischen Jesus (above, p. 135, n. 59).

But this norm is not a criterion within our control, and it is not the case that simply with the help of Old Testament quotations as "*dicta probantia*" it can be shown on a Biblical basis what must be regarded as right and wrong preaching of doctrine. We agree that the appeal to the Old Testament not seldom is exercised by verbal quotations, even if the non-literal allusions to Old Testament passages are far more numerous.[32] But even literal quotations can at times be used by different authors to demonstrate opposing doctrines even on points of quite central importance (e.g. Gen. xv. 6, in Rom. iv. 3, and Jas. ii. 23). The needed agreement and consistency with the preaching of the Old Testament cannot simply be reached by literalistic references to the Old Testament itself, because this agreement exists only with the Old Testament as interpreted by Jesus. The endeavour to find this concordance thus becomes the task of theology in the quite specific sense that the subject of enquiry is how far the preaching of Jesus Christ is in accordance with the preaching of Jesus as the Christ of the Old Testament. Theology disposes of no definite principles as norms for the fulfilment of this task, but it places itself within the process of the historical development flowing from the Christ whose Gospel proclaims and authenticates Himself, and in which the person of Jesus Himself is basic as the critical norm. But in this process the word of Jesus cannot be controlled. Rather it strikes the preacher and teacher in the tradition of proclamation in order itself to normalise the latter. The New Testament theologian who within this circle is seeking the true message and proclamation has at his disposal the Scriptures together with the rest of Judaic *paradosis*, as well as the critical interpretation of them by Jesus Himself, as that interpretation is mirrored in the *paradosis* of the Church. He cannot amplify and explain this *paradosis* in detail simply by measuring it against the Old Testament in any literalistic way, but, on the contrary, must elaborate the critical interpretation of the Old Testament by Jesus Himself, in order to discover by this means the desired concordance. There is no one factor in the whole development which would guarantee this consistency of Christian

[32] On this cp. the index to *Novum Testamentum Graece*, ed. Nestle, 1952, pp. 658 ff.

preaching with the true meaning of the Old Testament. The sole guarantee is the Lord Himself who is the Spirit (II Cor. III. 17), who both can and will make evident to the hearer the word of preaching, and who by this means alone verifies and authorises it. In the last resort the endeavour of the theologian to find true Christian preaching lives by the power of this promise alone.

Within this theological discipline are contained as the two most essential phases: preaching and teaching. But since both preaching and teaching always take place within a definite tradition in which what has been received is handed on, there is added as the third phase the transmission of traditions. We now turn to enquire about the relation of preaching and teaching, still within the framework of the New Testament.

CHAPTER VI

PREACHING AND DOCTRINE

THE ideas κηρύσσειν and διδάσκειν are widely used in the New Testament not only alongside of each other but also almost synonymously. In any event, it is hardly possible to distinguish preaching and teaching as two distinct activities and to keep them separate.

With regard to this, Bultmann, as we have seen, attempts to distinguish *kerygma* and doctrine: "*Kerygma* or summons is hence a doctrine in so far as it implies a certain new understanding." [1] The task of doctrine is, then, "to clarify the concepts of the believing mind." In theology "*kerygma* is present as debated doctrine." [2] It "must repeatedly be disentangled from the state of theological elaboration in which it always faces us, to such an extent, indeed, that in practice it is never possible to distinguish clearly between *kerygma* and doctrine. It must be disentangled so that it may be understood as furnishing the possibility of man's self-understanding and so mediating a call to decision." [3] This limitation of the idea of *kerygma* to the Scriptural word which summons us is not, however, as we have seen, true to the New Testament. [4] The same criticism might be urged in regard to Bultmann's idea of doctrine. According to Bultmann the business of the theological formulation of doctrine may only from time to time be taken in hand when justified by a definite polemical occasion, whereas in the New Testament it is a function that is constantly practised in conjunction with preaching. Hence we cannot assent to the distinction between *kerygma* and doctrine as drawn by Bultmann.

(a) Doctrine as an aspect of preaching

The real reason for the impossibility of distinguishing the two ideas lies, as we have seen, in the specific meaning attaching to

---

[1] Bultmann, *Glaube und Verstehen*, VOL. I, p. 180.

[2] Bultmann, *op. cit.*, p. 186.

[3] Bultmann, *Theol. des N.T.*, p. 581.　　　[4] See above, p. 131.

διδάσκειν in the New Testament, which cannot be explained by secular linguistic use, which equates διδάσκειν and δεικνύναι, the latter connoting the attempt to convince intellect and will of the evidence of a truth which compels recognition by its inherent authority. All such associations are in any case lacking to the διδάσκειν of the Synoptic Jesus. The latter continues rather the traditional method of teaching characteristic of the Rabbis, which consists in the handing-on and explication of the Law, which was revealed at the same time as the establishment of the covenant. But Jesus corrects the corruption of doctrinal teaching for which the Rabbis are responsible, inasmuch as they treated the Law as an absolute, in isolation from the action of the Covenant God, and He once more restores doctrine to its place within the pattern of the gracious action of God proclaimed in preaching. From this point of view it will *not* be possible to enquire how teaching is to be distinguished from preaching, but the question must rather be what is the special function of teaching within the process of preaching from which it cannot be separated. In this connexion we must first enquire how the use of διδάσκειν develops in the rest of the New Testament, and how far this development remains consistent with what we have found in the Synoptics.

In what follows, the idea of κηρύσσειν must constantly be taken into account.[5] Jesus, outside the Gospels, is no longer referred to as διδάσκαλος. This is no doubt connected with the fact that now the Synoptic order of κηρύσσειν and διδάσκειν is reversed: at the heart of the Gospel stands the witness to the Cross and Resurrection, and for the primitive community the teaching of Jesus has as its presupposition the fulfilment through the Cross of the promises given in the Law and the Prophets. Thus in Acts there results on the one hand the continuation by the disciples of the teaching of Jesus Himself, in accordance with the command of the latter, hence teaching in the name of Jesus. In this regard we find διδάσκειν alongside καταγγέλλειν and εὐαγγελίζεσθαι, and its essential content is the call to penitence and the offer of forgiveness (Acts IV. 18, V. 28-31, XV. 35, XX. 21). On the other hand they teach τὰ περὶ τοῦ Ἰησοῦ (XVIII. 25, XXVIII. 31), which includes

[5] See above, pp. 112 ff.

the whole narrative material relating to Jesus as the centre of Gospel proclamation (II. 23, III. 26, IV. 2, V. 42). Here the bridge between the teaching of Jesus which the disciples continue and the teaching about Jesus lies in the use of Scripture for argument and demonstration. Thus κηρύσσειν and διδάσκειν belong together, as we see from the following phrase referring to Paul in Rome: κηρύσσων τὴν βασιλείαν τοῦ Θεοῦ καὶ διδάσκων τὰ περὶ τοῦ Ἰησοῦ Χριστοῦ (XXVIII. 31). Here again it is not a question of Scriptural proof in the strict sense of a verification of the facts which mediate our salvation. Rather the purpose which in teaching is served by this Scriptural exposition and interpretation is to face the hearer with the necessity of deciding either to accept the proclamation about Jesus or to become involved in the contradiction of Scripture. Hence it is an indirect proof of the rightness of the preaching about Jesus that opponents must see in it a blasphemy against the Law (VI. 13, XXI. 18).

In Paul's Epistles, and then further in the Pastoral Epistles, the meaning of διδάσκειν and διδάσκαλος is determined by the fact that here a new *paradosis* is springing up. Teaching from now on has the twofold task of proving the agreement of this new tradition with Scripture, and then of handing on the tradition, whence teaching comes to coincide almost with παραδοῦναι. In Paul's life διδάσκειν is firstly the instruction which he himself gives in his missionary activity (cp. II Thess. II. 15, where it is the call to hold fast to τὰς παραδόσεις ἃς ἐδιδάχθητε εἴτε διὰ λόγου εἴτε δι᾿ ἐπιστολῆς ἡμῶν, similarly Col. II. 7 and Eph. IV. 20); and, secondly, it is a permanent function of Christianity exercised within the life of the Church (Rom. XII. 7, Col. I. 28, III. 16), and similar references are to be found in the Pastoral Epistles (I Tim. IV. 11, VI. 2; II Tim. II. 2; Tit. I. 11). According to this scheme the διδάσκαλος receives a special function within the Church alongside the offices of Apostles, Prophets, Evangelists and "shepherds" (I Cor. XII. 18 f.; Eph. IV. 11, Acts XIII. 1), the order in which the ministries are enumerated having no significance. On the other hand, in the Pastoral Epistles the idea of instruction shows a further development in that the διδάσκαλος in virtue of his call specially guarantees (I Tim. II. 7; II Tim. I. 11) the καλή and ὑγιαίνουσα διδασκαλία (I Tim. I. 10, IV. 6, VI. 3; II Tim. II. 1, 10, IV. 3;

Tit. I. 9), in contrast to the ἑτεροδιδασκαλεῖν (I Tim. I. 3, VI. 3).

(b) The formation of doctrine

Here we are faced by the important question as to how a doctrine arises. Both διδασκαλία and διδαχή denote in an active sense the giving of instruction (Rom. XII. 7, XV. 4; I Cor. XIV. 6, 26; frequently in the Pastoral Epistles; Acts II. 42, V. 28, XVII. 19; II Jn. 9 f.), but are used also with reference to the objective content of instruction (Rom. VI. 7, XVI. 17, Eph. IV. 14; likewise in Pastoral Epistles; Acts XIII. 12, Heb. VI. 2, XIII. 9) and it is often difficult to decide which of the two is the real meaning (especially in the Pastoral Epistles, but also, for example, Rom. XII. 7), since they merge into each other. But the fact that such a transition is possible is in quite a special way characteristic of teaching. The basis of it is the Scripture as the witness to the saving action of God and the newly developed *paradosis* about the action of God in Jesus Christ. On this basis the teacher does *not* make statements about truths (general or revealed) but about contingent happenings. It should be noted that by their essential nature such happenings require to be reported and handed on in a special way, by which alone one can be rightly instructed in them. This instruction is neither a mere historical report nor teaching about wisdom in the Greek sense, but witnessing to an event which for its transmission requires an authorised and competent witness. "This excludes formally and materially the Greek idea of teaching . . . since the self-consciousness of the teacher is here subsumed in the New Testament consciousness of mission." [6] Since the happening which forms the object of doctrine and teaching can only be handed on by proclamation and witness teaching cannot be separated from proclamation. This is not only true of such texts as II Tim. I. 11, where the author of the epistle describes himself as both κῆρυξ καὶ ἀπόστολος καὶ διδάσκαλος, since at this stage of the development the teacher takes the place of the now defunct Apostle, but also in those passages where teaching is mentioned as a specific function along with other functions (Rom. XII. 7; I Cor. XII. 28 f.; Eph. IV. 18). In such passages we may well

[6] Kittel, VOL. II, p. 167.

think of a certain division of labour between the teacher, on the one hand, and, on the other, the Apostles and Evangelists called to the special ministry of proclamation, but within the New Testament period there can be no rigid line of demarcation between the two functions. The ministry of διδάσκειν cannot in any case be detached from that of κηρύσσειν (and this latter understood in its real sense as an event lying within the process of saving history), and in fact it tends to merge into it. This is the material reason also why the two meanings of "teaching"—"to instruct" and "the content of teaching as doctrine," cannot be kept separate.

All this must be borne in mind for the right understanding of those passages in which διδασκαλία and διδαχή denote objective doctrinal content. Among these belong too those texts where the idea πίστις in the sense of "credo" or *fides quae creditur* is used as a summary of the content of belief (which is obvious in Rom. x. 8, xii. 7; Col. ii. 7; Tit. i. 11; ii Pet. i. 1-5). In addition, there belong also to this category the fixed formulae of the faith, which in the New Testament are either cited literally as part of the tradition (e.g. i Cor. xi. 23 ff., xv. 3), or are readily recognisable by us as such.

(c) Adolf von Harnack's explanation of the process of doctrinal formation

Again and again critics have attempted to see and evaluate this development as a "process of petrifaction." Thus Karl Heinrich Rengstorf says: "The linguistic usage of the primitive Church reflects the result of the transformation undergone by the term διδάσκαλος up to the time when it was taken into the storehouse of ecclesiastical words; διδασκαλία now denotes the summary of Church doctrine, of what the Apostles by their teaching handed on to posterity. . . . what is here visible as linguistic development is nothing less than the transformation of the Apostolic message into a tradition of doctrine and so the early stages of the hardening of the original Christian *kerygma* until it becomes early Church dogma." [7] Rengstorff sees the corresponding change in the idea of the διδάσκαλος effected especially in the Church province of Egypt. "Here Alexandrian wisdom penetrates into the

[7] Kittel, vol. ii, p. 165.

Church, and the Church takes over at the same time διδάσκαλος as a description of the one who represents and expounds such wisdom exactly as we find to be the case in Philo. The activity of the early Church schools in Alexandria is not a continuation of the function of the primitive Christian teachers, but the adoption by the Church of a Greek institution in a Christianised form. In accordance with this, the task of the early Christian apologists and teachers was 'to expound and demonstrate Christianity by means of ordered and methodical instruction.' [8] Quite consistently, therefore, the intellectualisation of the Christian faith among these teachers has as its consequence the reappearance of a phenomenon against which Jesus and Paul and the first Christian teachers struggled with all their might for the sake of God and His absolute and immediate sovereignty." [9] It is notorious that the meaning of "teacher" and "instruction" underwent a change from the period of primitive Christianity to that of the Alexandrian catechetical schools as a result of which it became increasingly assimilated to the Hellenistic idea of teaching. The question can only be whether, as Rengstorf thinks, the rise of formulated doctrinal ideas and of a tradition of instruction in the faith marks the beginning of this deviation. In this respect he is typical of the exponents of that scheme of thought which has gained the ascendancy through the influence of Harnack and Lietzmann,[10] and according to which the transition from New Testament proclamation to early Church crystallisation of doctrine is a process of petrifaction and intellectualisation affecting the original *kerygma* and faith, so that the whole history of dogmatic development may be viewed as a progressive decline from New Testament Christianity. This scheme of thought has caused not a little embarrassment to Evangelical theology. It compels the historian of dogma to exclude the New Testament from the history of the formation of dogma. The path of New Testament critics is blocked by the gap which it tears and they can render no help to the historian of dogma. And it means that the latter has not only lost from under his feet the ground of the New Testament,

[8]   Harnack, *Mission*, 373 A 3.
[9]   Rengstorf, in Kittel, VOL. II, pp. 161 f.
[10] Cp. Diem, *Theol.*, VOL. I, p. 128.

M

but has also lost the roots of the history of dogma which in this way is prejudged.

Wilhelm Schneemelcher,[11] shows how this point of view took its rise with Harnack. Harnack's point of departure is "that at the beginning of dogmatic history is to be found not dogma itself, but the Gospel."[12] The question is, however, what is to be understood by "gospel." He points out that "in the Church the word 'gospel' is used in a twofold sense. For it means not only Jesus's own warm message" but also "the proclamation of the Christ who was crucified and rose again for our sins and has brought the forgiveness of sins and eternal life. These two meanings are quite distinct and yet in their conjunction and association lies the peculiarity which determines the inner tensions and the richness of the Christian religion." [13] But this determines also the embarrassment of the historian of dogma, who has to bring together these two distinct meanings of the word "gospel" and to show how and at what point in this process dogma arose. It would seem obvious to suppose that the process of the development of dogma began with the transformation of Jesus' Gospel into the Gospel about Jesus Christ. But Harnack thinks that the Gospel in its twofold sense includes this transformation. Only after this period does dogma develop in opposition to the Gospel in both senses. Hence the Gospel forms the presupposition underlying the development of dogma, but the latter begins a process which is essentially something new and contradictory to the essence of the Gospel. For Harnack defines dogmas as follows: "I. Principles of doctrine which are formulated in conceptual terms, form a unity, and present the content of the Christian religion as an exposition of truth and as a system of the knowledge of God, the world, and the history of salvation [centring in Christ]. II. They appeared at a specific stage in the history of the Christian religion; both in their conception as such and in many details they show the influence of this stage, which is in fact the period of the

[11] W. Schneemelcher, *Das Problem der Dogmengeschichte*, *Z. Th. K.*, 1951, pp. 63 ff.

[12] Schneemelcher, *op. cit.*, p. 65.

[13] Harnack, *Dogmengeschichte*, 4th edn., 1909, cited below as *Dogmengeschichte*, VOL. I, pp. 65 f., quoted in Schneemelcher, *op. cit.*, p. 67.

ascendancy of Greek thought, and they have retained this character in succeeding epochs despite all the mutations and additions they have received." [14] An essential characteristic of all this is that Harnack sees theology at work for the first time in the construction of the edifice of dogma and not in the Apostolic explanation of the Gospel of Jesus: "Dogmas arise, develop, and are used for the service of new ends; in every case this happens through the activity of theology." [15] The relation between dogma and theology is then defined in the following way: "The product of theology assuming the form of dogma then limits and criticises the work of the theologian, both past and future," [16] which of course has as its consequence that dogma and theology are condemned "never to be clear what they owe to each other and what they have to fear from each other." [17] It would hardly be possible to caricature better than Harnack has done in this sentence the embarrassment which dogma and theology so understood inevitably prepare for each other. No doubt Harnack thought that he could afford to adopt this attitude of resignation in regard to dogma and theology because he saw the acute Hellenisation of Christianity resulting from the early Church formation of dogma counteracted by the Lutheran Reformation: "This whole presentation of Christianity which he [Luther] outlined with such a sure hand stands out in relief not only against this or that particular dogma but against dogmatic Christianity as a whole; Christianity is something other than the sum of traditional doctrines. Christianity is not Biblical theology nor the teachings of the Councils, but the disposition of mind and heart awakened by the Father of Jesus Christ through the proclamation of the Gospel. In face of this all the authorities of which dogma constitutes the basis are torn down—how in the presence of this spirit could dogma consider itself a body of infallible teaching, but what is dogma if it is not infallible?" [18]

Harnack's thesis that the morbid phenomenon of dogmatic Christianity was eliminated by the Reformation did not find

[14] *Dogmengeschichte*, VOL. I, p. 17.
[15] *Dogmengeschichte*, VOL. I., p. 12.
[16] *Ibid.*   [17] *Ibid.*
[18] *Dogmengeschichte*, VOL. III, pp. 896 ff.

acceptance in the Evangelical Church; and in theology, also, a movement arose in Harnack's own lifetime which gave a fresh positive valuation to the dogmatic side of Christianity.[19]

In spite of this Harnack has not only as a consequence of his challenge held the discipline of historical theology under his ban so far, he seems also to have been justified by the event in his classical formulation of the relation between dogma and theology. But it will never be possible to destroy his ban as long as we see in the rise of a tradition of doctrine as such the beginning of the baneful deviation.

(d) The question of the normalisation and authorisation of doctrine

The first point we must establish in criticising this thesis of the petrifaction and intellectualisation of the Gospel message, is that the idea of such increasing rigidity is not a theological category, and hence cannot properly be used to assess the phenomenon of a growth of formulated doctrinal material. Moreover, it is not at all clear why the rise of such firmly formulated statements as such should in any way demand a negative evaluation. The development of them certainly cannot, as Rengstorf says, be regarded as a transformation of the Apostolic message into a tradition of doctrine, for the simple reason that the Apostles themselves enter into such a tradition, which lies behind their preaching of the Gospel, and which they further elaborate by means of such preaching. The idea of tradition stands in indissoluble connexion with the New Testament idea of teaching, as long as this teaching itself is a development within the framework of Gospel proclamation. If we wish to discover at what critical point doctrine and instruction in the New Testament sense threaten to merge into the Greek idea of teaching, then in any event we shall *not* find it in the handing on of firmly formulated statements of doctrine, but only at that stage where such doctrinal instruction becomes severed from the event of preaching, with the result that the teacher has nothing more to do with the evangelists and witnesses of the New Testament but becomes a teacher of

[19] Cp. the correspondence between Adolf Harnack and Erik Peterson, 1932, repr. in E. Peterson, *Theologische Traktate*, 1951; and also the debate between Karl Barth and Adolf Harnack in *Christliche Welt*, 1923.

wisdom in the Greek sense. There cannot, for example, be any doubt that this critical point has been passed by the apologists. On the other hand, the question whether this juncture also already occurs within the New Testament is not so easy to answer. The observation, so fashionable today, that early Catholicism is already to be found within the New Testament means nothing so long as it is not made clear and precise what is to be understood by this deterioration into early Catholicism.

If we wish to describe this critical stage as the line of demarcation separating the Gospel from early Catholicism, then in any case we shall feel it to be illegitimate to regard the overstepping of this line as a lapse that has taken place once for all. In this respect we must not think in periods: primitive Christianity —post-Apostolic period—early Catholicism. The essential question is rather in what the substance of this lapse consists. Once we are clear about that, then we shall have a definite criterion which can be applied to all periods. We might consider, for instance, that the overstepping of the critical limit has occurred where the attempt is made to verify doctrine in a way which clashes with the whole spirit of Apostolic proclamation. The change from the New Testament to the Greek idea of teaching must especially have operated to overstep this limit. In order to be able to establish the character of this change we must first become clear as to how doctrine and the tradition of instruction are normalised and authorised within the New Testament itself. As we have seen, this is effected primarily by the fact that the Church enters into the tradition of teaching and proclamation in the Old Testament and affirms that it continues this tradition. Now if this claim is made the decisive argument in the presentation of doctrine, the appeal is not to any kind of general truth which can be demonstrated, but to a specific contingent happening, namely the revelation of God attested in the Old Testament Scriptures. This can only, however, be done if it is presupposed that the Scriptural witness stands in an adequate relation to the event which it attests. In their use of the Old Testament the New Testament authors do in fact assume this to be the case; and in certain texts the assumption is even expressly defined as the fact of the *inspiration* of the Old Testament.

(e) The inspiration of Scripture

We wish to emphasise that we are here concerned only with the fact of the inspiration of the canon as a given datum. In Judaism at that time there did not yet exist any explicit dogmatic definition of the canon of Scripture nor any corresponding doctrine of Scripture. This arose only subsequently about A.D. 100 at the Synod of Jamnia. Hence all that the New Testament itself says about the inspiration of Scripture must be kept distinct from later doctrines of inspiration. This will have to be regarded as true also of II Peter, even though the latter is estimated as a late document, because late Jewish influence on what it says about inspiration is hardly probable. In II Tim. III. 13 ff., we find mentioned the ἱερὰ γράμματα as a γραφὴ θεόπνευστος and in II Pet. I. 20 ff., it is said that no προφητεία γραφῆς "is a matter of one's own interpretation, because no prophecy ever came by the impulse of man, but men moved by the Holy Spirit spoke from God." Now, of course, both these texts belong to the latest writings of the New Testament; and since Ernst Käsemann described II Peter as "a document of early Catholic type and probably the most questionable of all the books of the canon," [20] one is no longer so ready to appeal to it as an authority. But this would be of importance for our question about the meaning of Scripture for the system of New Testament teaching, only if these two texts stated something contrary to the manner in which the earlier New Testament authors in fact use the Scriptures. This, however, would not seem to us to be the case even if we had not the Pauline parallels in II Cor. III. 4-18, where Paul gives an explicit account of this use of Scripture.[21]

Käsemann comments on II Pet. I. 20 ff. as follows: "In a quite classical formulation of the strictest doctrine of inspiration, vs. 21 declares the whole of the Old Testament to be inspired. The men of God spoke under the dictation of the Holy Spirit." [22] Now, of course, it is possible to build a doctrine of inspiration on II Pet. I. 20, and this has in fact been done. But we must not suppose from the outset that the

---

[20] See E. Käsemann, "Apologie" (above, p. 137, n. 69).

[21] Cp. Barth, K. D., VOL. I. 2, pp. 559 ff.

[22] Käsemann, "Apologie," p. 289.

author's purpose was to formulate such a specific doctrine, even at this early stage, in its strictest form, together with the idea of the dictation of the Holy Spirit. The text contains nothing of all this, and the author probably had no surmise of it. His purpose is to show his readers that the promise by which they "become partakers of the divine nature" (1. 4) rests on the knowledge of the Lord Jesus Christ (vs. 8). He wishes to remind them (vs. 12) of the truth which is already with them and in which they have been instructed and confirmed. Thus he is talking about something which is past, present, and future; about the δύναμις and παρουσία of our Lord Jesus Christ (vs. 16), whose proclaimers, among whom the author reckons himself as "servant and Apostle of Jesus Christ" (vs. 1), narrated to them no cunningly devised fables, but as eyewitnesses have reported the μεγαλειότης conferred on Him at His baptism and transfiguration. Together with this witnessing function of the Apostle which obviously is not sufficient in itself, the author ranks, "introducing it with a very remarkable comparative, βεβαιότερον the word of prophecy, which he calls a light shining in a dark place until the day dawns and the daystar arise in your heart. That we have (ἔχομεν) this word and that we shall henceforth do well to take heed of it (προσέχοντες) is the substance of his exhortation." [23] This προφητικὸς λόγος is now described as προφητεία γραφῆς (vs. 21) with emphatic repudiation of "false prophets" and "false teachers" who "promise them freedom but they themselves are slaves of corruption" (II. 19). Käsemann says correctly that "this is an attack on the enthusiasm of the gnostics, who refer their πλαστοὶ λόγοι (II. 3) and σεσοφισμένοι μῦθοι (I. 16) to the authority of the Holy Ghost." [24] Hence the προφητεία γραφῆς is opposed to the enthusiasm of the "lying prophets," and capricious individualistic appeal to the Holy Spirit is repudiated on the ground that genuine prophecy, such as we find in Scripture, never happens ἰδίας ἐπιλύσεως but through the fact that men speak "from God (ἀπὸ Θεοῦ)" moved by the Holy Ghost (ὑπὸ Πνεύματος Ἁγίου φερόμενοι). Käsemann comments on this: "In the same breath in which the Church is exhorted to pay more heed to Scripture, it has to be pointed out that private exegesis undertaken by individuals, and

[23] Barth, loc. cit.   [24] Käsemann, "Apologie," p. 278.

unauthorised by the guidance of the official teachers of the Church, is not allowed." [25] The ἰδία ἐπίλυσις stands here in contrast to the exegesis of the Πνεῦμα Ἅγιον but not to an exegesis prescribed by the official teaching of the Church. This latter interpretation of the passage is rejected for example by the *Confessio Helvetica posterior*, in our opinion rightly.[26] To the uncontrolled appeal to the Spirit is opposed the unique authority of Scripture which is a work of the Spirit, and therefore—we may infer the essential meaning to be—alone mediates the Spirit. As regards a specific doctrine of inspiration, we may not read more out of the ὑπὸ Πνεύματος Ἁγίου φερόμενοι than the mere fact that the writing prophets in their work stood in a special relation of obedience to God, and by the agency of the Spirit performed a special and exclusive function assigned to them by God. How we are to think of this work in its relation to their humanity, whether for instance the latter was eliminated by the "dictation of the Holy Ghost," cannot be decided on the basis of this text alone despite the οὐ γὰρ θελήματι ἀνθρώπου (vs. 21).

Much the same applies to II Tim. III. 16. Timothy is urged to remain steadfast in that which he has learnt and believed, especially in view of the one from whom he has learnt it (vs. 14) —which is primarily a reference to the writer of the epistle himself (vs. 10)—and in fact, at the same time, to Apostolic teaching in general. Then is added, linked by the simple copula καὶ and without the βεβαιότερον of II Pet. I. 19, though otherwise exactly as in the latter text, the mention of Holy Scripture the ἰερὰ γράμματα which from a babe he has known, and which can make him wise unto salvation through faith which is in Jesus Christ (vs. 15). Scripture can make more deeply effectual in him what he has learnt and believed, because πᾶσα γραφὴ is θεόπνευστος: i.e. "the whole of the Scriptures are, literally, instinct with the Spirit of God, in other words inbreathed, filled, and controlled by the Spirit of God; or, expressed actively, Scripture breathes, diffuses, and makes aware of, the Spirit of God. It is clear that this phrase is decisive for the meaning of the whole passage. Just because

---

[25] Käsemann, *op. cit.*, p. 292.

[26] *Bekenntnisschriften und Kirchenordnungen der nach Gottes Wort reformierter Kirche*, ed. W. Niesel, 2nd edn., p. 224, 13 ff.

it is so powerfully true that the Spirit of God precedes, exercises its sway over and lives in the word of Scripture, therefore Scripture has been and will be able to do what is claimed for it in the previous and following verses. But it is equally clear that here at the centre of the period a statement is made about the relation of God and Scripture, which is interpreted simply as a decree, act, and decision of God Himself, and which as such cannot therefore be further enlarged upon, but to which only reference can be made—and it is not for nothing that the reference is so brief. All that can be said on this point can only consist at the decisive juncture in underlining and marking the mystery (inaccessible to us) of the free grace of God by which the Spirit of God is effectually present preveniently to, and controlling both from above and within, the words of the Bible." [27] Hence from this text again we receive no further answer to the various questions raised by every doctrine of inspiration.

And now for the parallel in II Cor. III. 4-18. Here, in antithesis to the function of the New Testament οὐ γράμματος, ἀλλὰ πνεύματος (vs. 6), the Old Testament is qualified as διακονία τοῦ θανάτου ἐν γράμμασιν. "This description does not imply any disqualification of Scripture. This is said to bring out the superiority of the Spirit, but not in opposition to Scripture, or only to Scripture if understood and read apart from the Spirit." [28] For it is expressly said of the written code which kills διακονία τῆς κατακρίσεως that it too had δόξα (vs. 9), which is to say that it too was and is a witness to the self-disclosure of God. Hence it is not the fault of Scripture as such—which has δόξα—if the children of Israel read it with a veil on their hearts that is not lifted. The reason is rather that they are unable to see the δόξα Κυρίου (vs. 18) because they do not read Scripture through the Spirit which is the Lord (vs. 17). If Paul knew the Jewish doctrine of the inspiration of Scripture we should have to see in this text no doubt a correction of that doctrine, to the effect that such inspiration (not disputed but assumed by Paul) is not only meaningless but actually works death as a result of the emphasis on the letter, as long as the Spirit does not unlock for us the true sense. All this however does not amount to

[27] Barth, *K. D.*, VOL. I. 2, p. 559.   [28] Barth, *op. cit.*, p. 571.

anything like a hermeneutical method for the right exegesis of Scripture. Rather it is simply claimed for the διακονία τῆς δικαιοσύνης (vs. 9), and hence for the service in which the Apostle stands over against the Synagogue: "We all, with unveiled face, reflecting the glory (δόξαν) of the Lord, are being changed into his likeness ἀπὸ δόξης εἰς δόξαν, for this comes from the Lord who is the Spirit" (vs. 18).

We have undertaken this study of New Testament statements about the inspiration of Scripture in connexion with our question concerning the verification and authorisation of Apostolic doctrine and Gospel proclamation, in so far as the latter rests upon a Scriptural basis. Our study has brought us constantly face to face with the circular argument that the Spirit which has inspired Scripture can be recognised only by the Spirit which they alone have who are ἀπὸ Κυρίου Πνεύματος (II Cor. III. 18). Nowhere is there given any definite hermeneutical method of exegesis such as would furnish secure grounds for this recognition, nor can one be subsequently inferred from the practice of New Testament exegesis, which works with all the resources of contemporary hermeneutics. Moreover, it is not the isolated individual believer nor the theologian, in his interpretation of Scripture, it is rather the Church as such (cp., for example, I Cor. II. 6-16) which moves within this circle. But the Church is never confronted immediately by Scripture in its bareness. Just as according to the Synoptics Jesus Himself must open to the disciples the mind of Scripture, so the later Church has Apostolic doctrine which with Apostolic authority appeals to the Lord Himself as the key to the right understanding of the Bible. Hence we receive no hard and fast hermeneutical principle for the exegesis of Scripture, but a new tradition of proclamation and doctrine which claims to be the right understanding and exposition of Scripture and also to test Scriptural exegesis. Hence our question about the authorisation of Gospel teaching and proclamation must be addressed to this Apostolic tradition itself.

CHAPTER VII

THE APOSTOLIC TRADITION

At a very early stage in the liturgical or catechetical usage of the Church, there arise fixed formulae, which are accepted by the Apostles and further elaborated by them. In this matter however it is important to notice that in the New Testament these are never treated as fundamentals of doctrine which have to be scholastically explained, but rather as texts for preaching which are interpreted in the proclamation of the Gospel message.

(a) The paradosis in its meaning as a theme for preaching

The meaning of this fundamental distinction can best be realised by considering the work of Heinrich Schlier,[1] for the reason that he does not observe it. For Schlier these credal formulae are, "in accordance with their origin, pre-symbols, and so symbols in general proceeding from the self-revelation of the Risen Lord reflected in the words of the Apostolic witnesses," and indeed, "in a literal sense, were the outcome of the self-attestation of the Risen Lord in the presence of witnesses." Thus "the credal formulae have, in accordance with their origin, the dignity of revelational statements grasped, crystallised, and formulated by the general consensus of the Church under the inspiration of the Holy Spirit." [2] Hence the growth of credal formulae is removed from the sphere of public Church proclamation and referred to an esoteric communion between Christ and the Apostles. Nor does the needed consensus of the Church make any difference, because the latter springs not from open συζητεῖν which Schlier rejects as a factor in the rise of Apostolic doctrine, but signifies only an assent to the already developed *kerygma* "which remains outside of and prior to all human seeking and

---

[1] See Schlier, "*Kerygma und Sophia*" (above, p. 43, n. 3); and on the following, cp. above, pp. 46 ff.   [2] Schlier, *op. cit.*, pp. 44 f.

enquiry." [3] For these reasons it becomes plain why for
Schlier there is no continuity between the exegesis of the
Old Testament and the growth of New Testament *paradosis*.[4]

No doubt the Apostolic doctrine, because it has the dignity
of a revelational statement, can subsequently check Old
Testament exegesis; but it did not arise through the interpretation of the Old Testament in Gospel preaching. Furthermore,
Apostolic doctrine is not dependent for its verification and
testing on preaching which was inspired by the Holy Spirit,
in which it had to make its truth clear and persuasive. Faith
in this doctrine rests rather on "the acceptance of the validity
of a presupposition, namely the presupposition that in the
resurrection of Jesus Christ through the power of God is
contained the authentic disclosure of ultimate reality," i.e. in
obedient acceptance of the self-revelation of God in the affirmations of the *kerygma*. This means, further, that dogma as later
developed in the Catholic Church is nothing other than the
kerygma in a later stage of elaboration; that is, it is a learned
and scholastic explanation of the *kerygma* considered as a body
of principles and *fundamenta*, and hence it has not arisen, more
indirectly, through preaching. In this process it is of no
importance, and in any case cannot alter in the least the
scholastic character of the *kerygma*, that the object of the latter
is the contingent event of revelation rather than universal
timeless truth. What is really of decisive importance here is
the dissociation of the *kerygma* as it passes into dogma from the
concrete process of Evangelical proclamation.

But the situation is entirely different if the statements of the
paradosis within the New Testament have the significance of
texts for preaching, and if the ample exposition in which they
are embedded provides the relevant sermon (though in this
connexion of course the idea of preaching must not be taken in
too literal a sense, nor confined to its associations with Church
worship). Examples are, for instance, 1 Cor. XI. 23-5 as text,
and 26 ff. as the preacher's commentary on the theme, and
1 Cor. XV. 3-5 with the extended commentary of vss. 6-58;
while in other cases the text is quoted during the course of or
even at the end of the elucidating sermon (e.g. Phil   5-11;
Tim. III. 16), which makes no essential difference. Since the

_____
[3] Schlier, *op. cit.*, p. 45.   [4] Cp. above, pp. 48 ff.

rise of the *paradosis* is here in flux the use of it only in a few texts assumes the form of express quotations. For the most part it is worked into the texture of the discourse without being specially marked out, while the comments form classical formulations which are handed on further. Hence it is hardly justifiable to attribute to the pre-symbols as distinct from the remaining text a special dignity of their own, as Schlier does. In this process text and sermon are but rarely clearly distinguishable from each other; and eventually the whole text of the New Testament becomes a text for the preacher. No doubt it is historically correct to suppose that certain formulations harden into pre-symbols and symbols and, by a development which takes place concurrently with the formation of the canon become the *regula fidei*; and the question how the *regula fidei* which thus arises is related to Scripture will have to occupy our attention later. But within the New Testament itself there is no adequate basis for distinguishing between the two lines of development, so that—to use our terms once more—it might be possible to separate points of doctrine, on the one hand, from texts for the preacher, on the other.

(b) *The significance of tradition, according to Karl Barth*

At this point we must make some reference to the arguments of Karl Barth about παραδοῦναι.[5] He proceeds from the New Testament datum that παράδοσις on the one hand is used to describe the deed of Judas, who thus perverts his Apostolic office, and, "on the other hand, indicates the nature of the Apostolic ministry in so far as the latter consists in handing on the knowledge about Jesus, the report of His deeds and words, His death and resurrection, the knowledge of the will of God, revealed in Him, concerning the existence and order of the Church, and acts as the channel through which all this is transmitted, faithfully and fully, unchanged and undiminished, from the first human hands which received it to the hands of others, of successors who did not originally receive it."[6] In fulfilling this function the Apostles formally enter upon the activity of teaching tradition associated with the Scribes (cp. II Thess. II. 15 and Mk. VII. 13) and are faced with the same danger of annulling the command of God by

[5] Barth, *K. D.*, VOL. II 2, pp. 533 ff.   [6] *Op. cit.*, p. 535.

this tradition. But this danger, which they must inevitably risk, "is obviously now, this side of the Resurrection, a danger which essentially has been done away. That Christ dies no more (Rom. VI. 9) is now true in the sense that He has nothing more to fear from a new surrender into the hands of wicked men, and that He now wills to triumph through this very surrender that once took place. Hence, now, after sorrow has been expressed about the traitor Judas and the Jews who delivered up their Messiah, there has arisen in the power of the resurrection of Him Who was so delivered up, a new righteous and saving tradition of Jesus." [7] To the παραλαμ-βάνειν of the Lord there now corresponds the παραδοῦναι of the Apostles (1 Cor. XI. 23, XV. 3), which again requires a παραλαμβάνειν of their παράδοσις (II Thess. III. 6) Barth points out that in 1 Cor. XI. 23 the word παραδοῦναι: in one and the same sentence is used in its twofold sense of "betray" or "deliver up," and "hand on": "I received from the Lord that which I also *delivered* to you, that the Lord Jesus on the night when He was *betrayed*. . . ." and adds: "These *two* 'deliveries' obviously lend force to each other, so that Paul is placed just as much in the shadow of Judas as Judas stands in the light of Paul." [8] Thus the faithless act by which Judas and the Jews surrendered their Messiah is now by the power of the death and resurrection of Jesus renewed in another sense, in the tradition of the Apostles which throughout the whole world summons the Church into being. But—and it should be noted that Barth goes into this point in the section on the doctrine of election—"that Paul, also involved in this act of surrender, is by the grace of God what he is, Paul with his special background, it is that fact which justifies Judas and gives a positive meaning to his act of treachery, it is that which characterises his deed in accordance with his election as an Apostolic function and signifies the triumph of the election of this reprobate over his reprobation, although it is forbidden us—and we must acquiesce in this—to diminish in the slightest degree the gravity of his reprobation. It justifies him only in his capacity as the holder of the place for him who was destined to fill it so very differently from the evil

[7] Barth, *K.D.*, VOL. I. 2, pp. 535 f.
[8] *Op. cit.*, p. 536.

way in which it was filled by himself. But it does justify him none the less and that is the sole justification for the Jewish treachery, for Israel as a whole rejecting in its disobedience the fulfilment of the promise, the manifestation of the grace of God precisely to itself. . . . Israel is and remains the shadow of those future things centred in Jesus Christ and His Church. . . . It remains, of course, true that the Jews *betray* the word and command of God—in that they abandon, neglect and annul it —but in any case they do not cease to *hand it on*, they cannot cease to do so, and obviously also they may not." [9]

One might perhaps be inclined to see in all this only a witty word-play on the dual semantic use of παραδοῦναι which would make it seem questionable whether the two meanings of the word can be brought together in this way. Barth himself deals with this possible objection and says: "But the whole argument only becomes quite clear when we realise that according to the New Testament there exists apart from the παραδοῦναι of Judas and the Apostolical παραδοῦναι, in parti- cular a divine παραδοῦναι as the prototype of both, in which the integral connexion of the two and the light which the one throws on the other cannot, in fact, be mistaken, however much we are dismayed by the contrast in intrinsic meaning, and in consequence the formal correspondence of the two cannot in fact rest upon a mere linguistic accident. Here we have in fact the prototype of both meanings." [10] In this act of divine surrender also are included the two complementary aspects of the matter: the wrathful surrender (Acts VII. 42; Rom. I. 18) and the surrender which brings salvation (Rom. IV. 25, VIII. 32; Gal. II. 20; Eph. v. 2-25). In view of this Barth considers the connexion between the delivering of Paul and the delivering of Judas confirmed, and says "Clearly the urgency, the power and the meaning of *all* delivery is rooted in this *primary* radical action, by which God in the person of Jesus or Jesus as the Son of God makes Himself the object of an act of surrender." [11]

Unlike Schlier, who is especially concerned about the fixed content of the tradition, Barth vigorously emphasises the act of handing-on, the Apostolic transmission of tradition. About

[9] *Op. cit.*, p. 537.   [10] *Op. cit.*, p. 538.
[11] *Op. cit.*, p. 543.

1 Cor. XI. 2-23, XV. 3 Barth says: "What Paul as a representative of these things has to do and what in this capacity he has done for his readers, was the act of passing on to them the knowledge he received at first hand, the act of conveying it to them. As a result, according to Rom. VI. 17 they were no longer slaves of sin but servants living in obedience. This change in them has come about as a result of the act by which he delivered over to them the traditional teaching, and in any further relation with them Paul can and must refer back to this act, anything further that he has to tell them can only consist in a more emphatic repetition of this act, in an explanation and clarification of what as an Apostle he imparted to them." [12] Hence in addition to the παραδοῦναι of Lk. I. 1 ff. Barth refers to Jude 3, where Christians are urged to "contend for the faith which was once for all (ἅπαξ) delivered to the saints." What then is implied in Barth's emphasis on this act of delivering, which cannot be separated from the content of the delivery, and how are the two aspects of the matter related to each other? The Apostle does not merely remind his hearers of the action of delivering something to them, but also of the content of what was delivered, especially if we consider the particular passages in question Lk. I. 1 ff. and Jude 3. Just as we found in regard to διδασκαλία and διδαχή, where the two meanings of active instruction and the content of the teaching may merge with each other and are inseparable, so the παράδοσις always contains the idea of the action of delivering and the substance of what is delivered. In this emphasis on the action, we can see nothing else but a way of emphasising that the tradition consists not in the mere handing-on of principles of doctrine, in which case the action of imparting would have no essential significance, but in the highly qualified *event* of proclamation which constitutes both the Church and the individual Christian as such.

(c) *Apostolic teaching and the tradition of the churches*

In this matter we must not by any means forget what Hellmut Traub emphatically points out, namely that this present event of preaching takes place within an earthly history of preaching, marked by geographical and historical dates in

[12] Barth, *K.D.* VOL. I. 2 p. 536.

which the work of Christ is realised.[13]   The process of
proclamation has its historical starting point in Jerusalem
which has symbolic significance for the growing Christian
community. "For the saving history does not live in the power
of a message as such, its eschatological character does not
remove the necessity of its taking historical shape—to suppose
that would be Gnosticism—but it lives in the power of an event
which was declared to it, an event whose sole qualified witness
became the first Church at Jerusalem." [14]   Thus the Apostolic
epistles always speak relevantly to a specific historical process,
and at the same time create Church history themselves. "The
history of the growing churches is both the occasion and the
content of these letters. It is so in all its concrete manifestations, as the object and not merely the occasion of ever
renewed thanksgiving and prayer, and the story of the one
Church is from time to time communicated (in the fullest
evangelical sense) to other churches. Thus in Paul's Epistles
the discussion of the most realistic and practical questions
stands in immediate, concrete and indissoluble connexion
with the purely kerygmatic texts. In fact for Paul there is
no such thing as a pure *kerygma* without history. Nor can
there be such a thing, because *kerygma* both proclaims history
and makes history." The individual kerygmatic formulae
"receive their kerygmatic significance only in and through
the life and development of the Churches." [15]   In addition
there is the great part which alongside the history of the
churches is played by the individual story of the Apostle as an
example and type of the working of the Christian Gospel.
Hence the Gospel "cannot be distinguished and separated from
the life and history of the Apostles and churches which bear
witness to it." [16]

The event of preaching is therefore qualified by the following
factors: (1) that Christ Himself is the operative subject of
it; (2) that the Apostles were commissioned to promulgate in
preaching what had been delivered to them; (3) that in this
process of preaching the subject that is preached is actualised

[13] H. Traub, "Botschaft und Geschichte," in *Theologische Studien*,
XL (1954), p. 10.
[14] Traub, *op. cit.*, pp. 9 ff.   [15] Traub, *op. cit.*, p. 12.
[16] Traub, *op. cit.*, p. 16.

N

as present event in that it either awakens faith and so creates
the life of the Christian community, or has the effect of hardening the hearts of the hearers.   Hence there is a decisive act
occurring at a definite point in time, as Barth stresses, in the
sense that this παραδοῦναι which demands the παραλαμβάνειν,
takes place in the stream of earthly history, in which there is
for every Christian a beginning when he was faced by the
preaching of the Gospel for the first time, with the consequence
that he can always be referred back to the epoch-making
event. The emphasis on the act of conveying tradition would
then be equivalent to emphasising that the establishment and
the practice of the apostolic ministry of proclaiming tradition
is an aspect of the revelational process itself (cp. Lk. xxiv. 47)
—occurring always within the history of the Church, which is
itself part of earthly history.

But how is this related to the content of Apostolic tradition?
Must we add as the fourth feature qualifying the event of
preaching, the fact that, as Schlier maintains, the Apostle
possessed as the content of tradition a kerygma which was fixed
in substance and formulated as the authorised *veritas revelata*?
It is true that in 1 Cor. xi. 23, xv. 3, Paul cites fixed formulae.
But whence did he receive them?

In 1 Cor. xv. 3, he says simply: "I delivered to you that
which I also received," obviously through the tradition of the
Church. In 1 Cor. xi. 23, on the other hand, we read that he
received the word from the Lord. In this connexion it seems
hardly justifiable to think of a revelation made to Paul personally in which the Lord "repeated to him the words He used in
instituting the Last Supper . . ." as Barth [17] seems to suppose.
Cullmann,[18] in his discussion of the whole controversial
literature on the subject, comes to the same conclusions as
ourselves. Ernst Lichtenstein [19] tries to explain the origin of
the formula in 1 Cor. xv. 3 ff. by reference to diverse currents

[17] Barth, *Die Auferstehung der Toten*, 1924, p. 34.
[18] See O. Cullmann, "Die apostolische Überlieferung und der zur
Rechten Gottes erhohte Herr," in *Tradition*, 1954, pp. 8 ff, the most recent
discussion.
[19] See E. Lichtenstein, "Die alteste christliche Glaubensformel," in
Zeitschrift für Kirchengeschichte, henceforth cited as *Z. K. G.*, LXIII (1950-1),
pp. 1 ff.

of tradition. In this respect Barth is concerned above all to maintain that Paul does not wish to furnish an historical proof of the truth of his formula by appealing to the age of the tradition on which it rests. We feel that Barth's opposition to the idea of a historical argument is just as unnecessary here as in regard to 1 Cor. xv. 3 f.[20] Would it be then so very extraordinary if Paul had wished to do something of this sort? Barth says: "The Κύριος lives for him not in the oldest the most authentic or most credible tradition—why should it be precisely the Κύριος who lives and speaks there?—but in an extremely real and actual self-revelation of the Lord to His Church, *in concreto* in the kerygmatic *task* imposed on him, Paul. He reports directly from the source: the Lord *Himself* is the tradition." [21] But does the Lord speak to Paul in this matter concurrently with and independently of tradition? When in 1 Cor. VII. 10 Paul says against divorce and re-marriage: "To the married I give charge, not I but the Lord," and in VII. 25, concerning the unmarried: "I have no command of the Lord, but I give my opinion (γνώμη)," the meaning can only be that as regards the first question a word of the Lord had been handed down in the Church and was recognised also by Paul, while for the second question this was not so. And if it was believed that a word of the Lord existed in the Church and its traditions, then it was also presumably considered to be historically authentic. Nevertheless we may suppose that the Church did not wish to base the validity of such a word on an historical proof, but that it was felt to be verified by the fact that the Lord who is the Spirit had legitimated just this opinion as distinct from others. Thus we might agree with Barth's statement that "the Lord Himself is the tradition," in the sense that He confirms the legitimate as opposed to the illegitimate tradition, which of course is equally current. But it goes without saying that a tradition which is authenticated in this way by spiritual means would also be considered historically genuine, since that would be only natural for an historically primitive mentality such as we must presuppose here. Hence the problem posed by Barth may not legitimately be raised in connexion with these texts. Such a problem only arises at a much later stage of the

[20] See above, p. 124. [21] Barth, *Die Auferstehung der Toten*, p. 34.

development when there was an attempt to give an historical
proof of the canonicity of the New Testament texts by referring
to their Apostolic authorship, with the consequent danger
that the historically assured tradition was opposed to an appeal
to the Spirit.

But the question still remains open how the Apostle's own
special preaching mission is related to the general tradition of
the Church.   Barth too seems to agree that the Apostle, even
when he "reports *directly* from the source," draws, in so doing,
on the common fund of Church tradition, into which his
sayings flow back again, for he says: "That each of the individual sayings in which he discharged his mission had its
human earthly genesis, history and conditioning, and that even
those words of the Lord which were communicated directly
to him, to his lips, and his pen, became inseparably mingled
with the flood of contemporary ideas, he would himself have
been the last to dispute.   But this had not, and has not, either
positively or negatively, the least to do with the genesis,
history, and conditioning in virtue of which as a man of the
Graeco-Roman period he was an Apostle of Jesus Christ.
Thus Paul does not *prove* but he *attests* what as regards the
Last Supper celebrated by the Church, the will of its Founder
was." [22]   But this says nothing other or more than that "Church
tradition is in fact validated by Apostolic preaching which
stems from the authority of the call of the Apostle."   In that
case there is no difference as regards the validity of the
paradosis between the παρέλαβον ἀπὸ τοῦ Κυρίου of 1 Cor. XI. 23
and the mere παρέλαβον of 1 Cor. XV. 3 (cp. on the other hand,
Ernst Lichtenstein: [23] "Between tradition in the sense of
1 Cor. XV. 3 f., and in the sense of 1 Cor. XI. 23 f., a sharp
distinction must, however, be maintained").   In both passages
Paul is not proving but bearing witness, and that on the ground
of his Apostolic authority, which—as we must suppose—in an
exceptional way enables him to discriminate between the
spirits within the current *paradosis*.   In this endeavour he does
not on the one hand scorn to avail himself of an historical
reference to the paradosis of the Lord, where that seems
possible, as in 1 Cor. VII. 10 and XI. 23.   On the other hand, it

[22] Barth, *op. cit.*, pp. 34 f.
[23] Lichtenstein, in *Z. K. G.*, LXIII (1950-1), p. 3.

makes no essential difference to the authority of his witness as regards form and content when this possibility does not exist, as in 1 Cor. vii. 25 and xv. 3, since he is acting under the command of the Lord who is the Spirit. In both cases he does not appeal to his own Apostolic authority in face of the congregation in the sense that the latter must accept his unproven opinion, but in declaring it he appeals to the authority of the Spirit which rests on the congregation also. And he can do this no less freely than confidently because he can add when he declares his own judgment: "And I think that I also have the Spirit of God"(vii. 40).

Apostolic authority in the exercise of the παραδοῦναι does not therefore mean that the formulae declared by the Apostles to be truths of revelation are superior to the common fund of Church tradition, but rather that the text for preaching carries more weight than the preaching itself. Where the Apostle in addressing the congregation appeals to this admitted weightier element of the tradition, he can do so as in 1 Cor. xv. 3 by referring to a fixed formula, hence a specific sermon text. But even apart from such a specific text he may appeal to the authority of his preaching itself and as a whole, which in Gal. 1. 11 ff. he calls "the Gospel"—a gospel which he received from no man, nor was taught, but which came to him through revelation of Jesus Christ. Or again, in Rom. vi. 17 it is described as τύπος διδαχῆς, by which (with Schlier) we may understand a "preliminary stage of a later credal symbol" used in the practice of baptism.[24] In any case the decisive factor in all this is, as Barth says with regard to 1 Cor. xv. 1 ff., that the παραλαμβάνειν corresponding to the εὐαγγέλιον "is, from the first and in virtue of its object, an acceptance that is binding, irrevocable, and commits the recipient once for all. It is not possible subsequently to feel free to adopt a different attitude. 'Aeternam haec acceptatio obligationem involvit,' is Bengel's interpretation. To accept and then to claim freedom later, as if one had merely accepted so much Paulinism, is impossible." [25] What has been received is rather the *paradosis* which the Lord Himself commits to the Church through the

[24] Schlier, "Die Taufe nach dem 6. Kapitel des Römerbriefs," in *Ev. Th.*, 1938, p. 343.
[25] Barth, *Die Auferstehung der Toten*, p. 71.

ministry of the Apostles, in whose Gospel-preaching the Lord
is present and makes Himself known.

This Pauline use of "*paradosis*" is not essentially modified in
the later writings of the New Testament. The strong emphasis
on adherence to the delivered doctrine characteristic of the
Pastoral Epistles would in fact only go beyond the Pauline
attitude, if Schlier were right in his interpretation of παραθήκη
as specially authorised Apostolic *paradosis* in a fixed form of
words.[26] Then the preponderance of *paradosis* over preaching
would not merely mean the greater authority of the text as
compared with the sermon, but, as Schlier contends, the
paradosis could become the foundation principle of a new
wisdom which would have to be scholastically developed out
of revealed doctrine. For this point of view we find no basis
in the texts. At least we should expect in this case that the
content of the παραθήκη, on whose literal and fixed form so
much stress is laid, would also be literally quoted. But this
never happens apart from the two passages of I Corinthians,
which are hardly sufficient to fit the description. We might
also expect that there would at least be some allusion to the
content of the παραθήκη as the *regula fidei* confessed by the
Churches and universally recognised as authoritative, but this
again does not happen, no doubt because at the time of the
composition of the Pastoral Epistles this development had not
yet taken place. It is obvious that Schlier has projected back
into the New Testament the later stage of early Catholicism,
because he needs to do so in order to derive from the New
Testament itself the Catholic idea of dogma.

The question is whether—as Schlier does here from a
pro-Catholic tendency—Käsemann has not done likewise
from an anti-Catholic tendency in his interpretation of
II Peter and Jude. We refer to the ἅπαξ παραδοθείσῃ τοῖς
ἁγίοις πίστις of Jude 3 and the παραδοθείσῃ ἁγία ἐντολή of
II Pet. II. 21, with which is identical the πάρουσα ἀλήθεια of
I. 12, texts in which Käsemann finds emphatic expression of
early Catholic views: "Just as faith here means traditional
Christian instruction, so ἅπαξ in the New Testament is used
with original force and is intended to bring out the once-for-
all and final character of the eschatological event. But this

[26] See above, p. 46.

implies in the context that eschatological meaning is ascribed to the Christian tradition of teaching as such. This teaching has a once-for-all character which shows its divinely ordained inviolability and absolute finality." [27] But what is there really so bad about this, and how does it show a deviation from the position of Paul towards that of early Catholicism? That an attack is here being made on the enthusiasm of the Gnostics by an appeal to traditional teaching is quite as true as the further deduction: "the Church guards the historical character of the revelation, the contingency of the eschatological event, by insisting on the Apostolic authority of its teaching tradition. In this connexion, therefore, the Apostles are not primarily prototypes of saintliness, but essentially those who have authoritatively transmitted the instructions of the Lord and Saviour." All this we may agree to and Käsemann himself continues: "It is clear that in such theories original Christian motives are being retained. Paul himself emphasises in the strongest terms the eschatological character of his Apostolate, insists that the Apostle should be seen solely in the light of revelation and should be accepted as the very embodiment of the Gospel." In just this way on the basis of the rest of the New Testament we have interpreted the meaning of the Apostolate and of Apostolic teaching. But what is there really so catastrophic about II Peter which makes it appear as "a document of early Catholic tendencies and probably the most questionable writing in the whole canon?" [28] Käsemann adduces the following reasons: "The formula of St Vincent of Lerin '*quod ubique, quod semper, quod ab omnibus creditum est*' is only a reflexion of what is already intended in Jude 3 and is taken up again in II Peter i. 12 to counter the deviations from orthodox established truth. The motive which urges the coining of such formulae and the adoption of such an outlook is the desire to withdraw the *fides catholica* from individual caprice. The truth may be expounded and developed, but as the deposit of saving truth once for all committed to the keeping of the Church it can no longer be changed or completed." [29] But precisely what is reflected here, and in what? We do not understand with what right

[27] Käsemann, "Apologie," p. 278.   [28] Käsemann, *op. cit.*, p. 272.
[29] *Op. cit.*, p. 278.

Käsemann imputes to the author of II Peter the doctrine of Vincent of Lerin. In order to justify this he insists that the decisive difference between Paul and II Peter lies in the following point: "In place of the co-ordination of Apostle and Gospel, we see in II Peter the co-ordination of Apostle and the Church tradition of doctrine." [30] What this distinction is intended to imply and how he purposes to develop it in detail is not clear from the results of our examination so far. But he continues: "The effect of this is that the Apostles no longer appear in the light of assailed and harried men, as in I Cor. IV. 8 ff., II Cor. IV. 7 ff., XI. 23 ff., XIII. 4, or as in I Thess. II., where they have to fight against the reproach of being cheats." [31] Here the Apostle, formerly "the tempted and tried, has become the bringer of *securitas*." [32] In all the passages quoted the trial consists in the fact, as Käsemann himself says, that the Apostolate of Paul "is enshrouded in peculiar obscurity," [33] shown in the suffering and persecution to which he is subject, and in his failure to find clear recognition. This may indeed have been a trial for Paul himself, but we nowhere are told that it ever impairs the certainty of his Apostolic teaching and preaching, or that his claim to authority over his churches has thus been relativised. Rather, this obscurity means something quite different, namely that he can never furnish satisfactory proof of the authority of his Apostolate. This absence of direct proof, which has nothing to do with the certainty of Apostolic teaching, becomes for Käsemann the cause of his troubles, and the latter are made a criterion for the legitimacy of his Apostolic doctrine—a point of view which is hardly consonant with the New Testament. Käsemann sees this false *securitas* also in the fact that the author claims to be an eyewitness of the earthly life of Jesus, and on this basis purposes to guarantee the historical continuity of his teaching with that of Jesus Himself. We shall have to go into this in detail later.

The difference between Paul and II Peter in regard to the Apostolic tradition of doctrine seems to us mainly that the claim of the Apostles to be the reliable bearers of tradition— a claim which as we have seen Paul vigorously pressed—has in the meantime become generally recognised. Hence legiti-

[30] *Ibid.*　　　[31] *Ibid.*　　　[32] *Ibid.*　　　[33] *Op. cit..* p. 279.

mate preaching needs to stem from the authority of an Apostle. "Of course writers claimed the sanction of individual Apostles such as Peter or Paul, not as individually colourful and significant personalities, but as undoubted authorities whose individual differences do not count. Apostolic authority is at bottom the authority of the college of the Twelve, to which only Paul was added as a peer; it is characteristic that the first system of morals and Church discipline was drawn up under the title Διδαχὴ τῶν δώδεκα ἀποστόλων." [34]

But how could Apostolic authority be concretely effective after the deaths of the Twelve and of Paul? There was, in the main, oral tradition as transmitted by the pupils of the Apostles and by the duly appointed elders. "But how uncertain this was is shown in the struggle with Gnosticism; for the latter too appeals to oral tradition, to the ἀποστολικὴ παράδοσις ἦν ἐκ διαδόχης καὶ ἡμεῖς παρειλήφαμεν.[35] And it was *gnosis*, above all, which made oral παράδοσις suspect." [36] In proportion as oral tradition was discredited by Gnosticism, the weight and influence of written tradition increases. This consisted, apart from single words of the Lord, in the Gospels, whose reading in Church worship is already attested by Justin, as also in the Paul's Epistles, which were likewise read in Christian services, and of which a collection must very early have existed. But this implies no essential change as regards the Pauline practice with reference to Apostolic *paradosis*. It means merely that the writings which were sermons amplifying traditional material used as texts, are now regarded in their entirety as texts. This brings us face to face with the problem of the canon of Scripture.

[34] Bultmann, *Theol. des N.T.*, p. 484.
[35] Ptolemy the Gnostic, *Ad Floram*, x. 5.
[36] Bultmann, *loc. cit.*

CHAPTER VIII

THE CANON OF HOLY SCRIPTURE

IN proportion as written Apostolic tradition gained in importance by contrast with the oral tradition to which the Gnostics referred, and as a canon of Apostolic writings was established for the purposes of Church proclamation, the idea of Apostleship became narrowed, and whereas it had sometimes been used in a broader sense with reference to evangelists and missionaries (Acts IV. 4; Rom. XVI. 7; 1 Cor. XV. 7), its use was now restricted to the Twelve and Paul. What distinguishes this circle as a whole from all other bearers of *paradosis* is in particular the fact that they hold their commission from the risen Lord, while their second characteristic, their status as eyewitnesses, they share with a much wider circle. But one difference between the Twelve Apostles and Paul is that the former alone fulfil the requirement of having been with the Lord from the beginning (Acts I. 21 ff.) while Paul can appeal only to the fact of his encounter with the risen Lord. The whole life of Paul testifies to the fact that because he did not join the Christian community until later, and then under such suspicious circumstances, it was more difficult for him to gain recognition as an Apostle. But he felt himself in no way to be an Apostle of lesser authority because he had not been an eye-witness of the pre-Resurrection life of Jesus (cp. 1 Cor. IX. 1) and he is nowhere in the New Testament regarded as being of inferior rank.

E. Käsemann,[1] draws, it is true, a different conclusion from the testament of Peter in II Peter I. 13 ff. and in connexion with III. 15: "Thus the Twelve are the real Apostles whatever Paul's merits may be. In our letter he can be considered as the author of canonical writings and described by Peter with the honourable qualification 'our beloved brother,' so that he is very near to the Twelve. Again, he too sanctions the

---

[1] Käsemann, "Apologie" pp. 272 ff.

Churchly tradition of doctrine reaching back to the beginnings. But he has no power to give an authoritative basis to this tradition; only the companions of Jesus can do that. His Apostolate, as in Acts, is wrapped in a curious twilight; it cannot be denied that the Gentile churches are essentially his work. But orthodoxy cannot count him as belonging to the true foundations of the Christian movement, because, unlike the Twelve, he is unable to assure continuity with the historical Jesus, in which true believers see the guarantee of traditional doctrine." [2] Käsemann sees in this very different evaluation of Paul's Apostolate a fundamental change in the conception of an Apostle, which would consist in the fact that now exclusively the eyewitness of the earthly life of Jesus has become the guarantor of tradition, the witness of the Resurrection has become the witness of the *historia sacra*, the bearer of the eschatological action of God has become the founder of an institution mediating salvation, while the tempted and tried Apostle has become the guardian of *securitas*.[3] Thus Käsemann poses certain fundamental questions into which we must go, whether we agree with his interpretation of II Peter or not.

(a) Tradition and Apostolic succession

The first point is the connexion of tradition with an Apostolical succession. Primarily this means nothing more than that the Apostolic *paradosis* by its very nature demands transmission from one preacher to another, so that a successor can always appeal to the authority of his predecessor from whom he has learnt the traditional faith. There can be no doubt that the New Testament writings as a whole imply Apostolic succession in this sense and in fact exercise it. In this respect II Peter makes no exception. What is *not* found in the New Testament is the *securing* of Apostolic succession by means of an historically demonstrable list of office-bearers, guaranteeing the uninterrupted process of ordination from Peter through the Roman Bishops to the duly appointed clergy, and so making pneumatic succession and the apostolicity of the Church dependent on an historically and juridically proved set of facts or rather replacing the former by the latter. There is no trace of this even in II Peter.

[2] Käsemann, *op. cit.*, p. 279.   [3] *Ibid.*

A second point is the primacy of Peter among the Apostles. Even if the author of II Peter had been mainly concerned to emphasise this primacy, he would not have had to go beyond statements to be found elsewhere in the New Testament. The emphasis on Peter's primacy is to be found (apart from Mt. XVI. 18 ff.) in Jn. XXI. 15 ff., for example, or in the tendentious comparison between Peter and Paul in Acts. What is *not* found in the New Testament is the mechanical conveyance of this primacy to Peter's successors in office. Of this even II Peter bears no trace. Moreover, in the Roman Church the primacy of Peter is nowhere founded on a greater fidelity of Peter as an eyewitness by comparison with Paul or the other Apostles, but solely on the fact that Jesus invested Peter with the precedence in the administration of the Church. And even in this regard the ultimate authority cited is that of the risen Lord, so that in dogmatics one can distinguish between the promise to Peter according to Mt. XVI. 18 and the fulfilment of this promise by the risen Christ recorded in Jn. XXI. 15-17.[4]

In this matter II Peter is not really of importance for Käsemann in respect of Peter's primacy, but rather because he sees in the author's choice of Peter's authority something of significance in connexion with the changed conception of Apostolic teaching: "It is not for nothing that the pseudonymous author entrenches himself behind the authority of the prince of the Apostles" [5]—his object in fact being to play off Peter against Paul. And the transformation of the idea of Apostolic teaching which he has taken it in hand to bring about is "what has driven him to assume the cloak of pseudonymity. Where Apostolicity is the criterion of legitimate traditional doctrine, it is natural as the defender of such traditions to stand in the shadow of the Apostles." [6] It all looks as if the author, and not indeed *bona fide*, merely in order to sell successfully an idea of doctrine which is no longer Apostolical, "camouflages himself with brazen immodesty behind the mask of the prince of the Apostles." [7] One might even go a step further than Käsemann and in explanation of the epistle adopt the view that it was very probably written

---

[4] Cp. Bartmann, *Lehrbuch der Dogmatik*, 1926, VOL. II, p. 171.
[5] Käsemann, *op. cit.*, p. 279.   [6] *Op. cit.*, pp. 279 ff.   [7] *Op. cit.*, p. 280.

in Rome and at a time when Rome was setting about the task of asserting its primary position by appealing to Peter's primacy, and that it was just this letter which was intended to serve as a means to this end. In that case we might imagine the author to be the leader of a group in the Roman See which would be comparable to that later group of associate forgers who were responsible for the concoction of the pseudo-Isidorian Decretals. Why should we not suppose that in the history of the Church where almost everything has been deemed possible, something of this sort might have been contrived at an early period, just when orthodoxy in its fight against heresy could not afford to be fastidious in its choice of means? [8] For the sake of clarifying the problems by which we are faced, let us suppose our extreme hypothesis to be historically true. Would it even then be possible to recognise in II Peter the authority of an Apostolic writing? In any case, from a purely formal point of view, this question must clearly be answered in the affirmative. We cannot disregard the author's consciousness of representing legitimate Apostolic tradition, and hence of speaking rightly *in* the name and thus, according to Old Testament models, *under* the name of an Apostle. Further the special feature by which he emphatically prefers Peter to Paul is to be explained, apart from the special situation in Rome, in the light of the fact that the Gnostics whom he is attacking apparently appeal to the authority of Paul. The question whether in doing this he has changed the essence of the Apostolic idea should not be confused with the formal question of the pseudonymous authorship as Käsemann confuses it.

(b) The Apostolic authorship

A further point for discussion is the character of the Apostles as eyewitnesses. This is quite clearly throughout the New Testament the presupposition for the transference of the Apostolic commission by the risen Christ, in which respect Paul, as we have seen, is everywhere estimated as equal in status to the eyewitnesses of the pre-Resurrection life of Jesus. But the character of eyewitness is never stressed in such a way as to suggest that it is the factor which secures

[8] Cp. Walter Bauer, *Rechtglaubigkeit und Ketzerei im ältesten Christentum*, 1934, pp. 134 ff.

that continuity with the historical Jesus, in which, as Käse-mann says "orthodoxy saw the guarantee of the correctness of traditional doctrine." [9] The eyewitness as such guarantees nothing at all if he is not at the same time an Apostle; and the Apostle guarantees this continuity by his commission and by Apostolic succession. But not even "orthodoxy saw the guarantee of the correctness of traditional doctrine" in the establishment of continuity with the historical Jesus by means of eyewitnesses as such. In any case it was not the intention of the author of II Peter to adopt this view, otherwise he would have appealed to less esoteric and more clearly established historical facts than the transfiguration of Jesus and the heavenly voice at His baptism (i. 16 ff.) by means of which he might indeed (as was probably his intention) have rivalled the secret esoteric traditions of the Gnostics, but could hardly have brought forward an historical proof. But that he did not intend such facts to serve as an historical proof is shown by the context of the following verses, in which is adduced as the sole possible guarantee of the Apostolic witness (if there can be such a thing) the witness of the Old Testament prophets who spoke, being moved by the Holy Ghost (i. 21). Here we find exactly the same co-ordination of Apostolic witness with the Old Testament Scriptures which we have found in II Tim. III. 16 ff.[10] In either case it would be a very curious type of historical proof, which would rest ultimately on the witness of the Holy Spirit and require for assent to it a faith which would be equally dependent on the working of the Spirit. Here one must agree, even from a purely historical point of view, with what Karl Barth says about the Apostles: "As such they represent above all the indissoluble unity of the new with the old people of God, and the origin of the former in the latter, as in its true root. And thus oddly enough they are primarily a confirmation of the authority of the Old Testament," and, moreover, what he adds is not unimportant: "It is remarkable that the symbol of 381 accepted the connexion with the Old Testament not mainly in its definition of the Church but rather in its description of the Holy Spirit as the founder of the Church: *qui locutus est per sanctos prophetas*." [11]

[9] Käsemann, "Apologie," p. 279.   [10] See above, p. 176.
[11] Barth, *K. D.*, VOL. IV. 1, pp. 805 f.

In spite of all this it cannot be overlooked that in the collection and examination of the New Testament canonical writings the historical question of Apostolic authorship played an essential part. This is understandable in so far as an historically naïve type of thought would inevitably infer from the legitimate standpoint of Apostolic succession that those writings which in fact, by their use in Church worship, had become normative must also be historically the oldest, i.e. of Apostolic authorship. Both points have for us become questionable as a result of the conclusions of historical critical science. Of course it is undeniable that most of the canonical writings are also historically the oldest; but in all probability II Peter is later than the First Epistle of Clement or the *Didache*, neither of which were received into the canon. And the question of Apostolic authorship was left open in the early Church inasmuch as the possibilities of authorship by an Apostle himself and his pupil were considered equally good entitlement.[12] This is only an historical confirmation of the fact that the legitimate standpoint of Apostolical succession, and the illegitimate standpoint that genuine Apostolic tradition can and must be historically secured, were even at that time not compatible and never will be. But we must realise that this observation has serious consequences for the question of the justification of the New Testament canon and its demarcation against later tradition.

*(c) The demarcation of the canon against later tradition
and the doctrine of verbal inspiration*

In this matter there are no difficulties for the Roman Church, which regards the canon merely as a specially important element of tradition but not as something normative and qualitatively distinct from the subsequent living tradition of the Church.[13] Here the apostolicity of the Church is based not only on the Apostolic witness of Scripture, but also and equally on the apostolate of the Episcopal Church secured by the Roman Bishop as the successor of Peter and the authorita-

---

[12] Cp. W. G. Kümmel, "Notwendigkeit und Grenzen des Neutestamentlichen Kanons," in *Z. Th. K.*, 1950, p. 293, n. 3.

[13] For the following, cp. Diem, "Das Problem des Schriftkanons: Die Einheit der Schrift," in *Ev. Th.*, 1953, pp. 385 ff.

tive source of Church doctrine and teaching. Hence it felt no difficulty when critical research revealed the growth of the canon in its historical conditioning, and in particular demonstrated that the acceptance of Apostolic authorship for all the various writings was untenable. On the other hand, since the establishment of these conclusions the Evangelical Church has experienced considerable embarrassment in regard to the exact nature, limits, authority, and unity of the Scriptural canon, because it regards the latter as qualitatively distinct from the later tradition of the Church, and as the valid criterion of all later developments. In view of the conclusions of historical criticism must the Evangelical Church simply surrender its claim for the unique authority of the canon and, as in practice many of its theologians have long since implicitly done, be content with the Catholic view regarding the relation of Scripture and tradition? That would at any rate be a solution to the problem. But before we adopt it, let us first enquire more closely into the real nature of the embarrassment.

It is to be noted that the difficulty did not exist for the Reformers, although at that time, above all in the Protestant world, the limits of the canon were becoming somewhat fluid, not yet for critical reasons but for certain material reasons: part of the Old Testament Scriptures was excluded as "apocryphal," and Luther especially made distinctions of valuation within the New Testament itself and very definitely relegated certain of its writings to the borders of the canon. It was, on the contrary, the Roman Church which in reply sharply re-established at the Council of Trent not only the limits of the canon,[14] but also declared as authentic for Church use the specific text of the Vulgate [15] and that in the very Session IV of 8 April 1546 in which was first discussed the co-ordination of Scripture and tradition, as being of equal authority,[16] whilst later the interpretation of Scripture was reserved for the official teachers of the Church.[17] It is very striking that it was left for the Roman Church, where the importance of Scripture was so severely restricted by tradition and Church teaching, to establish the security of the canon, whilst the Evangelical Church, which based everything upon Scripture, had this considerable freedom with regard to the canon. But obviously

[14] Denz. 784.   [15] Denz. 785.   [16] Denz. 783.   [17] Denz. 786.

this freedom was lost later when the clash between historical research and dogmatic teaching about the Scriptures caused difficulties which did not exist for the Reformers.

The Evangelical Church gave up this freedom only when orthodox Protestantism introduced the doctrine of the verbal inspiration of Scripture, from late Jewish sources and from Roman Catholicism, a doctrine which is not to be found in Scripture itself. The relevant passages in this regard, II Tim. III. 15 f. and II. Pet. I. 20,[18] are concerned chiefly with the Old Testament. But as in both texts the divinely inspired proclamation of the Old Testament is quoted to authenticate Apostolic *paradosis*, which is itself amplified in the writings of the New Testament, what is here said about the inspiration of the Old Testament does in fact cover the whole Biblical Prophetic-Apostolic witness. Karl Barth defines the criterion of any doctrine of inspiration as follows: "The doctrine of inspiration must in any event describe the relation between the Holy Spirit and the Bible in such a way that the whole reality of the unity between the two is brought out just as vividly as the fact that this unity is always a free act of the grace of God and therefore for us always essentially a promise." [19] But there is not to be found in the Bible itself any detailed doctrine of inspiration which explains this relation between the Holy Spirit and the letter of the Bible with reference to the problems involved. We can only observe the fact that in regard to the witness of the Old Testament, with which he places his own witness on an equal footing, the Apostle invokes the exclusive working of the Holy Spirit both as regards the genesis of this witness and its intended effect. Again, with Barth, we may summarise the situation as follows: "The witness stands alongside all other men in face of the mystery of God and the grace of His revelation. In the sheer marvel of his existence as a witness the first thing is that this mystery reveals its secret to him, and the second, that he may communicate it. But once more the mystery of God, now entrusted to a human witness, would have to remain a mystery, as happens with the Synagogue, which has only the γράμμα, and as happens with the life of the world, for which

[18] See above, p. 174, and Diem, *Theol.*, VOL. I, pp. 87 ff.
[19] Barth, *K.D.*, VOL. I. 2, p. 571.

O

the word of the Apostle is and remains folly—if the self-disclosure did not go further, in the form of human witness which it has now assumed, if the same Spirit who created the witness did not bear witness of its truth to the men who read and hear it. The whole process of this self-disclosure may be termed Θεοπνευστία, the inspiration of the word of Apostles and Prophets." [20] As far as the two texts quoted are concerned, there can be no doubt that a verbal inspiration is intended which refers not merely to the thoughts and opinions of the witnesses in a general way, but to the very words they use—not only their meaning. But beyond this nothing is said in the New Testament about a possible change in the human nature of the witnesses, or about an elimination of their personality as authors through the operation of the Holy Spirit, and thus about a material inerrancy of their statements as the later doctrine of verbal inspiration asserts.[21] The lack of theological inerrancy, or inerrancy in other respects, is not contradictory of verbal inspiration as the New Testament understands it, because the unity of God and man realised in Prophetic-Apostolic witness is the work of divine grace, which is and remains free from human control, and hence cannot be materially proved in the Biblical word as such. We cannot reverse the order of events and say that because God binds His word to this testimony, therefore in this testimony we can touch and handle the Word of God Himself. As far as we are concerned "Θεοπνευστία" has reality only as a promise that through this witness and this witness alone the Word of God will disclose itself to us as hearers and readers. Inspiration may not be broken up into its single moments nor "freed from the circle described by the movement in which God reveals Himself by the Spirit and illuminates our minds by the same Spirit. . . . But the question is just this, whether we have not already taken it out of the circle and understood it in terms of verbal inspiredness which we recognise that we owe to the grace of God but which we no longer really feel as grace but

[20] *K.D.*, VOL. I. 2, p. 573.

[21] On the development of this doctrine, cp. Barth, *op. cit.*, pp. 574 ff., where, however, there is no mention of the extremely interesting history of the Jewish doctrine of inspiration relating to the O.T., which is rich in surprising parallels with the history of the N.T. doctrine of Scripture.

rather as a bit of higher nature?" [22]   It is clear why, in consequence, for Catholic theology with its understanding of
Scripture as the *summa veritatis revelatae* there could be no
difficulty, that on the contrary it was exactly such a doctrine
which Catholic theology needed, whereas for Evangelical
theology, even though there had never been such a thing as
critical research, this doctrine must have caused the greatest
embarrassment.

In any event, within the New Testament itself the idea of
verbal inspiration has not yet developed into a doctrine of
verbal inspiredness. So much is clear not only from the few
texts which speak explicitly or implicitly of such inspiration,
but above all from the whole character and practice of Apostolic
proclamation, which is grounded in the self-evidence of the
Word of God in the testimony of Prophets and Apostles. In
this Prophetic-Apostolic witness, which, as Scripture understands it, is the foundation of the Church (Eph. II. 20), lies both
for the historian and the theologian the same state of affairs.
And if the historian endeavours to understand it as it wishes
to be understood, then having regard to its exclusive character
he will not be able to explain it on the basis of general religious,
psychological, or sociological grounds, but he will realise
that he must understand it theologically i.e. as an utterly
underivable, contingent phenomenon—viz. the speech of God
in His self-disclosure through human witnesses. On the other
hand, this will not hinder him—and the theologian least of all
will be allowed to hinder him—from seeing these witnesses in
all their rich humanity and investigating their historical
conditions and circumstances.

Nevertheless, the question remains, both for the historian
and the theologian, how the demarcation of this Apostolic
witness in the canon of Scripture by contrast with later
traditions is to be explained and understood. In this connexion
we must first of all institute an historical enquiry as to how this
demarcation came about. [23] Despite all our efforts it will not
be possible historically to do more, at bottom, than to conclude
that in this process of acceptance or rejection, the canon of

[22] *K. D.*, VOL. I. 2, p. 575.
[23] Cp. on this point, Diem, "Das Problem des Schriftkanons," (above,
p. 199, n. 13), pp. 4-6.

Scripture simply and spontaneously arose on the lines of demarcation eventually fixed, and hence we shall have to agree with Karl Barth, who says: "The recognisable nucleus of the formation of the canon is then simply this, that certain parts of the oldest tradition, amid all sorts of vacillation, gradually in fact established themselves in the appreciation of Christendom, within the various churches—an event which due and formal canonisation by the resolutions of synods and so on could but subsequently confirm. At some time and in some degree (together with everything accidental which this high esteem may have sanctioned) just *these* writings in virtue of the fact that they *were* canonical took care that later it was they which were recognised and proclaimed to be canonical." [24]

(d) The basis of the canon of the New Testament, according to W. G. Kümmel and O. Cullmann

It was not to be supposed that historians would simply accept this theological explanation of the formation of the canon. In particular Werner Georg Kümmel [25] thought it necessary to oppose it on historical grounds. In so doing he himself proposes an historico-theological solution which is so interesting on account of its methods of procedure and so characteristic of the present situation in Evangelical theology that we must examine it in some detail. He considers that Barth's interpretation of the rise of the canon is false and says: "To be sure the Church did not manufacture the canon; but in finally fixing its limits it did not simply observe what *was* canonical as a result of having proved itself to be such, but it set aside by an *authoritative* decree the doubts about the Apostolic authorship of certain writings which had been felt in whole sections of the Church, and thus for the first time *made* those writings widely known to be of canonical status." [26] Since Kümmel agrees with Barth on the decisive issue, viz. that the Church, to be sure, did not manufacture the canon, the controversy would seem to turn simply on the point to what extent the Church acted self-consciously and authoritatively in declaring

---

[24] *K. D.*, vol. i. 2, p. 525.

[25] Kümmel, "Notwendigkeit und Grenzen des Neutestamentlichen Kanons," in *Z. Th. K.*, 1950, pp. 277 f.

[26] Kümmel, *op. cit.*, p. 302, n. 1.

what was canonical. Kümmel does not want to say "that the New Testament canon was in general a conscious creation of the Church." Its growth was rather "a part of the process by which the Church developed and organised itself and not a conscious creation of the Church." [27] It is only with regard to the closure of the canon that he observes: "Thus in its final, irrevocable form the canon is doubtless a conscious creation of the Church; thus in regard to the canon as a fixed entity the organised Church is primary." [28] But what exactly is the meaning of "primary" in this connexion? No one will dispute that the Church was the subject in this process of acceptance and rejection. But the Church did not first as an unorganised quantity, unselfconsciously, and, so to speak, receptively, listen to the reading of the writings and feel their canonical quality while later from a particular moment of time and as a self-conscious body it took the matter into its own hands and fixed the limits of the canon. Canonisation was always rather a conscious process in so far as the adoption of individual writings in the practice of preaching always required either consent or the reverse. What altered, or rather widened, in the course of this process was merely the active subject of these decisions; from individual hearers and readers to churches and groups of churches up to persons and *gremiales* representing the Church as a whole. But at every stage the actors were very conscious of acting as the Church. Hence what can it mean that not in the growth but in the final fixation of the canon the Church was "primary"? What we have here historically is nothing other than the reciprocal influence of the Scriptural canon shaping itself and on the other hand the Church constituted by the preaching of this canon and in turn authorising it. If there must be in this matter a distinction between "primary" and "secondary" then in any event the Apostolic witness would be primary and the demarcation of it by the Church secondary.

But the real opposition between Barth and Kümmel does not arise at the point where Kümmel thinks it necessary to raise his objection. He considers the whole process of the formation of the canon from the point of view, so characteristic of his whole type of thought, of "the development of the form of

[27] *Op. cit.*, p. 294.   [28] *Op. cit.*, p. 215.

the Church,"[29] which explains nothing theologically but merely confuses everything, and says "that the canon of the New Testament must be defined if it is to fulfil the task for which it was created. . . . The canon can secure for the Church the undistorted *kerygma* of the Apostolic age and thus give access to saving historical events only if it is not made superfluous by the fact that oral or written tradition is co-ordinated with or ranked superior to it." [30] Here we see that confusion of historical and theological points of view which is thoroughly typical of the whole present-day discussion of the question.

If we approach the formation of the canon from the point of view of history and the sociology of religion, then we shall conclude that its fixation was necessary. In this case we must agree with Harnack's judgment about the final settlement of the canon: "The age of enthusiasm is past and for the present the Spirit is really—to adopt the phrase of Tertullian (*Adv. Praxeam* i)—banished: it has been banished into a book!" [31] But it is this very point of view which Kümmel does not like. The final closure of the canon should not be regarded as a regrettable mistake in this process of development, but on the contrary he tries to show that it is *essentially* necessary if the canon is to be sharply distinguished from later tradition—a thesis which he adopts in emphatic opposition to the Council of Trent. But in proceeding thus he is making a *dogmatic* judgment which in no way follows from a purely historical survey. He himself seems to have noticed this, and hence he continues: "The necessity for the canon to be essentially fixed can only be appreciated and approved when the once-for-all character of the saving action of God in history is not challenged by the co-ordination with the Apostolic witness of the later Church and its traditions. This view does not make Christianity into a book religion, but, on the contrary, takes seriously the unrepeatableness and the foundation character of primitive Christian history. The witness of the Spirit promised to the Church (Jn. xiv. 16 f., xvi. 12 f.) does not create a new revelation but simply makes possible an ever

---

[29] Kümmel, *op. cit.*, p. 294.

[30] *Op. cit.*, p. 300.

[31] A. V. Harnack, *Die Entstehung des Neuen Testament*, 1914, p. 25, quoted in Kümmel, *op. cit.*, p. 301, n.

new encounter with the unique historical revelation." [32]   In this argument he has of course combined the historical and dogmatic standpoints, and he does so precisely in the same way as Roman Catholic theology, for which the canon is historically the oldest part of tradition, and must be defined for the very reason that Kümmel himself gives, viz. that "the unrepeatableness and foundation character of primitive Christian history" is thereby to be secured. [33]   Kümmel differs from Catholic theology only in the fact that he does not maintain such a neat and systematic historico-dogmatic combination as the latter, but argues somewhat capriciously, now historically, now theologically, and now with a mixture of the two. This is shown in the way in which he thinks of "the ever new encounter with the unique historical revelation," which means, for him, "with the unrepeatable primitive history as it comes before us within the fixed canon." Naturally he will not adopt the Catholic view of the mediatorial role of the Church and its traditions, for he cannot admit that the historical revelation as finally fixed within the limits of the canon can in this way be extended through the history of the Church. How then does he proceed?

He asks first of all whether the canon as traditionally fixed has been *appropriately* "limited or not, and whether we can and must retain this limitation in the sense intended by the early Church." [34]   In this connexion, the reference of the writings to Apostolic authorship, which even in the ancient Church could not fully succeed, must, in accordance with critical conclusions, be completely surrendered as a valid criterion of canonical quality. [35]   It follows irresistibly that we can no longer pose the question of the limits of the canon of the New Testament by resuming the discussions of the third, fourth, and sixteenth centuries, [36] as contemporary dogmatics still try to do. [37]   It is no longer merely a question of the right limitation of the canon

---

[32] Kümmel, *op. cit.*, pp. 300 ff.

[33] For this combination of historical and dogmatic judgments in the Roman argument, cp. Diem, "Das Problem des Schriftkanons," pp. 7 ff.

[34] Kümmel, "Notwendigkeit und frenzen des neutestamentlichen Kanons," p. 301.

[35] *Op. cit.*, p. 304.   [36] *Op. cit.*, p. 305.

[37] He instances E. Brunner and W. Elert.

with respect to the writings which up to recently have been subject to debate. "Rather the decisive point is whether the traditional canon of the ancient Church has been appropriately limited or not, not merely with reference to certain of its writings but *as a whole*." In this respect everything depends on what Kümmel understands by the word "appropriately".

He then attempts to establish a chronological criterion, and once again turns to historical arguments. Since the canon is for him the testimony to early Christian history,[38] "it is clear that writings which were composed after a certain point of time, for instance after the first quarter of the second century, can no longer be regarded as original witnesses and hence cannot be included in the canon," [39] for which reason the Muratorian Canon rightly excluded the *Shepherd of Hermas*. Naturally this chronological test can only be used negatively, as a ground for exclusion, but not positively, since otherwise the First Epistle of Clement and perhaps also the letters of Ignatius would have to be included. By this formal criterion "the Church must be granted the right to exclude again any document which finally found its way into the New Testament if it can be *securely* proved that such a writing dates from a period outside the chronological limits of the Apostolic *kerygma*." [40]   But, "on the other hand, as is clear from the example of the First Epistle of Clement, the question whether a newly discovered document should be accepted or one hitherto regarded as canonical should be excluded should in no case be decided merely by the chronological factor, but must in decisive fashion be clarified by consideration of the content of the writing concerned" [41]—a concession which makes the whole formal criterion practically useless. Besides this, Kümmel says—and now he is again arguing theologically —"such an act modifying the canon of the ancient Church could only be more than a further fortuitous historical event if the whole of Christendom agreed to it, which is hardly conceivable." [42]   If, however, such an act modifying the canon were today completed with the consensus of the whole Church, and thus were more than a further fortuitous historical event, then it is really difficult to see why the original fixation

[38] Kümmel, *op. cit.*, p. 301.   [39] *Op. cit.*, p. 306.
[40] *Op. cit.*, p. 307.   [41] *Ibid.*   [42] *Ibid.*

of the canon which was effected in this manner was not itself such an act, and therewith the whole elaborate argument becomes unnecessary. But perhaps Kümmel wished to bring this chronological criterion into the discussion in order to show how its use leads to an absurdity. In any case he once more gives up the question of an appropriate limitation of the canon and says: "We must recognise the authoritative decision of the ancient Church with regard to the canon as a given fact and admit that we are unable to justify, by intrinsic reasons, its precise extent." [43] It is simply not clear whether he establishes this point resignedly as an historian, or whether as a theologian he values the "authoritative decision"—or whether in the end he does both at the same time—especially as he goes on, "we do not mean that the decision of the ancient Church should have for us the character of a binding norm," and indeed— and now again he argues historically—"for the simple reason that this decision was not universally recognised right into the sixteenth century, but especially because we know that it was made in view of materially untenable opinions concerning the Apostolic origin of particular writings." [44] That decision is only for us "the sole possible starting point for a necessary consideration of what must be the norm for faith within the limits of the canon as given." The questions as to how we can find an appropriate limitation of the canon and as to "the living encounter" with "primitive history" have now been reduced to this once more theological question. Now the situation is, as Luther's formula puts it, "that that is canonical 'which preaches and practises Christ'." [45] The diversity of the various Biblical testimonies makes no difficulty for Kümmel —unlike Käsemann in this respect; rather it is necessary "because only a collection of varied witnesses, i.e. the canon, can adequately bring us into contact with the primitive Christian kerygma," though it should be noted "that this manifold testimony has normative significance for all times not because it stands in the canon but because it stands in a temporally and materially near relation to the historical revelation of Christ." Thus there arises as the critical criterion that a writing or a section "must be reckoned all the more surely as part of the regulative canon, the more plainly the

[43] *Ibid.*   [44] *Ibid.*   [45] *Op. cit.,* p. 308.

text points to the historical revelation of Christ and the less it is modified by extra-Christian thoughts and later Christian problems." [46] The application of this criterion consists in a comparative study "of the message and figure of Jesus as we find it in the oldest form of the Synoptic tradition, of the oldest form of the *kerygma* in the primitive Christian community, which interpreted the life and Passion of Jesus and bore witness to His Resurrection, and of the first attempts to think out the implications of this *kerygma* in the theology of Paul. . . . If as a result of strict historical and theological research it can be shown that there follows from the composite view of these three oldest forms of the New Testament kerygma a Gospel proclamation which is unified in its main features, then we have reached the establishment of a central Gospel message by which the rest of the New Testament witness can be measured." [47] By the use of this criterion resulting from historical work, there can no doubt be shown a difference in the degree to which the single writings of the New Testament approximate to the central *kerygma*—"only the brief Epistle of Jude contains no central proclamation of the Christ" [48]— and also more or less considerable contradictions to it. But there can be no question of rejecting specific writings from the canon for these reasons, if only because similar contradictions and divergences can also be found among the exponents of the central body of the *kerygma*. "Thus the real line of demarcation for the canon of the New Testament runs through the midst of the canon itself," [49] and must be recognised and defined ever afresh. "The limit of the canon of the New Testament is thus historically fixed, but in fact it must be determined ever anew." By this approach we gain the freedom to regard and use as a real norm the central proclamation of the Christ which we can establish on the basis of this historical perspective . . . and without having to succumb to the temptation to consider every word of the New Testament as normative simply because it was accepted as part of the Church collection of Apostolic writings." [50]

In this way, and by means of his strict historico-theological approach, Kümmel seems to have succeeded in restoring the

[46] Kümmel, *op. cit.*, p. 309.   [47] *Op. cit.*, p. 310.   [48] *Op. cit.*, p. 311.
[49] *Op. cit.*, p. 312.   [50] *Ibid.*

position of the canon which, as a dogmatic factor, historical criticism had attacked, and in securing it, if not acceptably to any doctrine of inspiration, yet in its essential character. Since his conclusions are relatively conservative with regard to the traditional limits of the canon, and since he represents also and especially the Evangelical interest in defining the canon as against later accretions of tradition, accepted by Catholicism, his solutions are likely to be welcomed. We, however, are of the opinion that these are only apparent solutions which evade the real problem. This applies in the first instance to questions of historical science. This today, as in the work of Vielhauer and Käsemann, reaches far more radical conclusions with regard to the possibility of finding a unified witness to Christ in the New Testament and we cannot imagine how Kümmel can contradict such opinions on the basis of his own presuppositions. Moreover, Kümmel must join issue with the historians as regards the valid usefulness of his "historico-theological" method. In the sequence of our own argument we are especially concerned about whether he has succeeded in defining the canon as against later tradition and in polemic against the Council of Trent.

We must once more return to his polemic against Karl Barth. He says with regard to Barth's thesis that in the growth of the canon what in the last resort was accepted as canonical was that which had proved itself to be such: "Barth's assertion, while it corresponds to the Catholic view, overlooks the fact that the canon in its final form is a fortuitous historical factor and thus is contingent like every historical factor." [51] But it is just this contingence which is stressed as strongly as possible by Barth, since he does not, like Kümmel, consider the Canon as essentially closed but only as factually so. Hence Kümmel cannot legitimately proceed: "If the Church had merely established what already had proved itself to be canonical, then even Barth should not later require that 'the Church does not from the outset close its mind with regard to further enlightenment concerning the scope of what has been entrusted to its keeping as canonical'." [52] One should say exactly the opposite: just because the Church only established what had

[51] *Op. cit.*, p. 302, n. 1.
[52] *Op. cit.*, p. 302, n. 1.

already proved itself to be canonical, and did not delimit the canon according to its own specific principles, it should fundamentally be prepared for the possibility of a change in the situation with regard to the canon.

We must now enquire more closely what is meant by the fundamental as opposed to the factual finality of the canon. When for instance Kümmel stresses "the necessity for the canon to be in principle closed " [53] he is, as we have seen, concerned that the "uniqueness of the saving action of God in history should not be imperilled by the co-ordination of later Church tradition with the Apostolic witness," he wants to secure "the unrepeatability and the foundation character of primitive Christian history." [54]   But in this respect the Roman Church, which also regards the canon as in principle closed, could fully agree with him.   And this very fact shows that a fundamental finality of the canon is of no avail to protect Scripture from being overlaid by later tradition at all events.   But this simply means shifting the ground of the problem to the next question, which is how revelation in its historical uniqueness and contingency can later become a vivid present reality.   And how magnificently the Roman Church succeeds in doing this through the *praesens perpetuum* of the Church can be followed in the work of Gerhard Ebeling.[55]   But with regard to the question of the fundamental finality of the canon, if this is affirmed, it cannot primarily be a matter of for what reasons this is considered essential, but on what grounds it can be based.   Kümmel and the Roman Church would really have to base it, by the exigencies of their thought, on the view that in the canon are contained in complete form the Apostolic testimonies to primitive Christian history and hence that the Church has included in the canon all the relevant witnesses and that therefore there can be no question of a revision of limits.   This presupposition is implicitly contained in the decisions of the Council of Trent with regard to the canon, and hence the argument of Catholic theology can proceed in such a way that the historical and theological reasons support each other and yet the burden of proof lies in the last resort on dogma

[53] Kümmel, *op. cit.*, p. 300.   [54] *Op. cit.*, p. 301.
[55] See G. Ebeling, "Die Bedeutung der historisch-kritischen Methode," in *Z. Th. K.*, 1950, p. 20.

alone. But Kümmel cannot make the same presupposition,
and thus in his corresponding combination of historical and
theological reasons he cannot go beyond merely probable
historical judgments by which a fundamental finality of the
canon can never be securely grounded.

Quite a different attempt to justify the canon and to secure
it against the Roman principle of tradition has been made by
Oscar Cullmann.[56] He thinks that he can observe around the
year 150 not only a far-reaching consensus of the Church as
regards which writings were worthy of acceptance into the
canon, but a decision of the Church in favour of the canonical
principle: "When the church of the second century demanded
a canon (it is a question of the principle underlying the
canon rather than of its final form) she did not merely resolve
to meet prevalent dangers and especially that of *gnosis*. She
made a decision which involved the whole future of the
Church." [57] "By introducing the principle of the canon the
Church recognised that from now on tradition in itself was
not a criterion of truth. She underlined Apostolic tradition
and thus declared that henceforth every later tradition must
be checked by the tradition of the Apostolic age." [58] If this
is supposed to be an historical judgment one must ask in what
way the Church in this connexion, which "itself created in
principle the canon," [59] can have acted thus as subject and
have made decisions of this fundamental nature. One may
well imagine that in individual churches the need arose
gradually to acquire a basic form of Gospel proclamation
which would be binding on all Christians and thus would help
in the struggle to resist the pullulation of eccentric traditions.
But the question would still remain by what organs the Church
of that time could emerge effectively in action, and in virtue of
what competence it could have made a decision of this kind
involving the whole future. But Cullmann goes further and
wishes to establish the fact of a fundamental decision not only
with regard to the "what" but also with regard to the "that"
of the canon. And he insists on deriving this decision not only
from needs connected with the sociology of religion but from
causes of an historical-theological nature: "Is it, however,

[56] See O. Cullmann, *Tradition*, 1954.   [57] Cullmann, *op. cit.*, p. 47.
[58] *Op. cit.*, p. 45.   [59] *Op. cit.*, p. 44.

permissible to ascribe to the growth of the canon such a degree of importance for the process of saving history? Are we not thus attributing to the Church of the second century, from which the idea of the canon arose, a quite unusual kind of importance? It must be recognised that this was a decisive event for the age of the Church. On the one hand, *c.* 150 the Church was near enough to the time of the Apostles to be able, with the help of the Holy Spirit, to sift oral and written tradition. On the other hand, the frightening proliferation of Gnostic and legendary traditions had made the Church ripe for this act of humility, for the submission of all later inspiration to a certain norm. In no other period of Church history could the formation of the canon have been carried out. At that time God endowed the Church with grace to recognise the distinction between the age of the Incarnation and the age of the Church.'' [60]

We are here again faced by a combination of historical and theological arguments, by means of which it is attempted to justify, in opposition to the Roman Church, the superiority of Scripture to later tradition, and this time by the use of the idea of saving history which rests on the distinction between the age of the Incarnation and the age of the Church. Here, too, the Roman Church might agree, though for other historico-theological reasons, and with an intention opposite to that of Cullmann. The latter wishes to establish Scripture as a norm and thus make it superior to later tradition, while the former, by its dogmatic attitude towards the canon of Scripture, wishes so to foreshadow the later doctrine and tradition of the Church as to make it impossible for such accretions to be called in question by Scripture itself. The only question is which of the two succeeds the better. Cullmann buttresses his historico-theological idea ''that the time of the Apostles is the centre of all times'' with the historical consideration that the problem of ''Scripture and tradition'' is really the problem of ''Apostolic and post-Apostolic tradition,'' and in this connexion he uses the word ''Apostolic'' in a strictly historical sense.[61] Thus he comes to the conclusion that the Church established the canon, taking care to accept only writings of Apostolic origin,[62] and in regard to the historically dubious

[60] Cullmann, *op. cit.*, p. 47.   [61] *Op. cit.*, p. 7.   [62] *Op. cit.*, p. 34.

origin of some of these writings he gets out of his difficulty by suggesting that even those "which were not composed by Apostles themselves intend to be a direct expression of the eyewitness accounts and testimony of Apostles," [63] which, however, some of the non-canonical writings also intended to be. Is Apostolic authorship really essential or not in the strictly historical sense, if non-Apostolic writings could also become canonical? But we may not question Cullmann so sharply, otherwise he simply shifts from his historical line of thought to his idea of saving history, where such historical exactitude is no longer relevant, where the deciding factor is rather belief in an age specifically qualified as the time of the Incarnation. Both currents of thought run together again when he remarks "that the Scriptural principle on account of the natural consequences which it implies for theological method is in harmony with the scholar's motto 'ad fontes'. This is the true place of meeting between historical science and Protestant theology." [64]

We fear that neither historical science nor Protestant theology are well served, and that there can be no genuine contact between them when the position of the question is changed in this way according to convenience. That Catholic theology can do this much better, and that even the "ad fontes" solution is better adapted to it, was soon noticed by humanists, such as Erasmus, of the Reformation period. But as in the case of Kümmel's primitive Church there arises for this "time of the Incarnation" the problem of its present realisation, and on this Cullmann says: "If we believe with the early Christians that the divine institution of the Apostolate had the purpose, in the economy of salvation, of conveying directly the divine revelation in Christ, to the exclusion of all intermediate links which would have been an inevitable source of misrepresentation, then we must pay heed to this plan of God and entrust to the Apostolate in our modern Church the same task. Hence there is secured for us in the New Testament the real presence of the Apostles in the Church of all time, but we can only recognise it in so far as we ourselves, excluding all intermediate links, seek the immediate encounter with these witnesses." [65] How are we to conceive of this

[63] *Ibid.*   [64] *Op. cit.*, p. 35.   [65] *Op. cit.*, p. 36.

twofold *immediacy* of realisation? In the first place what is
implied is that the divine revelation was conveyed to the
Apostles directly and in such a way as to exclude the possibility
of error, but by this we can imagine nothing else than a
revelation taking place under the verbal dictation of the Holy
Spirit which must have the effect of excluding especially the
worst source of error, namely the humanity of the Apostles,
and thus producing a text that is absolutely inerrant. Did
Cullmann really mean this? And in the second place what is
implied is our own immediate encounter with the Apostolic
witnesses which eliminates all intermediate links. Frankly we
cannot imagine what this can mean. For even if we suppose
this to mean the vivid presentation of Apostolic witness in
the word of preaching we cannot eliminate as intermediate
links the preacher himself in his humanity nor the whole
tradition of exposition and proclamation in which he stands.
What Cullmann has in view here seems to us something
impersonal and inhuman, for it does not reckon with the fact
that "the Word became flesh" and so became involved in a
human history, which, however, we do not wish to interpret as
Kümmel does when he concludes his study with the words,
which mean everything and nothing: "For the believer the
uncertainty with regard to the limits of the New Testament
Canon is a reflexion of the Incarnation of the *Logos*." [66]

(e) *The Reformers' re-discovery of Scripture in its significance as a theme for preaching and the repudiation of this view by the Council of Trent*

We cannot admit that either of these attempts, so characteristic
of the present theological situation, to delimit the canon of
Scripture as against later tradition, has succeeded in giving
a satisfactory reply to the Tridentine conception of the relation
between Scripture and tradition. We can and must agree
with them in so far as they endeavour to understand the
formation of the canon as a once-for-all contingent event, as
of course the Catholic Church does likewise. But instead of
leaving this historical fact in its contingency, they destroy it,
since each in its own way tries to connect it with historical

[66] Kümmel, "Notwindigkeit und Grenzen des Neutestamentlichen
Kanons," p. 313.

and theological reasons, and so in the place of a *factual* closure of the canon they set an *essential* closure—again like the Catholic church. If we, on the other hand, remain satisfied with the contingent event of the formation of the canon, we ourselves have to answer the question how we propose to define the canon as against later tradition, and also the further question how today we can realise the truth of the canon as thus delimited. If in considering these questions we turn to the Reformers we must notice that for them the second question came first. Gerhard Ebeling says: "The opposition between Protestantism and Catholicism rests on their different understanding of the way in which the ἅπαξ (the uniqueness) of revelation is to be made real for us today. The Reformation takes the colossal step of reducing the present realisation of the historical ἅπαξ to faith alone." [67] With the Confession of Augsburg, Art. V, we might define this "in faith" more closely by saying that this realisation is effected by that faith which is born in the heart of the hearer as he listens to the preaching of the Gospel. The decisive objection of the Reformers to the Roman Church is that the latter can no longer *preach*. In that Church the voice of Christ has passed into Scripture and, indistinguishably from the latter, into the tradition of the Church, and now it can merely be heard speaking through the mouth of the Church, but it can no longer critically address the Church. Proclamation made by the teaching office of the Church, which has incorporated into itself Christ and the Holy Ghost, can now reflect only the communing of the Church with its own tradition, it cannot transcend such self-communing. Hence the whole effort of the Reformation was concentrated on restoring the real *event* of Gospel proclamation in preaching; that it thus rediscovered the significance of Holy Scripture as the basis of preaching was its essential service and it also clearly raised the question of the relation of Scripture and tradition. The Reformers only incidentally and peripherally appealed to the argument of the historical priority of the canon to the later tradition of the Church, and they did so only under the influence of the humanists and their cry *"ad fontes."* This was not their fundamental standpoint. They did not attack the doctrine

[67] Ebeling, *op. cit.* (above, p. 212, n. 55), p. 20.

P

of the Roman Church about the relation of Scripture and tradition, which in fact was first defined only by the Council of Trent in its desire to counter the Reformation, but by going back to Scripture as the basis of preaching they in practice neutralised the Roman custom of setting tradition above Scripture. With this discovery of Scripture as the basis for preaching they at the same time went back historically behind the degeneration of primitive Christianity into Catholicism to authentic Scripture itself in its self-understanding, for they realised that in the Catholic world Scripture was no longer allowed to preach its true message. In this work they did not need to evolve a doctrine of the canon of Scripture and its relation to later tradition, or to establish historically the exact moment of the degeneration of primitive Christianity, as we with our more precise knowledge of the growth of the canon are tempted to do. Nor did it occur to them to see in such epochs moments of significance in saving history. All this they could quietly leave to their adversaries. They were fully satisfied with faith in the self-evidencing authority of Scripture as it makes itself felt in the event of preaching. For this purpose they did not need any doctrine about the essential foundations of the canon, but they simply made practical use of its contingent givenness and took all sorts of liberties with its limits.

But of course it was inevitable that both sides should give account theologically of their relation to Scripture. As we have seen the Catholic Church did so first by its comprehensive theological definition of canonical Scripture in the Council of Trent. By this doctrine it neutralised the event of preaching as the living voice of Scripture, for it replaced the idea of the canon as something empirically given by that of the canon as something essentially determined, and adapted it to its doctrine of tradition by explaining it to be the oldest part of tradition. And it had to do this because it could not allow everything to depend on the preaching of Scripture and thus let Scripture become established as the criterion of Church doctrine and teaching. This event has its exact parallels as far as the Old Testament is concerned in the Synod of Jamnia c. A.D. 100, where in the debate between Pharisees and Sadducees the following points were accepted as marks of the canonical: (1) inspiration, (2) sanctity, (3) the number of the books, and (4) the firmness and purity of the text. Just as in pre-Tridentine Christianity, there were also in Judaism, prior to this synod, all kinds of controversial doctrines about Scripture and its relation to tradition, but no comprehensively defined and officially promulgated dogma. Up to that time the unity of the Old Testament Synagogue and the New Testament Church rested on the empirical existence of the canon and the preaching of it. After the canon had in fact found acceptance in the Church, Athanasius in his Easter letter of 367 counted 27 writings as necessarily to be accepted as part of the canon, and this is generally regarded as the terminal point in the growth of the canon. But of course he had not the competence to speak in the name, and with the authority, of the Church as a whole. Later on, certain provincial synods decided to accept the canon as thus defined without any Ecumenical Council confirming their decision. This took place for the first time in the Council of Florence of 1441, where, in the interests of negotiations for reunion with the Eastern Church, the doctrines of the unity of the Old and New Testaments, of the inspiration of Scripture, and its extent, were dogmatically formulated, and then at the Council of Trent this formulation was more comprehensively renewed for the purpose of countering the Reformation. Thus the dogmatic definition takes place pre-eminently—again in exact parallel to the canonisation of the Old Testament at the Synod of Jamnia—at a time when the unity of the Church as based on the unity of Scripture can no longer be taken for granted, but when the Roman Church, which in practice has become a single confessional Church, feels compelled to make this dogma into an article of faith—*fides quae creditur*—in order to maintain over against the other confessional churches its claim to be the true Church of Christ.

(f) The theological justification of its use of Scripture given by the Church of the Reformation

How did the Church of the Reformation justify its own use of Scripture in reply to this teaching? Let us compare with the Roman doctrine of Scripture the Confession of Württemberg, for example, of 1551, which is especially important for our question, because not only do the definitions of the 1546 Council of Trent lie before it, but also because it was intended to represent the Reformed position at the subsequent council. It says, in Art. XXVII, concerning Holy Scripture: "Holy Scripture we call the official confirmed books of the Old and New Testaments about whose authenticity [68] there has never been any doubt in the churches." [69]   After thus simply accepting the factual givenness of the Scriptural canon, it goes on: "Further, we believe and confess that this Scripture is a true and certain preaching of the Holy Ghost, which is so authorised by heavenly witnesses that if an angel from heaven were to preach otherwise he should be cursed. For the same reason we reject all teaching worship and religion which are contrary to this Scripture." Thus the authority of Holy Scripture lies in its character as proclamation, which rests on the inspiration of the Holy Spirit speaking through the Apostles: "What, however, the Apostles received from Christ they spread abroad by their preaching throughout the whole world and conveyed to posterity in their writings. Hence it is clear that everything which is necessary for our salvation is contained in the writings of the Apostles and Prophets." [70] This is proved by means of a quotation from Chrysostom, among others: "I have been assured that in his day he revealed his word through the office of the preacher, in discourses. For the Gospel contains in itself everything, both present and future, the honour of God, the service of God, faith, in fact all has been included in preaching." Thus as regards the relation of Scripture and subsequent tradition it is simply observed without further justification, that as a matter of fact Scripture alone is given to us as the text for preaching. And in reply to the attempt to reserve the right of interpreting Scripture to the official teachers of the Church, it is said: "Thus the gift of interpreting Scripture shall not be so confined to the Papacy that any one who became Pope would be deemed to expound Scripture aright, but the true understanding of Scripture is implicit in Scripture itself and is found in

[68] Or "power and authenticity" (v.l. "de quorum auctoritate").

[69] Confessio Virtembergica: Das württembergische Bekenntnis von 1551. ed. E. Bizer, Stuttgart 1952, cited below as Conf. Virt., p. 178.

[70] Conf. Virt., p. 179.

those who are so inspired by the Holy Ghost that they seek to expound Scripture in the light of Scripture." [71] Thus Scripture empirically given in the canon as the theme for preaching proves its authority not merely by the fact that it is actually preached, but makes the truth of its witness evident in so far as it is interpreted in its own light.

Thus the authors of the Confession of Württemberg in no way allowed themselves to be misled by the confessional self-definition of the Roman Church in its Tridentine doctrine of Scripture, nor were they tempted to occupy the same ground in their repudiation of that doctrine, by establishing, for their part, any excessively specific articles of belief about Scripture, as *fides quae creditur*. The theological justification which they give for their own use of Scripture, in contra-distinction to later tradition, consists simply in the observation of the actual givenness of Scripture for preaching, its all-sufficiency and self-evidencing authority. Hence at the decisive point the authors were faithful to the claim of the Reformers "to have remained in and of the Church, to have remained in the one common order of Christendom, and to have founded no new order. [72] This gives them the right to say in the foreword, corresponding to the final affirmations of the Confession of Augsburg, "that in our churches no ground has been yielded to any other teaching than that of the right, true, Apostolic, Catholic and orthodox doctrine of Christendom." [73]

Other Reformed confessions follow the same lines in so far as they at all contain any special doctrine of Scripture, and this is especially true of the Reformed Church. We may cite, in this respect, the *Confessio Helvetica prior*, 1536, Arts. I-III, but much more detailed is the *Confessio Helvetica posterior*, 1566, Art. I: "*Credimus et confitemur scripturas canonicas sanctorum prophetarum et apostolorum utriusque testamenti ipsum verum esse verbum Dei: et authoritatem sufficientem ex semetipsis non ex hominibus habere. Nam Deus ipse loquutus est patribus, prophetis, et apostolis, et loquitur adhuc nobis per scripturas sanctas. . . .*" This present speech of God addressing us takes place through Holy Scripture: "*Proinde cum hodie hoc verbum per praedicatores*

[71] *Conf. Virt.*, p. 180.   [72] Cp. Diem, *Theol.*, VOL. I, pp. 261 ff.
[73] *Conf. Virt.*, p. 138.

legitime vocatos annunciatur in ecclesia, credimus ipsum Die verbum annunciare, et a fidelibus recipi, neque aliud Dei verbum vel fingendum vel coelitus esse exspectandum: atque in praesenti spectandum esse ipsum verbum, quod annunciatur, non annunciantem ministrum, qui etsi sit malus et peccator, verum tamen et bonum manet nihilominus verbum Dei. . . ." All heresies are rejected, including those of the Manicheans, Valentinians, Marcionites, etc., *"qui negarunt scripturas e Spiritu sancto profectas: vel quasdam illarum non receperunt, vel interpolarunt et corruperunt."* The Apocrypha is distinguished from the other writings of the Old Testament in the same way as happens with Luther. About the interpretation of Scripture Art. II says: *"illam . . . scripturarum interpretationem pro orthodoxa et genuina agnoscimus, quae ex ipsis est petita scripturis . . . cum regula fidei et caritatis congruit, et ad gloriam Dei hominumque salutem eximie facit."* Church traditions cannot be recognised as apostolical if they deviate from Scripture. *"Sicut enim apostoli inter se diversa non docuerunt, ita et apostolici non contraria apostolis ediderunt. Quinimo impium esset asseverare apostolos viva voce contraria scriptis suis tradidisse."* [74] The Scots Confession of 1560 speaks of the doctrine of Scripture in Art. XVIII ("Of the Notis, be the quhilk the trewe Kirk is decernit fra the false, and quha sall be Judge of the Doctrine." The three characteristics of the true Church are defined as "the trew preaching of the Worde of God, . . . the right administration of the Sacraments of *Christ Jesus* . . . and Ecclesiastical discipline uprightlie ministered," all on the basis of the Word of God, "into the quhilk God hes revealed himselfe unto us, as the writings of the Prophets and Apostles dois declair." The Scottish Reformers claim to have restored this true Church in their sphere, "for the doctrine taucht in our Kirkis, conteined in the writen Worde of God, to wit, in the buiks of the Auld and New Testamentis, in those buikis we meane quhilk of the ancient (*ab infantia usque Ecclesiae*) have been reputed canonicall. In the quhilk we affirme, that all things necessary to be beleived for the salvation of mankinde is sufficiently expressed." About the exposition of Scripture it is said: "The interpretation quhairof . . . neither appertaines to

---

[74] *Bekenntnisschriften und Kirchenordnungen der nach Gottes Wort reformiertne Kirche*, ed. W. Niesel, 2nd edn., 1930, henceforth cited as *Bek. Schr.*, pp. 222-5.

private nor publick persone, neither zit to ony Kirk, for ony preheminence or prerogative, personallie or locallie, quhilk ane hes above ane uther, bot apperteines to the Spirite of God, be the quhilk also the Scripture was written. When controversie then happines, for the right understanding of . . . Scripture, or for the reformation of ony abuse within the Kirk of God, we ought not sa meikle to luke what men before us have said or done, as unto that quhilk the halie Ghaist uniformelie speakes within the body of the Scriptures, and unto that quhilk Christ Jesus himselfe did, and commanded to be done. For this is ane thing universallie granted, that the Spirite of God, quhilk is the Spirite of unitie, is in nathing contrarious unto himselfe." [75] Hence if some opinion contradicts another Scriptural text then it cannot be right. The essential point is, as we are told in Art. XIX, "Of the Authoritie of the Scriptures," that this authority depends "nether . . . on men nor angelis" but is the authority of God Himself. For this reason it is blasphemy to concede to Scripture only so much authority as the Church admits it to have. For the Church "alwaies heares and obeyis the voice of her awin Spouse and Pastor [Jn. x. 27]; bot takis not upon her to be maistres over the samin." [76]

[75] *Scots Confession (Confessio Scoticana), 1560*, ed. G. D. Henderson, Edinburgh 1937, pp. 73 f.
[76] *Op. cit.*, p. 79.

CHAPTER IX

THE UNITY OF SCRIPTURE

THE pivot of this theological justification of the use of Scripture is clearly the strong emphasis on the unity of the Bible which in fact is implicit in the capacity of Scripture to interpret itself. But in what way can this unity be best exploited in Scriptural exposition, and then further in preaching and doctrine? Reformation thought on the doctrine of the Scriptures continues to develop through the endeavour to answer this question of hermeneutics. On this subject, G. Heinrici writes: [1] "The Reformers contented themselves with the formulation of leading principles which were summed up in the doctrine *'Scriptura scripturae interpres'*. But this formula is not immediately clear. If the text of Scripture is from the start paraphrased and distorted by dogmatic postulates, then such a formula opens the door to the penetration of strange feats of finesse or very unbalanced points of view. And in fact the Protestant doctrine of Scripture did not escape this danger, for to the principle *'Scriptura scripturae interpres'* was added as something of equal value *'Omnis intellectus ac expositio scripturae sit analogia fidei'* (Rom. XII. 6). After Luther this is done most decisively by M. Flacius,[2] who with A. Hyperius [3] is the greatest theoretical exponent of classical Protestant hermeneutics. Even when he is speaking of a *'sensus mysticus'* or *'compositus'* or *'duplex'*, he does not consider that the Holy Spirit intended us to see independently of the literal sense a second meaning; it is merely a question of applying the literal sense. But the *analogia fidei*, just because of its clear-cut definition, becomes increasingly a handy touchstone which is used either concurrently with or preferably to scripture itself; the former when

[1] In *Realencyclopaedie für protestantische Theologie und Kirche*, 3rd edn., VOL. VII, pp. 718 ff.

[2] See M. Flacius, *Clavis scripturae sacrae*, 1567, II, reg. xvii.

[3] See M. Hyperius, *De recte formando theologico studio*, 1582, I. IV.

as the '*harmonia dictorum Biblicorum*' (Hollaz) it fetters the interpretation in detail, the latter when it is plainly regarded as the '*summa quaedam coelestis doctrinae*' (J. Gerhard), especially when this *summa*, as though this were a matter of course, is equated with the contents of the symbolic books. . . ."

(a) The post-Reformation deviation from the unity of Scriptural proclamation to the unity of doctrine

This method of solving the hermeneutical problem dogmatically successfully established itself in classical Protestantism and for a long time determined the relations of dogmatics to Scripture. Thus the unity of Scripture was resolved into the unity of a doctrinal system, which was superimposed on the texts of Scripture. In the course of this development the rule was in principle retained that all doctrine was to be tested by Scripture. But it became ever more dubious how Scripture was in practice to fulfil this function of arbitration if from the outset it was presupposed that its interpretation must correspond with a specific *summa doctrinae*.

It is obvious that the authors of the *Konkordienformel* were no longer aware of this contradiction, since they gave as the heading to the introductory section of the *Solida Declaratio*: "*De compendaria doctrinae forma fundamento, norma atque regula, ad quam omnia dogmata iuxta analogiam verbi Dei diiudicanda.* . . ." [4] It must be accepted that the body of doctrine here expounded has already been put together by inference from the Word of God, *iuxta analogiam verbi Dei*, and hence yields the criterion by which all doctrinal controversies can be settled according to this analogy. Thus it cannot be of much use when later among the other writings contained in the *corpora doctrinae* Holy Scripture is expressly mentioned in the first place and it is said with regard to it: "*sacras litteras solas unicam et certissimam illam regulam esse credimus, ad quam omnia dogmata exigere et secundum quam de omnibus tum doctrinis tum doctoribus iudicare opporteat*," [5] and then after enumerating individual writings which "*in purioribus ecclesiis et scholis semper habita fuere pro compendiaria hypotyposi seu forma sanae doctrinae*," [6] it is added that this body of doctrine was founded on God's word by D. Luther,

[4] *Bek. Schr.* (above, p. 222, n. 74), p. 833.
[5] *Op. cit.*, p. 834.   [6] *Op. cit.*, p. 836.

who in his writings *"hoc discrimen (inter divina et humana scripta)*
perspicue posuit, solas videlicet sacras litteras pro unica regula et norma
omnium dogmatum agnoscendas, iisque nullius omnino hominis scripta
adaequanda, sed potius omnia subiicienda esse." [7]　The question
remains whether this *"sana doctrina"* which Luther brought to
light, and which was approved in pure schools and churches,
was once for all tested by the criterion of Scripture and stood
that test, or, if not, how Scripture can in practice still fulfil its
function of arbitration with regard to it?　In fact, it cannot
be otherwise than that the *norma normans* of Scripture has been
absorbed and rendered inoperative by the *norma normata* of the
confessional documents, as the history of the Lutheran Church
shows up to the present time.　In this respect the decisive
development undergone by the Reformation was effected by
the Lutheran confessional Church. [8]

As regards the Reformed Churches this development took
place on slightly different lines, since there the *regula fidei*, with
which, even according to the *Confessio Helvetica*, [9] the exposition
of Scripture must agree, was not considered to be so unassail-
ably secured in confessional writings.　For this reason the
Biblicist procedure of harmonisation in the interests of establishing correct doctrine played so much greater a part, with
the result that it was felt possible to read off doctrine from
Scripture.　As Heinrich Heppe (who summarises Reformed
doctrine on the basis of its sources) [10] observes, Holy Scripture
is "the principle underlying theology as a whole, the exclusive
norm of Christian doctrine, and the infallible judge in all
doctrinal disputes, and this implies that everything which the
letter of Scripture contains, or which can be indubitably
inferred from it, is dogma, while all that is contrary to Holy
Scripture is error, and all else, even though it does not actually
contradict Scripture, is a matter of indifference to the salvation
of the soul." [11]

In this way in both Reformation Churches the unity of
Scripture was resolved into the unity of a doctrinal system
which was supposedly read off from the text of Scripture,

---

[7] *Op. cit.*, p. 837.　　　[8] Cp. Diem, *Theol.*, VOL. I, p. 270.
[9] See above, p. 221.
[10] See H. Heppe, *Die Dogmatik der evangelisch-reformierten Kirche*, Stuttgart
1952.　　　[11] Heppe, *op. cit.*, p. 11.

though the process of inference took place in the one case by a more directly Biblicist procedure, in the other by reading Scripture through dogmatic lenses. As a result Scripture inevitably lost its character as a theme for preaching and proclamation (the rediscovery of which had been the great achievement of the Reformation) and became instead the basis and the summary of a theological system. Now it was no longer possible to be content with the fact that Scripture is its own evidence in so far as it is preached, but it was necessary to invest it with an authority *ante et extra usum* also, and this in consequence inevitably led to the development of the doctrine of verbal inspiration. Because in this way the Reformation Churches ceased to live by the actual givenness of the canon of Scripture, and in its place taught the doctrine of its essential and intrinsic finality, they defined themselves confessionally by their Scriptural doctrine just as much as their Tridentine partner had done.

But, above all, by this Scriptural doctrine the Evangelical Church ruined its own true foundation, namely preaching: the concrete event of preaching in which Scripture was proclaimed and its witness reanimated in the living witness of the preacher was now replaced by a didactic exposition and demonstration of its statements considered as so many truths and matters of fact. Moreover, faith, too, in its relation to Scripture, underwent a change: it was no longer faith awakened by the proclamation of Scripture and directed to the events which Scripture attests and their significance for salvation, but it was rather primarily an act of faith in the divinity of Scripture—faith understood as *fides quae creditur*—and in those predicates of Scripture which were implied in that conception or were considered necessary to maintain it. Of course preaching still continued to develop; and since true faith can be born even from false preaching, this deterioration in the Reformation went for a long time unnoticed. Nor in fact did the Evangelical Church improve in this respect as a result of the fact that it became anxious about the ever more apparent sterility of its preaching or the increasing weariness of its clergy in regard to their preaching duties and the inner tendencies to re-Catholicisation which were bound up with this development. The stimulus which compelled the Church to revise its doctrine of Scripture came rather from historico-critical science; and because the Church saw this to be an inroad into theology coming from without, and therefore illegitimate, it resisted for long enough, and indeed still resists the demand.

This controversy has been going on for the last 200 years and its history is well known. Here we need only concern ourselves with its present stage, and in this connexion it is significant that New Testament historians who have become especially active in this matter cannot so easily be regarded as intruders in theology as was perhaps more obviously possible at an earlier period. The reason for this is first that present day New Testament scholarship on the basis of its critical conclusions stresses in general the proclamatory character of New Testament writings, and hence stands with the Reformers and confirms the rightness of their use of Scripture. Further, its main objection to the prevalent use of Scripture is that the latter allows dogmatics to guard the interpretation of Scripture, and thus modern criticism makes its voice heard just in connexion with that process by which, as we established, the Reformation degenerated into classical Protestant dogmatics. Hence from this point of view it will have to be seen whether the true and genuine use of Scripture is not better maintained by the Reformers themselves than by the post-Reformation dogmatists. The latter, as we have seen, support their whole doctrine of Scripture by the contention that Scripture forms a doctrinal unity. The modern historian tries, however, to show that this doctrinal unity of the New Testament is imaginary.[12] We can leave open here the exegetical question whether the doctrinal differences between the various writings of the New Testament are in fact so great as, for instance, Vielhauer and Käsemann contend, and we grant that a harmonisation of the doctrinal statements of the New Testament would only be possible if some violence were done to the text. We are even of the opinion (which we have given reasons for above) [13] that these divergences are necessarily implied in the proclamatory character of Scripture. Once

[12] For the following, cp. Diem, "Das Problem des Schriftkanons" (above, p. 199, n. 13), and above, pp. 39 ff.

[13] Pp. 143 ff.

this is conceded, then not only is the interpretation of the relation of Scripture and doctrine suggested by post-Reformation dogmatics impossible, but the whole theological justification for the Reformers' use of Scripture must be thought out afresh and on different lines.

(b) Justification as a hermeneutical canon in the work of Ernst Käsemann

Such an attempt was made by E. Käsemann.[14] He takes up the distinction between the Reformed formal principle (*sola scriptura*) and material principle (*sola gratia*, *sola fide*) which had become usual in the nineteenth century, and says that "we can never speak rightly of the sole authority of Scripture as of a formal principle, although this has been done long enough."[15] It was only possible to speak of this sole authority in critical debate with Churchly tradition, "if Scripture was understood primarily in the light of its actual environment and of the message of which it is the precipitate, hence in the light of the Gospel." We cannot hope to understand Scripture rightly on the basis of the canon as such, since the latter in the totality of its writings does not form a real unity.[16] The situation is rather that "by a decision of faith which must appear arbitrary to an outsider" it is recognised that in Scripture "we have to do with a dynamic and at times self-contradictory historical process which has compelling authority over us and not with a dogma or an idea which might make a very dubious claim to timelessness and unequivocalness. This once more brings us up against the fact of a contingent happening to which the Church is essentially related."[17] But Käsemann is concerned above all to emphasise that this "must not be interpreted in the sense of a miracle." The Bible, he maintains, is "neither God's word in an objective sense, nor a system of belief and doctrine, but the precipitate of history and the proclamation of early Christianity. The Church which canonised it nevertheless asserts that it is the bearer of the Gospel in just this way. The Church asserts this

[14] See E. Käsemann, "Zum Thema der Nichtobjektivierbarkeit," in *Ev. Th.*, 1952-3, pp. 455 ff.
[15] Käsemann, *op. cit.*, p. 460.
[16] *Op. cit.*, p. 462.   [17] *Op. cit.*, p. 463.

because it sees the history which is here firmly integrated and proclaimed, unified under the standpoint of the justification of the sinner, and since its assertion is at the same time a witness and a confession it is also a challenge to us to place ourselves with our own private history under the claim of this event in which the sinner is justified. Thus we are led to make a decision not only as to whether we will or not accept this challenge but also as to whether such a confession penetrates to the heart of Scripture."

Thus Käsemann, too, takes it as his point of departure that in regard to the self-proclaiming history which lies before us in the Bible, we are faced by "the fact of a contingent happening" to which the Church is essentially related. When he at the same time stresses that it cannot here be a question of "the recognition of a miracle," this no doubt implies that "the contingence" of the event does not signify a supernatural saving penetration into history, as is suggested by Cullmann's time of the Incarnation,[18] but simply the underived, unrepeatable character of the fact in its uniqueness, in which respect it is like all other events.[19] But to what extent then can this historical process be made of "compelling authority"? He says that the Church which canonised Scripture has effected this and could only so effect it because it sees the "self-proclaiming history unified under the standpoint of the justification of the sinner." If this is supposed to be an historical judgment about the formation of the canon, it must certainly be contradicted, for the Church of the second to the fourth centuries, which was responsible for the process of canonisation, did not work with this category. Otherwise all that which Käsemann objects to in the canon could not have crept into it. But obviously he does not intend to state historically what has taken place in the historical formation of the canon but to state theologically how the Church should view this process or more precisely how the Reformation has viewed it. He is concerned about the question how the "*sola scriptura*" is to be made effective as against Church tradition; and since this can no longer be done with the formal principle, then it must

---

[18] See above, p. 214.

[19] Cp. the application of the idea of "contingence" discussed above, pp. 134 ff.

be done by recourse to the material principle. There can then no longer be any question of the history and proclamation of primitive Christianity attested in the canon being made of "compelling authority." This history as such has no general and essential implication. What is "authoritative" is simply the principle of interpretation in the light of which this history is to be viewed. The authority which the canon exercises over its readers or hearers results from the application to the canon of a specific principle of exposition without regard to the history of the canon itself. The reader or the hearer is challenged by the testimony or confession of the canon to decide whether he is willing to yield to the power of that event by which the sinner is justified and to recognise it to be the heart and centre of Scripture. "In other words, and in New Testament terminology, we are compelled to test the spirits also in the matter of Scripture," [20] which in practice can only mean that this material principle (Käsemann does not use this particular expression) forms the critical touchstone by which the validity of Scriptural statements is to be tested.

In this way Käsemann has given very pregnant expression to something which haunts the minds of many modern New Testament critics as a possible solution to the question of the canon such as would enable them to counter the work of the post-Reformation dogmatists: the establishment of a canon within the canon by means of the doctrine of justification as a hermeneutical criterion. But this solution does not at bottom suggest anything new, it simply goes back to Luther, who wished to have Scripture examined in the light of the principle "the preaching of Christ," by which in the last analysis he, too, understood nothing other than the "*sola gratia*" and the "*sola fide.*" Hence it is thought that by this means we may return to the Reformers' use of Scripture and overcome its distortion in the work of the classical Protestant dogmatics. Is this correct?

Above we have pointed out how the Catholic Church parried the Reformed discovery of Scripture as the theme of Gospel proclamation by paralysing through its doctrine of Scripture formulated at the Council of Trent the living event in which Scripture proclaims itself. And we have further seen how the

[20] Käsemann, *op. cit.* (above, n. 14), p. 463.

Reformed Churches in their controversy with this opponent allowed themselves to be pushed in this same direction, and how the two parties in their dispute with each other at this point defined themselves confessionally. Now the very same thing happened in regard to the doctrine of justification, as it bears upon the doctrine of Scripture. The "*sola gratia,*" too, for the sake of which the living proclamation of Scripture had been restored, was very soon on both sides erected into a specific doctrine of justification which became its primary aspect. For years Ernst Wolf has again and again been calling attention to this extremely important point: "The conception of the doctrine of justification as a 'material principle' distinct from the '*sola scriptura*' as a 'formal principle' signified a not inconsiderable foreshortening; and to declare the doctrine of justification to be a foundation dogma conceals the danger that as 'object of faith' it might be resolved into a Protestant *theologoumenon.*" The Catholic Church certainly so understood it when at the Council of Trent it defined its own doctrine *de justificatione*, of which Wolf says: "Here the doctrine of justification has become an object of faith in the strict sense, *fides quae creditur.* But in the movement of the Reformation itself the position occupied by the *doctrina de justificatione* is something quite different; it formulates representatively, so to speak, and at one particular point, historically determined or chosen, what might thus be formulated in regard to the whole of the Christian life and the being of the Church: namely the message of the Gospel in its critical aspect, the witness to that word which slays or makes alive, and for which the death and resurrection of Christ in their ἐφάπαξ reveal the unity of the Creator and Redeemer God." [21]

If we propose to use the distinction between the formal and material principles as an aid, then it must never be forgotten that the two can only convey "the message of the Gospel in its critical aspect" in so far as they are indissolubly bound up with each other. As we must repeatedly stress it is a question of the living event of preaching in which the "*justificatio impii*

[21] See E. Wolf, " 'Erneuerung der Kirche' im Licht der Reformation," in *Ev. Th.*, 1946-7, pp. 327 f.; cp. also his articles "Die Rechtfertigungslehre als Mitte und Grenze reformatorischer Theologie," in *Ev. Th.*, 1949-50, pp. 298-308, and "Sola gratia?" in *Peregrinatio*, 1954, pp. 113 ff.

per fidem sola gratia" is not taught, but happens as a result of the fact that there is imputed to the hearer a righteousness which lies not in his own merits but in the merits of Christ *extra nos*. And the objectivity of the word secured by the living process of preaching guards this righteousness against becoming a *habitus* within the control of man.   But if the "*sola scriptura*" is a norm presupposed by preaching, and therefore distinct from it and and not first legitimised by the decision of the hearer, and if it were to fail, then the "*sola gratia*" conveyed in the event of preaching would necessarily fail at the same time, even though the doctrine of justification which is both preached and believed were indisputably Pauline.[22]

Now Käsemann would certainly deny that he has made the "*sola gratia*," considered as an object of faith, into a foundation dogma, and hence resolved the doctrine of justification into a Protestant *theologoumenon*.   He might even point out that he expressly rejected the possibility of adopting a dogma or system of doctrine, because he was concerned about a certain attitude towards Scripture in which we do not believe in the doctrine of justification as such but bring ourselves with our own private history under the power of that redemptive event in which the sinner is justified.   But our question is whether he really does or can submit to the power of this self-proclaiming history, or whether he paralyses and must paralyse the authority of this event conveyed to him through the preaching of Scripture by the fact that he makes of it a history with compelling power only after first testing it critically and assenting to it sub-sequently.   Certainly this happens in his mode of thought quite differently from the way in which the Roman or post-Reformation dogmatists render illusory by their doctrine of Scripture the living event of preaching, or make nugatory by their doctrine of justification the event of justification itself. The "*sola gratia*" is for him no dogmatic principle of the *fides quae creditur* type but (if the expression may be allowed) an existentialist principle.   But perhaps this attempt, so very widespread today, to make the self-proclaiming history existentially authoritative is the modern form of erecting a *theologoumenon* in the place of the event itself.

[22] On this, cp. Diem, "Est autem ecclesia congregatio sanctorum . . .," in *Barth-Festschrift*, 1936, pp. 113 ff.

Q

This compelling process of self-proclamatory history consists in the fact that the Church has exclusively heard, in the proclamation of these witnesses, the Word of God, and we must therefore continue to proclaim and hear just as exclusively through these witnesses. This fact can only be recognised; it cannot fundamentally be justified. The only possible theological justification in this matter consists in using the Scriptural canon appropriately by preaching on its themes with confidence in its self-evidencing power. In the empirical use of the canon in this way lies also the only theological possibility of defining it against Church tradition. In this way we stand once more at the side of the Reformers.

(c) The importance of the situation in which the Gospel is proclaimed: Paul and James

Only in the light of the above considerations can the question of the unity of Scripture be correctly framed and answered. If we preach Scripture with faith in its self-evidencing authority, this can now no longer imply that its statements may be incorporated into a unified doctrinal system. Any attempt to prove such doctrinal unity within the Bible would be just as desperate an undertaking as to disprove it, since the unity of Scripture does not consist in its unity of doctrine. The self-evidencing authority of which we speak means rather that in the proclamation of these witnesses Jesus Christ is to be heard proclaiming Himself; and the fact of the canon bears witness that the Church has in fact unequivocally heard in these witnesses the proclamation of Jesus Christ, and we too can and must, likewise, hear it there. Now this self-evidence of the Biblical witnesses palpable in preaching is not the same thing for all times and in every situation, as would be the case with the evidence of doctrinal propositions. We have explained the manifold variety of the witnesses to be grounded in their proclamatory character. As Biblical testimony was proclaimed from time to time by particular men in particular circumstances and with particular aims in view, that is again the case when today it continues to be proclaimed. Hence the modern preacher must be first of all concerned to come to grips with the particular texts in which the self-proclaiming history confronts him, with the greatest possible historical precision. In this respect critical research has achieved much for the preacher, and the freedom of its activity neither can nor must in any way be circumscribed. The further task of the preacher is to make these Biblical witnesses effectively and suitably heard in the present-day religious situation. In the performance of this task it will always be the case that in view of the concrete exigencies of the modern situation certain testimonies are preferred and others put aside. But there is an essential difference between the current use of the texts being governed by the practical needs of the contemporary situation and its being decided by the preacher himself on the basis of fundamental viewpoints and in accordance with specific criteria of exposition.

To take the classical example, Luther was not able to endure the Epistle of James, as compared with those of Paul, because of the religious situation in his own day. Hence there cannot be much objection if some theologians today take the point of view that because of inner tendencies towards re-Catholicisation in modern Protestantism, a decision must be made, in the presentation of the Christian message, between Paul and Luke. But whenever such an appraisal of the value of the various witnesses is made, the significance of the fact of the canon must be taken into account. This demands the recognition that the witness neglected by us did in fact bear witness to Christ (within certain historical conditions, for how could it be otherwise?) and did find a hearing in the Church, and thus spoke under the inspiration of the Holy Spirit. We might perhaps go as far as Luther—though this is going rather far— who in his September Bible of 1522 clearly dismissed the Epistle to the Hebrews, the Epistle of James and the Epistle of Jude together with the Revelation of John, and would not have them reckoned among the "right certain main books." Yet he did not exclude those writings from the canon, and the Church quite rightly did not adopt his evaluation as fundamentally valid. In this respect, the whole point is that an appraisal governed by particular circumstances should not be made into a fundamental appraisal, that therefore the canon of Scripture must be recognised as the *text* which in any event is permanently binding, and that all our attempts at exposition, on the other hand, are only *commentaries*, which with their constantly changing conclusions cannot take the place of the text itself.

The fact that the canon itself cannot be modified by the temporary degree of our insight has, however, not simply a prohibitive but primarily a positive significance. The fact of the canon protects the expositor from his subjective, arbitrary judgments, and from the constant danger that instead of letting the texts speak for themselves in their concrete actuality and historical uniqueness he may do violence to them in the name of a preconceived principle of exegesis, and for that very reason fail to do justice to their character as witnesses and as texts for preaching. The canon does not thus by any means fetter the expositor in his work, but implies simply that in these various witnesses the unequivocal testimony to Christ is to be heard. Just this becomes clear from the dispute between Paul and James. With Paul's Epistles, the Church has also given us the Epistle of James, and has thus suggested that this, too, is a theme for proclamation and a witness to Christ. Yet it is impossible to establish doctrinal unity between the two. In II. 14 ff. James discusses the relation of faith and works in frank polemic against what he has heard of Paul and in such a way as to arrive at formulae diametrically opposed to those of Paul. In the course of his discussion he even appeals to Gen. xv. 6, the very text which Paul had quoted in Rom. IV. 3. A direct harmonisation of the two sets of statements is quite impossible. We may not suppose that the arguments of James about hearing and doing, about a faith that is dead without works and living with works, can be adapted to the Pauline antithesis of grace and works. His point of departure is not this way of stating the problem, which is so characteristic of Paul and is worked out by him to its extremest consequences: it is rather that he is opposing a faith which is imagined to take the place of works, and he stresses, on the other hand, the indissoluble connexion of the two. He does this in a polemical situation in which he feels it his duty to resist in his own way the danger arising from the Pauline presentation of the Gospel—the danger of an abuse of grace which Paul himself had striven against in his arguments in Rom. VI. 1 ff. In this situation we must first see and listen to what he has to say, rather than complicate his more unreflective statements by reference to Paul's far more complicated point of view, as for example by considering how in the works required of us the grace of God and human achievement are related to each other, and what man's own achievement in this matter (by contrast with the idea of work accomplished in faith of Jas. II. 22) signifies in respect of man's justification before God.

Even the exegetical realisation of this situation will be difficult if we approach the Epistle of James with a criterion of exposition that we have derived from a study of the Pauline doctrine of justification. It will then be difficult to appreciate adequately that James, with his emphasis on the necessary fruits of faith, expresses a not inconsiderable aspect of Scripture, and even of Paul himself, and in any case it will be hard to avoid disparaging his testimony by contrast with that of Paul. But the difficulty only then becomes acute when we are called upon, as the canon bids us do, to preach both texts in conjunction with each other, and when it is thus not possible for us to reject the one or the other by appealing to their incompatibility. Hence in proclaiming one text we must at the same time listen to the voice of the other. But in any event this must not happen in such a way that by one text we blunt the point of the other, and so level down the two of them, as, for instance (and this is commonly done), by expounding a Pauline doctrine of justification *sola fide* and then afterwards by reference to James correcting Paul's one-sidedness and explaining that the faith which justifies must of course prove itself by its fruits. Any weakening or completion of the *sola fide* doctrine in this way can only have the effect of nullifying it and undermining the whole Pauline teaching at the very roots. Nor will it do to correct James by Paul and to weaken and qualify his contention that the faith of Abraham "was completed by works" (II. 22)—which sounds extremely bold to minds trained in the Pauline school—by the *sola fide* doctrine, which was not envisaged in his framing of the problem. Rather we must take seriously and give undivided attention to each text as it stands, and try to understand each of these witnesses in the context of its unique historical situation. The great merit of critical research is that it helps us to do this and excludes the possibility of toning down the various texts by the concordance method. An

excellent example of this type of exegetical study is provided
by the work of Georg Eichholz,[23] who not only brings out the
contours of the Epistle of James by contrast with Paul, but
proceeds to ask what these two, Paul and James, have to say
to each other, and what they have together to say to us.[24]
"The '*quo jure*' of a theological exposition is not simply detachable from the concrete circumstances of the hour for which it
is a relevant message.   And this time-situation is obviously
different in the case of Paul and James.   Paul's formula is
heard in the hour of James, and in that context becomes
twisted.   In the hands of those who now use it it is warped.
Here James puts us on our guard against this formula and
enquires beyond it to the heart of the matter, i.e. seeks the
word which is relevant to the new hour.   Here we see the
earnestness with which Gospel preaching wrestles for the soul
of man.   In this way James makes himself responsible *for*
Paul in the canon." [25]   But "it is equally true that James does
not stand alone on his own responsibility.   The '*quo iure*' of
the witness is no isolated '*quo iure*'." [26]   "By the particular point
which Paul in the exigencies of his hour gave to the Gospel,
he stands surety *for* James in the canon.   Thus each protects
the other because the message of any one witness cannot find
protection in itself.   This means that in the very message that
it bears each word of a witness points beyond itself and does
not live confined within its own message." [27]   And what the
one has to say to the other, each from the point of view of his
own time and its demands, they have to say to us conjointly
because the hour of the one is as little a thing of the past for us
as the hour of the other.

Eichholz quite rightly emphasises that the question what
James and Paul have to say to each other, and conjointly to
us, is not specifically a problem for systematic theology but
belongs also to the work of the exegete.   Unfortunately, in
this respect exegetes render their task far too easy, and think
that it is finished when they have brought out in the sharpest
possible contrast the distinctive traits of the various witnesses,

---

[23] See G. Eichholz, "Jakobus und Paulus: Ein Beitrag zum Problem
des kanons," in *Theologische Existenz heute*, n.s., xxxix (1953).

[24] Eichholz, *op. cit.*, p. 48.   [25] *Ibid.*

[26] *Op. cit.*, p. 49.   [27] *Op. cit.*, p. 50, n. 25.

leaving it to the systematic theologians or to our pastoral guides to bring the whole together again into a unity. In that case they should not be surprised or complain if an unbridgeable gulf remains between the work of the exegete and that of the systematic theologian, with the result that there is no longer any co-operation between them.

What the exegete can and must contribute to overcome this severance is that he should pursue his enquiries as far as possible to discover whether and in what sense the individual Biblical witnesses in their mutual protectiveness become responsible for each other. If he does this his work will quite spontaneously merge into that of systematic theology. For it must be the business of the latter to ask this question first if its concern is to say anew for us today what the manifold witness of the Bible says in common. In proportion as the exegete thus prepares the way for the systematic theologian he will guard the latter from the danger of levelling down the individual witnesses and systematising them from a standpoint that is foreign to the texts themselves. On the other hand, the exegete, too, is dependent on the systematic theologian, whose business it is to prevent him from neglecting the concurrent testimony of other witnesses and to remind him of other aspects of Scripture to which he must give heed. But in order to be able to say more about this and more concretely, we must first elucidate the essential aim of systematic theology in its relation to exegesis.

CHAPTER X

THE TASK OF SYSTEMATIC THEOLOGY CONSIDERED AS A PROBLEM OF SCRIPTURAL EXEGESIS

THE question of the essential function of systematic theology has in the course of the history of theology been posed from many and varied points of view. But in consequence of the conclusions which we have reached so far we are unable to select any one of these possible points of view arbitrarily; we must rather approach the problem as we have become aware of it in our consideration of Scriptural exposition. Thus for us it means, in practice, the requirement that in the exposition of the individual Biblical witnesses we should always be prepared to take into account what the others have to say to us. But we felt unable to adopt the solution of the problem which consists in levelling down and harmonising Scriptural statements and so seeking to impose on them a doctrinal unity by Biblicist-dogmatic methods. Hence we must avoid that departure to the right which began already with the *Konkordien* formula and was taken by post-Reformation theology. We felt it equally wrong to deviate to the left, as was done in the attempt to establish Biblical unity by means of a canon within the canon, by applying to Biblical statements a specific principle of exegesis as a critical criterion. And we felt these deviations to be wrong not because of any dogmatic teaching about the Scriptural canon—we have not formulated anything of the sort—but because of the historical fact of the formation of the canon itself within the history of Biblical proclamation. This development forbids us to disconnect any one of the witnesses from its historical continuum and to erect it into an absolute authority. In turning, now, to enquire what solution there can be other than these two possibilities which have been excluded, we must remember that Scriptural exposition implies for us a second task, namely to consider what common message these manifold witnesses have for us today. We must deal with the second point at the same time as we reflect on the first, while excluding the two possibilities to which we have referred.

(a) The problems of systematic theology

We must now discuss in more detail the function of systematic theology which we have thus precisely defined. The question is: (1) To examine more closely the Biblical witnesses to God's revelatory action, and to seek to discover beyond their conditioning by the person of the witness and his circumstances the nature of the revelatory event itself to which they point and which they reflect; (2) To enquire what possible contact there is between the event thus attested and our present existence as hearers and exponents of the Scriptural witnesses; and (3) On the basis of this contact, to formulate such statements as will be generally valid and authoritative (as distinct from those statements of the witnesses and exponents which are conditioned by particular circumstances), and may therefore be used as a *norm* for further exegesis of the text.

In this matter we have intentionally spoken merely of systematic theology and not of dogmatics. The two are not the same; and it is probably one of the worst signs of the lack of a sense of direction in present-day theology that it no longer appreciates this distinction—or even refuses to appreciate it. Just because it is necessary to discover again the true basis of this distinction, we enquire first about the function of systematic theology. It will have to be shown in the course of our study itself how we can and must distinguish from this discipline the function of dogmatics.

It will immediately be realised that each of the three special tasks that we have defined coincides with a significant problem in the history of theology. Expressed briefly and straightforwardly it is a question (1) of revelation in its historical aspect, (2) of the problem of hermeneutics, and (3) of the *regula fidei*. We may try to discuss these problems separately, or at least to place one or the other of them in the foreground, as has happened from time to time in the history of theology. But we may not lose sight of the context in which in the course of our consideration of the problem of Scripture we have been confronted by the question of systematic theology as a whole and in its single phases. This means that we should not isolate any of the three problems, as we might be tempted to do by the fact that in the history of theology each of these problems has been treated in some polemical situation, and thus has necessarily been viewed with one-sided emphasis. The classical example of this is provided by the debate between orthodoxy and pietism. The strongest influence in modern theological discussion flows from the example of Kierkegaard, who could say that the doctrine of the Church was in good order and that he therefore need not concern himself about it. He was much more concerned about the question of the subjective appropriation of the objectively established faith. And we have seen what consequences [1] this one-sidedness of interest inevitably had for the supposed objectively secure doctrine. In present-day theological discussion the question of the *regula fidei* is thrown into the background completely by the prominence of concern with hermeneutics. Even the emphasis on revelation in history serves this one-sided approach to the problem, because as a consequence of the historical view of the Bible there is no longer any possibility of formulating such statements as used to be called dogmatic, and hence the function of systematic theology is primarily or even exclusively sought in the solution of the hermeneutical problem. We shall be prevented from adopting such a one-sided approach if we firmly envisage the function of systematic theology as part of the problem of Scriptural exposition as we have defined it in its three phases.

On the other hand, it may be objected that the preference of particular problems in modern theological discussion does not imply a one-sided treatment and thus a foreshortening of the problem, but rather a "reduction" in the literal sense, and hence a referring back of one set of problems to another. This kind of reduction, which must not imply any real curtailment, is not only possible, but even from time to time necessitated by changes in the historical development of ideas. Thus, to take one of the most important examples, the surrender of the subject-object pattern of thought in philosophy has completely shifted the position of the problem of historical

[1] See above, Ch. I.

reality, which can now only be posed from within private existence as an enquiry into what has meaning for such existence. Now of course it will never be possible to say in advance whether a "reduction" of the problems concerned involves also a real diminution in scope and meaning. Rather the question of intrinsic appropriateness can only be answered in relation to the specific object involved; and since we have enquired into the function of systematic theology as part of the problem of Scriptural exegesis, the problems implied are posed for us in quite specific definiteness of content.

Thus, to begin with the first set of problems, we have met the question of revelation and history in the course of our concern with Scriptural exegesis not as a general question about the essence of history or the historical bearing of human existence. We were confronted rather by a specific historical process, namely the history of Jesus Christ who proclaims Himself. Our encounter with this set of historical facts did not therefore in the first place mean that we were asked how we wished to relate ourselves to it, and whether with our private existence we wished to enter into relation with it or not. Rather it was declared to us in this encounter, i.e. authoritatively disclosed, that this proclamatory series of events which actually happened, and is ever being enacted afresh, implied a decision about our own existence and destiny. Hence we were prevented from examining this historical process in the light of our own prior conception of the historical, and enquiring whether in this process we have to do with real history or not. On the contrary, we were challenged to consider whether we were willing, or not, to recognise the decision which these events implied about ourselves, and hence whether—answering the question affirmatively in faith—we were willing to be delivered from our purely natural existence and development and to become engaged in God's action towards ourselves, or whether—answering the question negatively in unbelief—we were going to continue to vegetate unaffected by this process and so harden ourselves in an unhistorical existence. Thus in our confrontation by this proclamatory history as it has disclosed itself to us and wishes to be understood, we are not free to measure it by any of our criteria of history and what constitutes the historical, but on the contrary as *index et iudex sui et falsi*, this proclamatory history itself determines what history and historical existence are, it declares that the historical is the interaction, embodied in this process, between God and the world, on the one hand, and between the witnesses to the revelation and the hearers of their words, on the other. That and only that may be regarded as the historical.

Thus we are here faced by an exceptional historical process which wishes to be understood as true history and which neither seeks nor admits in justification of its claim any authentication outside itself. This means that with regard to the function of systematic theology an important prejudgment has been made, and one which will exercise its effects at every point of theological enquiry and method. Hence we cannot, in the attempt to adhere to our own form of enquiry, go back behind the contingent fact of the Scriptural canon in which this history confronts us, no matter whether we question the significance of that fact or justify it and explain its rationality. In either case we should necessarily miss the true starting-point for systematic theology. This is the object of theological problematics in the light of which it must be shown whether a "reduction" of one set of problems to another is intrinsically appropriate or whether it means an inappropriate curtailment of the problems involved. We propose to illustrate this by certain examples drawn from modern theological discussion.

(b) The systematic conception of Rudolf Bultmann in his exegesis of St John's Gospel

In what follows we propose to adduce only Bultmann's exegesis of St John's Gospel as an example.[2] We have said that the proclamatory history neither seeks nor admits any authentication outside itself. This is also the determining point of view in Bultmann's exegesis, for which he can quote the Evangelist's own authority, especially the rule he gives in VII. 17: ἐάν τις θέλῃ τὸ θέλημα αὐτοῦ ποιεῖν, γνώσεται περὶ τῆς διδαχῆς, πότερον ἐκ τοῦ Θεοῦ ἐστιν ἢ ἐγὼ ἀπ᾽ ἐμαυτοῦ λαλῶ.

But in view of this principle Bultmann proposes to answer at one and the same time both the question as to the verification

---

[2] Cp. Bultmann, *Theol. des N.T.*, §§ 41-50, and *Das Evangelium des Johannes*, 1949.

of this διδαχή and that with regard to its content, and in fact
with the implication that the content of what Jesus teaches or
proclaims is one with the very fact of His proclaiming it. In
the same way, the two aspects which we have distinguished
in this history—the interaction between God and the world
on the one hand and that between the message and its hearers
on the other, in other words the action of God and the proclamation of this action—coincide, too, and the verification
of the whole proclamatory history lies in the conduct and
attitude of the hearer. Thus the question of revelation in
history is transposed and becomes the question of the history
of the hearer. In this consists the reduction about the
appropriateness of which we have to enquire.

We cannot make this enquiry otherwise than by asking
what the text in which the history confronts us wishes to say.
The proclamatory history, according to St John, is "written
that you may believe that Jesus is the Christ, the Son of God,
and that believing you may have life in his name" (xx. 31). The
preaching of Jesus is preceded by the prologue, which does not
merely express an *idea* of creation.[3] Rather it tells the *story*
of creation, how everything was created by the *Logos* who "in
the beginning" was not only "with God," but was God. In
the *Logos* was "life" which was "the light of men" (I. 1-4).
This light came into the world, inasmuch as in Jesus "the
Logos became flesh" (I. 14). It is probably not without a
recollection of Gen. I that the description "*logos*" is given to
the pre-existent one, whom not only John the Baptist testifies
Jesus to have been (I. 15-30), but whom Jesus declares Himself
as being (VIII. 58, XVII. 5-24). Again, Jesus bears the title
"*Logos*" because He is both distinct from God and yet identical
with God (I. I), because in the creation of the world He was
active. In this Gospel the distinction and the identity between
God and the *Logos* is reflected in that between the Father and
the Son. The Father loved the Son πρὸ καταβολῆς κόσμου
(XVII. 24). But He also loved the κόσμος, and indeed in such

---

[3] Cp. Bultmann, *Das Evangelium des Johannes*, pp. 20 f.: "The radical
nature of this idea of creation is shown in the fact that there is not given
to the world, as it were, in the beginning, as its very own, the factor which
later sustains it, but both the beginning and also the continued existence
of the world are ascribed to the activity of the *logos*."

fashion that τὸν Υἱὸν αὐτοῦ τὸν μονογενῆ ἔδωκεν (III. 16) in
order to show mankind that He loves them even as He loves
the Son (XVII. 23). Thus Jesus cannot be understood from
within this world, but it is continually stressed that His
manifestation in this world must be understood as a "being
sent" by the Father. Even His coming into the world does
not make Him belong to this world; it has its counterpart in
His departure from this world. He came as the one sent by
the Father in order to return to the Father (III. 13, cp. VI. 63).
But it is equally true of His own that they likewise are not "of
the world" (XVII. 14) and that though they yet remain in the
world, they must some time be where He is in order to behold
His δόξα (XVII. 24). This history of the pre-existent and the
post-existent *Logos*, which, on the one hand, represents an event
taking place in the interaction between God and the *Logos*-
Christ, and, on the other, between God-Christ and the world,[4]
and which, as Bultmann repeatedly says, is reported in mythological terms, constitutes the framework within which the
drama of the incarnate Word is unfolded. John testifies to
the whole history in the hope, and with the expectation, that
what God wills to accomplish by this series of events, namely
to impart eternal life to the believer, will in fact be achieved
as the reader or hearer is confronted by this proclamation.
Our question now is (1) whether this framework, which shows
God acting towards the world through Jesus Christ, can be
made coincident (as Bultmann makes it) with the drama of the
incarnate Word, and (2) whether the history can be equated
(as Bultmann appears to equate it, at least here and there)
with the proclamation of it; and we put these questions as
exegetical questions to the Evangelist himself.

In any case, we cannot make a distinction in this matter in
the sense of distinguishing between the proclamation itself and
the events which it attests as though the latter were historically
provable. This is impossible, especially in regard to the drama
of the incarnate Word, because John, above all, as is well
known, handles the historical dates of his story with great
freedom, and more than any other Evangelist completely
subordinates the historical report to the proclamatory exposition of it. But it is equally impossible in regard to the frame-

[4] Bultmann, *Das Evangelium des Johannes*, p. 18.

work presentation of the pre-existent and post-existent one, because here there can be no witness other than Jesus Himself, and it therefore can have no historical ground in the usual sense. Hence here we have no saving events, on the one hand, distinguishable from their proclamatory interpretation, on the other. But the Evangelist, in any event, distinguishes between the framework itself and the proclamation of it in the drama of the Incarnation. For if it is declared to man that by faith in the one whom God has sent, he can come to the knowledge of the truth, and that if he does not so believe because he loves the darkness of this world more than the light, then he denies the reality of God and by his lie falls a prey to death, the message presupposes that God has created this world through Jesus Christ and for that reason has sent His Son into the world which is His own—that God has loved this world and therefore has sent His Son into it in order to manifest to it the love of God. Hence the themes of the creation of the world and the love of God towards it are not thoughts or concepts about the being of God, but are concerned with an action of God the truth of which can only consist in its having happened. We must not conceal this exegetical observation of the matter (or simply disregard it) because it is impossible to grasp ontologically this series of events, since they are only presented to us in the proclamatory exposition. The reality of these events does indeed confront us here as objective truth.

Bultmann evades this implication by pursuing the observation, accurate enough in itself, that with Jesus words and works are identical, and then he proceeds to ask: "But what is the content of the word or words of Jesus? Jesus speaks of what He has seen or heard in the bosom of the Father—or, as we may put it in view of the identity of His words and deeds, He shows or enacts these mysteries (I. 18, cp. VI. 46). . . . But the amazing thing is that the words of Jesus never communicate anything specific or concrete with regard to what He has seen or heard in the bosom of the Father. He nowhere imparts mysteries or events of which He has been the witness. Nowhere do we find that the theme of His discourse is the heavenly world; nor does He disclose cosmological or soteriological matters as did the Gnostic saviours. The theme of His discourse is ever only the one thing, namely that the Father has sent Him, that He has come as the light, the bread of life, as the witness of the truth, etc., and that He will go away again and that men must believe on Him." [5]   From all this it is by no means clear to us that, as Bultmann infers, "the mythological statements have lost their mythological meaning." Even if, according to Bultmann's philosophy of the mythological, the proclamation of this history were couched in mythological terms, it would still be necessary to ask whether the history itself is no more than a mere myth.   What is Bultmann's attitude to this question, and what meaning can he still give to these mythological statements?   "Jesus is not seriously presented as a pre-existent divine being who visited the earth in human form in order to disclose unheard-of mysteries."   On the contrary, we think the text gives no grounds for thinking anything but that the Evangelist did in fact seriously believe this to be the truth and could not well have thought otherwise when he makes Jesus impart no "cosmological and soteriological mysteries" but "the unheard-of mystery" of iii. 16, that God not only thinks of the world lovingly and hence does not merely reveal His love for it, but embodies this love in action by the sending of His Son.   But Bultmann thinks differently from the text when he says: "The purpose of the mythological terminology is to express the absolute and decisive significance of His word; the mythological conception of pre-existence is used in the service of the thought of revelation.   The word of Christ comes from the beyond . . . and hence is utterly removed from human control, it is an authoritative word which faces the hearer with the choice between life and death." [6]   Thus it is suggested that John has used a specific terminology in order to invoke images which enforce the thought of revelation.   But in this interpretation what has become of the revelatory *action* which the evangelist without a doubt intended to convey?   As action, in the sense of iii. 16 at any rate, it is missing, and what remains finally is simply the fact that "Jesus as the Revealer of God reveals nothing except that He is the Revealer, which means that He is the one for whom the world has been waiting and who in His person brings that for which all men long: life and truth as the reality by the inspiration of which man can

    [5] Bultmann, *Theol. des N.T.*, p. 408.   [6] *Op. cit.*, p. 409.

exist, light which makes life transparent and puts an end to
questioning and perplexity. But how does He embody all this
and communicate it to the world? In no other way but that
He says that He embodies and communicates it—He, the Son
of Man speaking human words and demanding faith without
any special legitimation. Thus in his Gospel John expresses
only the fact of revelation without illustrating its content." [7]
Thus "the 'mythological' framework is reduced to and equated
with the story of the incarnate Word; and the latter again is
reduced to the sheer fact of revelation. But the revelatory
history thus diminished in scope is fused with the proclamatory
account which testifies to it and in which the hearer is starkly
confronted with the sheer ineluctable fact of revelation in the
person of Jesus of Nazareth in such a way that faith is needed
to overcome the offence, and to submit to the negation—
faith which recognises its own blindness in order to become
seeing" (IX. 39).[8]   Hence in the proclamatory message the
hearer encounters, not, as in John's Gospel, an account of the
saving action of God towards mankind, which by the mere
fact of its having happened authorises and proves the message
—the account of the salvation of the κόσμος resulting from the
τετέλεσται (XIX. 30) of the actuality of which the παράκλητος
must remind the Church as though it were the history of the
Church itself (XIV. 16 ff., 26, xv. 26, XVI. 7 ff.). The situation
here is rather that in the sheer fact of Christ he is confronted by
a claim which promises fullness of life, and which is rooted in
history only in so far as he meets it in a historical person, but
it is a person whose whole personal history is without significance beyond the fact that its historical emergence is the
"eschatological event."   Thus the revelational history is
distinguishable from the proclamatory exposition only inasmuch as the stark revelational fact is needed in order to set the
Gospel proclamation in motion.   It is now the believing
hearer himself who has to authorise and verify the fact of
revelation and the whole Gospel message by means of his own
personal history. This brings us back again to the principle
enunciated in VII. 17, but with the difference that the διδαχή
has been abstracted from the event to which it bears witness,
except in so far as it is an eschatological event.

[7] *Op. cit.*, p. 413.   [8] *Op. cit.*, p. 414.

R

It cannot be denied that this exegesis of Bultmann's conceals a particular systematic conception. There is no reason to make this an objection against Bultmann, for no exegete can make shift without such. But he must be able to give an account of the systematic conception he uses. This, too, Bultmann has done, because his systematic ideas stem from a specific solution of the hermeneutical problem. Hence the question whether his exegesis is correct or not must be discussed mainly with the purpose of testing his hermeneutical presuppositions by the facts of exegetical findings. But how could such a thinker break the vicious circle of his hermeneutics? He cannot interpret the "history" which we have found in St John's Gospel otherwise than as he does, if he is to stick to his hermeneutical rule that "in order to evaluate these events as historical, I must of course have a prior understanding of the historical possibilities within which they gain their character and significance as historical." [9] Hence we must agree with Karl Barth when he says: "Bultmann is an exegete. But I do not think that we can argue with him on an exegetical level, because at the same time he is a systematic theologian of such a type that there can hardly be a text in the treatment of which certain axioms of his thought do not become at once so obviously predominant that absolutely everything depends on the question of their validity." [10] But neither can one argue with him about his systematic presuppositions, since for these he refers us back to the conclusions of his exegesis, and can do so by means of his hermeneutical principles. Thus his hermeneutical circle makes him unassailable by any enquiry whether with his reference of systematic theology to hermeneutics he has done justice to the object of theological enquiry. Only within the circle of his presuppositions is it possible to argue with him.

But we refuse to move inside this circle because in that case we would no longer be allowing the text to say what it wishes to say. If this is already obvious in his exposition of the Gospel of St John, from which Bultmann insists that in the first instance he derived his presuppositions, then it must be

[9] Bultmann, "Das Problem der Hermeneutik," in *Z. Th. K.*, 1950, pp. 47 ff.
[10] Barth, *K. D.*, VOL. III. 2, p. 534.

still more plain in regard to other New Testament writings. Thus, for example, Günther Bornkamm says about his exegesis of Paul: Christ "not only makes possible for me the decision of faith, which I have to make, but prior to that He is the reality of a decision which God in His saving grace has made about me. He not only gives me the possibility of understanding myself anew in my own life and history, but He opens up to me a totally new life and history by drawing me into the sphere of His eternal life. In this way, Bultmann's interpretations are (in my opinion) no longer sufficient, for they do not enable us to grasp the reality of the new life in Christ." [11] They are not sufficient because they do not enable us to grasp the life of Christ in its historical aspect: "Hence it is by no means sufficient to describe redemption in such a way that it means nothing more than a new qualification of my own life and history. Paul means in fact a new history which far transcends my own life. This is the purpose of the characteristically local expressions of Rom. VIII, which are of course exposed to mythological abuse (*gnosis* provides sufficient examples of this) but which must not be surrendered as being mythological and replaced by philosophical ideas which may be inferred from existence as such. The new life in Christ into which I am incorporated begins and ends in heaven, in its foundations and end it radically surpasses my own life history and the understanding of my own existence. Like all history it has its past, its present, and its future. Its past, the whence from which as a believer I come, now means 'God sent His only Son'; God *has* given Him up for us all; its present, its effectual operation, means 'Christ dwells within you, God *is* for us, Christ *is* with us . . .'; its future, its whither, means 'How *shall* He not freely with Him give us all things, who *will* separate us from the love of God?'" [12] And with regard to Bultmann's systematic theology as a whole Bornkamm says quite rightly: "The retention of the saving event, of the saving action of God in Christ, thus preserves Bultmann's theology from becoming a mere Christian existentialism. But his insistence on an existentialist approach as a hermen-

[11] See G. Bornkamm, "Mythos und Evangelium," in *Theologische Existenz heute*," n.s., XXVI (1951), pp. 24 ff.

[12] Bornkamm, *op. cit.*, p. 25.

eutical principle makes it impossible for him to understand the
speech of the New Testament about the person and history of
Christ as speech in any objective sense. It is transformed into
a system of significance, it is dissolved into a mere '*significat*'
and has lost the force of the '*est.*' . . . The theological thinking
out of the reality implied by the Gospel message and faith is a
task which still has to be performed." [13]   This difficulty about
Bultmann's inadequate idea of the reality implied in the
gospel is shared also by Ernst Fuchs in his discussion of
Bornkamm's work.[14]   Yet he thinks that the "problem can
be terminologically elucidated without any necessity for the
attempted re-interpretation of the idea of history which
Bornkamm wants" [15] though this is hardly the intention of
Bornkamm, who instead of proposing any new solution
wishes to frame the question in different terms in opposition
to Bultmann.   In our opinion what is needed here is no
"terminological elucidation," and no new "idea of History";
it is simply a question of whether a specific history is to be
grasped or not as actual.   In any event Bultmann has failed
to do this, hence his reduction of the systematic problem to a
hermeneutical question is not intrinsically right and justified.

(c) Gerhard Ebeling's reduction of the systematic problem
to a hermeneutical one

Ebeling [16] begins with the observation that the object of
theology belongs to history: proclamation develops within
the tradition of the Church. The preacher is bound to a text
which is a specific document within a process of historical
tradition. In order to become proclamation this text requires
exegesis, with all the translation work linguistically and
ideologically necessary for this. A type of proclamation
which confines itself to merely repeating the text or in a
Biblicist manner derives from it a series of timelessly valid
propositions, in order to present them as universal truth, by

[13] Bornkamm, *op. cit.*, p. 19.

[14] See E. Fuchs, "Frontwechsel um Bultmann?" in *Th. Lit.-Z.*, 1952,
11-20.

[15] Fuchs, *op. cit.*, 17.

[16] See G. Ebeling, *Die Geschichtlichkeit der Kirche und ihrer Verkündigung
als theologisches Problem*, 1954.

disregarding the continual transformations within the historical process, necessarily misses the constant factor, namely the Word of God. But in saying this Ebeling is not really referring, as we have done, to a history, or an exceptional history, as object of theology, but to a "theology which is determined by the problem of the historical," [17] or to the taking seriously of the historical character, to bringing out its historical values,[18] to the theological problematics of the historical, etc. With regard to this difference, i.e. that Ebeling, unlike ourselves, is not speaking of *history* itself, but of the problem of *the historical* as the true object of theology, it might be said that he is thus taking the necessary next step. For this datum of historical fact must become for theological thought the problem of the historical. With reservations this might be granted; but then we must take care that the actuality of the history is not dissolved into the general problem of the historical. We think that Ebeling runs this risk, and, warned by the example of Bultmann, we see the danger especially in his conclusion that the emergence of the problem of the historical in all its theological depth *"comes to the same thing* [italics ours]" as "the problem of hermeneutics." [19] In view of "the phenomenon of Church history as a whole," Ebeling proposes to "consider the problem of the theological relevance of the historical nature of the Church and its proclamation." [20] We wonder if it can turn out well when he tries to come to grips with tradition, with which we have to do in the history of the Church, by means of a "general analysis of the essence of tradition." [21] The tradition with which we are concerned in Church history, means, at any rate in so far as Apostolic tradition is concerned, that God surrenders Himself and His word into the hand of a human process of tradition.[22] Certainly this process of transmitting tradition, even at the Apostolic stage, as a human thing, brings us face to face with the problem of "the combination of change and persistence," [23] in which Ebeling sees the essence of all tradition. But this problem concerns only a secondary aspect of the matter which need not have much theological relevance. What is theologically relevant above

---

[17] Ebeling, *op. cit.*, p. 25. [18] *Op. cit.*, p. 29. [19] *Ibid.*
[20] *Op. cit.*, p. 30. [21] *Op. cit.*, p. 31.
[22] See above, Ch. 7. [23] Ebeling, *op. cit.*, p. 31.

all is the essentially *precedent* question, namely by what features
this process of tradition is marked out as the self-surrender of
God and His Word. Only after considering this can we rightly
go on to the *next* point, concerning the enduring element amid
the vicissitudes of this history.

Tradition is "an event which combines the past and the
present into a unity and continues to operate in an historical
continuum," [24] in which the obligations arising from the past
give direction to the future. It challenges man to accept it
and to guard it critically in its purity and so to shape his own
present within the limits set by this decisively moulded process,
though with the freedom for which he has scope within this
framework. Then after this phenomenological analysis of the
problem of tradition Ebeling proceeds to deal with its theological aspect,[25] by considering the attitude to tradition
characteristic of early Catholicism, modern Catholicism and the
Reformation. Of especial interest to us is the way in which he
brings out the contrast between the Reformation principle of
Scripture and the Catholic principle of tradition. He says:
"The best thing about the early Catholic doctrine of tradition
was the formation of the canon of the New Testament, with
which after all the early Catholic Church could least manage
to deal, and moreover the canon in all its breadth and polyphonic texture, laden as it is with tensions and contrasts. For
in this form the so-called Apostolic tradition was best calculated, not simply to provide an answer to the question
of tradition, but to keep alive its challenge, and thus to
point beyond itself to Jesus Christ, as the Founder of the
Church." [26]   There may yet be more to be said about
Apostolic tradition reflected in the canon than that the Church
itself (so to speak) laid a cuckoo's egg in its nest in order to
keep alive criticism of its traditions. The important point
here is in what way Scripture in its polyphonic texture alludes
to Jesus Christ. In our own study of the question of the canon
we understood this to mean that we may not dissociate any
one of the various witnesses from the historical continuity, of
which, together with the other witnesses, it forms an integral
part, and that no one witness may in this way be given
absolute value.   Because the individual witnesses in their

[24] *Op. cit.*, p. 33.   [25] *Op. cit.*, p. 38.   [26] *Op. cit.*, p. 44.

mutual protectiveness stand responsible for each other in the proclamatory tradition, they point beyond themselves to the voice of Christ and the Word of God to which they wish to testify in common. And we could not disregard the fact that they believe themselves to be inspired in their witness in a quite specific sense, which however is to be carefully distinguished from the later doctrine of verbal inspiration.[27] But on this point what is Ebeling's attitude? Does the contingent fact of the canon mean for him, as for us, that Jesus Christ has spoken in the individual voices of this polyphonic composition and wills to go on speaking because God has surrendered Himself to just this stream of tradition? Or is it simply that for him the canon is a specially outstanding piece of Church tradition because it is best calculated to call in question from time to time this very tradition? The question might also be put in this pointed way: is the canon in its contingent factuality to be understood as a characteristic product of that stream of history in which God has surrendered Himself to a human process of tradition, or is its historical contingency only a constant reminder of the fact that "everything of which theology speaks is drawn into the vortex of the historical?"[28] This question will have to be decided by the conception of the Reformation principle of Scripture. It is not yet answered when Ebeling on the one hand says, "The limit of the canon must essentially be regarded as an open limit," but adds, on the other hand: "We see in the adherence of Protestantism to the canon of early Catholicism, assuming it was done with true understanding, the capacity to think historically and to respect a datum of Church tradition which it was felt should not be revised except under the stress of necessity, though it was not made into an absolute dogma."[29] We think this is too ambiguously put—what is the meaning of "absolute" and "dogma"?—and it admits all sorts of answers to our question. With regard to the theological basis of the canon he says: "The insight which was already realised at the Reformation, and then lost sight of, to be clearly formulated only in the theology of the Enlightenment, namely that the content of Scripture is authoritative not because it stands in

[27] See above, pp. 200 ff.   [28] Ebeling, *op. cit.*, p. 8.
[29] *Op. cit.*, pp. 52-3.

Scripture, but that Scripture is authoritative because of its content, compels us to bring our understanding of the canon into accord with it. This raises the question of the canon within the canon." [30]   Hence, as we said, the sole possible basis for the existence of the canon lies not in its sheer givenness, but the fact of the canon means no more than a piece of Church tradition which is to be respected and not to be revised except under the stress of necessity. Scripture receives its authority not from its givenness but from its content. But what is the nature of this authority which Ebeling seeks to discover by establishing a canon within the canon? In this respect it is not a question of authorising the canon as a whole and as such, but only of discovering a hermeneutical criterion for the exegesis of the individual writings within the canon. This enquiry is justified historically by pointing out that already in the formation of the canon by early Catholicism a hermeneutical principle was at work, as a result of which the genuine Pauline Epistles were (on the one hand) made capable of canonisation, and were (on the other), at the same time, to be interpreted in an early Catholic sense. "The point of canonising the deutero-Pauline writings was to set up a hermeneutical principle for the interpretation of what was genuinely Pauline, i.e. a piece of post-Apostolic development was put forward as genuinely Apostolic and by its incorporation into the canon all discussion was forbidden. Thus already in the early Catholic canon there is to be found a definite element of interpretation determined by the self-understanding of the early Catholic Church." [31]   In face of this historical judgment we might ask on purely historical grounds, incidentally, how Ebeling conceives of this consciously acting and planning subject which was responsible for the process of canonisation. But apart from this point, and supposing even that only the common sense of the Church was at work, the meaning of canonisation is here understood to be the introduction of a specific hermeneutical criterion. With this Ebeling contrasts the Reformers' understanding of the canon, for which the decisive question is "whether the exegesis of the New Testament is freed from this principle of interpretation involved in the early Catholic formation of the canon and

whether in lieu of these early Catholic elements the real centre
of the New Testament is admitted as the hermeneutical canon
for the exegesis of the New Testament as a whole." [32]   But if
the canon of Scripture owes its very existence and meaning to
the early Catholic hermeneutical canon, then the latter
cannot be simply replaced by another hermeneutical canon,
and indeed one with precisely opposite tendencies, while at
the same time it is desired to maintain the canon of Scripture
as a whole.   But Ebeling clearly thinks that he can do this.

In spite of its dubiety as the canon, the New Testament
retains for Ebeling its significance as "the original witness to
Christ," [33] on the basis of which "the eschatological action of
God" in Jesus Christ continues to be proclaimed and through
the proclamation is ever again re-enacted in the present.   But
in view of the manifold variety of the New Testament witnesses
what becomes of the unity of Scripture and thus of the unity of
proclamation and the Church?   "With the surrender of the
Catholic principle of tradition, and limitation to the Reformers'
principle of Scripture, the question of the unity of the Church
becomes dependent on the task of expounding this original
and varied witness to Christ.   We might go so far as to say
that the Reformers' reliance on Scripture alone makes the
unity of the Church depend on the problem of hermeneutics,
and stakes the unity of the Church on the bold venture of
existing solely by its connexion with the original witness and
without the security offered by the broader basis of tradition
—a connexion which is wholly at the mercy of Scriptural
exposition." [34]   In this matter Ebeling appeals to the authority
of Luther: "Scripture is *per sese certissima, facillima, apertissima,
sui ipsius interpres, omnium omnia probans, iudicans et illuminans.*
Scripture alone is therefore the *principium primum* of its own
exegesis." [35]   But *why* is it all this, and *why* can Luther dare to
rest the whole unity of proclamation and the Church on the
self-exposition of Scripture?   In view of the manifold variety
of Scriptural testimony he could hardly have done so in virtue
of the fact that it is the original (in the sense of "historically
the first") witness to Christ, and we who are so much better
acquainted with this manifold variety than he was could do

[32] *Ibid.*   [33] *Op. cit.,* p. 66.
[34] *Op. cit.,* p. 69.   [35] *Op. cit.,* p. 71.

so much less.   Rather he must in some way have assumed that
the "originality" of Scripture consists not only in its historical
priority to Church tradition, but that Jesus Christ in a special
and exclusive way surrendered Himself to these witnesses and
that *for this reason* they point to Jesus Christ as their originator.
Thus for Luther the "*solus Christus*" is fused with the "*sola
gratia*" and the "*sola scriptura*."   But as far as we can see
Ebeling repudiates any such suggestion, because he fears the
tendency to "isolate a specific part of history from the rest of
history, as a process of ontological and absolute significance,
i.e. as a sphere of the historical which is *sui generis*." [36]   Yet
without some such "separation" we can hardly do justice to
the testimony.   In this connexion we would prefer not to speak
of a sphere of the historical which is *sui generis*, but of a process
of history which is *sui generis* and yet would in no way need to
be of ontological and absolute significance and distinctiveness.
Its distinctive quality could be indicated rather only in
dogmatic terms, which, as we shall see, is something different.
But for this very reason Ebeling is concerned that the canon
should not be made a dogmatic datum as opposed to a datum
of Church tradition and history. [37]

In place of this dogmatic datum he puts Church history
itself, which refers us to Holy Scripture, the testimony to
Jesus Christ the Founder of the Church, and this is a final
court of appeal. [38]   "It is *de facto* the case in the history of the
Church that without reference to Holy Scripture there can be
no answer to the question as to the meaning and nature of our
relation to Jesus Christ.   Hence every attempt at an answer
must be tested by Holy Scripture." [39]   Thus it is the fact of
Church history which makes Ebeling stake everything on the
exegesis of Scripture: "Because in the whole course of its
history the Church is bound to this text, the task of theology is
not subjective and arbitrary, and an understanding in the
sphere of theology is not a hopeless prospect.   For exegesis is
a work which can be checked and is subject to generally
binding rules.   What professes to be exegesis must yield itself
to careful scrutiny.   And difficult as the problem of exegesis
and its scrutiny may be, it is in any case a problem which

[36] *Op. cit.*, p. 60.   [37] *Op. cit.*, p. 53.
[38] *Op. cit.* p. 78.   [39] *Op. cit.*, p. 79.

admits of intelligent and generally acceptable solution." [40]
But the history of the Church that is bound to this text runs
its course within history as a whole and hence is subject to
the general laws of persistence and change which govern all
tradition. "The category of exegesis in its structural continuity understands how this variability is bound up with
identity and how identity must merge into variability." [41]

How is this structural continuity related to the historical
element in Scripture and what criteria does it yield for the
testing of exegesis? "The enduring element in the vicissitudes
of Church history is the origin of the Church, the witness to
which makes the Church what it is: Ἰησοῦς Χριστὸς ἐχθὲς καὶ
σήμερον ὁ αὐτός, καὶ εἰς τοὺς αἰῶνας (Heb. XIII. 8)" [42] The
changing element is this witness itself in its historical development. But the persistent self-identical element is nowhere
separated from the ever-changing, not even in Scripture
itself, for this too is an historical witness to Jesus Christ, and as
such is subject to the laws of change. Nevertheless it is the
original witness which—as even Ebeling must suppose—is
fitted, in an exclusive way, by its continued proclamation,
to maintain the Church in continuity with its Founder and
in identity with itself. At the same time, there is a self-
identity of the world "which consists in the fact that the world
in all its historical changes remains the world, or, expressed
in other terms, that mankind at all times remains essentially
the same, in so far as it is of the world, self-identical in virtue
of its origin and understanding its being in terms of the
world." [43]   In this self-identical world the history of the
Church, self-identical through the proclamation of Scripture,
unfolds itself as a history of the exposition of Scripture,[44] as
Ebeling earlier defined the essence of Church history.[45]

Now, does Ebeling use this definition of Church history as a
critical criterion to evaluate Church history, or is it for him
simply a means of understanding the phenomenon of Church
history? Clearly he uses it in both ways, and if we understand
him rightly, the hinge of his whole conception lies in just this
—that this definition can insensibly pass from the phenomenological understanding of Church history to a theological and

[40] *Ibid.*   [41] *Op. cit.*, p. 82.   [42] *Op. cit.*, pp. 81 f.
[43] *Op. cit.*, p. 84.   [44] *Op. cit.*, p. 81.   [45] Cp. above, p. 146.

critical understanding. It grasps the phenomenon in so far as it observes that all churches, even though they use different hermeneutical criteria, appeal to their exegesis of Scripture, and from this stem both the features they have in common and their differences. But if the definition is to go further than this and become a theological and critical evaluation of Church history, then it requires a definite and authoritative hermeneutical canon. This is, for Ebeling, the Reformers' understanding of Scripture. For him "it is not the isolated single word of Scripture as such which is of binding authority—not even, in our opinion, the single word in its connexion with Apostolic proclamation as a whole and as an aspect of the latter"—but rather "the words of Scripture receive their authority purely from their relation to the focus of Scripture as a whole. The function of exegesis is to illuminate this relation to Jesus Christ as the radiating centre of Scripture." [46] But what are the marks of this relation to Jesus Christ, which, as we have seen above, was concealed in the early catholic approach? Ebeling does not explicitly express himself on this point. But obviously this relation would be more readily discovered, in any event, by a reversal of the early Catholic criterion, by setting up the genuinely Pauline as against the deutero-Pauline. This, however, in the first instance, would have the effect of making the genuine Paul, whose testimony moreover is somewhat complex, rather than Jesus Christ, the centre of Scripture. Or should one say (what is probably Ebeling's opinion) that with Paul this relation to Jesus Christ is least obscure, just because a criterion of exegesis derived from Paul best enables us to understand the structural continuity of identity and variability, persistence and change, and, consequently, the historical character of the New Testament witnesses as a whole. But to what extent does this disclose that the relation to Jesus Christ is the focus of Scripture? Probably because this universally valid structural continuity must be taken as vouching for the historicity of the testimony to Jesus Christ and its interpretation (though a link in the argument is missing, which should have shown how a particular and infallible principle of interpretation could take the place of Jesus Christ Himself). In the history of the Church this testimony is proclaimed

[46] Ebeling, *op. cit.*, p. 57.

with the effect of opening up the possibility of faith.   The
hearer whom it endeavours to persuade in the world, "is not
only the unbeliever but also the believer who exists historically
in the world and who must constantly be reminded that his
being has its origin not in this world but in God." [47]   The aim
of the proclamation must be, therefore, to reclaim from
worldliness a Church and a world constantly exposed to the
danger of secularisation, and the interpretation of Scripture
discloses to it with vivid relevance the ever new forms of this
continual danger, in order to overcome it again and again by
pointing to the testimony of Jesus Christ.   But this critical
criterion must be applied not only to the exposition of Scripture
in the history of the Church, but also to Scripture itself, which
already is part of Church history, and is therefore in danger of
the same process of secularisation.   Thus by the circuitous route
of Church history this hermeneutical canon is ultimately
derived from Scripture itself, since it is at the same time
applied to the exposition of the latter.   Scripture therefore
seems to need no legitimation beyond itself, since it authorises
itself by the application to it of this hermeneutical canon.   In
this way Ebeling dares to stake the unity of the Church and
its proclamation on the "category of exposition" alone, and by
means of it to investigate the "theological relevance" of the
phenomena of Church history.   The phenomenological use of
the definition of Church history as the "history of the exposition
of Holy Scripture" has apparently become transformed into a
critical criterion.

But this is only apparently so.   In fact Ebeling has surrepti-
tiously filled his formal category of exposition with the content
of the Reformers' understanding of Scripture, and thus—
quite apart from the question whether he is historically
justified—has made a particular period of Church history and
its spirit the criterion for the true interpretation of Scripture.

He bases this procedure not on a dogmatic but on an historical
consideration.   "The fact that nevertheless the Reformation
of the sixteenth century is a unique, unsurpassable, and ever
normative event of Church history is one of those inexplicable
secrets of the historical process in which, despite many detailed
changes, there are but few periods of fundamental and decisive

[47] *Op. cit.*, p. 81.

significance. Such a unique period of fundamental importance
was the sixteenth century because then a new understanding
of Scripture emerged and overcame the approach to Scripture
which had controlled the whole of the previous course of
Church history." [48] This theological interpretation of the
significance of critical periods in Church history has thus
made it possible for him to dispense with a dogmatic judgment.
At the same time Ebeling emphasises that "the Evangelical
Church also can only be true to itself if it attempts to secure
itself historically," for which reason it, too, must always
subject its own traditions to the critical process of Scriptural
exposition. [49] Ebeling distinguishes three such crises of fundamental importance in the history of the Church: "(1) The rise
of early Catholic hermeneutics; (2) the rise of the Reformers'
hermeneutics; and (3) the total reconstruction of hermeneutics
which coincides with the inauguration of the modern epoch in
the history of ideas and the challenge of which has been
occupying us theologically up to the present." [50] Adding
that this "third chapter in the history of hermeneutics, unlike
its two predecessors, did not give rise to a confession," he
puts the question: "Is this because it was of the very essence
of this modern critical approach to Scripture not to constitute
but to dissolve Church life? Or is it because between the
Reformation and modern hermeneutics there exists, in spite
of all that seems to contradict this, a close inner connexion,
which would explain also the different attitude of the Catholic
and Protestant churches towards the question of historical
critical methods? Or are these two possibilities not mutually
exclusive? Might it be the case that Protestantism as such
already called in question the whole conception of the Church
as a factor which was concerned to secure and maintain itself
within history, because the Reformation placed Scripture
above tradition and the Word of God above the Church?
That is the question which confronts us today." [51]

It is clear that Ebeling wishes to answer the question in the
third way and so to overcome the alternative of a factor
disintegrating to Church life or strengthening to Church life.
But does not this simply resolve the Reformation understanding
of Scripture and its hermeneutical canon into a matter of

[48] *Op. cit.*, p. 90.   [49] *Ibid.*   [50] *Op. cit.*, p. 91.   [51] *Ibid.*

eternal dialectics as a result of which the Church, securing itself historically by means of its tradition and forced to do so by the very nature of historical life, is again and again deprived of this security since all such attempts, made by means of doctrine and Church order, are called in question by Scripture? Was not this the meaning of the sixteenth-century Reformation? We confess that we are simply puzzled by Ebeling's procedure in this respect, because we cannot understand why he, above all, who lays such emphasis on the historical being of the Church, concludes with such a remarkably unhistorical idea. Should it not be possible to show that within Church tradition there is also a theologically legitimate development of Church life, that doctrine and Church ordinances do not *merely* serve the purpose of self-security within history, if only because it is necessary to have a critical standard by which to resist that kind of false security? Otherwise all Church tradition must be explained wholesale by the motive of attaining security as Ebeling does. With him this is probably the result of the fact that he classes Church tradition with the general pheno-menon of historical tradition, and also sees in the canon a Church tradition to be respected and not to be revised except under the stress of necessity.[52] It is of no avail that sub-sequently he wishes to base Church tradition on Scripture, and at the same time to make of the latter the critical criterion of tradition. His real criterion is not, of course, the contingent historical fact of the Scriptural canon, but the hermeneutical canon, which is an abstraction from Church history and derived from the epoch-making significance assigned to the Reformation, and which again only applies the general category of exposition to the special case of Scripture. Thus Scripture gains a twofold function, both constitutive of the Church and disintegrating to the Church. But the fatal thing is that, according to Ebeling's outlook, it operates to strengthen the Church where its exposition is theologically wild, where it is guided by no criterion or by a false one; on the other hand it is disintegrating to the Church where its exposition is theologically correct. Surely there may be something not quite in harmony here.

Since Ebeling refers the whole problematics of theology to

[52] *Op. cit.*, p. 53.

the problem of hermeneutics, we must still enquire what his solution of the problem signifies as regards exegetical discussion. He says that the problem of exegesis is a problem which admits of intelligent and generally acceptable solution.[53] But on his own assumptions, it can only be true that exegesis is, as he insists, a work which can be checked and is subject to generally binding rules [54] if we accept his own hermeneutical canon. If we do so, then a verification and comparison of exegesis will be possible; and one can and must speak of wrong and right exegesis both in regard to exegetical procedure and detailed conclusions. If we represent Ebeling's point of view we have *the* right exegesis because scientifically verifiable and demonstrable, although of course as is seen within the school of Bultmann, there still remain enough possibilities of controversy. But, on the other hand, any possibility of understanding with Catholic theologians on the matter of Scriptural exposition would be from the outset excluded. In this case, however, what becomes of the unity of the Church, which is promised to us, even though as an historical reality it has never existed? We have been told: "The Reformers' Scriptural principle surrenders the unity of the Church to the hermeneutical problem" since this unity is staked wholly on the nexus with the original testimony to Christ in Scripture, i.e. "a nexus which is wholly bound up with the problem of interpreting this original testimony." [55] But the common nexus with Scripture can bear fruit only so long as there is a possibility of understanding about Scriptural exposition. It is just this, however, which is excluded by the Reformers' understanding of Scripture which hazards the unity of the Church not on the link with Scripture but on the link with a "category of exposition," or in other words; not on the canon of Scripture but on the hermeneutical canon. As regards the question whether this view is truly that of the Reformers, Ebeling has shown himself a specialist by his studies in Luther's hermeneutics. But if we grant that he can appeal to the authority of Luther in justification of his conception, then the Church of the Reformation could no longer repudiate the reproach which is constantly being made against it, that it made a new

[53] *Op. cit.*, p. 79.   [54] *Ibid.*
[55] *Op. cit.*, p. 69.

departure and started the break-up of Christendom.[56]   If
this is the case, then it would be Luther himself who made out
of the Reformation a new confessional church. Of course this
would involve an ecclesiastical *novum* among the confessional
churches only in so far as its characteristic would be that it
was the only confessional Church based on a principle which
permanently called in question all points of view from which
a confessional Church might spring. As regards the promised
unity of the Church, it would be in the same position as the
other confessional churches which require their own basis
to be adopted by others if the unity of the Church is to be
realised.   The only difference would be that this Lutheran
principle would have the effect not of aspiring towards a
universal Lutheran Church but of questioning the *raison d'être*
of every single confessional church.   And the latter would
have to surrender their churchmanship not to a new unsecured
Church—such a Church cannot exist—but to a critical
principle which is disintegrating to all churchmanship and
deprives all churches of their basic security—namely, the
principle *"ecclesia semper reformanda."*

But in order that this whole dialectic might once more be
firmly rooted on the soil of ecclesiastical history, this new
confessional Church, which desires not to be a Church, would
be forced to—shall we say, excuse or justify—its existence by
appeal to the "Pauline principle of ὡς μή, having as though we
had not." [57]   And this brings us again to the question of
correct Scriptural exposition and the usefulness of this
hermeneutical canon; for we consider it exegetically impossible
simply to apply the ὡς μή in 1 Cor. VII. 29 ff., which there
refers to οἱ χρώμενοι τὸν κόσμον (vs. 30), to relationship to
Church tradition, as has become quite usual nowadays.   This
can only be done if, like Ebeling, we classify Church tradition
along with the general phenomenon of tradition.   In any case,
Paul himself would not have allowed the ὡς μή to be applied
to Apostolic tradition. Ebeling's whole theory might once more
become distinctly questionable in the light of this by no means
unimportant detail of exegesis, which would show that one
inevitably thinks on these abstract and unhistorical lines if

---

[56] Cp. Diem, *Theol.*, VOL. I, § 20 ("Die Einheit der Kirche"), pp. 261 ff.
[57] Ebeling, *op. cit.* (above, n. 16), p. 90.

S

one insists on reducing the question of revelation as history to the problem of the nature of the historical.

(d) History and the historical in Friedrich Gogarten

Friedrich Gogarten's systematic theology [58] moves essentially in the same circle of problems as that of Bultmann and Ebeling, with the result that our initial question concerning revelation as history stands in the main at the centre of his thought. He reduces all other problems to this one. He too regards this revelatory history as the history of Jesus Christ who in his message proclaims Himself, as we ourselves have insisted,[59] and he also lays the greatest stress on the fact that we have here something which has become actual fact, and for that reason alone is being constantly re-enacted. In *Entmythologisierung und Kirche*, in which he discusses the work of Ernst Kinder,[60] he declares that he is in agreement with those theologians who say, like Schieder, that the saving acts of God "are indestructibly, indissolubly, immovably given as prior to all human existence." [61] According to him "the question which is debatable and calls for decision, is rather that of how, in what way, the action of God in history is prevenient to all human being and doing. On the one hand, the objective factuality of this saving action is emphasised, while, on the other, it is said that the action of God, embodied in the destiny of one concrete historical man and accordingly a once-for-all action, strikes men as something prevenient to their life, through the medium of the New Testament *kerygma*." [62] Thus the alternative is the priority of this history as "objective factuality" or as an experience mediated through the *kerygma*. Of course in modern discussion the question is framed in this way; and this simplification may well enable Gogarten to carry on the debate with his partner. If, however, it is assumed (as we have consistently done) that the divine saving action meets us only in the *kerygma*, then the question of

---

[58] See F. Gogarten, *Entmythologisierung und Kirche*, 1953, cited below as *E. und K.*
[59] See above, pp. 114 ff.
[60] E. Kinder, *Ein Wort lutherischer Theologen zur Entmythologisierung*, 1952.
[61] Quoted by Gogarten, *E. und K.*, p. 56.
[62] Gogarten, *E. und K.*, p. 56.

revelation as history can no longer be reduced to this simple alternative. In that case the question is framed more precisely from within the history of proclamation, and it is asked what actualised history precedes the event of proclamation. In this case it still remains an open question as to what medium is proper for grasping this history which precedes proclamation and by its actuality authorises and verifies proclamation; for that is just the point. Should it turn out that talk of "objective factuality" or of historically verifiable saving acts is not the appropriate medium for grasping this history, as with Gogarten we assume to be the case, then the question itself still remains to be settled.

When Jesus declares Himself to be the one whom the Father has sent, the statement implies "a unity between God and Himself, which concerns more than the words He speaks. What kind of unity is this?" [63] The question is whether the relation between Jesus and God should be understood metaphysically as in early church Christology, or whether "it should be understood historically." [64] When we speak of the "historical character of this turning of God towards us in and through Jesus," [65] we are not alluding to what is meant by "saving facts" and "objective" happenings. "Rather this question about historical character is concerned with the ultimate mystery of revelation, which early Church dogmatists tried to understand by means of the concepts of late Greek metaphysics, which were the only means at their disposal, and thus through the mystery of the unity of the divine and human natures in the one person of Christ, or, as we might more correctly express it, they tried to symbolise it thus since they were well aware that they should retain the element of mystery. Because they realised that here and only here—in the hiddenness of the unity of the Father and the Son—salvation is actualised both in time and eternity, their whole thought and devotion was orientated by this conception. For here tower up "the hills of God unshakably and with unbreakable rock-like solidity, *pro nobis*, but also *sine nobis* and *contra nos* in spite of the world's unbelief." [66] We agree with Gogarten that "here, in relation to the ultimate mystery of revelation, the unity of the Father and the Son, the question of the

[63] *Op. cit.*, p. 58.   [64] *Ibid.*   [65] *Op. cit.*, p. 59.   [66] *Ibid.*

historical aspect of salvation is to be posed and takes on its full seriousness." [67]   But Gogarten thinks that it is no longer possible for us today to express this unity by means of the ancient Church dogma, because this uses the Greek idea of φύσις and hence cannot speak of an event. We will set aside the question whether Gogarten is correct in thinking that it is impossible to make any further use of the ancient dogma on account of its metaphysical nature, and can the more readily do so seeing that Gogarten has no intention of surrendering its meaning, namely the mystery of the unity of the Father and the Son. "A historical approach to the matter is of just as little use as the metaphysics of the ancient dogma. Rather, the former, like the latter, only attempts to preserve the mystery of the saving event as a mystery, which, seeing that it takes place between God and Jesus, is a divine-human event. Yet it preserves this mystery as something historical." [68]

This historical aspect means, he continues, "two things and yet one. Firstly, it happens in eternity between God and Jesus; secondly, it happens in time between Jesus and the world. . . . In Luther's hymn 'Rejoice, O ye Christians,' is expressed in an unsurpassed way the theme of this drama which is one and yet has a twofold bearing. In its first phase the theme runs, 'He spake to His dear Son: the time draws nigh to have mercy'; and in its second phase, 'He spake to me: hold fast to Me.' And Luther expresses the unity of the two by saying, 'The Son became obedient to the Father'." [69] For Gogarten everything depends on the two aspects of the event, the temporal and the eternal, being held together in a unity: "Here we have, however, neither two mysteries nor two events, but one mystery, that of God's turning towards us in mercy in Jesus Christ. And it manifests itself as such precisely in that we neither can nor may speak of it except inasmuch as its two phases are mutually involved." [70]   But, granted that it is a question of one and the same mystery, and that in speaking of the one event we must always speak of the other, must we not see in Luther's hymn, regarding what happens in eternity between God and Jesus and what happens in time between Jesus and the world, a reference to two events,

[67] *Op. cit.*, p. 60.   [68] *Ibid.*
[69] *Op. cit.*, pp. 60 f.   [70] *Op. cit.*, p. 60.

if not separable, at least clearly distinguishable? Again we grant that "in what happens in eternity between the Father and the Son the world and we men are implied, and only in thus far does it concern us. In what happens in time between Jesus and the world, in His earthly destiny and course of life, the eternal unity of the Father and the Son is involved, and only so is there actualised in that earthly destiny the unity of Jesus with the world and of the world with Him." But before we can unreservedly go on with Gogarten to say that "this oneness is in both cases something historical in character," [71] we must ask: "Is this event which is both temporal and eternal legitimately to be regarded as one and the same event—that of God's turning towards us in mercy— though described now in one aspect, now in the other?" God's merciful condescension towards us takes place in the Incarnation of the Word. This divine condescension is an action of God, an event, a definite act, in relation to which there is a before and an after and the idea of revelation as history depends on the actuality of this event in which God as He is in Himself becomes God for us. Only so can the oneness of God and Jesus, and of Jesus and the world become, as Gogarten says, "a historical happening." [72] But if we blur this distinction which alone makes possible revelation in history, then it is a question whether Gogarten's argument can prevent the inference that the Incarnation of the Word is not a real historical event which in its actuality is prevenient to my own history, but something which has merely the implication that it qualifies our temporal history as having an eternal bearing and thus gives it an historical significance.

Wilhelm Kamlah [73] gives a philosophical criticism of this sequence of ideas, which is of such decisive importance for the whole argument. Asking whether we really are faced by "the decision between historical and metaphysical thought," he says, "The language in which the unity of God and man has sometimes been expressed is not under discussion here. Here we are merely concerned with the point as to what can be the meaning of Gogarten's repeated and urgent qualification

[71] *Ibid.*　　　　[72] *Ibid.*
[73] See W. Kamlah, "*Die Entscheidung zwischen geschichtlichem und meta-physischem Denken,*" in *Ev. Th.,* 1954, pp. 171 ff.

'but precisely as something historical.' [74] If anyone speaks, as Gogarten does here, of the oneness 'which combines eternal and temporal history indissolubly together,' [75] I might suppose that I understood to some extent what he means if he were then to add that he was speaking of the unity of the historical and super-historical. But Gogarten thinks that such a phrase would be inadmissible because suspect of metaphysics. It is a question not merely of temporal but in all seriousness of eternal history also. But what can this mean if it is not to have metaphysical implications? If it is to mean history in the strict sense and furthermore in Heidegger's sense? I do not see that Heidegger, despite his arbitrariness, meant anything else by 'history' than temporal history, for of course 'being and time' was his problem, certainly not 'time and eternity.' Nor do I see how by history, 'if language is to have any meaning at all,' [76] anything but temporal history can be intended. Thus, if we are not content to leave the *mysterium fidei*, but wish to reach an understanding of it, or even a 'conceptual' understanding, I do not at all see how the comprehensive idea of 'the historical,' on which Gogarten so much insists, can be of much help in this direction. Least of all do I see how this can still be regarded as the same idea which Gogarten had earlier developed on the lines of Heidegger—the idea which he developed like Heidegger, yet less in consequence of a genuinely Christian type of thought, than of his preoccupation with the historical, of which he can say: 'For this is the insight which we owe to the historical outlook that man, however else he may be defined, is himself determined by history'." [77] Kamlah concludes with the question, "which now first arises, whether we can really understand the historical from the point of view of the 'historicity' of the existence of the individual, of which it is said that it is the background for the supposition 'that there is such a thing as history'." [78] In his reply, Gogarten says on this point: [79]

[74] Gogarten, *E. und K.*, p. 60; see above.

[75] Gogarten, *op. cit.*, p. 61.   [76] Gogarten, *op. cit.*, p. 35.

[77] Gogarten, *op. cit.*, p. 81, quoted in Kamlah, *op. cit.*, p. 176.

[78] Gogarten, *op. cit.*, p. 33, quoted in Kamlah, *op. cit.*, pp. 176 f.

[79] F. Gogarten, "Zur Frage nach dem Ursprung des geschichtlichen Denkens; Eine Antwort an Wilhelm Kamlah," cited below as "Antwort," in *Ev. Th.*, 1954, pp. 226 ff.

"Now in truth everything for me depends on understanding this happening to be in the most genuine sense historical. This means: if this happening is other than what we normally call history—and this it obviously is—yet the governing difference must not be of such a kind as can only be described by an altogether different conception of history—namely that of super-history. The difference must rather be defined within the limits of the historical. In exactly the same way as the qualitative difference of the man whose relation with God is the subject of this happening does not consist in His being something like a super-man. . . . Only so long as He is 'true man' does the community between Him and ourselves remain, without which He could not be understood as Saviour in the sense in which the Christian faith understands Him. The latter understands Him to be Saviour because it believes in Him as the man who is at one with God. What I am concerned about is the genuinely historical character of this unity in the sense I have described." [80] In our opinion this does not answer Kamlah's question how this historical value can embrace both time and eternity.

But Gogarten stresses that this unity is brought about by the Son's obedience: "As this obedience is the link which binds together eternal and temporal history into an indissoluble unity, it indicates both the oneness of Father and Son, and that which subsists between Jesus and the world." [81] But what is to be understood by this obedience? Of it Gogarten says: "If we enquire into the 'history which was there enacted' and which is enacted unto the end of the world, then we must examine the attitude of obedience and all that it implies. Otherwise we are faced only with the *res gestae* which in themselves are not the object of belief in any way." [82] If we think again of the Luther's hymn, we see that there the obedience of the Son is preceded by the decision and command of the Father who sends Him into this world, or, to use Gogarten's phraseology, the Father's "appeal" to the Son, which the latter answers by His obedience, and from this is distinguished the action between Jesus and ourselves, in which the summons of His preaching requires our obedience. Since

[80] Gogarten, "Antwort," pp. 230 ff.
[81] Gogarten, *E. und K.*, p. 61. [82] *Op. cit.*, p. 62.

Gogarten insists that the two events are not to be distinguished, the process of revelation in history and the process of proclamation merge into each other and show the attitude of obedience which consists in "responsibility" in face of an "appeal," as Gogarten understands these ideas from Heidegger. In this view of things we must not ask whether it is a question of the obedience of Jesus or of our own obedience, or of both, or how the obedience of Jesus is distinguished from our own or precedes it as the ground which makes it possible. In the first place it is simply a matter of obedience as such which is a specific mode of being, "the historical," corresponding to revelation in history, and through which, therefore, "the unity of the divine and human is realised." [83]

Responsibility means "not an undetermined, arbitrarily chosen attitude, but the answer called forth by a word that is spoken and which can only be given by the whole power of one's being." [84] A man who is responsible for the world and its form, and is therefore historical, cannot express his relationship to the world in the subject-object pattern, because then an isolated subject would stand face to face with an isolated object, and man's original relationship to the world would no longer be realised. The same is true if, in the pattern of this type of thought, history is conceived of as an object. There is no way from this conception of history as an "objective" reality to the "historical dimension" of man's being. This for Gogarten is "*the* point at which so-called modern thought must be overcome, and at which theology must strive to attain an exact and penetrating type of thought appropriate to it." [85] The ideas of "responsibility" and "historicity" enable us to grasp "a relationship of man to the world which is original and in which he always finds himself, and which he does not need to invoke subsequently in reflexion, as in the case of the subject-object pattern, where he has to prove the reality of the world or believe in it." [86] Here the "world" is not to be understood as something already existent, but as the element in which man is immersed or out of which he exists, which corresponds formally to the Pauline use of prepositions when he speaks of man as being in sin or under the Law. Because sin "reigns,"

[83] *Op. cit.*, p. 41.   [84] *Op. cit.*, p. 43.
[85] *Op. cit.*, p. 44.   [86] *Op. cit.*, p. 45.

to be "in sin" is the same thing as to be "in the world." This can be expressed existentially as the confession of sin. But if we wish to give a theological account of this, "then we must do so conceptually, and since sin affects not only the doing but also the being of man, this means in respect of the existential structure of the inner life of man, as the Apostle Paul does, in terms that are universally known." [87] But this self-understanding, existentially interpreted, must in no event be transposed into the subject-object scheme of thought, otherwise there would necessarily arise all those misunderstandings which have been brought out in the demythologising debate, which see in this self-understanding only an "immanentist consciousness," [88] or a "subjective phenomenon which as such is without relation to reality or indeed dissolves the latter." [89]

Gogarten thinks that such mistakes are made not only by Bultmann's enemies but also, occasionally, by his friends, e.g. Günter Bornkamm [90] in the passage quoted by us above.[91] It is very significant for Gogarten's own position that he inevitably sees such a misunderstanding in the fact that Bornkamm distinguishes between the history of the obedience of Christ and my own history and does not try to interpret the Pauline text in such a way that the two coincide. Moreover, Bornkamm speaks of the new life which is opened up by the fact of Christ, whereas Gogarten, up to the present, has spoken of existence under sin. Hence Gogarten ought first to show how the new existence is related to the old, or how his idea of historicity characterises the new existence also. Hence he should give material reasons why Bornkamm ought not to make this distinction.

The "existential structure" of the old and the new life is in any case the same, in support of which Gogarten appeals to Heidegger.[92] The mark of this structure is "responsibility," through which man answers by his whole being a call addressed to him, and so becomes "historical." But even though this whole existential structure must be the same in the old and new existence, and hence both can be designated by the concept of historicity, the further question arises as to the

[87] *Op. cit.*, p. 46.   [88] *Op. cit.*, p. 47.   [89] *Op. cit.*, p. 48.
[90] Gogarten, *op. cit.*, p. 47, n. 1.
[91] Above, p. 251.   [92] Gogarten, *op. cit.*, p. 46, n. 1.

meaning of the fact that this call means different things at different times. With Heidegger it is conscience which addresses man by appealing to his own true being.[93] But in this case who calls and who is the one addressed? "Ontologically it is by no means sufficient to answer that being is both the one who calls and the one who is called. *Is* then being, as summoned, not otherwise there, except as the summoner? Does man's own deepest capacity for selfhood function as the summoner? " [94] In anxiety about capacity for selfhood, being grows afraid, for it sees itself faced by the nothingness of the world, and dispeace is revealed in this foundation feeling of anxiety. Thus "being finding itself grounded in anxiety and dispeace becomes the summoner of conscience."[95] With Gogarten it is the summons of sin which by appeal to the law accuses me, who examine my life, and in the face of which I must give account of myself by my whole existence. Here the "mode of existence made possible is that of corruption." [96] Thus it is in the old existence; and although Heidegger calls the summoner dispeace and Gogarten calls it sin, yet they refer to the same ontic phenomenon, the only difference being that Gogarten, with the help of Paul, gives it another name. But what are we to say about the call which was addressed to Jesus and which He answers with His obedience, and further of the call addressed to us through the proclamation of the Gospel of Jesus and summoning us to new life?

To refer back to Luther's hymn Jesus is summoned by His Father and He answers the summons by His human existence in filial obedience to the Father. This existence of Jesus must formally be in its existential structure the same as that which receives historical value by the call of anxiety or of sin. Otherwise the being of Jesus would not be that of a man. But apart from this formal similarity, what is the meaning of the difference that (in the one case) sin makes its voice heard in a corrupt mode of existence and (in the other) it is the merciful God who expresses His will to save from this corruption? It would seem obvious to answer that in the latter case the

[93] Cp. Heidegger, *Sein und Zeit*, 1927, pp. 272 ff.
[94] Heidegger, *op. cit.*, p. 275.   [95] Heidegger, *op. cit.*, p. 276.
[96] Gogarten, *E. und K.*, p. 47.

call does not, as in the former, spring from human immanence, but that—since it must be a question of divine self-revelation— it springs from God's action towards man as distinct from the action of man's self-understanding. But this cannot be so, since we would then have the relation between a divine and a human process which could scarcely be understood otherwise than by means of the forbidden subject-object scheme of thought. Hence the difference in this summons must consist in the fact that it makes possible a new and quite other order of human existence, in such a way that it "individualises and interiorises it to its very depths." [97] But it is just this which was lacking to the existence of man as springing from an immanent call, as a result of which it became a corrupt order of existence. As Christian faith lives only in "purest subjectivity" [98] so it can become aware of God only in "extreme subjectivity." [99] And "In subjectivity alone are we faced by the reality of God. Only through it does God become for us God." [100]

We think, of course, that were it a question of the *event* of God's self-revelation, then we could not ask how "God becomes God for us," and establish in the requirement of the "purest subjectivity" those conditions under which alone we have to do with the reality of God. It would rather have to be the converse, namely, that God by His action becomes God for us, and by His manner of doing so Himself makes the conditions under which we can encounter Him. But according to his whole approach Gogarten can express the matter only as he does, and therefore he argues not from the actuality of revelation, but from the idea of subjectivity, which alone makes possible the encounter between God and man: "The subjectivity which we are seeking is that in which man becomes aware of reality; the latter by its very essence cannot become an object, and, in face of it, man cannot be the controller of himself or a being grounded in itself. *Here* lies subjectivity of personal being." Thus once more the circle of the argument closes and the conclusion confirms that man may not think in the scheme of the subject-object relation, and also explains why.

[97] F. Gogarten, *Die Verkündigung Jesu Christi*, 1948, cited below as *Verkündigung*, p. 493.
[98] Gogarten, *Verkündigung*, p. 493.   [99] *Op. cit.*, p. 494.   [100] *Ibid.*

This means, of course, that revelation as event has been surrendered and reduced to a new self-understanding of subjectivised and individualised existence, in the historical dimension of which the factuality of revelation is dissolved. The actual history of Jesus Christ is a presupposition for this historicity of existence only in so far as, through the proclamation of that history which alone makes the history effectually present, the call of God becomes a reality.

From this point of view we neither can nor must enquire into the event itself as distinct from its proclamation, since that would mean a lapse into the subject-object mode of thought which is to be overcome. History must rather be freed from every sort of objectivisation in thought. Hence the purpose of systematic theology is not to attain objectively valid statements, whether in the sense of objectively proved statements about the facts concerning Jesus, or in the sense of dogmatic statements about the action of God in Jesus Christ. The aim is, on the contrary, to discover the genuine subjective truth of the faith in the ever-changing situations of the mind and spirit which human development brings, and by unfolding this truth in the struggle against all that threatens it, to help towards an ever new self-revelation of the word of God. In this way it is possible for Gogarten to take up our third circle of problems, the question of the *regula fidei*, and by discussing historicity to lead the argument back to the first set of problems, the question of revelation as history.

Gogarten sees here, too, a means of overcoming an abstract historicism. He describes the latter as a type of thought in which "all historical patterns and norms are recognised to be 'merely' historical, with the result that their validity is confined to their actual historical limits," and thus personal responsibility in the face of history is lost sight of.[101] This lifeless historicism is overcome if "we understand history and the historical dimension in its true historical essence, or, as we should rather say, since a word of verbal force is required, in its vital control."[102] And this general conception of the historical is also applied to the events of revelation: "What is thus generally true of history and the historical, no matter

[101] F. Gogarten, *Der Mensch zwischen Gott und welt*, 1952, p. 454.
[102] Gogarten, *E. und K.*, p. 66.

what the nature of the events in question, is no less true of the history with which the theologian is concerned." To the objection that the process of revelation, in contradiction with its essential character, has been subsumed under a general view of history and the historical, Gogarten might reply that this very understanding of history springs from the Christian faith and that it brings out the vital essence of the historical, since "it illuminates the genuinely Christian understanding of human existence and of the world of man as a historical world." [103] He might say that he has done nothing but bring to light the New Testament understanding of history which was obscured by the medieval conception,[104] because Greek thought, which was the starting-point for medievalism, tried to grasp the reality of the world, not in its changes, and thus not historically, but in its changeless being.[105] At the root of this medieval view of history lie "both the metaphysical approach to the Christian faith, which was expressed in its classical form in the Christological and Trinitarian dogmas of the early Church as elaborated by the Fathers and the first four General Councils, and also Roman Catholic sacramentalism, which cannot be separated from this metaphysical approach." [106]

Here—in the same way as we found in the case of Ebeling —we come across what is in the last resort the decisive link in the argument of Gogarten, namely interpretation in terms of an epoch of absolute significance. Thus he says that "the total reinterpretation of human life in terms of the historical which makes its appearance in the modern age is not something in the nature of a new theory or one of the many world views among which we can choose and which we may adopt, according to our interests: but one might almost say that it represents the original understanding of human life by which we all live, whether we are Christians or not. . . ." [107] Here a new responsibility of man for the world as his world is indicated, and "although we must admit that the special expression of this responsibility, as it has evolved in the development of modern life, owes its origin to the beginnings of the modern epoch, the same is not true of this responsibility in itself. What is true of it is rather the amazing fact, which even yet has

[103] Gogarten, *op. cit.*, p. 18.   [104] *Ibid.*   [105] *Op. cit.*, p. 19.
[106] *Op. cit.*, p. 21.   [107] *Op. cit.*, p. 23.

hardly gained recognition, that it has its origin in the Christian faith itself." [108] On this point again, the philosopher Wilhelm Kamlah says: "That all this is amazing who would wish to dispute? Hence to repeat: we are to think historically and no longer metaphysically because the historical approach understood as responsibility for the world and its development belongs to the original essence of human life. This moulding of the life of the world in responsibility is foreign to the Middle Ages, it only emerges as the spirit of modern times, but in such wise that thereby there springs to light again what is the original Christian understanding of man. In this account, it is the historian who is chiefly surprised and who enquires: If the birth of the modern age meant a renewal of genuine Christian thought, why did not the Reformation suffice for this genesis? The fact that modern enlightenment took shape within the sphere of Christendom gave it no doubt a radical character which was foreign to antiquity. But this paradoxical influence of Christianity on the formation of modern civilisation does not really make Christianity the sole historical root of the latter, and does not make that renewal of genuinely Christian thought which Gogarten, like every one else, finds in Luther rather than Descartes, the same thing as the emergence of the modern epoch. Of course, Gogarten, too, wants to criticise modern thought, and in particular Cartesianism with its subject-object cleavage," [109] for he points out "that the modern development of the world has not remained on the lines it originally took (moreover when and where is this original form to be found?) but has lapsed from its ideal 'as far as world-responsibility is concerned,' more precisely because it has departed from the historical and has sought refuge once again in the metaphysical. According to this the spirit of the modern age in its original essence was legitimate both from the point of view of Christianity and also philosophically, and its subsequent perversion is to be understood as a lapse into the obscurities of metaphysics—but can such theories conceal the doubt whether we are not again here faced by a reconstruction of history which in spite of its apparent historical mode of thought does not do justice to the living spirit of history? And must we not further fear that

[108] *Op. cit.*, pp. 24 f.   [109] Kamlah, *op. cit* (above, n. 73), p. 174.

this Christianising interpretation of modern historical thought will block the way by which we might hope to achieve a satisfying critique of this thought and its Cartesian idea of reality? In fact, is not the alternative of 'metaphysical' and 'historical' which Gogarten establishes only, perhaps, a variation of the precisely similar Cartesian dualism of reality and consciousness (or nature and history) which Gogarten rightly considers to be the root evil of contemporary thought? Gogarten of course says that 'historical thought' itself implies the overcoming of this dualism," [110] and tries to show this by illuminating the mystery of the unity of God and man in the process of salvation against the background of his idea of the 'historical'—an attempt which Kamlah, as we saw above,[111] considers unsuccessful.

It still remains for us to point out that Gogarten has also drawn our second set of problems, the question of hermeneutics, into his systematic theology and in the same way has linked it up with the first problem, revelation as history. His circular argument from systematic conception to Scriptural exposition has far greater scope than is the case with Bultmann, because it is not simply that a specific existential understanding and the New Testament *kerygma* are brought into relation with each other, but that the whole history of ideas and of theology is involved, and, conversely, made the basis for the systematic conception. But essentially, in both cases, a systematic conception supposedly taken from Scripture itself furnishes the critical criterion for a demythologising of the New Testament: "If it is a question of a critical interpretation of New Testament mythology, then it is not—as some theologians in their unhappy fear of knowledge immediately suppose as soon as they hear the word 'critical'—that this criterion is taken from an alien world view, but rather is it taken from the New Testament understanding of history plainly enough expressed in spite of mythological elements in New Testament language. And the critical interpretation tries, by means of this criterion, to show what the New Testament intends to say by means of the mythology to be found in it." [112] This means that we cannot exegetically discuss the systematic conception

[110] Kamlah, *op. cit.*, p. 175.   [111] Above, pp. 269 ff.
[112] Gogarten, *E. und K.*, p. 63.

of Gogarten any more than that of Ebeling or Bultmann because every controversial issue, and indeed every point, unless we constantly refer one-sidedly to certain texts and leave others out of account, must at once lead to a debate about the systematic presuppositions.

(e) Retrospect

In consequence, is there no other course but to accept or reject as a whole the contemporary systematic position together with the hermeneutical circle it involves, or are there possibilities of criticising it from within? That is to say: Must we resign ourselves to the present comfortless position of modern theological discussion which means that we must become pupils of a master (who of course may be not only Bultmann or Gogarten but also Barth) or adherents of a definite theological movement, at the cost of no longer being able to speak with or read the works of a member of the opposing party, or even needing to read him and so not in fact doing so? We should note that this state of affairs prevails not only between exegetes and systematic theologians, as is continually complained, but, according to our present conclusions, has been made all the more hopeless by the work of those systematic exegetes who proposed to overcome it through their attempt to reduce the whole problematics of theology to the hermeneutical problem. As a result, the evil has now spread from systematic theology to every section of theology.

What possibilities then remain of criticising these systematic conceptions from within? Naturally these always exist. We have ourselves given a few examples and quoted others. Such critical objections can introduce nuances and variations, can make more precise the framing of a question or formulate other questions, dispute principles and methods or replace them by others, reject certain interpretations, etc. But this achieves nothing so long as the debate is carried on on both sides by instruments of thought, and for the sake of instruments of thought, the choice of which can be shown to be justified for material, historical, and personal reasons, but must appear arbitrary when measured against the theological object. In this way we attain no common theological basis of discussion and no serviceable norms for exegetical and systematic discussion. Now we have seen that all three of our systematic theologians were careful to avoid all such questions and statements as are commonly called dogmatic; and, on the other hand, we had to make our objections just at those points where we had the impression that they missed the essence of the matter precisely through the avoidance of dogmatic thinking. If we wish to take our debate with them further and not confine ourselves to an ultimately useless criticism from within, then we must now go on to enquire what is the real meaning of dogmatic thinking and whether and to what extent systematic theology must merge into dogmatics.

T

CHAPTER XI

SCRIPTURAL EXPOSITION AS THE THEOLOGICAL FOCUS OF DOGMATIC THOUGHT

(a) The idea of Dogma in the New Testament

THE ideas denoted by δόγμα and δογματίζειν occur but infrequently in the New Testament,[1] and two connotations of the term can be distinguished. I. In Lk. II. 1, Acts XVI. 7, and Heb. XI. 23, δόγμα connotes a decree of government. In Acts XVII. 4, where the decisions and ordinances of the Apostles and elders in Jerusalem, especially those of the Apostolic Council, are called δόγματα, this meaning is taken over to express the directives of Church-government, and this is continued later in the use of δογματίζειν with reference to the enactment of canonical law by the Church Councils. II. In Eph. II. 15, the δόγματα are commands of the law drawn up in detailed regulations, those regulations of the "bond which was against us" of Col. II. 14. Here we see a continuation of the linguistic usage of Hellenistic Judaism where δόγμα is used to denote the divine ordinance of the Mosaic Law—a connotation which in Josephus and Philo overlaps with the meaning of "doctrine" or "point of doctrine" characteristic of Hellenistic philosophy: "The Torah becomes a system of sacred doctrines contained in a divine philosophy and comparable with the δόγματα of secular philosophy."[2] But δογματίζεσθαι, or submission to regulations (Col. II. 20) given in these δόγματα, has come to an end with Christ. This meaning of δόγμα cannot, therefore, be positively continued by the Church without further question. Nor does this anywhere happen in the New Testament. On the other hand,

---

[1] On this cp. Kittel, VOL. II, pp. 233 ff.
[2] Kittel, VOL. II, pp. 234 f.

we find the Apostolic Fathers already speaking of the δόγματα τοῦ Κυρίου and τοῦ εὐαγγελίου. We shall have to consider whether in such terminology we have merely a formal continuation of the language used to denote the divine ordinance of the Torah and an application of it to New Testament doctrine, or whether here, too, as is the case with Josephus and Philo, we are faced by a linguistic usage which overlaps with that of Hellenistic philosophy. In the latter event, we should have to go on to ask whether such a use of the idea of dogma in itself suggests a change from the Judaic to the Greek conception of teaching.[3] This question cannot be decided semantically, since "dogma," from a purely formal linguistic point of view, is an authoritative and normative pronouncement, and as such can equally well be applied to an authorisation and standardisation of doctrinal statements in the Judaic —New Testament sense—as to the Greek conception of such things. Thus an investigation of the meaning of the word is of no further help to us in our consideration of the theological focus of dogmatic thought and so we must endeavour to come to grips with our subject in a different way.

(b) The New Testament witnesses as witnesses to facts and witnesses to truth

Let us therefore take as our point of departure, as we did in the case of the problems of systematic theology, the general aims of Scriptural exposition. According to the understanding and point of view of its writers, Scripture contains statements made by witnesses. Let us remember, in this connexion, that in speaking of witnesses and testimony the New Testament took over from the usage of the Greek world the twofold connotation of witnessing, namely the giving of evidence about facts and the making known of views or truths with regard to those facts.[4] Since in the Gospel it is a question of the revelation of God in history, the two aspects of witnessing here coincide. Now, in regard to witnessing, truth is not intrinsically contained in the testimony itself. The latter can only be demonstrated as true by the object to which witness is borne. This means, as far as witnesses to facts are con-

---

[3] Cp. above, Ch. 6 ("Preaching and Doctrine").

[4] Cp. above, p. 118.

cerned, that the testimony is true as a result of the fact that
the thing attested did actually happen. As far as the witness
to truth is concerned, it means that what he declares to be his
opinion as to the significance of the event can only be verified
by the event itself, and only so can his declaration be
authorised; and this is so regardless of the fact that the New
Testament witness to the truth stakes his own existence on the
truth of what he attests, for even that does not in itself make it
true. The witness, in both these senses, does not appeal to a
criterion of truth which is at the hearer's disposal. If, as
regards the event attested, it is a question of "what no eye
has seen, nor ear heard, nor the heart of man conceived"
(1 Cor. II. 9), then its truth cannot be judged by our "prior
understanding of historical possibilities," [5] nor can it be
verified by the resources of historical science. The plain
truth is rather that it must be accepted as history merely in
virtue of the fact that it has happened. And because its sheer
factuality is its final and sole legitimation, the question of its
meaning cannot be dissociated from that factuality. The New
Testament witnesses are agreed in declaring that the meaning
of the event was disclosed to them only in the light of the
actuality of the event, and this in the strictest sense, with the
result that it was the sheer happening of the event which made
possible and conditioned their recognition of its meaning.
Paul expresses this as follows: "God has revealed to us through
the Spirit. For the Spirit searches everything, even the
depths of God" (1 Cor. II. 10). By this he means that this
Spirit is not a principle for the discovery of truth or a mediator
who brings into a system of coherence what is true for God
and true for man. The Spirit of which it is here a question, is
rather an aspect of the event itself in its momentous actuality,
it is an act of God by means of which God makes Himself
understandable to man, for at the same time He makes man
a being who is capable of understanding Him. John expresses
the matter thus: "But to all who received him, who believed
in his name, he gave power to become children of God;
who were born, not of blood nor of the will of the flesh nor of
the will of man, but of God" (Jn. I. 12-13). Thus a new birth

[5] R. Bultmann, "Das Problem der Hermeneutik," in *Z. Th. K.*, 1950,
p. 66.

is required to achieve this insight of faith: "Unless one is born anew (γεννηθῇ ἄνωθεν) he cannot see the kingdom of God" (Jn. III. 3; cp. Mt. XVI. 17). But in this connexion the revealer comes εἰς τὰ ἴδια (Jn. I. 11), i.e. to men who already stand in a special relation to Him, which distinguishes them as men from other creatures. Thus it is fully presupposed that in virtue of this original relation to God they have the possibility of (φύσει . . . ποιῶσιν, Rom. II. 14) a purely natural awareness of God and understanding of His will (Rom. I. 18 ff.; Acts XVII. 16 ff., etc.). The *idea* of natural theology is by no means disputed. What is disputed is, on the other hand, any possibility that this natural knowledge of God might be conducive here and now to the recognition of the revelatory event in any other way than by making man inexcusable in the presence of it (Rom. I. 21, II. 1). But if by the agency of the Spirit man has divined in the actuality of the revelation its significance, then it cannot subsequently occur to him, transposed as he is into the καινὴ κτίσις (II Cor. V. 17) to apply values and criteria of truth which belong to the past ἀρχαῖα. All that now belongs to the οὐδένα οἴδαμεν κατὰ σάρκα of II Cor. V. 16. Thus neither immediately nor on reflexion has man any possibility of recognising the significance of the event other than what is given as a prior condition in the sheer happening of the event itself.

(c) *Existential and dogmatic accrediting of Biblical testimony*

We have seen that in regard to Biblical testimony the event and its significance are fused together into a unity. This fusion could have two reasons. It could arise, firstly, because the witness has appreciated in the actuality of the event its significance and by his acceptance of it has testified to its truth. This means that by the operation of the Holy Spirit what has happened is something which Paul expresses in the statement (Rom. VIII. 16) that "it is the Spirit himself bearing witness with our spirit that we are children of God," or which is implied in Jn. VII. 17, where the doing of the will of God does not mean individual actions on the part of man but must be understood rather to connote the act of decision to accept the attested διδαχή—a decision which involves the believer's existence as a whole. We might describe this first possibility as the *existential* verification of the Biblical testimony. The second possibility of explaining the coincidence of significance and actuality in the Biblical testimony would be that these two aspects are fused in the event itself which is being attested and *therefore* must also be fused in the testimony. To refer again to Jn. VII. 17, the θέλημα Θεοῦ is what God designs in history and what—since with Him the will and the performance are the same—He carries out in the sending of His Son. The διδαχή of Jesus is the teaching about, or the proclamation of, this saving counsel of God which is always at the same time a saving action and event; and such teaching is continued in the witness of the Evangelist. But what exactly does this διδαχή mean by contrast with the γινώσκειν? Does it in fact mean, as was the case with our first possibility, a verification by the attitude and response of the hearer? In his article on γινώσκω [6] Bultmann comments on the "apparently dogmatic way in which ὅτι sentences suggest the content of the γινώσκειν: what is being contended for is a dogma (a διδαχή, VII. 16 ff.): the dogma that Jesus is the Son of God (VII. 26, X. 38, XIV. 20, XVI. 3, XVII. 7 f., XXIII. 25, etc.). In truth what is at stake is the historical character of the revelation; but what follows from it is the offensiveness of a dogmatic recognition—and this latter may not legitimately be ignored in the Johannine γινώσκειν." [7] If in this way the content of the διδαχή is understood as a dogma and its appreciation is described as a dogmatic recognition, then this cannot mean anything else but that what is here taught or witnessed is, from a purely formal point of view, a truth *sui generis* which demands primarily not understanding but acknowledgment, in view of its authoritative character, though subsequently the acknowledgment may lead to understanding. This formal conception of dogma and dogmatic recognition has in the text its concrete content and quite specific meaning. The content is the will of God as revealed in the actuality and the significance of the sending of Jesus and as recognised in the indissoluble union of these two aspects. Thus in those of the Evangelist's sentences which are in question we are faced not merely by statements which are of an apparently dogmatic character, but by statements in which the idea of the dogmatic acquires quite a special meaning

---

[6] In Kittel, VOL. I, p. 688 ff.   [7] *Op. cit.*, p. 712.

in virtue of the thing expressed. The "dogmatic character" of the Johannine knowledge results from the fact that it is concerned with a διδαχή or a witness, the truth of which springs solely from the object attested. And since this testimony always involves both meaning and fact in indissoluble connexion, a dogmatic statement in this specific sense always concerns as Bultmann says "the historicity of revelation," or as we would rather say, revelation as history. Conversely no statement can be made about revelation in history which does not involve the offensiveness of a dogmatic recognition. Thus the γινώσκειν cannot imply a verification of the διδαχή by the hearer's existential attitude and response, but must denote primarily the acknowledgment of its dogmatic truth. Accordingly πιστεύειν precedes γινώσκειν. "In the relation of man with God, i.e. God in His self-revelation, πιστεύειν connotes the initial inclination of the heart, which, if maintained, receives the promised γινώσκειν (Jn. VIII. 31 ff., x. 38, cp. XIV. 20). True faith, i.e. faith which is steadfast, as such contains in itself the seed of γινώσκειν (cp. 1 Jn. II. 4 with 6); the latter in fact is an integral part of faith, and is indeed the understanding proper to faith, identical with that χαρά which no longer needs to ask (Jn. xv. 11, XVI. 22-4), and for which the words of Jesus no longer have the character of παροιμία but that of παρρησία (XVI. 25-9)." [8] If we described the first possibility as an existential verification of the Biblical testimony, this second possibility may be termed the dogmatic verification.

Thus within the context of Scriptural exposition we have discovered the theological focus of dogmatic thought, which we must now consider in more detail. First of all, we must enquire whether these two possibilities of accrediting Biblical testimony which we have described as the "existential" and the "dogmatic" are mutually exclusive. In any event this cannot be true of John, since for both possibilities we could appeal to Jn. VII. 16 f. It will become still more plain that it cannot be here a question of alternative possibilities when we observe "that obedience (ἀγαπᾶν) is described as the criterion of γινώσκειν";[9] it is "clear, therefore, that γινώσκειν does not mean a type of knowledge which investigates and examines

[8] *Op. cit.*, p. 713.   [9] *Op. cit.*, p. 712.

nor anything in the nature of speculation, nor yet mystical vision, which loosens the bonds of connexion with temporal history and action, but in fact γινώσκειν is fulfilled through action within history." [10]   Also what has been said above about the relation between πιστεύειν and γινώσκειν excludes the idea of an alternative between these two possibilities.   On the contrary, they would seem to belong to each other.   How indeed do they do so?

For the existential possibility we have referred to Rom. viii. 16.   But the same text may also be quoted in support of the dogmatic possibility.   That we attain the certitude of being the τέκνα Θεοῦ only through the συμμαρτυρεῖν of the πνεῦμα υἱοθεσίας (vs. 15) is only true under the presupposition that by the saving counsel of God we *are* already such.   Only if that is true can we *become* such by the surrender of our mind and spirit.   Otherwise, of course, we would have made ourselves sons of God by our own action.   But in what way is this status already assured to us by the saving counsel of God?   This intention of God towards us, revealed by His action in history, cannot be grasped in the form of a universally valid truth concerning mankind as the family of God.   That would be a mere speculation, which might appear both in the form of a theological statement about the being of God conceivable only in his turning towards man, in His "*pro nobis*" as also in the form of an anthropological statement about the being of man and his divine destiny.   In either of these ways we should be failing to appreciate the fact that the Biblical texts make no ontological statements about the counsel of God but only historical ones.   God has fulfilled His counsel concerning our status as sons.   This fulfilment took place inasmuch as through Christ we as sons were made heirs—κληρονόμοι μὲν Θεοῦ, συγκληρονόμοι δὲ Χριστοῦ (vs. 17)—or as, for example, this θέλημα of God is expressed in Eph. i. 5 ff.: προορίσας ἡμᾶς εἰς υἱοθεσίαν διὰ 'Ιησοῦ Χριστοῦ εἰς αὐτὸν . . . ἐχαρίτωσεν ἡμᾶς ἐν τῷ ἠγαπημένῳ.   Thus, to adhere to the metaphor of Rom. viii, this foundation of our sonship consists in our being called to be joint heirs with Christ.   But this does not mean that a universally valid truth about humanity has been replaced by an objective historical fact through which the saving

[10] *Op. cit.*, p. 711.

counsel of God has been realised and completed. It is rather
that the fulfilment of it continues to operate in our own life
when, in VIII. 17, Paul goes on to say εἴπερ συμπάσχωμεν ἵνα καὶ
συνδοξασθῶμεν. Hence we may not withdraw ourselves from
the process of the action of God directed towards us in order
to objectivise it, i.e. to make it an object of our own reflective,
considering, or even existential attitude, and that not because
we are forbidden on philosophical grounds to think in "subject-
object" terms, but because we must become utterly involved
in the actual process of this history in order that it should
reach its appointed goal. This becomes still clearer when we
see that the realisation of the counsel of God is described
(VIII. 14) as the operation of the Spirit: ὅσοι γὰρ Πνεύματι
Θεοῦ ἄγονται, οὗτοι εἰσιν υἱοὶ Θεοῦ. In this Πνεύματι Θεοῦ
ἄγεσθαι (cp. also Gal. v. 18, Lk. IV. 1-9) the πνεῦμα is the active
subject within man. This is more precisely described as πνεῦμα
υἱοθεσίας in contrast to the πνεῦμα δουλείας (VIII. 15), i.e. as the
spirit which the son of the house enjoys and not the slave, for
this Spirit not only reveals to us that the purpose of God is
to make us sons, but makes effectual this filial adoption so
that by the same Spirit (ἐν ᾧ, vs. 15) we can address God as
Father (cp. also Gal. IV. 5; Eph. I. 5). Thus the Spirit is
God in action, in fact, God Himself acting to realise and
accomplish His counsel. Once again it is not we who have to
realise imaginatively this historical process of God's action
as though it were an object outside ourselves, but we have to
place ourselves in all the actuality of our existence within it,
or rather allow ourselves to be placed within it. Thus far
there is just as little opposition between the existential and the
dogmatic approach as we found to be the case in St. John's
Gospel.

But it does *not* follow from this that these two points of view
condition each other. The συμμαρτυρεῖν of Rom. VIII. 16
might be taken to suggest this, were it a question of such a
συμμαρτυρεῖν as takes place, according to Rom. II. 15 and IX. 1,
between man and his συνείδησις. In our text however there is
no suggestion of reciprocal action; it is said that the πνεῦμα
υἱοθεσίας testifies to *our* spirit, but not the reverse. Such an
idea is not only excluded by the clear wording of the text, but
is materially excluded by the presupposition of the counsel of

God working itself out in His dealings towards us in history, as they are effected by Jesus Christ and the Holy Spirit. We may say, therefore, that the dogmatic truth includes the existential in so far as the will of God reaches its goal only through the existence of the believer as transformed by the work of the Holy Spirit, which means that the ring embracing God and man is closed by God Himself. We cannot, however, say, conversely, that the existential possibility also includes the dogmatic one, that therefore the accrediting of the Biblical testimony by the hearer's existential attitude also authenticates the thing attested both as to its factuality and significance. Such a thing is impossible.

(d) Exegetical difficulties

Now, of course, it might be that an exegete, in spite of the clear wording of the text, understood the συμμαρτυρεῖν to imply the existential possibility. He would not even need to assume this as an alternative to the dogmatic possibility, but he might suppose that in the πνεῦμα the two possibilities are fused, and the history of theology offers examples of this wherever the *testimonium Spiritus Sancti internum* is invoked as the *ultima ratio*. How obvious this interpretation is is seen immediately we appreciate the complexity of the problems involved in the συμμαρτυρεῖν. The first, and always the most difficult, of these problems is that of the relation between the indicative and imperative: we *are* children of God and yet we are to *become* so. Between the two there must lie an act of decision which presupposes freedom to decide. Does this mean God's freedom to decide for us, or our own freedom to decide for Him? If it were a question of the first freedom, there then arises the further question whether and to what extent it involves the second freedom. This again leads to the question about the relationship of the Holy Spirit to our own human spirit; whether there is a point of contact between the two at which the agency of the Holy Spirit might begin to operate or whether this point of contact is only established through the medium of Gospel proclamation. There might be yet a third possibility, namely that through the work of the Holy Spirit a capacity in man that exists only in a state of potentiality is once more roused into fullest activity. The answer given to these questions will not only decisively influence anthropology itself but will also be disclosed in the position assigned to anthropology within theology. We are here faced by questions of central importance, but which obviously cannot be decided on merely exegetical grounds, i.e. on the sole basis of the Biblical testimony. No doubt we might, with some degree of probability, infer from the Biblical testimony as a whole how the witnesses have answered these questions in so far as they were aware of them, and also to some extent how they would have answered them had such questions been put to them. But in so doing we are making inferences and suppositions conditioned by our own approach to systematic theology. Furthermore, our own questions are often framed in the context of other questions and in the light of other ideas than those which were current among the Biblical witnesses and accordingly cannot without more ado be applied to the text.

As an example of these exegetical difficulties we quote from Bultmann's *Theologie des Neue Testaments*: "It is perfectly clear that the πνεύματι ἄγεσθαι (Rom. viii. 14; Gal. v. 18) does not mean a rapture in which the will of man plays no part (cp. Cor. xii. 2), but presupposes just an act of decision between the either—or of σάρξ or πνεῦμα (Rom. viii. 12-14; Gal. v. 16-18). Likewise behind the apparently mythological expressions of the φρόνημα of the πνεῦμα (Rom. viii. 6-27) and its ἐπιθυμεῖν (Gal. v. 17) there is concealed this unity of resource for action and divine requirement. For the point of such expressions is to suggest that the πνεῦμα creates a new power of willing the origin of which lies not in man himself, but in the divine work of salvation—a willing which has a specific direction, which is emancipated from the σάρξ and is engaged in a struggle against it, since it is led by the divine demand. Again, the difficulty is overcome by the fact that, on the one hand, the πνεῦμα is imparted to all Christians in baptism, and, on the other, sometimes becomes manifest in special deeds of power." [11] In saying this Bultmann has reduced the exegetical questions to a certain common denominator: what is at issue in the problem of the agency of the Holy Spirit is the relation between the divine act of redemption and the fruits it produces

[11] Bultmann, *Theol. des N.T.*, p. 333.

in the inner life of man. The two must be envisaged in co-ordination with each other, even though the prevenience of the divine action must be safeguarded. The point at which the co-operation between God and man becomes effective is found in human decision, which (on the one hand) is released by the divine requirement and (on the other) consists in the answer which man gives by his "new power of willing." Thus is achieved the unity of divine will and human power of action. But in what exactly consists this human power of action bestowed upon man by the working of the Holy Spirit? Bultmann considers that Paul has two opinions about this: "In regarding the Πνεῦμα as a wonder-working energy Paul unreflectively shares those popular ideas according to which 'wonderful,' i.e. extraordinary phenomena, distinguishable from the course of normal life, are felt to be the direct mani-festation of the energy of the Spirit, and to this category belong such things as glossolaly, prophecy, miracles of healing, etc. (§ 14, 1)." [12] However, he also calls attention to a difference in the way in which such phenomena are conceived: "Accord-ing to the *animistic* mode of thought, the πνεῦμα is imagined as an independent subject, a personal power, which like a demon can seize upon man and take possession of his being, em-powering or impelling him to accomplish extraordinary and powerful actions," and for this point of view it is just Rom. viii. 16 which we find quoted along with other texts. "According to the *dynamic* mode of thought on the other hand the πνεῦμα appears as an impersonal power which like a fluid fills the personality of man. The one or the other conception may here and there and incidentally be vividly brought out, but in general no particular emphasis is placed on either and in one and the same author both points of view may be in-extricably mingled." [13] But Paul differentiates himself from this popular outlook "above all by the fact that he reckons the activities of charity within the sphere of the Church as belong-ing to the manifestations of the πνεῦμα . . . and by the fact that he connects moral conduct with the πνεῦμα. . . . This does not mean that he is giving to the πνεῦμα idea a spiritualising, ethicising twist, but indicates that he considers free ethical obedience to have its origin in sheer miracle, consistently with his

[12] *Ibid.*   [13] *Op. cit.,* pp. 153 ff.

view that man must be freed from the fetters of the flesh and sin and rendered obedient by the redeeming work of God." [14]

What answers to our questions are given by these exegetical conclusions which we are willing in the main to accept as correct? Clearly, so far, none. We have merely been told that in the writings of Paul we find, on the whole, two different ways of conceiving the mode of operation and the effects of the πνεῦμα in human life. According to the animistic-dynamistic type of thought we have a magical transformation of man which results in his endowment with supernatural powers. According to the other type of thought it is a question of the miracle by which through an act of decision there comes to birth in man a free ethical obedience and a new power of willing. Since these new resources which come to him are not to be conceived as magically imparted, the sole possibility which remains is that previously they were potential in him and now have been released into effective operation by this miracle. But which view is the correct one? Or perhaps one should not ask this question, since both views are to be found in Paul, and indeed in immediate juxtaposition with each other; for as regards the power of the πνεῦμα to bring about capacity for decision Bultmann refers, for example, to Rom. viii. 12-14, and as regards the animistic view he invokes Rom. viii. 16. Let us therefore ask what Paul really meant by speaking of one and the same thing in these different and inconsistent ways. We might suppose that he was not clear about the matter himself, or, if we do not want to suppose that, that he was faced by a mystery which could not be precisely and adequately expressed with the resources of thought at his disposal. In any event, we ourselves are confronted by the question how we are going to represent the matter, which apparently cannot be resolved exegically. We might, for example, see in Paul's second view his real opinion and by this second view, in consequence, demythologise the first view on broadly existential lines. Again, we might combine both views, as is done in the sacramental teaching of the Roman Catholic Church in combination with its doctrine of grace, and could then interpret the texts on that basis. But in both cases we should have expounded the texts by means of

[14] *Op. cit.*, pp. 333 ff.

a systematic theology which we ourselves had applied to them. We could then, by pursuing the same train of systematic thought, give an answer to all the questions which arose in the course of exegesis. But this would not of course be the answer of the texts but the answer yielded by a specific systematic approach which is suggested by the very fact that the various answers can only be discussed systematically, not exegetically. In this connexion there would in fact be no essential difference between the Roman Catholic systematics and those of Bultmann or Gogarten, quite apart from the fact that in certain vital questions, for example in the sphere of anthropology, their answers would be the same. The systematic theology of the Roman Church is by no means transformed into a dogmatic type of thought merely as a result of the fact that it makes a claim to dogmatic inerrancy. Otherwise, as we shall see, it would have to permit itself to be discussed on an exegetical basis too.

(e) The method of dogmatic exegesis

Let us now enquire what difference results when in exegesis we think no longer on systematic but on dogmatic lines. Once again, our point of departure is that the Biblical testimony can be authenticated as true only by that to which it bears witness: God's eternal plan, in its indissoluble unity of fact and meaning, as a consequence of which the revelation becomes an historical process that both has happened and is happening, as the witnesses attest. This gives a specific method to the exegetical search for truth. This method we have not freely thought out for ourselves, but have established it as a result of and in the course of exegesis itself and have of course applied it to the task of exegesis. We have beome involved in a hermeneutical circle in which the testimony is only to be interpreted by the thing testified and, again it is only the witnesses who can inform us about the latter. We have deliberately become involved in this circle because we consider that this is the mode of hearing and understanding the message which the text itself requires, and which alone corresponds to the testimony as an ἀκοή, a momentous declaration which demands to be listened to, and indeed as an ἀκοή πίστεως requires the obedience of faith (Rom. x. 14 ff.;

Gal. III. 2-5). In this connexion is to be noted the point to which Hellmut Traub draws our attention, namely, that ἀκοή connotes both "the shock of a strange message" and also "the possibility and the act of hearing it." The "ears which hear," and which Jesus opens (Mk. VII. 35), and the event of present hearing (Mt. XIII. 14), are linguistically and conceptually identical with what is heard, with the declaration and the communication, the preaching (Rom. X. 17).[15] The ἀκοή, which in its meaning as preaching (λόγος ἀκοῆς, I Thess. II. 13; Heb. IV. 2) comes close to ἀγγελία and κήρυγμα, is therefore a moment in the historical process of revelation which the latter both attests and effects. In our "hermeneutical circle" what is in question is nothing else but that in our Scriptural exegesis we must go to the place of ἀκοή because only there can we encounter the history which the text certifies, only at that centre can we appreciate it truly. And when we speak of a method of exegesis, this method cannot consist in the application of a principle, but quite the contrary, it can mean only the renunciation of all systematic thought about the event in order that we may stand at the locus of the event itself. This does not mean that we have made the faith of the exegete, which no one can control, the condition of sound exegesis, although it is certain that the true understanding of the text requires faith. We have also observed the distinction between the expositor and the preacher of Scripture, although all exposition must be tested against preaching. But whether the exegete stands at the locus of the ἀκοή, which again no one, not even he himself, can control, or whether he refuses to stand at that point in order to reserve to himself what he supposes to be his critical freedom over against the text—in any event it is true of him as the mere expositor, who neither is nor desires to be a believer or preacher, that he can appreciate the text only in the light of what happens at that locus.

What then happens at this locus in regard to the συμμαρτυρεῖν? We can no longer critically establish this simply from the point of view of the scientific history of religion, nor seek to explain and note it by referring to the "animistic type of thought." The πνεῦμα conceived as an "independent subject"

[15] See H. Traub, "Die Predigt von Kreuz und Auferstehung Jesu Christi," in *Theologische Existenz heute*, n.s., XLIII (1954), p. 5.

and as "a personal power" does perhaps here bear the appearance of a "demon," if we take the point of view of the phenomenology of religion. But it is clearly not the intention of the witnesses to describe a demonic phenomenon, but to proclaim the mighty action of God which they have encountered in the history of His dealings with men. For the Biblical writer this God is distinguished from all demons by the fact that as the God of Abraham, of Isaac and of Jacob He was already at work in His covenantal dealings with Israel; from which it follows that in his witness he can differentiate this God from all demons who deal otherwise only by calling Him the God of Israel and nothing else (cp. Rom. IX-XI). Furthermore, we may, with Bultmann, say that this God "seizes upon" man and "takes possession" of him, in which connexion we may remind ourselves of the experience of Paul at Damascus, as also of less dramatic but equally significant examples like the call of the disciples or other followers according to the reports of the Synoptics. In any case, however, the Apostle in the sequence of his thought in Rom. VIII wishes to say that in the πνεῦμα we encounter overwhelmingly not the fluid substance of impersonal power, but God Himself as the subject of a mighty action, or, as we may also say, as person, though in this connexion we are using that highly ambiguous term merely to indicate a contrast to something fluid and impersonal. In the ἀκοή God Himself as active subject turns to the hearer and is manifested through the πνεῦμα υἱοθεσίας, the hearer, for his part, realising his filial status and his partnership in the heritage of Christ according to the saving counsel of God, by an act of πνεύματι ἄγεσθαι accomplished in the power of the πνεῦμα. This whole process is summarily described as the συμμαρτυρεῖν, as a process which takes place between God as the bestowing subject and man as the receiving subject, and in such a way that the divine and the human come into closest communion without the human subject as such being dissolved.

If, now, we wish to represent to ourselves in conceptual terms what has taken place in this process of συμμαρτυρεῖν, then we are faced in regard to this action of God towards man with a history *sui generis*, in the light of which all possible analogies and comparisons fail, and which can only be understood in its unique character. God is here manifested as acting in three distinct modes of being: as Father, Son and Spirit, and in all three modes as the self-identical subject of this process. The ancient Church expressed what happens in such a process, as attested both in this text and in many other places of Scripture, by the construction of the dogma of the Holy Trinity. It did not simply read off this doctrine from Scripture —I Jn. v. 7, the only text which might be formally cited in support of the doctrine, not having been inserted before the fourth century—but rather the doctrine gradually arose through a long-drawn-out process of debate. In any case the Church's original intention, in the light of which we have to understand and critically appraise the whole process of the formation of dogma, was to give thereby a necessary help in the matter of Scriptural exposition. We have tried by this example to show how dogmatic pronouncements arose in their essential phases, though in so doing we have disregarded other, not directly relevant phases, which might possibly have had some influence here too.

(f) Dogmas as a means of orientating Scriptural exegesis

How then does this aid to exegesis work out in practice? The question of such an aid arose, as we saw, because the Biblical testimony does not contain intrinsic truth, but is dependent for its verification on that to which it bears witness. If a dogmatic pronouncement is made about the truth which is attested, for example, as is the case with the doctrine of the Holy Trinity, it is intended to fulfil a twofold purpose, formal and substantial. Just in the case of this fundamental dogma we can leave aside the question which aspect of this purpose is primary and which secondary, since they are in fact inseparable. The formal aspect of a dogmatic pronouncement consists in making clear that the only legitimate point of view which can orientate Scriptural exegesis is that the Biblical testimony can be verified both as to its factuality and significance (which are inseparable) solely by that to which witness is borne. From this it follows that every dogmatic pronouncement has certain essential characteristics. (1) A dogmatic statement is distinguished from every statement of a philosophical, metaphysical, mythological, or historical kind by the fact that in

U

the last resort its truth rests upon the contingence of an event, which may not be so co-ordinated with the system resulting from affirmations of these other categories that it is dissolved in them.   (2) This contingent event is essentially something *sui generis,* for the reason that its factuality is determined by its significance and *vice versa,* which is not true of any eternal truth emerging fortuitously as a truth of history, for in this case the eternal truth is essentially separable from its historical mode of manifestation.   (3) The dogmatic pronouncement has arisen in the course of the actual happening of the ἀκοή. If, now, we turn from these formal characteristics of the dogmatic pronouncement to their substantial aspect, as illustrated by the content of the doctrine of the Holy Trinity, the following norms for the exegesis of our texts follow: we are not told what the texts must say, but from what point of view we must approach them.   Thus in the instance we are considering we have to examine the texts to see whether and how far they speak of the *opera Trinitatis ad extra,* though the same texts will always, of course, have to be examined at the same time with reference to other dogmatic and Christological statements. We must not expect that we shall find in any one statement an explicit or quite complete *doctrine* concerning these *opera.* But the Church, which has given us this doctrine as an aid to exegesis, thereby leads us to expect that in all the texts we shall find the *opera* themselves attested.   To go back again to the passages quoted in Bultmann's *Theologie des Neuen Testaments,* even though in Rom. VIII. 16 the πνεῦμα may have been described in terms of "an animistic type of thought," such an observation is not yet a theological exegesis.   Nor does it become such even if we compare this passage with others in which we find the πνεῦμα understood as a summons to decision, and then according to our own standards, whether they arise from existential understanding or the insight of faith or whatever else, establish what really must have been "meant." Exegesis will only become theologically relevant and secure against arbitrary questions when we ask whether we do not find the *opera Trinitatis* attested in the συμμαρτυρεῖν and its context, hence whether, in order to put the matter quite plainly, God the Creator is not here making Himself understood by man whom He has created and whom in Jesus Christ

He has redeemed, and to whom He is thus attesting Himself through the Holy Ghost, with the result that through Jesus Christ man *may* once more address God as Father, and *can* so address Him because his life has been struck by these *opera Trinitatis.* Or let us think of the "union of strength for action and divine demand" and the question as to the solution of the difficulty arising from the relationship of the indicative and imperative. If the dogma of the Holy Trinity constitutes the point of view from which we should approach the texts, then the tension arising from the fact that we are addressed as those who already are children, and yet are required to become so, can no longer be explained by referring to the tension between the ideal and the actual, between objective and existential truth, or between the objective events of salvation and their subjective appropriation, and so on. All such terms of reference are shown to be not only inadequate but misleading, when it is realised that this tension corresponds simply to the relationship existing between the individual *opera trinitatis* and therefore can be overcome only through the operation of this relationship itself. But a further consequence is that we can now rightly frame the question concerning the power bestowed upon man as he decides through the marvel of the πνεῦμα and its relation to his own inherent possibilities, whether there is here conveyed to him a new potentiality through magico-sacramental means or whether a power already latent within him is now released into effective operation. This question, again, is shown to be wide of the mark and misleading, because the point is not that the πνεῦμα effects in man a transformation of his inner personal being by means of an additional *habitus*, but rather that through the πνεῦμα man receives personal being as a joint heir with Christ. It is not, indeed, a question of a capacity being bestowed on man, whether it be conceived as something poured into him from without or merely some latent power roused into new energy; rather the power which is active in that "free ethical obedience" is Christ Himself who is the ἄγων in the πνεύματι ἄγεσθαι. That here (as so often in the New Testament) the *opus Christi* and the *opus Spiritus* in the last analysis coincide, is consistent with the rule derived from the dogma of the Holy Trinity: *opera trinitatis ad extra*

sunt indivisa. This situation—μορφωθῇ Χριστὸς ἐν ὑμῖν (Gal.
IV. 19)—which must simply seem paradoxical and incompre-
hensible to any anthropology which is not grounded in the
doctrine of the Trinity, is expressed in Biblical statements
such as that "it is no longer I who live, but Christ who lives
in me" (Gal. II. 20), or that "your life is hid with Christ
in God" (Col. III. 3). We should consider how such texts are
capable of interpretation if we begin with the being of man
and not with the action of the triune God towards him, or
even if we try to combine both points of view, as Roman
Catholic theology attempts to do. It was not for nothing
that the Reformers fought so bitterly against Catholic
anthropology, and in opposition to it emphasised that man is
not to be defined by reference to the characteristics of his
essential being but only by reference to an event which happens
to him: that is, only in the light of the "hominem iustificari
fide." [16] They also realised that this event can only be
prevented from becoming dissolved into a self-initiated act of
human spontaneity under the guise of the *testimonium Spiritus
Sancti internum*, when it is understood in its proper context of
the *opera Trinitatis*. It is widely supposed today that one is
secure against such uncontrolled subjectivity if it is emphasised
with the *Confessio Augustana*, Art. V, that the Holy Spirit
cannot be experienced *"sine verbo externo."* But this is only true
if Word and Spirit are correctly distinguished in the Trinitarian
doctrine itself, as Art. I shows. If it is falsely taught in such
quarters *"quod non sint personae distinctae, sed quod Verbum significet
verbum vocale, et Spiritus motum in rebus creatum,"* then no longer
does the externality of the Word save us from subjectivising the
Spirit; and all Scriptural exposition remains a conversation of the
reader or hearer with himself, for which preaching as the mere
verbum vocale provides only the necessary instigation.[17] We can
appreciate from this interpretation of the Nicene Creed by
the authors of the *Augustana* how only a true dogmatic approach
can protect us from the arbitrariness of systematic theology,
and hence from an equally arbitrary exegesis.[18] In a far-

[16] Cp. Diem, *Theol.*, VOL. I, p. 244.
[17] Cp. Diem, "Est autem . . ." Barth-Festschrift 1936, pp. 320 ff.
[18] On this, cp. J. Koopmanns, *Das altkirchliche Dogma in der Reformation*,
to H. Quistorp, Beiträge zur *Evangelische Theologie*, VOL. XXII, 1955.

reaching study of the history of dogma, Jan Koopmanns, on this point, comes to the conclusion that the Reformers were the first theologians to formulate adequately the doctrine of the Holy Spirit by setting it within the context of the doctrine of the Holy Trinity. "By this means the Protestant teaching about salvation does in fact construct the first dogmatics which assign to early Church dogma the function that is proper to it. Justification and election, those essential elements in Protestant doctrine, are not only inconceivable apart from the basis of the early Church doctrine of the Trinity and early Church Christology: they are the necessary outcome and application of the latter." [19] This book will play a significant part in present-day discussion about early Church dogma and will dispel a number of prejudices: "Instead of regarding dogma itself as a product of the Greek mentality sprouting on the soil of the Gospel, we must affirm that the traces of Hellenism which survive obscure the whole meaning of dogma." [20]

These examples, to which we might add, as we please, others taken from every sphere of dogmatics, suffice to show how exegesis develops when it is orientated in its approach to the text by the dogmatic point of view. For what reasons might an exegete decline to use this resource? A representative of the historico-critical method might conceivably object that this type of exegesis is not scientifically exact. But what does this objection amount to? We can and must make use of all the resources of historical and critical knowledge together with its ancillary disciplines, in order to appraise as exactly as possible and in the clearest outline the historical context of the Biblical testimony. But after this has been done, the task of theological interpretation begins, which must perforce accept the situation that it is the object of the testimony which authenticates the latter. Dogmas arose in the process of ἀκοή, and in the course of such theological exposition as alone is congruous with its object and therefore alone is truly scholarly. For what valid reasons, then, should a later expositor decline to avail himself of the work of his predecessors on grounds of principle? This attitude by no means relieves him of the duty of himself initiating enquiries afresh about the object attested

[19] Koopmanns, *op. cit.*, pp. 114 ff.
[20] Koopmanns, *op. cit.*, p. 114.

as reflected in the testimony; and if we have rightly understood the essence of dogmatic statements and their fundamental import, then they not only permit but demand an ever new exegetical testing. This must not be taken as a mere empty assertion. Rather we shall have to show in detail how the presupposed dogmatic structure *and* its critical exegetical investigation belong together, when it is once more possible to institute a free exegetical and dogmatic discussion.

CHAPTER XII

THE SYSTEMATISATION OF DOGMATICS

(a) Dogma and dogmas

A DOGMATIC affirmation bears witness to the saving action of God both as regards its actuality and meaning. We have knowledge of this saving process only through historical human traditions, primarily through Apostolic *paradosis*, to which—as the Apostles themselves assert—God in His saving action has surrendered Himself. Just as certainly as Christ Himself is the subject of this historical stream of proclamation and tradition, so the counsel of God which is realised in the process is not thereby exhausted but remains distinct and transcendent. The history of the Church, too, runs its course amid the history of the world, and hence is involved in the history of mankind. For this reason, too, the counsel of God is not to be considered as exhaustively contained in any dogmatic statement. In every such statement the divine counsel is refracted in a twofold way: to begin with, through the human personality of the Apostle (and here we are using the term "Apostle" canonically to denote authors of the received New Testament text) and then again through the human personalities of those theologians (and also *per nefas* of those statesmen and Church politicians who influenced the growth of dogma) who have formulated such dogmatic statements and have obtained their recognition by the Church at large. *Pace* Schlier and the Roman Church [1] we are nowhere promised that through the Apostles God has either explicitly or implicitly delivered His counsel over to us in the form of *veritates revelatae* which then could and should be straightaway formulated as dogma. A dogmatic pronouncement can never be taken as a statement fully adequate to the counsel of God, because it is only the precipitate on the

---

[1] See above, p. 43 ff.

human plane of the saving work of God, which always remains transcendent to the tradition in which it is reflected. However, since the idea of transcendence might here lead to false impressions as though it were a question of something like the relation of the "thing in itself" and its phenomenal appearance, whereas in reality it is a question of the accomplishment of an event, it would perhaps be better to say that every dogmatic statement is to some extent an attempt to picture the bird in its flight. But this image, too, is unsatisfactory since in regard to this historical process there cannot be an observer or a sketcher capable of observing the process from some fixed standpoint, for the dogmatist himself as one personally concerned in the process is forced to take up his stand at the locus of the ἀκοή. Hence let us renounce all metaphor and simply hold fast to the truth that dogma is the divine counsel itself and that we can never adequately grasp dogma in any of our dogmatic statements.

But this means that dogmas are always insecure and essentially debatable. The only question is from what point of view they can be assailed and on what basis discussed. They can only be disputed from the standpoint of a better understanding of the Biblical testimony springing from the ἀκοή itself; and the only ground on which this can happen is that of exegesis. In order that this may be possible dogmas must never be used to forestall the results of exegesis. The latter orientated by dogma in its approach to the testimony will always be *eo ipso* a critical challenge to dogmatic statements. But this challenge cannot spring from the exegesis of any one particular Biblical passage, but only from a comprehensive survey of the Biblical testimony as a whole. Dogmas do not invoke any isolated texts as *dicta probantia*—it may be that they cannot even cite any specific text at all for their formal legitimation, as is the case with the dogma of the Trinity—but rest upon the testimony of Scripture as a whole.

(b) Concordance hearing as distinct from concordance method

This explains why, though we repudiate the concordance *method* for the exegesis of Scripture, we insist on concordance hearing.[2] We understand the distinction between them to be

---

[2] See above, pp. 234 ff.

that as a result of the concordance method the varied statements of the witnesses are reduced to a common denominator derived from a basic principle discovered in systematic thought with the consequence that their unique historical characteristics are violated. On the other hand, concordance hearing means that the varied statements are made comparable through some unifying point of view which is the ultimate end orientating our approach to them. This latter approach is compatible with the recognition as a given fact of all possible divergences in the testimony. It presupposes only that all these statements in their various ways *intend* to testify the same thing, but not that they in fact do so. This latter supposition is a prejudice springing from the fact that the Church has heard in all this varied testimony the clear and unequivocal witness to Christ and hence has received it into the canon for further proclamation. This prejudice requires from us nothing more than respect. It is just as true of the doctrine of the unity of Scripture as of all other dogmas that as a guide to Scriptural investigation it must be tested by exegesis itself. Hence it will depend on the answer given by exegesis to this textual enquiry whether we do in fact find that this Biblical testimony is united as regards the object to which it bears witness. The fullest freedom of exegesis consists in the fact that it has the freedom to interpret Scripture by Scripture.

Of course, whether there is in practice an essential difference between concordance method and concordance hearing as thus defined must in the last resort be decided by our opinion as to whether, and in what way, there is a systematic consistency and completeness about dogmatic statements. This is a question which it is not easy to answer, in view of the special character of dogmatic statements. It is not only a question of statements about the actuality of a happening which essentially aim at completeness of description. But neither is it a question only of statements about the *meaning* of this happening which essentially tend towards systematic unity. It is rather that both aspects are involved at one and the same time and that in such wise that they are inseparable and reciprocally conditioning. Hence it would follow that dogmatic statements must aim at both completeness and systematic consistency. But what can be the meaning of completeness in this connexion? The counsel of God which is realised in the *opera Trinitatis ad intra* and *ad extra* concerns not only a past and present happening but also a process which extends to a future as yet unrealised. Thus this partly fulfilled and partly (as yet) merely promised course of events can have a complete description only in God's saving counsel itself, which embraces the whole process of God's dealings with the world and mankind from the divine plan of salvation πρὸ καταβολῆς κόσμου (Eph. i. 4) to that future state when God shall be πάντα ἐν πᾶσιν (1 Cor. xv. 28). The complete description of the fact must therefore rest ultimately on the unifying meaning. Only at that point can it be grasped, not in a completeness of the testimony to the event. But what can be the meaning of a systematic consistency and finality in relation to the unifying significance? In the last resort it can only consist in the one and self-identical will of God as it makes itself known in the event. This systematic principle of unity can therefore be nothing other than what is implied in the statement "God is God." From the point of view of formal logic this statement of course expresses merely a tautology. But as a statement about this God who fulfils His counsel in history it must be understood not from the point of view of formal logic, but only from that of dogma, and therefore of history. But then it means that God does that which corresponds to His inmost being and that He is in Himself what He does. This can also be expressed by saying that the triune God *ad intra* is the same as He is *ad extra*.

(c) *Systematising event or systematic principle*

To what an extent this principle "God is God" lends systematic finality to the edifice of dogma can be appreciated if we consider the passage Col. i. 9 f., where in the συνέστηκε (vs. 17) we catch a suggestion of systematisation. The Apostle prays for the Colossians, ἵνα πληρωθῆτε τὴν ἐπίγνωσιν τοῦ θελήματος αὐτοῦ ἐν πάσῃ σοφίᾳ, καὶ συνέσει πνευματικῇ (vs. 9), not that thereby they may gain secret knowledge but rather with a distinct anti-Gnostic intention, περιπατῆσαι ἀξίως τοῦ Κυρίου (vs. 10). From this point of view the Apostle himself expounds this spiritual wisdom, and indeed he does so in such a comprehensive fashion that his points furnish the outlines of a whole dogmatic system, which culminates in the sentence καὶ αὐτός [ὁ υἱός, vs. 13] ἐστιν πρὸ πάντων καὶ τὰ πάντα ἐν αὐτῷ συνέστηκε (vs. 17). What then is the systematic principle contained in this συνέστηκεν? We may seek it nowhere but in the action of the Son Himself, which is universally embracing and unifying, for which reason we had better not speak of a systematic principle but rather of a systematising event. Also this corresponds exactly with the linguistic use of συνίστημι. The word which in vs. 17 is employed intransitively is used in the language of Hellenistic and late Jewish religious philosophy and also by the Apostolic Fathers, in a middle sense "sum up, effect, prepare," and with reference to the creative activity of God.[3] This means, therefore, that the συνέστηκεν τὰ πάντα ἐν αὐτῷ is only valid because God ἐν λόγῳ συνεστήσατο τά πάντα.

But we might also say as much of a Gnostic speculative system; and the fact that the finality of this dogmatic structure lies not in a systematic principle, but in a systematising event, would not differentiate it fundamentally from a Gnostic system centred in some metaphysical happening. The very ease with which Christianity fell a prey to *gnosis* is an indication of a basic affinity between them. How then does the Apostle differentiate the dogmatics with which he intends to attack *gnosis* from the latter itself? According to II. 8, the Gnostic error against which he warns his readers consists in a philosophy κατὰ τὴν παράδοσιν ἀνθρώπων, κατὰ τὰ στοιχεῖα τοῦ κόσμου, καὶ οὐ κατὰ Χριστόν. But both religions live by a *paradosis* concerning Christ which is handed on by men; and the great difficulty which the Church experienced in its controversy with the Gnostics lay just in the fact, as the second Epistle of Peter shows, that the latter also trace back their *paradosis* to the Apostles. The question therefore is why that is legitimate for the Church which with the Gnostics is a κενὴ ἀπάτη or "vain deceit" (II. 8). Clearly it is not without some allusion to Gnostic talk of the "*pleroma*," which however remains worthless, that Paul opposes to them ὅτι ἐν αὐτῷ κατοικεῖ πᾶν τὸ πλήρωμα τῆς Θεότητος σωματικῶς (II. 9). Here everything depends on the fact that this κατοικεῖν (cp. also I. 19) receives historical embodiment in that Christ Himself is ἡ κεφαλὴ τοῦ σώματος, τῆς ἐκκλησίας (I. 18), and that this bodily indwelling is effected

[3] Cp. W. Bauer, *Wörterbuch zum N.T.*, 4th edn., 1952, 1438.

in the real present in and through the life of the Church, especially the preaching ministry of the Apostle, to which the latter is commissioned κατὰ τὴν οἰκονομίαν τοῦ Θεοῦ (1. 25). Thus in spite of all formal similarity the Apostle's discourse is not vain like that of the Gnostic because the *pleroma* proclaimed by Paul is secured through the real presence of Christ in the Church and its Apostolic preaching ministry.

(d) Dogmatics or gnosis

But might not the Gnostic claim precisely as much for himself and his Church? In any case he has done so. Then, however, everything depends ultimately on where legitimate Apostolical succession is to be found; and it would seem quite obvious and apparently almost unavoidable that the Apostle should take unreservedly the next step in the controversy and seek to prove historically the validity of his Apostolate, as in fact was later done in the early Catholic Church by the production of the theory of Apostolical succession, and, as Käsemann, on different lines, imputes *even* to the author of II Peter. But the fact is that the author of Colossians does not make this tiny yet momentous advance into early Catholicism. Instead he does something quite different. He constantly adds to his dogmatic affirmations the point that the latter do not constitute a *gnosis* complete in itself, but allude to a mighty happening which has as its goal the personal lives of the hearers, "in order to present you holy and blameless and irreproachable before him" (1. 22). Dogmatics has therefore to prove itself by its fruits in ethical conduct, and this can only be done "provided that you continue in the faith, stable and steadfast, not shifting from the hope of the Gospel which you heard, which has been preached to every creature under heaven, and of which I Paul was made a minister" (1. 23). Had the author made the transition to early Catholicism, then he would have transmuted his dogmatics into an ecclesiastical structure rivalling that of Gnosticism and would thus have set up an ecclesiastically authorised *gnosis*. But instead he surrenders his dogmatic affirmations for use in preaching and says that solely in the event of the ἀκοή can the question of their validity be tested and decided. In so doing he expressly warns his readers that in the debate with the Gnostics they should not leave the ground of preaching and move to that of πιθανολογία, or "persuasive speech" (II. 4), on which the Gnostics alone can effectively operate. Thus the author does the same as Paul in I Cor. I when he refuses to speak ἐν σοφίᾳ λόγου, ἵνα μὴ κενωθῇ[!] ὁ σταυρὸς τοῦ Χριστοῦ (I. 17), but instead relies on the ἀπόδειξις Πνεύματος καὶ δυνάμεως (II. 4).

Hence, to sum up, there corresponds to the transition from concordance hearing to concordance method that from a systematising event to a systematic principle, and, further, that from a dogmatics which is tested in preaching to a self-sufficient *gnosis*. But it would be a mistake to suppose that this transition has been made only once in Church history, namely in the crucial deviation to early Catholicism. Such a deviation is rather a danger by which all dogmatics is constantly threatened. It exists in the sphere of Protestantism just as much as in that of Catholicism; and therefore it is not possible to say that as far as Catholicism is concerned it has been made once for all and irrevocably with the crisis of early Catholicism. Otherwise, of course, there could no longer be any dogmatic discussion between Catholics and Protestants at all. Dogmatic discussion is possible and intelligent so long as this danger is appreciated and care is taken to avoid it. But in practice the ultimate test of how far this is the case must be to what extent the dogmatist is prepared unreservedly to surrender his affirmations to exegetical discussion.

(e) *The constant endangering of dogmatics by systematic theology*

This requirement cannot of course furnish the dogmatist with a simple and easily applicable rule of thumb in such a way that he is once for all shielded from these dangers. Even in the sphere of evangelical theology, where it is a matter of principle that dogma should be based on Scripture and be capable of Scriptural verification, we are by no means protected from the possibility of such deviations. The very fact that each single dogmatic pronouncement must emerge in a sequence of ideas with other such pronouncements, and in a way which gives rise to interconnected inferences, means that we are constantly confronted by the temptation to deduce the truth of these ideas from their systematic interlocking. This

temptation is perhaps less severe when in our dogmatics we are
content with the stringing-together of particular loci which
stand in no systematic interconnexion, as happened in the
early medieval collections of texts or the early editions of
the loci of Melancthon by contrast with the great *summae* of
theology.   But the danger essentially exists in regard to every
scheme of dogmatics, even the simplest, as, for example, that
of the Apostles' Creed.   The dogmatist will endeavour to meet
this danger by not allowing his systematisation to revolve
around some central abstract principle, but, as we have seen,
by making it reflect the unified process of the saving action of
God.   From this point of view it might be questioned whether
the redactors of the Apostles' Creed did not proceed somewhat
unadvisedly since, unlike the authors of the confessional
formulae in the New Testament, they did not begin with
statements about Jesus Christ, but with statements about God
the Creator.[4]   In so doing, at any rate, they encouraged the
misconception that one might make affirmations about God
quite apart from His self-revelation in Christ, and they failed
to note that such a statement about God the Creator cannot
be a dogmatic statement, i.e. a statement about the saving
work of God, but in fact must be a metaphysical statement
even though verbally it might coincide with the statement of a
dogmatist.   For this reason, many dogmatists prefer to begin
with Christology, or Trinitarian doctrine, or the doctrine of
the Word of God.   But from every scheme of co-ordination
we can deduce a systematic principle, or rather every such
scheme has an inherent tendency to become systematised.   On
one occasion, Karl Barth, in an attempt to characterise the
systematising danger in dogmatic work, said that systematising
theology was not like driving a car, in which case you can go
where you please and stay where you please, but rather like
travelling by train, where you are bound to specific lines which
lead you to specific stations at which the train stops.   We
might extend the metaphor and say that you can get into the
train at any station you like in order from that point to travel
over the whole network of lines.   And in regard to the possibility of exegetically discussing dogmatic statements, this
would mean that it must be possible to initiate such a discussion

<hr>

[4] Cp. Diem. *Theol.*, VOL. I, pp. 124 ff.

at any point we please at which we are confronted by testimony to the counsel of God, without feeling compelled to accept, as a preliminary, any systematic premises of the dogmatist or to discuss his system as a whole. Whether the dogmatist can do this at any time will constitute a proof to himself as to whether he has after all merely systematised and not reflected on an exegetic basis. There cannot, in the nature of the case, be any absolute security against this particular danger. Moreover, every dogmatic statement contains systematic presuppositions, not only because of its being interlocked with a total viewpoint, but because of the very fact that it must use specific concepts and ideas as means of expression, which stem from some philosophic or other general outlook. But the same is true also of every exegete. No doubt this is the main reason for the various kinds of deadlock in modern discussion where one reproaches another with using antiquated intellectual resources, or more often than not the exegete considers that this dead weight of material lies wholly on the side of the dogmatist and not with himself. If we are to meet these difficulties, then we must above all be clear about the fact that all who take part in the discussion are essentially in the same position, and not indeed only the modern dogmatist and exegete, but even the authors of the text of Scripture, even those who formulated the dogmas of the Church. Only if we are fully aware that all are speaking of God's plan with humanly conditioned resources of expression have we any hope of reaching an understanding about what they are all trying to say. For only if we have this awareness do their statements become comparable and intelligently debatable. Furthermore, we should at times consider the question of the greater or less usefulness of certain means of expression, and for the sake of general intelligibility replace antiquated by more efficient and better ones. But we must not allow the dispute on the theological theme to depend wholly on the dispute about the use of certain means of expression, however much we may think that the subject matter itself is befogged by the use of a particular technique of ideas. Thus, for example, Bultmann can consider that what the Scriptures intend to say is in many ways beclouded by what he calls "mythological" concepts, or Gogarten that the meaning of early Church dogma is obscured by the use of the Greek idea of φύσις. But in his discussion of this system of thought and expression Bultmann would have to leave scope for the consideration of the event itself—here proclaimed in the form of so-called mythology—if he is to be able to engage in an exegetic and dogmatic debate with some one who works with quite a different intellectual approach. The same applies to Gogarten in saying, for instance, that the overcoming of the subject-object scheme of thought "is the first step by which theology must acquire an exact type of thought appropriate to it."[5]   As we have already seen,[6] that the Trinitarian action of God Himself directed towards us forbids us to try to withdraw ourselves from it in thought in order to objectivise it and make of it an object towards which we react, thus that God Himself by His saving work has overcome the "subject-object" pattern.   Is not Gogarten's demand on theological thought precisely confirmed by the Trinitarian dogma itself? Yet it is obvious that this "false" conceptuality has by no means prevented the Trinitarian dogma from expressing the matter rightly.   Conversely we might ask whether Gogarten's "correct" intellectual approach which has given up thinking on "subject-object" lines really grasps the point which is in question here.   If in fact the overcoming of the tension between subject and object has been attained not by man but by God acting through the Spirit in the συμμαρτυρεῖν, then a theology which forbids us from the outset to think in subject-object terms at all will hardly be especially suited to appreciate this situation and can hardly legitimately claim to be the "appropriate and exact type of thought" to measure and express it.   On the contrary, the danger will rather be that this type of theology will have no means of appreciating the strongly emphasised tension between man and God which is grounded in God's action but is overcome by the work of the Holy Trinity, and therefore will miss the central theological issue here.

[5] Gogarten, E. und K., p. 44.
[6] Above, pp. 298 ff.

CHAPTER XIII

DOGMAS AS APPLIED TO THE PRACTICE OF SCRIPTURAL EXPOSITION

I N order to show how the problems hitherto discussed work out in practice we adduce a few examples of the way in which dogmas, orientating our approach to the text, are calculated to unlock its meaning. For this purpose we shall first of all carry out an exegesis of the *pericope* Eph. II. 4-10, chosen for our ordination. The theme then will be:

(a) *The doctrine of predestination*

After making in ch. I a comprehensive survey and exposition of the saving plan of divine predestination the Apostle makes a fresh start in ch. II and turns with a forceful directness of approach to the readers themselves in order to impress upon them that this saving history constitutes the essential meaning of their own lives. In vss. 1-3 he shows, in a series of aorists *perfectum*, what an overwhelming sway sin has exercised over them as over all men, to such an extent that no individual could resist it, and then resumes in vs. 4 with a "but": "But God, who is rich in mercy. . . ." This adversative conjunction does not introduce something regarded as an equivalent to the struggles of men against sin—and in any case he is not talking about such struggles—rather it refers back to the saving work and counsel of God which is the theme of ch. I, of which he now speaks as something accomplished, just as he has spoken in the past tense about their life in sin. This perfected work of salvation is compatible with a distinction of times which gives scope for the drama of personal life in those whom he is addressing: according to vss. 4 ff. this saving work is expressed in the fact that "God . . . even when we were dead, through our trespasses made us alive together with Christ . . . and raised us up with him, and made us sit with him in the heavenly places in Christ Jesus." Thus the theme is here the work of salvation as it has been accomplished through the death, resurrection and ascension of Christ. Again, all this contains an allusion—not to another and earlier saving action of God, for it can always be a question of only one divine action for the salvation of men—but to an earlier stage of the same action, a stage which has been described in detail in I. 3 ff., and which begins with our election "in him before the foundation of the world" (I. 4), which He has disclosed to us as "the mystery of his will, according to his purpose which he set forth in Christ as a plan for the fullness of time" (I. 9 f.). This allusion to his earlier theme is made to the accompaniment of the repeated emphasis: "by grace you have been saved" (II. 6), and "it is the gift of God—not because of works, lest any man should boast" (II. 8 f.). And once more all occasion for boasting is removed from this human drama in which the saving purpose of God has been fulfilled in the lives of believers, by the reminder in II. 10 that this miracle is grounded in the ultimate purpose of the Creator: "For we are his workmanship (ποίημα), created in Christ Jesus for good works, which God prepared beforehand, that we should walk in them."

The whole understanding of our *pericope* depends on how we interpret the repeated ἐν Χριστῷ ᾿Ιησοῦ of II. 6, 7, 10. God, who is the subject of the συνεζωοποίησεν τῷ Χριστῷ (II. 5) and of the συνήγειρεν καὶ συνεκάθισεν, has acted in all this ἐν Χριστῷ ᾿Ιησοῦ (II. 6). He has done so in order, as II. 7 suggests—and here there are two possibilities exegetically —to show towards us His grace which is in ἐν Χριστῷ ᾿Ιησοῦ or ἐν Χριστῷ ᾿Ιησοῦ, to manifest His grace which subsists in any event apart from Christ. The implications of this difference become clear once more in II. 10, where again God acts as subject, this time κτισθέντες, and likewise ἐν Χριστῷ Ιησοῦ. Here again we might try the same two possible lines of interpretation as in II. 7: *either* that God has created us "in Jesus Christ" in the sense that Jesus Christ is not only instrumental in creation, but is both its real ultimate ground and the medium of its recognition, *or* on the other hand, that He is the one who has revealed to us God's creative purpose, which from the beginning was aimed at our good, in which case He would be not the ground of creation but only the means by which we recognise its purpose. But this second possibility would do violence to the text, for the point here is not a mere κτίζειν, which as the creation of God would be inconceivable except as a creation of man for the good life, it is rather a κτίζειν ἐν Χριστῷ 'Ιησοῦ and further ἐπὶ ἔργοις ἀγαθοῖς, so that the emphasis that we "have been created for good works" is obviously rooted in the fact that this κτίζειν has taken place expressly ἐν Χριστῷ 'Ιησοῦ. With this κτίζειν is connected the προετοιμάζειν of God, with which the idea of predestination characteristic of ch. I, especially I. 4, is taken up again though it is not otherwise mentioned *verbis expressis* in our *pericope*. Thus we are faced by the same question as to the meaning of ἐν Χριστῷ or διὰ 'Ιησοῦ Χριστοῦ, "in" whom God has "blessed us" (I. 3) and "chosen" us (I. 4), "through" whom He has "destined (προορίσας) us in love to be his sons" (I. 5), "in" whom as "the Beloved" He has "freely bestowed on us" His grace (I. 6), "in" whom He "set forth" the purpose, according to which it is "the mystery of his will" (I. 9), "to unite all things in him" (I. 10), "in" whom "we who first hoped in Christ have been destined (προορισθέντες) and appointed to live for the praise of his glory" (I. 11). In all these texts we have the same alternative possibilities of interpretation as in II. 7. Sometimes the one interpretation seems the more likely suggesting that the election of mankind is primarily an action between God and Christ, in which case the question is how man is taken up into this inter-Trinitarian action of the divine being. At the other times the second interpretation seems the more likely, according to which the πρόθεσις of God which takes place κατὰ τὴν βουλὴν τοῦ θελήματος αὐτοῦ (I. 11) uses Christ as the means, the fulfiller, and above all the revealer of the divine action, in which case the question is in what relation the redeeming work of Christ stands to the election purpose of God, which is understood independently of it.

All these exegetical difficulties are reflected in the history of the doctrine of predestination, in which the first chapter of the Epistle to the Ephesians has always played a specially important part.[1] This *pericope* cannot be expounded without dogmatic reflexion and hence without some consideration as

---

[1] In this connexion, cp. Barth's treatment of the theme of God's gracious election in *K. D.*, VOL. II. 2, pp. 1-498.

to the consequences which the one or the other line of approach must have.

Both Reformed and Orthodox Protestants of the sixteenth and seventeenth centuries were largely agreed about the understanding of the ἐν Χριστῷ in the sense that Christ is the *speculum electionis*. "The reference to our election in Christ in regard to which Augustine and the Reformers were undeniably faithful and adequate to Biblical theology implies an unmistakable call to praise, in this connexion, and under all circumstances, divine *grace*—grace which has concretely been manifested in the person of the *mediator* between God and man. We are called to see the ground of our election not in ourselves and our own work but in this other person who is the Person of God Himself made flesh, and in that divine work which comes to man from without, alien to what he himself is and does, but drawing near to him and accomplished for his benefit. Man with his decision follows the decision that has been made about him in this wholly other person—a decision that has been made prior to him, without his aid, and in regard to him, and whose origin is wholly elsewhere than in himself. And just in so far as he recognises this decision, he recognises with universal reality the meaning and the essence of the divine election: it is the epitome of all divine blessings, and thus he recognises the import of the doctrine of election, namely that it is the *summa* of the Gospel." [2]

But the question still remains open whether Christ is only *noetically* or also *ontically* the ground of election: is the πρόθεσις (I. 11) a *decretum absolutum* of God, independent of the decision made in Jesus Christ, and precedent to it, so that Christ only reveals and executes this decision of the hidden God made apart from Him, inasmuch as He calls by His word and His spirit those whom God has already chosen? Or is Christ Himself the active subject of this decision about our election, so that in this matter our faith must be pinned on Him alone, because behind Him there stands no hidden God? In the history of the doctrine of predestination it is on the whole the first of these views which has prevailed, although the best exponents of the theme have again and again come very close to the second view as soon as they have taken seriously the

[2] Barth, *K. D.*, VOL. II. 2, p. 67.

statements of I. 4 according to which we were elected precisely in Christ Himself and not merely saved by Christ after being elected in a different way. Barth has developed these points of view to their logical conclusion and has triumphed over that "mystery play involving the unknown God and the unknown man" into which the doctrine of predestination had degenerated, by summarising the whole doctrine in the two sentences: "Jesus Christ is the electing God" and "Jesus Christ is the elected man."

In the light of this may also be explained the προητοίμασεν (II. 10) of our *pericope* which refers back to I. 4. It is not a mere matter of course, deducible from the idea of God, that God "has created us for good works"—a self-explanatory idea which, moreover, would explain nothing, in view of the actual condition of humanity enslaved by sin. Rather it is the God active in Jesus Christ, proving Himself by this action to be the gracious God, with whom we are here exclusively concerned, and both noetically and ontically. In the election of Christ as the archetype of humanity our own destiny is also involved and grounded, that we may be "holy and blameless before him" (I. 4). "The primal divine decision, the sanctification coming to man from all eternity in the election of Jesus Christ, and therefore once for all, demands that the life of the elect in all its human questionableness and frailty, should be an image, an echo, a testimony and a recognition of that divine decree. In this sense Calvin repeatedly and sharply emphasised: '*Electionis scopus est vitae sanctimonia.*' And likewise, '*quae in electis futura erat sanctitas, ab electione habuit exordium.*' [3] Election is the sun, sanctification is the radiance which streams from it—who would wish to try to separate them?" [4]

Only from this point of view does the repeated emphasis of this passage on salvation by *grace* take on its full scope and meaning. The intention is not to bring grace into relief against the background of human powerlessness to co-operate in the divine work of salvation, but rather to emphasise the grace with which, *before* all human striving for sanctity *and* its failure, God completed His saving work in Jesus Christ, in whom He has saved us. And, finally, in the same context of

[3] Calvin Inst. III, 23.12, 22.3.   [4] Barth, *K. D.*, VOL. II. 2, p. 568.

thought it also becomes clear what significance the *Church* has in this work of divine election. To be sure all mankind are potentially destined to blessedness in Christ. But the saving counsel of God is not directed immediately to all, but primarily to Jesus Christ, in whom man is elected, and then "in" Him and "through" Him to Israel and the Church as the fellowship through the existence of which the whole of humanity is summoned to believe. In the history which unfolds itself between the Church and the world, the election work of God is embodied as a present reality. In the προορίζειν of the elect to sonship in Jesus Christ (i. 5, 11) that which in the inter-Trinitarian action of God focussed in Jesus Christ is, as it were, a divine necessity, becomes a very real struggle of God to save a humanity estranged from Him. In this context are made the decisions of faith between the καὶ ὑμᾶς ὄντας νεκροὺς (ii. 1) and the ὁ δὲ Θεός (ii. 4), which are grounded in the decision of God in favour of these particular men; and thus the wisdom of God is made known to the principalities and powers διὰ τῆς ἐκκλησίας (iii. 10).

By this example it becomes clear how the dogmatic teaching about predestination does not, on the one hand, forestall the conclusions of exegesis, and how, on the other, it brings out vividly those problems which confront exegesis and reduce it to an impasse, while at the same time it attempts to win from exegesis a solution to them, with the result that exegesis again takes up a critical attitude towards dogmatic teaching. We propose to take further examples from the Apostles' Creed, and in fact the doctrines of the Descent into Hell and the Ascension of Christ, because both in their dogmatic implications and in their exegetical basis, these doctrines, in particular, are today especially disputed.

(b) Christ's descent into Hell

In his essay "Mythical Speech and saving History," [5] G. W. Kümmel deals, *inter alia*, with the "*descendit ad inferos.*" Over and above the particular question with which we are concerned this essay is of special interest to us because he discusses his particular theme in the context of a far-reaching debate with

[5] See G. W. Kümmel, "Mythische Rede und Heilsgeschehen im Neuen Testament," in *Kerygma und Mythos*, vol. ii (1952), pp. 153 ff.

Bultmann on the subject of the latter's programme of demythologisation, and, unlike ourselves, does not make use of
any dogmatic points of view, but seeks to gain from exegesis
itself his criteria of judgment. His critical objections to
Bultmann, whose insistence on demythologising the New
Testament he considers to be essentially justified, rest
principally on his contention that such a process of demythologisation "cannot be based on the needs of modern
man (nor on the essential nature of myth) but only on the
central core of the New Testament message itself. . . ."[6] And
this means that in the first place the question must be clarified,
whether mythological speech belongs necessarily to the central
core of the New Testament *kerygma*, or whether only certain
forms of mythological expression are an integral part of it,
while others show themselves to be inadequate or at least
susceptible of misunderstanding." Thus he considers that
Bultmann, "by eliminating the temporal aspect of the history
of salvation, does in fact eliminate a 'residuum of mythology,'
which even the older liberal approach thought it necessary to
discount, but that in so doing he sets aside the vital centre of
the New Testament proclamation." [7] It will not do "*completely* to eliminate mythical language from the New Testament, if we wish to retain the New Testament *kerygma*; and
just as little as the New Testament proclaims a myth, just as
little is it possible to free the very heart of its message from the
thought-forms and the language of myth which furnishes the
only possible means of expression by which to convey the
significance for faith of the *historical facts* concerning Christ." [8]
But how does Kümmel himself gain a criterion for the critical
examination of myth (which he thinks is justified) after he
has declined to use Bultmann's criterion?

"Since there can be no question of altogether effacing
mythical language, our task can only be to discriminate, or
separate out as problematical those mythical ideas or forms of
expression which do not fulfil the sole legitimate end, namely
that of furnishing an indispensable mode of expression (still
liable to misunderstanding) for the proclamation of God's
historical action in Christ The purpose of a critical examination

[6] Kümmel, *op. cit.*, p. 157.   [7] *Op. cit.*, p. 159.
[8] *Op. cit.*, p. 160.

of myth can therefore only be to expose the dubiety of such human expressions as are inadequate to convey the significance for faith of the Christ-*history*. And the direct consequence of this is that the starting-point and the criterion for a criticism of New Testament mythological language can only be the extent to which particular mythological forms of thought and expression agree with the central New Testament *kerygma*." [9] One wonders whether Kümmel is not thus treading upon very insecure ground. Is he not thus yielding to the arbitrary interpretation of the individual exegete what is to be counted as part of "God's *historical* saving action in Christ"? And further, what is to be considered inadequate or otherwise to the end of expressing the significance for faith of this history? He will hardly be saved from such exegetical arbitrariness by trying to "show the deviation of particular New Testament modes of thought or texts from the message which is common to the New Testament as a whole, and thus to establish the 'inner limits' of the canon and to expose the encroachments of early Catholicism or of completely un-Biblical thoughts." [10] But let us see how he applies his method to the myth of the descent of Christ into Hell, which is reported in 1 Pet. III. 19 ff.[11]

He refers to Bo Reike,[12] who has convincingly shown "that here the theme is quite certainly that of the preaching of Christ to the fallen angels whom Christ visited in the underworld during the time of his passage through the Cross to final exaltation in glory; he has further shown that this allusion to the preaching before disobedient spirits has, in the context of III. 13 ff., the purpose of supporting the fearless proclamation of the Gospel to the Gentiles by suggesting that these disobedient spirits to whom Christ preached are the instigators of all heathendom. Thus it should be clear that this allusion to the preaching of Christ in the underworld is no divagation in the context of 1 Pet. III. 13 ff., but an integral part of the admonition, the motive of which is continued on general lines in IV. 6 by the allusion to the preaching to the departed. Further, it is a very likely assumption that the whole admonitory context of 1 Pet. III. 13 ff. which has its parallels in

---

[9] *Op. cit.*, pp. 160 ff.   [10] *Op. cit.*, p. 161.   [11] *Op. cit.*, p. 167.
[12] See Bo Reike, "The Disobedient Spirits and Christian Baptism," in *Acta Sem. Neot. Upsal.*, XIII (1946).

1 Pet. ii. 19 ff. and Tit. iii. 1 ff., has been taken from a literary τόπος exploited by the author of 1 Pet."

So far Kümmel agrees with Reike's exegetical findings. They only part company in their critical appraisal of all this, for "Reike goes a step further and asserts that the preaching of Christ to the departed 'was possibly a fact well known to all Christians,' that the descent of Christ into the underworld 'was presumably a special point of the Christ drama at the very beginning of the history of Christianity.' But this is very questionable." [13] But what is really questionable for Kümmel about this? Obviously Reike's assumption that Christ's stay in the underworld and in particular his preaching there was in general an established part of the *kerygma* from the earliest beginnings of Christianity. Kümmel disputes this hypothesis by pointing out that in the other texts which allude to the descent of Christ into Hell after His death (Mt. xii. 40; Rom. x. 7; Eph. iv. 9; Acts ii. 27) the motive of 1 Pet. iii. 18 ff. is lacking. Also there are to be found only late and isolated allusions to the preaching of Jesus in the underworld and His triumph over its rulers (Jn. v. 25; 1 Tim. iii. 16). The motive of the preaching of Jesus is also missing in texts parallel to 1 Pet. iii. 13 ff. in 1 Pet. ii. 19 ff. and Tit. iii. 1 ff.; "and it is equally striking that in other texts, especially older ones where there is some mention of the victory of Christ over Hades (Phil. ii. 10 f.; Col. ii. 15 f.; Eph. i. 20 f.; Rev. i. 18) there is no sort of allusion to a *descensus Christi*." [14] Summarising these objections we see that the argument is that there are older texts which while speaking of a stay of Christ in the underworld do not mention His preaching there, or do not bring this stay into connexion with the victory of Christ over the rulers of that world, but at other times the argument is on the contrary that there are texts—once again, especially old ones—which speak of the victory of Jesus over those powers but not of His *descensus*. The two things were only first brought together in certain later texts: Jn. v. 25; 1. Tim. iii. 16; 1 Pet. iii. 18 ff. From all this Kümmel draws the conclusion that "the mythical representation of an activity of the risen Christ in the underworld developed only late and hesitantly into the thought that the death and resurrection of Christ

[13] Kümmel, *op. cit.*, p. 167.   [14] *Op. cit.*, p. 168.

also imply His triumph over the powers of the underworld." [15] This is a historical judgment of probability exactly like that of Reike; and as far as the theme itself is concerned it is of no particular importance whether Reike's thesis or Kümmel's is the more convincing.

Clearly Kümmel himself has the feeling that this *historical* judgment alone cannot decide anything.   Hence he adds a judgment about the thing in itself and goes on to say: "This hesitation is also quite understandable as regards the subject. The conception of various stages in the exaltation of the Crucified to the dignity of heavenly *kyrios* means a speculative materialistic embellishment of that faith in the exaltation of the risen Saviour to the Godhead which cannot be expressed apart from mythical language."   From this he concludes "that it is not philosophical objections on the part of the modern man which compel us critically to question the myth of the Descent into Hell, but rather the fact that *this* mythical conception was not from the beginning integral to the likewise mythically formulated faith in the exaltation of the Risen Lord and His victory over the powers inimical to God, and in fact stands in a relation of tension to the latter." [16]   Werner Bieder also emphatically agrees with this point as the result of his comprehensive survey *Die Vorstellung von der Hollenfahrt Jesu Christi*, but not without challenging Kümmel as to "what standard he accepts as a basis for distinguishing between adequate and inadequate myths in the New Testament." [17]

Obviously our fear that Kümmel's method of appraising and discriminating between the mythical forms of expression in the New Testament might lead to arbitrary exegesis was not altogether unfounded.   Let us consider first his *historical* judgment that these later mythical expressions "did not belong to the original core of the faith."   We will grant that the *kerygma* underwent a development in this respect.   Further, as Kümmel wishes, we will reckon seriously with "the possibility of erroneous developments within the world of New Testament ideas." [18]   But even so, Kümmel's historical

---

[15] *Ibid.*

[16] See W. Bieder, *Die Vorstellung von der Hollenfahrt Jesus Christ*, 1949, p. 207, n. 274 (*a*).

[17] *Op. cit.*, p. 207, n. 274 (*a*).   [18] *Op. cit.*, p. 168.

arguments can lead us just as well to conclusions opposite to his own, namely to the conclusion that the later texts continue and amplify the original *kerygma* in a quite legitimate way: we found a first series of texts which, while they mentioned the stay of Jesus in the underworld, did not bring it into explicit connexion with the victory He wrought there (which however is by no means true of Eph. iv. 9, in the context of iv. 8). Alongside these we have a series of texts which speak indeed about a victory of Christ over the underworld, but not of His descent thither. But what point can there be in playing off these two sets of statements one against the other, instead of allowing them to elucidate each other, especially when to some extent they spring from the same authors or even stand in the same writing? Further, the two series of statements clearly belong together from the point of view of meaning, since the writers would hardly have wished to make statements about the stay of Christ in the underworld unless they had wished to imply some meaning and purpose in that event. But there remain also the later texts (Jn. v. 25; 1. Tim. iii. 16; 1 Pet. iii. 18 f.), the point of which is simply to connect the two sets of statements without further modification. This applies also to the preaching in 1 Pet. iii. 18 f. which stands in exactly the same sequence of thought as the *"descendit ad inferos"* of the Apostles' Creed. Hence the historical objections made by Kümmel seem to us groundless. What are we to think of his objections made from the standpoint of meaning and content?

He takes exception to the "idea of various stages in the process of the exaltation of the Crucified," hence not to the mythical form in which faith in the exalted Lord is expressed, only to the "speculative materialistic embellishment" of this faith. But is it not just as arbitrary that at one time, in regard to the exaltation, he should accept this mythical language, while at another time, in connexion with the Descent into Hell, he should reject it? What exactly is the standard he applies when he brands mythical language as speculative only after it has exceeded a certain degree of materialistic embellishment? His criteria are not easily grasped and clarified, and above all they are not theological criteria; nor do they become so when combined with historical judgments, in a way which is typical of Kümmel, even though the historical judgments were less questionable than in fact they are. In any case it is impossible to deal with this subject adequately by means of such arbitrary discriminations in the mythical language of the New Testament. It is to be supposed that in nearly all the quoted passages the event of salvation has been elucidated with the help of Gnostic ideas and forms of expression, and that the writers were influenced by the Gnostic redeemer-myth concerning the pre-existent divine being who came down from heaven and assumed human form in order, after the completion of his earthly work, to be exalted to heavenly glory and win, through his conflict, dominion over the cosmic powers in the spiritual world. Now, as Bultmann points out, the Descent into Hell does not form part of this Gnostic redeemer-myth, but rather the cosmic powers are subjugated by the Ascension into heaven. "Thus, also, according to I Pet. III. 22, the ascent of Christ to heaven is at the same time the act whereby He obtains dominion over the demonic world-rulers, and III. 19 ff. where according to the original meaning (Bultmann thinks that vss. 18-22 are based on a hymn to Christ) the Descent into Hell is as little in question as in Eph. IV. 9, follows the Gnostic myth, which has it that the prison-house of the dead is not in the lower parts of the earth but in the regions of the air where the powers of the stars or of the firmament hold them captive." [19]   In this connexion Bultmann notes: "The author of I Pet. has understood v. 19 as an allusion to the Descent into Hell, as IV. 6 shows." Now of course in IV. 6 it is only said that "the Gospel was preached to the dead" while the φυλακή of III. 19 is not defined as "Hell." But, as in Eph. IV. 8, this does not need to be explicitly brought out, since according to Jewish and oriental religious thought generally "Sheol" or "Hades" was thought of as the sphere of the dead and was described as a prison. [20]   Hence we may say that the representation of "Hell" as the sphere of the dead is a very widespread notion found within the New Testament,

---

[19] Bultmann, *Theol. des N.T.*, p. 175.

[20] Cp. on this point, Christoph Barth, *Die Erretung vom Tode*, 1947, p. 78: "The definition and description of the sphere of the dead as a prison is meant to suggest the loss of freedom of action consequent upon death— a trait which recurs in the ideas of the underworld peculiar to nearly all peoples."

though the question remains as to where and how precisely it is localised, whether and to what extent therefore the Gnostic view which places this abode in the upper regions of the air is corrected by the Jewish view which localises it in the deeps, and whether, for instance, in regard to the κατώτερα μέρη τῆς γῆς of Eph. IV. 9 we are to think of the one or the other. At the same time it should be noted that this "localisation," as Christoph Barth shows [21] is by no means such a simple matter, and in any case cannot be appreciated on the basis of the somewhat crude scheme of the three-storied universe.

What, now, do these observations amount to as far as the exegete is concerned? Here as elsewhere he has essentially two distinct possibilities open to him, namely to expound the texts in the light of or without reference to dogma—in this case that of the *"descendit ad inferos"*—which we conceive as a guiding principle in exegetical approach to the text. If he wishes to expound the texts *without* reference to the dogma in question, then of course he can point to sources and parallels for the Biblical testimony as furnished by the scientific history of religions, and if he proposes to interpret and judge, he can measure this testimony by what he conceives to be the real core of Scripture; or he can interpret existentially the *mythologoumenon*, or simply, according to his taste or caprice, wholly or in part repudiate it or accept it. But in all these cases his exegetical conclusions will be beyond the reach of discussion, in so far as they do not permit or make possible any discussion about the texts themselves, but only about the presuppositions and criteria on the basis of which the exegetical study has been developed.

But all those observations which we have noted retain their full import when we go further and approach the texts in the light of the dogmatic assumption of the *"descendit ad inferos."* Yet merely to note the fact of the *descensus* would not help us very much to wrest from the texts their inner meaning. We could only go so far as to establish that several of the texts do in fact mention this *descensus*. What they intend to imply by this, whether it be an affirmation within the framework of the Gnostic redeemer-myth, the drama of which is thus carried a step further, or whether an invasion of the Jewish Sheol is

[21] Chr. Barth, *op. cit.*, pp. 80 ff.

intended, or how far it can mean anything at all for us moderns who no longer share the manifold views which characterised a now vanished picture of the universe—the mere fact of the *descensus* can yield no Biblical answer to such questions. We must pay heed to the "*descendit ad inferos*" within the context in which it occurs in the Apostles' Creed, where it stands between the "*crucifixus, mortuus et sepultus*" and the "*tertia die resurrexit a mortuis, ascendit ad coelos*"—as, moreover, is precisely the case also in the most detailed of the texts, viz. 1 Pet. III. This context reveals first the most decisive thing, which is that we here have to do with a statement concerning the saving work of God, who in the self-humiliation of Jesus Christ takes pity on man even when he is found in the extremest distance from God, with the result that the Incarnation, giving fullest effect to the divine pity for man, operates even in the midst of the last dread consequences and the direst working of powers inimical to God. Then it is further implied that because God Himself dies the death of man in Jesus Christ therefore this death, and therewith the whole realm of the dead, becomes qualified as the final destiny of man apart from the saving intervention of God—and so in fact is first taken in all its seriousness—but there is also the further implication that in the victory of the God-man, Jesus Christ, death and all those powers which hold man estranged in remotest distance from God are overcome, so that now our life, anchored in the person of the exalted Lord, "is hid with Christ in God" (Col. III. 3). Thus our task is to examine the texts in the light of this realised drama of the dealings of God with man in history, and in particular to consider whether and to what extent this *descensus* forms an essential moment in the saving happening of this triumphal progress of God. In pursuance of these questions we must now occupy ourselves with the text of 1 Pet. III. 19.

On the purely dogmatic side of the question we may compare the "*Konkordienformel*" which in Art. IX treats of "Christ's Descent into Hell." [22] The dogmatic controversy which arose among the theologians of the Confession of Augsburg, and to which an attitude is adopted here,[23] is not of course

---

[22] Cp. *Bek. Schr.* (above, p. 176, n. 26), pp. 812 ff., 1049 ff.
[23] Cp. also Bieder, *op. cit.* (above, n. 16), pp. 6 ff.

concerned with the question whether the article is to be struck out or not, but with the problems which we shall see recur similarly in regard to the Ascension: "whether it took place before or after the death of Christ? Item, whether in the soul alone, or in the Godhead alone, or with body and soul, spiritually or corporeally? Item, whether this article belongs to the Passion or to the glorious victory and triumph of Christ?" [24] This whole debate is summarily decided by an allusion to Luther's sermon at Torgau (1533): "But since this article as also the previous one (Of the Person of Christ") is not to be grasped with the senses nor with the reason, but solely by faith: our plain view is that it is not to be disputed and debated but in the simplest manner believed and taught." And from this sermon [25] the conclusion is drawn with the words: "Then it is enough for us to know that Christ descended into Hell, destroyed Hell for all believers, and redeemed them from the power of death, the Devil, and eternal damnation in the hellish pit. But how this happened we are not to enquire in this life. . . ."

One might see in this "it is enough" as in the quoted sermon of Luther a certain evasion of the dogmatic and exegetical problems. Werner Bieder sees it thus and calls it "an artistic achievement reviving the Melanchthonian and genuinely Lutheran points of view as regards the *descensus* by a consistent attestation of what they have in common and a concealment of their differences and an adaptation of Luther's Torgau sermon with its Melanchthonian colouring." [26] We feel, however, that we must judge this sermon otherwise. In describing the outward circumstances of the Ascension Luther speaks with the greatest ease and unconcern about "words," "thoughts" and "images," and says: "For such picture language shows the power and the usefulness of this article and brings home to us the fact that Christ has destroyed the power of Hell and robbed the Devil of all his might—as an event which indeed has taken place, is preached and is believed. If I have that then I have the right essence of the matter, and am not to enquire further and rack my brains as to how it

[24] *Bek. Schr.*, pp. 812 f.
[25] Printed in *op. cit.*, pp. 1050 ff.
[26] Bieder, *op. cit.* (above, n. 16), p. 11.

happened or was possible, just as in other articles of the faith
as well such busy pondering, such pretensions of the reason to
thrash it all out is forbidden us, and in any case can do no
good." [27] But it should at the same time be noticed that in
the very unconcern with which he refers to picture-language
he stands poles apart from the aims of modern demythologising
exegesis. This means on the one hand that he not only takes
no offence at what the modern critic is accustomed to call the
mythological mode of speech, but can even say: "For such
images can do me no harm nor lead me astray from the truth,
but are of service in enabling me the more firmly to grasp and
hold fast this article of our creed, and my understanding of it
remains clear and undistorted." [28] The same applies to the
other point, to what he calls "the force" and "the usefulness"
and "the truth" of the article. Here again all demythologising
exegesis is left far behind, even though it were anxious not to
discard the doctrine altogether but to save it in its power and
usefulness by means of the "*pro nobis*" of an existentialising
interpretation. For in speaking of the power and the usefulness
and the truth of the doctrine Luther, as we have seen, is
concerned about the point: "that it has happened, is preached
and is believed." Absolutely everything for him depends
on the interconnexion of these three: *happened, preached,
believed.*

But what can be the real nature of the event in question
here, if all the concrete details and circumstances by which it
is expressed may be surrendered as mere metaphorical speech,
and when it is expressly stated that "it cannot be grasped with
the senses nor with the reason?" We see then that it is an
event which cannot and must not be the object of speculative
thought but can and must be exclusively preached and
believed; and this means, to put it in the context of our own
ideas, that it is a type of happening about the actuality and
significance of which in their inseparability only a dogmatic
affirmation can be made. If that is so, however, the attitude
of "it is enough" represents no evasion, no *refugium ignorantiae*,
but rather indicates precisely that this event which is *sui
generis* requires as the only mode of speech appropriate to

[27] *Bek. Schr.*, p. 1050.
[28] *Op. cit.*, p. 1051.

render it the equally *sui generis* dogmatic statement. Moreover, it becomes clear at the same time why such a dogmatic statement is not a mythological one attempting to objectify the event in the form of myth. The affirmation "*descendit ad inferos*" is not a statement imparting information about some situation which can be objectivised in thought with the result that, upon reflexion, we might take up towards it an attitude of belief or unbelief. It is rather the proclamation of an event which so immediately concerns the hearer that both as regards its factuality and significance it simply is not, apart from faith, what it purports to be. Within the triad: event, proclamation and faith, there is no room for objectification if the "object" of that triad is to be "that Hell has been destroyed for all believers." We are not called upon to believe *in* Hell and the demonic powers—certainly not—but we are to preach and believe that for believers Hell is *destroyed* and the powers of evil *overcome*. This is the point which is aimed at by the summary statement "it is enough."

If we insist on enquiring further and refuse to accept that "such busy pondering and pretensions of reason are forbidden us and in any case can do no good," then we shall naturally have to ask the next obvious question and shall wish to know what objective reality can be assigned to Hell and the powers of Hell, and whether and in what way we can imagine them as really existing and feel compelled to accept their existence. This question can be answered in various ways, but since it means asking a question in a way which is theologically forbidden, no theological argument can be used to answer it; with the consequence that no limits are set to the caprice and taste—and incidentally tastelessness—of the thinker. If in view of certain experiences of our own we feel that we cannot deny the reality of these hellish powers, we shall not be prevented from believing in them by the mere fact that perhaps we cannot fit them in to the scientific world view which we hold, but we shall be inclined to objectivise them in terms of some mythology or other. Accordingly we shall feel it necessary to interpret the relevant passage of the New Testament in such a way as to suggest that these powers are realities which must be accepted as such.

Then one day a movement of enlightenment will come

Y

replacing the *"descendit ad inferos"* of our catechism by some such tag as:

> To God be eternal praise and honour,
> The Devil is no more!
> Where then has he hidden?
> Reason has him forbidden.

And how has reason managed this? It may quite simply have demythologised our picture of the world, so that there is no longer any room for these *mythologoumena* as realities, and therefore, whether he likes it or not, the Devil must depart from the scene. Again it may have succeeded in adapting these mythologically objectivised powers into some anthropological scheme, so that their evil effects are taken full account of, and become observable and explainable on an anthropological basis. In that case mythological objectification is replaced by that which takes the form of psychological phenomena and the contents of consciousness. In both these ways which for the most part are adopted alternately, reason is accustomed to cast out the Devil. All this is reflected in a certain type of New Testament exegesis which first, in mythological terms, objectivises Hell and all its powers in order then to destroy them by means of the process of demythologisation.

The demons of course usually refuse to be driven out in this manner. In fact belief in them has always flourished most in the wake of such a movement of enlightenment. We may go so far as to say that the retributive nemesis of all enlightenment which wants belief in God without the Devil is just that in consequence men come to believe more easily in the Devil than in God. Accordingly many signs suggest that as a reaction against demythologisation we shall witness a new and positive valuation of myth as a means to the apprehension of religious phenomena. In this connexion we may call to mind Karl Jaspers's debate with Bultmann,[29] or C. G. Jung: [30] "What can be the meaning of a religion without myth when all religion, if it means anything at all, means precisely that

---

[29] See K. Jaspers, "Wahrheit und Unheil der Bultmannschen Entmythologisierung," in *Schweizerische Theologische Rundschau*, June 1953.

[30] C. G. Jung, *Antwort auf Hiob*, 1952, p. 77.

it fulfils the function of uniting us to the eternal myth?" We may also foresee what effects this movement of reaction will exert on this particular article of the creed when gradually the theologians, too, dare once more to put a positive value on mythical thought, and when once more we come to believe in demons. Furthermore there exists the possibility of modernising the myth of Hell and its powers, i.e. of adapting it from the pre-scientific to the scientific world view. For this it would only be necessary to transpose the objectified mythological data from the domain of psychical to that of parapsychical phenomena, from the subjective consciousness to the world of the trans-subjective subterranean consciousness such as is constituted, for instance, by the archetypes of C. G. Jung, or into any newly discovered or rehabilitated metaphysical hinterland. There are many such possibilities. Then a corresponding exegesis will arise, which will feel no need to demythologise New Testament statements about Hell and its powers, but will view them as a reality which is to be accredited —whereupon after some time a demythologising process will begin all over again by way of reaction.

Dogmatics must make its voice heard against this vicious circle. Its objection, as we have seen, must be first of all that the very framing of the *question* implying an objectification of New Testament statements is excluded from the theological point of view and therefore from the start any *answer* must be described as capricious and theologically irrelevant. And this point of view was taken by no means by way of evading certain difficulties of apprehension but—in connexion with the triad "event, proclamation, and faith"—it was meant to emphasise that the *infernum* occurs only as a transitory aspect of this saving process and its proclamation, i.e. that only the idea of its destruction can be expressed linguistically and that it cannot and may not be understood in any other way. Thus it is only the conquest of the *infernum* which is to be believed in and in so far the *infernum* itself cannot be made an object of faith. If in spite of this we still wish to reckon with the existence of the *infernum* and its powers, quite apart from the saving event of the "*descendit ad inferos*," then one can merely say that these destroyed powers attempt to acquire reality by becoming objectified in some more or less mythological or demythologised form. We can counter these attempts at self-manifestation only with radical disbelief; and in this respect everything will depend on whether we refuse to believe in them because they can no longer exist at all from the point of view of demythologising reason, or whether, while recognising them in their possibility of self-manifestation, we think that for the believer they have lost this possibility of self-manifestation in consequence of the *descensus Christi*.

The only wider question which may legitimately be posed in this connexion is in what way Christ by His *descensus* has achieved this victory which enables us to believe that the self-manifestation of the *infernum* is no longer possible. The answer to this question is given in 1 Pet. III. 19, namely that Christ τοῖς ἐν φυλακῇ πνεύμασιν πορευθεὶς ἐκήρυξεν. Here the absolute use of κηρύσσειν is to be noted.[31] By the πνεύματα we may understand both the imprisoned spirits and the powers which hold them captive, and hence conclude that by the proclamation of the victory of God's μακροθυμία (vs. 20) both the imprisoned are freed and the powers cease to be able to manifest themselves. Here, in any event, is to be found the true and decisive point of contact between *kerygma* and myth: through the event of κηρύσσειν the powers which desire to manifest themselves in the form of myth, are "demythologised," and such exorcism is theologically the sole legitimate method of demythologisation. It takes place not by the instrumentality of the reason but by the power of faith responding to the *kerygma*.

In saying thus that it is not reason which has banished the *infernum* and its powers, but faith which has dispelled them by its efficacy, the question arises to what extent we may affirm this in the perfect tense. This exorcising process of demythologisation through preaching and faith is an event which is ever to be repeated by us, for according to 1 Pet. v. 8 our adversary the Devil prowls about as a roaring lion seeking someone to devour. But the exorcism can only be continually repeated because it has once happened through the *descensus* of Christ and His preaching. It should be noted that the whole section 1 Pet. III. 18-22 is included under the ἅπαξ of III. 18. Thus the event, the proclamation and the faith belong indis-

[31] Cp. above, p. 113.

solubly together in the sermon of Luther. For this reason it becomes clear also why, like all dogmatic statements, the "*descendit ad inferos*" cannot be simply a statement of belief. But it will *become* an affirmation of faith ever afresh in proportion as faith can in fact bear witness to the "usefulness and the power" of this doctrine out of the heart of its own living experience. But in order that the exorcism of faith might have this experience at all, the "*descendit ad inferos*" must be preached to it as a given happening conditioning both its belief *and* unbelief. But it is just this which is expressed by the "*descendit ad inferos*" as a *dogmatic* statement.

(c) The ascension of Christ

The Apostles' Creed says with reference to the ascension of Christ: "*Credo . . . in Jesum Christum . . . qui . . . ascendit ad coelos, sedet ad dexteram Dei, patris omnipotentis: inde venturus est iudicare vivos et mortuos.*" What does the New Testament say about this? The ascension of Jesus is attested only by Luke (Lk. xxiv. 51 and Acts i. 9 ff.) and by the spurious ending of Mark (xvi. 19). The sitting "at the right hand of God" is found both explicitly and implicitly in many texts but not in genuinely Pauline ones. On the other hand we find in the latter the expectation of the return of Christ from Heaven: 1 Thess. i. 10, iv. 16; Phil. iii. 20; 1 Cor. xv. 47 ff. This state of affairs might well raise the question whether the Apostles' Creed has not simply constructed the history of the post-Resurrection life of Christ by means of the method of concordance, and has taken Luke as the witness for the first stage, the deutero-Pauline texts as the witness for the second, and the genuinely Pauline ones as the witness for the third stage. This process of historicisation would then have taken place on impossible lines: for the Ascension, which none of the other witnesses mention, the quite singular account of Luke has been used—an account which is clearly legendary by its whole mode of presentation and which has been worked out with the crudest conceptions of the universe current at the time. For the sitting in Heaven, about which no one can possibly know anything at all since even in the New Testament the word "Heaven" denotes the sphere of the hidden and the limit of the knowable, affirmations drawn from a later stage of the early Christian kerygma have been utilised, a stage when the need was felt to fill the gap between the Resurrection of Christ and His future coming. To conclude this drama of the post-Resurrection being of Christ it was attempted to quote, along with other witnesses, Paul too, in whose world of ideas, however, this whole drama refuses to be fitted. And in making into a dogma this dramatic historicisation of the post-Resurrection Christ, is it expected that as a series of events which happened and still happen we shall believe in it?

A modern exegete might express himself in these terms with regard to the "*passus*" of the Apostles' Creed; and he would then presumably be inclined to say that the invitation to subject such a dogma to critical exegesis is senseless and absurd. He would do better, however, not to say this at the outset but rather to get down to his exegetical work, leaving open to question whether in fact we have here to do with a historicisation of the post-Resurrection being of Christ.

The exegete will always take it as his point of departure that in the oldest form of the *kerygma* of primitive Christianity the story of the Ascension is not to be found, but that there the Resurrection is viewed as being at the same time an exaltation. Bultmann says with regard to this: "According to 1 Cor. xv. 5-8, where Paul enumerates the appearances of the risen one as the παράδοσις furnishes them, the Resurrection implies the exaltation; it was only later that it was interpreted in terms of a temporary return to life on earth, and out of this interpretation arose the story of the Ascension (Lk. xxiv. 50-3; Acts i. 3-11)." [32] He supposes, therefore, that as a historian he can distinguish an early stage of the primitive *kerygma*, in which the Resurrection of Jesus was understood as an exaltation to glory without any return to earthly life, from a later stage, which included such a temporary return and consequent ascension to Heaven. If this be so, then not merely the Ascension but also the bodily appearances of the risen Lord must have been lacking to this early stage of the *kerygma*. But how can Bultmann appeal to the *paradosis* of 1 Cor. xv. 5-8 as evidence of this early stage, since that tradition enumerates precisely the appearances of the risen one, which in any event are emphatically understood by Paul in the sense of a return to earthly

[32] Bultmann, *Theol. des N.T.*, p. 46.

life? However, among these appearances referred to in vss. 9 ff. there is also mentioned the one which struck Paul himself and which nevertheless occurred after the "forty days." And from the fact that this is enumerated along with the other appearances, Bultmann must no doubt have concluded that the other appearances, too, must not be understood as signifying a return to the life of earth. It is indisputable that the Damascus experience of Paul offers a certain difficulty if we wish to distinguish the life of the risen Lord during the forty days from His exaltation by means of the Ascension. But in any case Paul has mentioned all these appearances as forming one series and did not therefore feel this difficulty. And if Bultmann does feel it and so concludes from the Damascus experience, which contrasts strikingly with the other numerous texts, that the latter, contrary to their unambiguous declaration, cannot have meant to suggest a return to earthly life, and further that there must have been an original *kerygma* which did not distinguish the Resurrection from the exaltation, then we must ask whether this supposed original *kerygma* has not been reconstructed by Bultmann under the influence of his own systematic point of view, which interprets as the exaltation the Cross itself, rather than the Resurrection as a second event distinguishable from the former. Unlike Bultmann, we ourselves feel cautiously that we are unable to say more than that the story of the Ascension is in fact lacking from the oldest *paradosis*, but not that it *must* be lacking because it could have had no place in it.[33]

The oldest form of the *kerygma* emphasises with all the intensity of expectation the coming of the Lord ἐξ οὐρανοῦ, which makes it understandable that it is concerned hardly at all, or only incidentally, with the state of being ἐν οὐρανῷ while the ascension εἰς οὐρανόν is altogether lacking. In the course of the development of this primitive *kerygma* there then seems to have taken place, if not a shift of emphasis, at any rate a broadening of the theme. In order to explain this we shall have to take as our point of departure the data of the oldest tradition as found in Paul. Here the resurrection of Jesus from the dead is integrally connected with His coming

---

[33] Cp. with regard to the following, H. Traub's article *s.v.* οὐρανός in Kittel, VOL. V, pp. 496 ff.

from the heavens to raise all the dead (1 Thess. I. 10, IV. 16, 1 Cor. XV. 20 ff.; Phil. III. 21). The resurrection of Jesus furnishes the possibility of His *parousia*, but not merely in the sense that in principle it is its necessary prelude. The appearances of the risen Lord (1 Cor. XV. 5-8) also play an essential part in it, inasmuch as they provide the ground and the assurance for that life which His coming again promises to bring to the dead, and inspire the hope of this eternal life. Although there is no special reflexion about the Lord's state of being in the intervening period, the thought of it is not wholly lacking. In Rom. VIII. 34 it is said of the ἐγερθείς: ὅς ἐστιν ἐν δεξιᾷ τοῦ Θεοῦ (which in connexion with Rom. X. 6 is an allusion to being in Heaven), ὅς καὶ ἐντυγχάνει ὑπὲρ ἡμῶν, which again corresponds to Phil. III. 20: ἡμῶν γὰρ τὸ πολίτευμα ἐν οὐρανοῖς ὑπάρχει. Thus in regard to the sitting at the right hand of the Father, the emphasis is not on the description of a state, but it is a question rather of participation in God's world-government, considered as His hidden saving work on our behalf, of His being μεθ'ὑμῶν (Mt. XXVIII. 20) in time until His coming again. From this point of view also the Second Coming takes on its true scope and meaning as the disclosure of what has hitherto been hidden in heaven. "The coming of Jesus Christ, i.e. the ultimate eschatological revelation, is in all these texts understood to be the breaking-through into space and time or the rending of the concealing heavens." [34] In the later texts this interpretation of Heaven *sub specie dexterae Dei* is at times overlaid with the linguistic usage and the world of ideas characteristic of Gnosticism (e.g. Eph. IV. 9 ff.; Jn. III. 13, 31); though at the same time the anti-Gnostic tendency is evinced in the very way in which these Gnostic means of expression are used. But is this interpretation of Heaven *sub specie dexterae Dei* decisive for the story of the Ascension?

How could it be understood otherwise? There is no room for any speculative interest within the framework of Luke's dominating conception of saving history. On the other hand, we might impute to him a special interest in the historicising of the single facts in the process of saving history to an extent which is in any case not typical of the other New Testament authors. His intention is in any event to report περὶ τῶν

[34] Traub, in Kittel, VOL. V, pp. 523 f.

πεπληροφορημένων ἐν ἡμῖν πραγμάτων (Lk. i. i), and here we are unable to associate ourselves with the disparaging judgment which is today usually made in connexion with this fact.[35] For mere reliance on historical reporting of the πράγματα is of no significance for Luke either; what he is essentially concerned about is that it is a question of fulfilled and established facts such as cannot be historically apprehended nor reported in a historical way, but only proclaimed and believed. With the fulfilment of these matters he announces that the mighty works of Jesus spell the dawning of the time of salvation. It is in this context that we have to view his proclamation of the fact of the Ascension, for it is an event integral to the course of this age of salvation and on its factuality he certainly lays all possible stress. Why he does so it is only possible to understand in the light of the meaning of the event. Again it is from the same point of view that we must judge the world of ideas which lies behind his reporting.

In discussions about demythologisation the story of the Ascension is the favourite illustration chosen by exponents of the theory. For in this instance they can not only point to the whole paraphernalia of an outworn world view in all its impossibility and absurdity, but also with the greatest ease convict their opponents of demythologising without being willing to admit it by the very fact that they themselves have ceased to make use of such conceptions. Such discussions are not of course a new thing, but were conducted on similar lines in 1564 at the Maulbronn Conversations between Württemberg and Palatine theologians. The Reforming opponents of the doctrine of ubiquity argued that Christ had bodily gone up into the heavens, which should be thought of as a specific place above the earth and the sphere of the stars, and that consequently He could not be corporeally present in the Eucharist. Previously this view had been reduced *ad absurdum* with furious scorn by Brenz,[36] who had said, among other things, that the spatial motion of a body could not suddenly and capriciously happen, so that after His disappearance

[35] Cp. above, pp. 118 ff.

[36] *De personali unione duarum naturarum in Christo, et ascensu Christi in coelum ac sessione eius ad dextram Dei Patris. Qua vera corporis et sanguinis Christi praesentia in coena explicata est et confirmata,* 1561.

behind the clouds, Christ must have gone further step by step. "The schoolmen however, calculated that the distance between the heavens of the fixed stars and the earth was so great that a leaden weight falling thence to the earth would take more than 500 years. Hence one should be careful to consider whether Christ were already in Heaven or was still on the way thither." [37] But how are the notions and images used by Luke to be assessed then? In Lk. xxiv. 51 ff. and Acts i. 9 f., where Jesus is represented as disappearing in the direction of the heavens, or the firmament, nothing is said about Heaven itself. But we are bound to infer from the description of the ascent in terms of spatial motion that Luke, in accordance with the idea of the universe prevalent in his time, pictured Heaven as situated in space. In Acts i the cloud forms the point of transition to the veiling heavens, whereas in Lk. xxiv. it appears as a kind of celestial means of transport. The occurrence of cloud-pictures in connexion with apotheoses and epiphanies is found everywhere in Christianity and Hellenism, as also in the Old Testament and in Jewish-Christian apocalyptic,[38] whence they have crept into this account without having any particular theological significance. The probably older and less crudely materialistic description in Acts i itself cuts short all interest in the phenomena of the Ascension and speculations to which it may give rise concerning the celestial abode of Jesus by the declaration that He will come again (i. 10 f.). And the same two heavenly witnesses appear as in the scene of the empty tomb (Lk. xxiv. 4; cp. also the function of the proclaiming angel in the Nativity stories, Lk. ii. 9 ff.) in order to declare the meaning of an incident which in its mere historical happening is obviously not self-explanatory. With this is connected Peter's preaching in Acts ii. 32 ff., where, with an appeal to the authority of Ps. c, the exaltation to Heaven is equated with the sitting at the right hand of God and His coming again is proclaimed as the fulfilment of Old Testament promises: $\H{\epsilon}\omega\varsigma$ $\H{\alpha}\nu$ $\theta\hat{\omega}$ (ii. 35), which is virtually identical with $\H{\alpha}\chi\rho\iota$ $\chi\rho\acute{o}\nu\omega\nu$ $\mathring{\alpha}\pi o\kappa\alpha\tau\alpha\sigma\tau\acute{\alpha}\sigma\epsilon\omega\varsigma$ $\pi\acute{\alpha}\nu\tau\omega\nu$ (iii. 21). Hence for the story of the Ascension, too,

---

[37] E. Bizer, *Studien zur Geschichte des Abendmahlstreites im 16 Jahrhundert*, 1940, p. 361.

[38] Cp. Oepke's article *s.v.* $\nu\epsilon\phi\acute{\epsilon}\lambda\eta$ in Kittel, VOL. IV, pp. 904 ff.

the "understanding of the οὐρανός *sub specie dexterae Dei* is decisive (cp. 1 Pet. III. 22; Mk. XVI. 19)." [39]

In the light of all this, we have now to enquire what is the nature of Luke's interest in the Ascension as a special event in the process of saving history, and why the Apostles' Creed shares this special interest of Luke, inasmuch as it places the *"ascendit ad coelos"* as a prelude to the two other relevant statements. The simplest explanation would be that Luke, with his desire for historical completeness, has added this story which he has taken from some special private source. If we are content with this explanation, however, we shall hardly be able to avoid eliminating the story both on account of its being an isolated witness and on account of its legendary form, and so striking out the corresponding clause in the Creed. But this explanation, even though it expressed certain intentions of Luke's, is in any case inadequate in the light of our exegetical findings. It is impossible to overlook the emphasis given to the event by the appearance of the two heavenly witnesses, as in the Resurrection narratives, and the fact that these witnesses are necessary in order to disclose the meaning of this incident, which while being presented as historical is not historically interpretable. The solemn meaning of their testimony lifts the reported event of the Ascension as, in the other case, the narrative of the empty tomb, out of the sphere of the indifferent material of history, and makes it an integral part of God's saving counsel which, although realised within history, is not recognisable from the historical point of view, and which alone makes this historical process an act of divine self-revelation. Thus, in its present literary form, which goes far beyond a mere historical account, the Lucan report already contains in the declaration of the heavenly witnesses a dogma which is intended to orientate our approach to the whole testimony of Luke. In detail this means that the exegete must enquire whether the text in the whole context of Lk. XXIV and Acts I and II (between which Luke probably felt no contradiction) has any other purpose than to declare that, by taking His place at the right hand of the Father, Jesus has entered upon a new mode of sovereignty and of presence with His own. If this sitting at the right hand of God is equated with being in

[39] Traub, in Kittel, VOL. v, p. 525.

Heaven, then the idea of "Heaven" here connotes the same circle of ideas as it does for example in the Lord's Prayer, "The heavenly Father is the God who, unhindered by earthly limitations, is omniscient, all-seeing, and omnipotent, and who therefore is accessible to all," [40] and likewise in the phrase βασιλεία τῶν οὐρανῶν, on which K. L. Schmidt says: "We should consider whether 'Kingdom of Heaven' has not a quite special meaning in that it is intended to imply the divine sovereignty which comes from Heaven and enters this world." [41] Hence the being ἐν οὐρανῷ is at the same time an expression of the point of departure for the ἐξ οὐρανοῦ; and the presupposition for both is the εἰς οὐρανόν as the special act of exaltation which closes the period of the forty days and inaugurates the intervening time of the Church characterised by the presence of God in Word and Spirit, for which reason the disciples before the Ascension itself are warned to look forward to the event of Pentecost (Lk. xxiv. 49; Acts i. 7 ff.).

It is no doubt in this context of thought that the Apostles' Creed has interpreted the triad εἰς οὐρανόν, ἐν οὐρανῷ, and ἐξ ουρανοῦ which it has expressed in the three members of its dogmatic pronouncement. If this sequence of ideas can be made dogmatically clear and tested and verified by exegesis, as we have seen to be the case, then the unique testimony to the first member—the "*ascendit ad coelos*"—plays no part of special importance in the establishment of the dogmatic conclusion. But on the other hand the "*ascendit ad coelos*" can and must serve to orientate our approach to the Pauline texts also, where an explicit witness to it is missing.

Although we have established that these disputed clauses of the Creed can be exegetically verified, many questions still of course remain open, and the dogmatic and exegetical discussion is by no means ended. We have only to think of the above-mentioned question of the "corporeal" ascension of Jesus and its implications for eucharistic doctrine in the controversy between Lutheran and Reformed. These and other questions are not decided dogmatically by any general consensus of Church teaching and must be further discussed in

---

[40] Johannes Haussleitner *s.v.* "Vaterunser" in *Realencyclopaedie für protestantische Theologie und Kirche*, VOL. XX, p. 436.

[41] K. L. Schmidt, *s.v.* βασιλεία, in Kittel, VOL. I, p. 582.

the explication of dogma and also in the ever renewed verification of dogmatic inferences through exegesis. For the performance of this task we are infinitely better equipped today than were the theologians of the sixteenth century. We need only study the above-mentioned report of Ernst Bizer about the Maulbronn Conversations of 1564 to realise how in this instance a dispute was carried on which could not possibly lead to any decisive conclusion so long as it was conducted alternately with the resources of Aristotelian syllogistics and an appeal to isolated Scriptural texts regarded as so many *dicta probantia*. In view of such examples we can only be thankful that the historico-critical approach to the Bible makes such arguments impossible for us, and has freed us for a better understanding of the Bible in the rich multiplicity of its testimony and thus its humanity. But we also owe it to the same scientific approach that we can today discriminate on quite other lines between a dogmatic and a syllogistic argument, now that the proclamatory character of Scripture has been fully brought out. The division of present-day theological work into dogmatics and exegesis, which makes theological discussion so very difficult, is therefore not really understandable. On the contrary, we have every reason to remain together and to work together in our theological studies and to adopt an attitude of fullest confidence in each other.

To sum up we may say: what makes possible genuine exegetical and dogmatic discussion and renders individual points of view comparable is that freedom in obligation which arises solely when the focus of all our thinking is the ἀκοή. We are bound to this centre in that we have to direct our enquiry solely to the proper object attested in the Scriptural texts, and must forbid ourselves to indulge in arbitrary questioning. Thus we take up our stand in the process of proclamatory history as those who pay heed and respond, and here no one is alone and no one can start afresh on his own, but each must pay attention to what other hearers of the message have said before him and say alongside him by way of response and understanding. And none must lay upon his partner in discussion or allow to be laid upon himself any other obligation than that each must recall the other to the focal centre of the ἀκοή where dogma *itself* is never dissolved in our subjective thinking, but, on the contrary, ever confronts us anew as both the original source and the touchstone of the systems we construct. Within this unremitting obligation, we have the freedom, in face of answers already given, to question the testimony anew as to the object attested, and to answer with new means of expression. Not only is this a *legitimate* freedom but it is one we are *obliged* to make use of because our theological work must further the purpose of that Biblical proclamation which must continue to be enacted and by which in the last resort it must be verified and authenticated.

CHAPTER XIV

THE AUTHORITY OF DOGMA
AND OF DOGMAS

THE ἀκοή is the primary and the sole legitimate focus for
the construction of dogmas. Only from this standpoint,
therefore, can the question of the effective authority
inherent in the formation of dogmas be answered. In this
matter it is always a question of the ἀκοή in its two senses
which may not be separated: of what is heard and the event of
present hearing, both being aspects of that revelatory historical
process and at one and the same time attesting the actuality
of the latter and effecting its operation.[1] In proportion as
ἀκοή takes place the circle is closed between the revealed
declaration of the will of God and man's heeding it with the
obedience of faith and the human responsiveness couched in
the form of the ὁμολογεῖν (Rom. x. 10), of a full assent to the
content of the ἀκοή. This act of confession, or ὁμολογία,
includes the activity of professing one's faith (ἡ ὑποταγὴ τῆς
ὁμολογίας ὑμῶν εἰς τὸ εὐαγγέλιον τοῦ Χριστοῦ, II Cor. IX. 13)
and the content of the profession (Heb. III. 1, IV. 4, X. 23),
though these two senses easily merge into each other, as we
found to be the case also with the διδασκαλία and κήρυγμα.[2]
Fixed formulae are used in connexion with the idea of the
ὁμολογεῖν (I Jn. IV. 2 ff.) as of the παραδοῦναι (I Cor. XI. 23,
XV. 3 ff.), frequently, however, without any special emphasis
in contrast to the rest of the text. Such formulae of confession
develop with the evolving tradition of the churches and are
used on various occasions: in the cult as part of the liturgy,
in instruction to catechumens, and in the sacrament of baptism,
as a formula for exorcisms, and in the refutation of opponents
from without, as of heretical teachers within. They arise
through the process of the ἀκοή and also serve and promote

---

[1] Cp. above, p. 294 ff.   [2] Cp. above, p. 164 ff.

that process.[3] We have now to concern ourselves with the *theological* question of the authority of these confessions of the faith, in order thus to gain a criterion of material importance for assessing this historical development.

(a) Dogmatic statements and confessions of the faith

In any event within the New Testament itself and also even in the sub-Apostolic age it is hardly possible clearly to distinguish between dogmatic statements, as we have defined them, and statements in which a profession of faith is made. The latter are dogmatic in so far as they give a critically theological account of what takes place in the ἀκοή in both its aspects. This kind of formulation is a work which neither can nor should be undertaken by every Christian, but which should be reserved for the preachers of the Gospel, who again may, but need not, specialise either in the work of evangelists whose task it is to proclaim the Christian message, or in that of teachers who theologically underpin the former. On the other hand, the profession of the faith is a matter for the Church as a whole, which by its consensus lends to confessional formulae a greater weight and so, if not in kind yet in degree, a different and a higher authority than that possessed by a dogmatic statement which is merely the product of individual theologians.

With regard to the manner in which this co-operation of preachers, teachers and hearers brings about a consensus of confessional opinion, there are hardly any principles which can be discovered within the New Testament itself. It is not possible to ascertain more than the fact that the co-operation of these various factors is necessary. The only pertinent account in the New Testament, the report of the Apostolic Council in Acts xv, contains, leaving aside for the moment the question of its historical reliability [4] no detail concerning the *modus procedendi*. On the other hand, we have here an important indication as regards the authority of the decision reached, in

---

[3] As regards the historical question how these various confessions of faith develop into a unified *regula fidei*, cp. O. Cullmann, *Die ersten christlichen glaubensbekenntnisses*, Zürich 1943; and, from the critical angle, Diem, *Theol.*, VOL. I, pp. 124 ff.

[4] On this point and on the following, cp. Diem, *Theol.* VOL. I, pp. 170 ff.

the sentence which introduces it: "It has seemed good to the Holy Spirit and to us" (vs. 28). Thus here men have acted in the faith that the event of the divine address to man has, in this particular human response, produced by divine inspiration a guidance which for its authorisation neither can nor will rest on anything but the sheer faith that the saving manward work of God has here *in concreto* reached its fulfilment. As regards the type of authority claimed it is important to notice that the decision is not simply laid down as a law for observation by the churches, but it is delivered to the Antiochenes as a verbal message through Judas and Silas, καὶ αὐτοὺς διὰ λόγου ἀπαγγέλλοντας τὰ αὐτά (vs. 27). And it is said of the recipients of the message in Antioch: ἀναγνόντες δὲ ἐχάρησαν ἐπὶ τῇ παρακλήσει (vs. 31). Thus no decree goes forth, but the decision is announced as a testimony of the clear and unanimous faith of the Apostles and thus the churches are requested and invited to give their assent to this testimony. And, consequently, in the whole matter there is no argument nor any playing-off of some authority, but there is a proclamation and admonition διὰ λόγου (vss. 27, 32). Nor is this an extraordinary act, but it is a type of activity which is continued in the διδάσκειν and εὐαγγελίζεσθαι τὸν λόγον τοῦ Κυρίου (vs. 35). The authority which is claimed and used, therefore, lies not by any means in the persons of those who take action or in their official status, but solely in the λόγος as the medium which stands at their disposal. And as the λόγος τοῦ Κυρίου this is not conceived of as the ground of truth immanent in the pronouncements and calculated to make them into a *veritas revelata* on the basis of which by argument and deduction further conclusions might be drawn. It is not here a question of the λόγος by which one might be persuaded through syllogistic procedure, but this λόγος is in the strict sense an address in which man concretely encounters the Κύριος as the truth of God which has become embodied in a living historical process and which demands a concrete answer. Accordingly the answer of faith consists not only and not primarily in a certain insight but in a certain attitude—in this case that of the χαρά for the παράκλησις (vs. 31) which involves as a consequence a certain insight expressed in assent to the witness of the Apostles. Hence in this process by which human state-

z

ments about the will of God become authorised the actual event of proclamation mediating a living summons and a living response must on no account be lacking if the essential nature of the statement and its authorisation is not to be radically altered. In this connexion it should above all be noted that even the Apostles, who here are assessing the paradosis of the Church at a debatable point and in tension with the paradosis of the Synagogue, who by their critical reaction develop it and by their decision create a new *paradosis*, at bottom wish to do nothing else but *expound the Scriptures*.[5] Thus far, we find, too, that Luther's thesis in the Schmalkaldic Articles is confirmed: "The Word of God must decide the articles of the faith and nothing else, even were it the angels." [6]

(b) The regula fidei

So far we have been speaking only of the dogmatic statements within the New Testament itself and of the various confessions of the faith only in so far as they have become reabsorbed in the proclamatory history of the New Testament. The question we have now to consider is whether all this is true of that development which leads to the embodiment of such confessions in a *regula fidei* existing independently of the New Testament, or whether there is here introduced some other authority than Scripture and a means of authorisation other than the ἀκοή.[7] Historical conclusions give us no reason to suppose that the dogmatic affirmations of the *regula fidei* in the Apostolic age gather their authority from any other source than that of the ἀκοή. Cullmann is no doubt justified in saying with regard to the development of the rule of faith: "The life of the New Testament Church is reflected in the selection made from the welter of tradition. It was not the Apostles themselves, but rather the Church of the Apostolic age, which detached from Church preaching those facts which we have noted in the various formulae, and which most accurately expressed the

[5] Cp. on this Chs. V and VII above, esp. the distinction between the Jewish-Christian and the Greek conceptions of doctrine, and the argument with H. Schlier.

[6] *Bek. Schr*, p. 421.

[7] For the following, cp. O. Cullmann, *op. cit.* (above, n. 3), and T. Zahn, *s.v.* "Glaubensregel," in *Realencyclopaedie für protestantische Theologie und Kirche*, VOL. VI, pp. 682 ff.

assurances of its inner Christian experience." [8] But it might
have been the fact that the confession of faith, even though
springing from responsiveness to the preaching of the Scriptures,
ceased gradually to be content with the natural intrinsic
authority of a widely recognised tradition and acquired an
authority which was ranked above that of preaching and
Scripture. The very use of the expression "*regula fidei*" might
be taken as an indication of this. But this seems primarily
not to have been the case. T. Zahn points out that ὁ κανὼν τῆς
πίστεως, "*regula fidei*," is used synonymously with ὁ κανὼν τῆς
ἀληθείας, "*regula veritatis*," and comments: "It goes without
saying that there can be no question of a canon to be applied
to the truth itself or of a pattern to which truth must conform,
and the idea of a touchstone by which to test what claims to be
truth would agree neither with the connotation of ὁ κανών
nor with that of ἡ ἀλήθεια. Hence the only possibility that
remains is that truth itself was conceived as the criterion by
which everything else was to be measured. . . . This is that
saving truth which was not only preached and taught by the
Church but also formulated. For this reason Irenaeus can
allow ὁ κανὼν τῆς ἀληθείας and τὸ τῆς ἀληθείας σωμάτιον and
ἡ ὑπὸ τῆς ἐκκλησίας κηρυττομένη ἀλήθεια to be interchangeable." [9] The situation is similar with regard to ὁ κανὼν τῆς
πίστεως. We have seen above in our study on the relation
between proclamation and teaching that within the New
Testament itself the idea of πίστις can pass from the connotation of the believing *attitude* to that of the *content* of what is
believed,[10] and that there is no reason to see in this an erroneous
development, since the two meanings are complementary.
The same line of development is continued in the rule of faith,
and to such effect "that it is not conceived as a law which
commands men to believe and also prescribes what they
should believe, but rather that it connotes the fixed communal
faith of the Church as the norm to which individual Christians
and Church corporations must conform in all that concerns
the Christian faith. Since, however, πίστις did not cease to
denote the subjective aspect of faith, the believing attitude,
the change in the idea 'rule of faith' by which it came to suggest

<hr>

[8] Cullmann, *op. cit.*, p. 29.   [9] Zahn, *op. cit.*, p. 683.
[10] See above, pp. 167 ff.

a law commanding belief was quite possible linguistically, and indeed a very natural one, in view of the legalistic conception of the duty of belief in general and of belief in certain points of revelation and Church doctrine in particular. It cannot be a matter of chance that Tertullian who was inclined to this view consistently speaks of '*regula fidei*' rather than of '*regula veritatis*'." [11] We ourselves would prefer to see the danger of deviation which here threatens or is perhaps already existent not simply in the "legalistic" conception as such. Our own conception of the function of dogma as the indispensable orientation of Scriptural exegesis is not compatible with the idea that dogma is merely something in the nature of a free-working hypothesis. And why should we not be regarded as being under the strictest obligation to listen to the testimony of the Fathers reflected in the traditional Scriptural exegesis, which is the voice of the Church that has hearkened, believed, and confessed before us? Hence we would by no means take exception if this patristic testimony were presented to us as a law which lays its obligation upon us. It is simply that this law should not be allowed to take the place of Scripture itself. But this seems already to have been the case with Tertullian, when he says that "we can investigate and come to individual opinions as much as we like about those questions which the Bible raises and which stand in a certain connexion with the life and the faith of the Church, *in so far as they have not already been settled by the rule of faith* [italics ours]. But we must not contradict either the letter or the spirit of the rule of faith.[12] Agreement with this latter is the condition of all true insight, and the faith which makes the Christian blessed lies in observation of and conformity with the rule of faith" [13] —a point of view which later found its classic formulation in the Athanasian Creed.[14]

(c) The formal authorisation of dogmas

The result of this development in fact is that, alongside of the preaching of the Church which authenticates itself by the power of the Holy Spirit, there is introduced as a new criterion of truth the *regula fidei*, the legitimacy of which we must now

[11] Zahn, *op. cit.*, p. 683. [12] Tertullian, praescr. 12 extr.
[13] Zahn, *op. cit.*, pp. 683 ff. [14] See above, p. 1.

investigate. If the consensus of opinion which arose through Church development and the formation of doctrine, and which led to the establishment of the rule of faith, was to be received as a critical norm for the settlement of debate with heretics outside the Church and for the interpretation of Scripture within it, then the legitimacy of this norm and of all that flowed from it had to be demonstrated and secured by historical proof. The early Catholic Church, and its consistent continuation in the Roman Catholic Church, adopted this procedure. The first efforts to furnish such historically demonstrable criteria are seen in the standardisation of confessional formulae taken in hand by the officers of the Church and connected with the firm establishment of doctrinal decisions through an episcopate legitimised by Apostolic succession. The next stage lies in the decisions of ecumenical councils which by their lawful constitution guarantee the concurrence of the Holy Ghost *ex opere operato*. Finally we have the declaration of the infallibility and irreformability of definitions of the faith as issued by the Roman bishop speaking *ex cathedra*. In this process of development we have to notice that it is not simply a question of those doctrines which have historically established themselves gaining *ipso facto* spontaneous recognition as dogma, but for this is required from time to time the express decision of the ecclesiastical teaching office. Accordingly the Vatican Council laid down with regard to the content of the faith: "*Porro fide divina et catholica ea omnia credenda sunt, quae in verbo Dei scripto vel tradito continentur et ab Ecclesia sive solemni iudicio sive ordinario et universali magisterio tamquam divinitus revelata credenda proponuntur.*" [15] The ecclesiastical teaching office has full competence in this matter because the *doctrina fidei* has been delivered to the Church by God as a *depositum* "fideliter custodienda et infallibiliter declaranda." [16] Thus it is expressly stated that the Holy Ghost has been promised to the successors of Peter, not "*ut eo revelante novam doctrinam patefacerent, sed ut, eo assistente, traditam per Apostolos revelationem seu fidei depositum sancte custodirent et fideliter exponerent.*" [17] Thus a direct line of development proceeds from Tertullian to the decisions of the Vatican Council.

[15] Denz. 1792. On the following, cp. Diem, *Theol.* VOL. I, pp. 15 ff.
[16] Denz. 1800.   [17] Denz. 1836.

(d) The authorisation of the content of dogmas

At the same time as the process of development which concerns the formal side of the authorisation of dogma, there runs through the history of the formation of dogma another line of development which concerns the authorisation of its content and is indissolubly connected with the former. This second line of development begins with the apologists and their attempts to justify Christian doctrine in the eyes of the pagan philosophers. For the apologists Christian doctrine is superior to philosophy because it rests on revelation and thus has a certainty which the latter lacks and cannot attain. Nevertheless, from this point of view, Christian doctrine itself becomes a revealed *philosophy*, and, as such, becomes susceptible of discussion by the philosophers. When in this context of thought the sum of Christian affirmations is called δόγμα τῆς ἀληθείας [18] it represents a development of that type of thought which we found not in the New Testament itself but in Josephus and Philo, where the Jewish use of the term δόγματα to denote the various ordinances of the Torah overlaps with the Helenistic implications of teaching and the principles of philosophy.[19] Here the Christian doctrines are in fact worked up into "a system of the sacred principles of a divine philosophy comparable with the δόγματα of heathen philosophy," and the change from the Jewish-Christian idea of doctrine to the Greek idea of teaching is palpable. The historical question as to how far this type of thought has already influenced the formulation of the rule of faith, for example in the co-ordination of the articles, or even in the very conception of them, and how far it has, through its *logos* speculation, moulded the development of the doctrine of the Trinity and of Christology, need not be traced here in detail. What it is important for us to notice is that we see here the starting-point for that whole cast of thought which has controlled the development of Roman Catholic dogmatics, and which regards dogmas as *veritates revelatae*. The latter, in any event, have in common with the principles of natural theology and philosophy the idea of *veritas*, and on this account can and must be brought into a systematic relationship with such principles. Here again it is a long way from the still

---

[18] Aristides, 2p. 10.   [19] Cp. above, pp. 282 ff.

largely primitive attempts of the apologists to co-ordinate reason and authority through St Thomas Aquinas to the carefully considered, classical formulations of the *Vaticanum*, which on the one hand declares, "*Si quis dixerit, revelationem divinam externis signis credibilem fieri non posse . . . anathema sit,*" [20] and on the other, "*Si quis dixerit, assensum fidei Christianae non esse liberum, sed argumentis humanae rationis necessario produci . . . anathema sit.*" [21]

(e) *The ecclesiastical teaching office*

In spite of the doubts which one must entertain about this structure of dogma, with its use of the Greek idea of teaching for the purpose of unfolding the truths of revelation, we must be careful to notice that the system still leaves full scope for the contingency of revelation and intends in the last resort to make the event of revelation the ultimate ground of authority on which dogma must rest, and to deduce the truths of revelation exclusively from that event. We might think that we see here step by step how from the insights of dogma about the fact and the meaning of the divine action for man's salvation there has evolved an ecclesiastically authorised *gnosis* which in fact depends on the authority of the truth inherent within it and no longer on the living Word of God. But the question is whether this amounts to a fundamental objection. We ourselves have noted above that even dogmatic thought as we conceive it is constantly threatened by the danger that the truth of its statements will be inferred from the continuity of the system in which they are embedded, because it cannot avoid using the concepts of some philosophic system and because the various affirmations are interlocked with each other. There is no absolute security against the danger that a dogmatics which has become independent of the revelatory event may take the place of this event, and, where only the action of the triune God and the testimony to it both will and can constitute truth, may endeavour to establish truth by means of some alien authority. Hence by the help of our critical criterion for dogmatic thought we can constantly point to specific junctures in the history of the Church and of dogma where the Church has at least been very careless of

[20] Denz. 1812.   [21] Denz. 1814.

this danger and on that basis assess critically the development that has followed. On the other hand, it will be difficult to say that at any one of these points, whether it be early Catholicism, Tertullian and the apologists, or St Thomas Aquinas, or the Vatican Council, there has taken place such a sinful lapse that in consequence the dogmatic thought of the Roman Church as a whole and in detail has become for us beyond the reach of discussion. We have always at least the possibility in discussing any particular dogmatic pronouncement, of pointing out the danger that arises from the very basis of all dogmatic thinking; and as long as Catholic theologians are in agreement with us —as may be to a considerable extent assumed—that here lies a danger to be avoided, then it is always possible for us to have discussions with them.

In that case, their answer to us will, above all, be that the Catholic Church itself has built into its system the strongest security against this very danger, by the fact that it connects the validity of its dogma with its proclamation by the official teachers of the Church. All the prudence with which the decisions of the latter are guarded against the caprice of man, flow from the fact that this *magisterium*, endowed with exactly the same authority as that of the New Testament Apostolate, with which moreover it stands in a historically demonstrable succession, is a moment in the revelatory action of the Triune God, and therefore by its proclamation of doctrine, exactly as we have asserted of the Apostolate, both attests and effects that action. Furthermore, our demand that this proclamation of doctrine must proceed from the focus of the ἀκοή seems also to have been satisfied thereby; and the Catholic dogmatist can say: "Through the Church we believe in Scripture (*fides ex auditu*), and by the latter can convince ourselves of the divinity of the former." [22] Moreover, it may even be attempted to show historically that the relationship between the official promulgation of dogma by the responsible teachers of the Church, and, on the other hand, the text of the Scriptures, is not one of mutual conditioning but that the teaching office of the Church was prior to and ranked superior to Scripture itself. For, it may be argued, the Church once existed before Scripture, which of course is only true if we leave aside the

[22] Bartmann, *Lehrbuch der Dogmatik*, 1926, p. 38.

Old Testament and disregard the fact that Apostolic proclamation was intended as an exposition of the Old Testament.[23] Further, it may be said, the first confessions of the faith and the *regula fidei* which arose out of them came into existence as a product of the Church before the rise of the canon of Scripture, and were used as a critical touchstone for the selection of Scriptural documents and their canonisation. Hence the teaching office of the Church existed prior to and superior to the Scriptures as the final court of appeal for their interpretation; and from this historical situation, by the gradual formation of doctrine concerning Scripture and tradition and the functions of the ecclesiastical teaching office, dogmatic conclusions were explicitly drawn.

(f) Fides ex auditu

In answer to this we can only say that we ourselves draw precisely opposite conclusions from this historical finding, namely that Scripture in the process of its proclamation, hence in the event of the ἀκοή, formed and still forms the critical norm for the elaboration of the *regula fidei* and the eventual canonisation of Scripture itself. And from this it follows dogmatically that there cannot be any Church teaching office having the competence to expound the Scriptures infallibly, but that Scripture must be interpreted in its own light and must supply the criterion by which all growth of doctrine is to be tested, for in the living process of the ἀκοή it stirs faith and engenders the confession of faith.

Here is the juncture where there arises a fundamental parting of the ways in dogmatic thought, and where, moreover, in controversial theology decisions must again and again be made with regard to particular points of dogma. The Catholic Church must adapt Scripture to its tradition and subordinate the justification of this tradition by the exegesis of Scripture to the authorisations of its official teachers. If, at the same time, it speaks of faith in its doctrinal promulgations as of a *fides ex auditu*, it is of course questionable whether this is the same thing as the ἀκοή τῆς πίστεως of Rom. x. 17, because in this case it would be impossible to continue straightforwardly: ἡ δὲ ἀκοή διὰ ῥήματος Χριστοῦ, for this ῥῆμα

[23] Cp. what was said above, pp. 48 ff., in criticism of Schlier.

Χριστοῦ has been absorbed into the Church and incorporated into its system of rule and authority. Nevertheless, we still must not say, for this reason, that the voice of Christ can no longer speak through the Church, and in fact the Catholic Church might, even in principle, assent to those words of Luther in the Schmalkaldic Articles to the effect that only the Word of God can establish what is to be believed—even though in this case the Word would be heard only through the medium of tradition and official teaching. But whether this is really the case can only be decided in the last resort by the extent to which the Church is prepared not only to attempt to *authorise* its dogmatic decisions in this circuitous way but on the contrary is also willing to allow them to be *tested* by Scripture. But it is just this which it can no longer do. Dogma has here ceased to be an aid to exegesis, which must in its turn be verified by the latter, but in principle it is no longer exegetically disputable. By exegesis it can now only be confirmed but not radically called in question. For this reason Catholic dogmatics has no further shield against those dangers to which we have drawn attention.

(g) The dogma of the Assumption of the Blessed Virgin Mary and an exegetical examination of its basis

As an example of our argument how it is at this juncture that decisions must be made in controversial theology both as regards principle and particular problems (the former in practice working itself out in the latter) we may consider the dogma of the Assumption of the Blessed Virgin Mary.[24] In Protestant polemics against this new dogma the principal objection brought forward is that it has no basis in Scripture —to disregard altogether for the moment the very defective proof from tradition, with which we are not in the main concerned. Of course it is asserted at the conclusion of the exposition of the bases of the definition: "All these proofs and considerations adduced by the Holy Fathers rest in the last resort on Holy Scripture." But it could hardly be said that this proof is made by appeal to particular texts of the Bible,

---

[24] For the following, cp. Diem, *Theol.*, VOL. I, pp. 144 ff., and K. G. Steck, *Das neue Mariendogma: Die Stimme der Gemeinde*, 1951, pp. 5 ff.

it is conducted rather by specious reasoning, as follows: Scripture "shows us the holy Mother of God as most closely bound to her divine Son and visibly sharing His destiny. Therefore it seems impossible to conceive that after this earthly life she would be separated from Christ, if not in the soul, yet in the body—she who conceived and bore Christ and fed Him at her breast and pressed Him to her heart. Because, then, our Saviour is the Son of Mary, He, the most perfect observer of the Law, must, in fact, as He honoured His Father, so also have honoured His dear Mother. Since He could do her the greatest honour in guarding her from the corruption of death, we must believe that in reality He has done so." [25] Such a "proof" is scarcely calculated to convince any one. But neither is it necessary, since according to the Catholic conception of the relation between Scripture and tradition and the authorisation of the latter by the official teaching of the Church, the exegesis of Scripture has no burden of proof to bear. Tradition has the same value as Scripture, and in a borderline case such as we obviously have here, it can even altogether replace the witness of Scripture.

For these reasons the Catholic Church cannot accept as a valid objection the defective Scriptural basis. On the contrary, it might point out with some reason that "proof from Scripture" must not in any case be conducted in a Biblicist way by means of *dicta probantia*, and it could even cite as an illustration the dogma of the Holy Trinity, which also springs solely from the teaching tradition of the Church (even though from a very early one) and is nevertheless universally admitted to be consonant with the Scriptures. Might not the same therefore be said with regard to the dogma of the Assumption? It is hardly possible to deny this *in principle*. What then can be our ground of objection? In any case we must not be simply content with asserting that the Scriptural basis is defective, but we must in practice make use of this dogma also as a means of orientating our approach to the texts, and at the same time, conversely, must submit it to critical questioning and challenge. That the Catholic Church itself has not taken into account the possibility of critical testing by application to Scripture need not bother us. The use of the dogma as a

[25] *Herderkorrespondenz*, Dec. 1950, p. 124.

norm for Scriptural exposition is in any event foreseen and practiced.

As an example of a Biblical passage which Catholics are fond of quoting for this purpose we take Gal. IV. 4: "But when the time had fully come, God sent forth his Son, born of woman, born under the law, to redeem those who were under the law, so that we might receive adoption as sons." Now let us compare with this what the Pope said in his sermon on this dogma: "We are all sons of one and the same mother, of Mary, who lives in heaven as that power which knits together the members of the mystical body of Christ as the new Eve and the new Mother of all that live, as the one who wills to lead all mankind to the truth and the grace that are found in her divine Son." [26] The mention of the woman, i.e. of Mary, in our text is intended to emphasise the completeness of the incarnation of Christ, and hence the fact that Christ shares the full destiny of man determined as it is by the curse of sin and of the law. In this context of thought Mary's function is by no means to serve as a *new* Eve, but precisely to symbolise the *old* Eve; and in this sense she represents humanity as such. The "born of woman" is quite clearly intended in this context to indicate through the very completeness of the Incarnation the deep radical need for humanity's redemption and to emphasise the exclusive nature and significance of the saving work accomplished by the incarnate Son of God. The "woman" has here as a single representative of the old un-redeemed humanity no sort of function to exercise in this work of salvation nor indeed any special affinity to it, for which reason she is not even mentioned by name. Nor in her capacity as wife and mother has she any such function or affinity, so that it is impossible to interpret the text as suggesting a glorification of wifehood or motherhood. We "receive adoption as sons" (vs. 5) as the sons of Eve, i.e. of the *old* Eve—and not, as the Pope insists, as sons of Mary, of the new Eve—and we receive it through the Spirit of the Son (vs. 6), who for our sakes became likewise a son of the old Eve. The text in itself gives neither occasion nor scope for the apotheosis of Mary which this dogma effects; on the contrary, the plain meaning of the text is inverted if Mary conceived as the new

[26] *Herderkorrespondenz*, p. 126.

Eve is taken to represent man co-operating in the Saviour's work of redemption, or in fact, as is sometimes said, "guaranteeing the fulfilment of this work": "the figure of Christ—let us say boldly—is not enough for us; for redemption is not accomplished by Christ the Redeemer alone and without the co-operation of man who is to be redeemed. . . . The realisation of the work of Christ is therefore in a certain sense guaranteed by the veneration which Christians give to Mary." [27] Gerhard Ebeling shows [28] that all this has its good sense and high significance from the point of view of the Catholic system of doctrine. Above all, he brings out the point that the controversy cannot concern this particular dogma in isolation: "What is here in question is something more than the dogmatisation of a miracle. What is at stake is the cornerstone in a whole ecclesiological structure. . . ."[29] There is no other dogma conceivable in which the Catholic Church could have expressed more forcefully what it believes. This Mariological dogma means that the very basis on which the edifice of Catholicism rests is exalted to the status of dogma." [30] But if we propose to use the dogma as a guide in our approach to the texts, then we find that, far from bringing out the meaning of the latter, it coerces them into saying something which is other than their intrinsic meaning. Examples of this could be increased at will, though of course the fact will not be able to shake the dogma nor to prevent the amplification of it that is expected to follow ("Mary as co-redemptrix"); for Scriptural exposition as a check on the elaboration of dogma is not taken account of in the Catholic point of view.

Now, however, we must allow the Catholic church to counter our argument with the question whether with our insistence on the ἀκοή we too have not set up in place of the ῥῆμα Χριστοῦ a doctrine of the Church, namely the doctrine of Scripture as a line of demarcation qualitatively differentiating the canon from the growth of later tradition. Have we not thus

---

[27] *Die leibliche Himmelfahrt Mariens*, Theologische Beiträge zum neuen Dogma der Seelsorge, Frankfurt am Main, 1950, p. 11; quoted in Steck, *op. cit.* (above, n. 24), p. 9.
[28] See G. Ebeling, "Zur Frage nach dem Sinn des mariologischen Dogmas," in *Z. Th. K.*, 1950, pp. 383 ff.
[29] Ebeling, *op. cit.*, p. 389.   [30] *Op. cit.*, p. 391.

essentially, and in precisely the same way, equated a human doctrinal authority with the Word of God itself, which in practice means that we have subordinated the latter to the former? We may not lightly dismiss this old Catholic objection to the "paper Pope" when we remember the development of post-Reformation dogmatics. It could hardly fail to be the case that the elaboration of dogma within the Protestant world, if only for the reason that it is encumbered with the weight of 1500 years of inherited Church tradition, is exposed to the same dangers as those to which we have drawn attention in connexion with the lines of development initiated by Tertullian and the apologists. And the challenge of the Catholic Church to ourselves must always be the question, how, with our quite different doctrine of Scripture and its relation to tradition, we propose to meet those dangers which we think Catholicism itself has gravely incurred.

(h) The endangering of Evangelical dogmatics by pura doctrina

The danger which threatens ourselves in regard to the *formal* authorisation of dogmas becomes plain if, for example, we compare the introduction to the Confession of Augsburg, I, "*Ecclesiae magno consensu apud nos docent* . . ." [31] with what the *Konkordien* formula states with regard to its attitude on disputed articles of doctrine: "*ut publicum solidumque testimonium, non modo at eos, qui nunc vivunt, sed etiam ad omnem posteritatem exstaret, ostendens, quaenam ecclesiarum nostrarum de controversis articulis unanimis fuerit esseque perpetuo debeat decisio atque sententia. . . .*" [32] The *ecclesiae* in the Confession of Augsburg understand themselves to be the congregations gathered around particular sees in various towns and countries, and through the more or less spontaneous and chance appointment of representatives expressing their agreement in matters of doctrine, whereas in the *Konkordien* formula the already consolidated Evangelical churches, territorial in character, speak through the representation of their lords and princes and the specialist theologians whom these appoint. This difference in the representation of Church consensus is, in practice, not so great, and in itself would not be of fundamental importance for the essential

[31] *Bek. Schr.*, p. 50.   [32] *Op. cit.*, p. 840.

question of the authorisation of doctrinal decisions, were it not for the fact that it led to other and more radical changes. In the first place, as regards the Lutheran Reformation, Church order did not in practice give rise to such congregations gathered to hear the preaching of the Gospel as Luther had in mind when he gave them the right to "judge doctrine." [33] In conflict with the fundamental principle of the Reformation, the Church was built up not on the basis of individual congregations but on that of the territorial Church. Therefore, in point of fact, the confessions were not drawn up as an expression of the consensus of doctrinal opinion among the various churches, but rather were imposed by the rulers of the Church under the guidance of specialist theologians, and were standardised as much as possible in order to achieve the greatest possible degree of unity among those who thought alike in matters of religion. This does not apply in the same degree to the Reformed Churches. In addition there took place a transformation in the idea of doctrine, the development of which did not proceed from the German understanding of Confession of Augsburg, VII: "For it is sufficient to ensure the unity of the Christian churches if the Gospel be preached profitably to souls in the light of a pure understanding . . .," but from the Latin understanding: *"satis est consentire de doctrina evangelii. . . ."* [34]   As Ernst Wolf puts it, "Luther's Declaration, *'Propter confessionem coetus ecclesiae est visibilis. . . Ex confessione cognoscitur ecclesia,'* is applied, as it were, to the formulated profession of doctrine! . . . To the idea of pure doctrine corresponds in fact the conception of the Church as the school of pure doctrine, a doubtful, though up to the present powerful, narrowing of the principle that the Church is the *creatura verbi*, through the interpretation of the *verbum evangelii* (as *pura doctrina*) as *doctrina de evangelio*." [35]   But in this type of thought how is it possible for Scriptural exegesis to check dogmas and to decide dogmatic controversies?   *Theoretically* it is no doubt emphasised in the *Konkordien* formula that all doctrine is to be measured by the test of Scripture.   But *in practice* this is rendered

---

[33] On the following, cp. Diem, *Theol.*, VOL. I, pp. 203 ff.

[34] On the following, cp. Diem, *Theol.*, VOL. I, pp. 248 ff.

[35] E. Wolf, "Okumenische Symbolik: Zur Aufgabe der Konfessionskunde heute," in *Peregrinatio*, 1954, p. 344.

nugatory by the fact that the conclusions of Scriptural exegesis must agree with a specific *summa doctrinae* [36]; and the ultimate verification of doctrine and Scriptural exposition by the living event of Gospel proclamation is provided for in this *"Church* as the school of pure doctrine" neither by Church order nor by Church theology.

(i) *The worship of the Church considered as a school of pure doctrine in the work of Peter Brunner*

In this connexion, it is not necessary to narrow down the conception of the school of pure doctrine to the sense of pure doctrinal activity, but the school can also be understood in the sense of Church worship, as for example Peter Brunner understands it.[37] We cannot here go into the implications of this for the form of Church worship as understood by Brunner, but will concern ourselves simply with its dogmatic basis. We may accept Brunner's point of departure, which is that Church worship is "a happening, an event," [38] and also his view that this worship "may not be limited to the cultic sphere divorced from the life of Christian obedience." [39] But as regards the "congregation of the faithful," i.e. Christian worship in the strict sense, the question must be asked how this ideal is to be fulfilled in practice, because here "man encounters the Word of God and the sacrament of Christ. Will this encounter prove of saving efficacy? Will it result in a pneumatic appropriation of the divine gift, and thus in a spirit-filled performance of the action of worship and so in the right *usus* of this sacrament?" [40] This is the question which Brunner asks and which he puts not only to the act of worship itself, but first and foremost to the doctrine of worship. For "if something false is taught or preached, or maybe nothing at all is said to the congregations and their ministers concerning what happens in the service of worship, how can there be a

[36] Cp. above, p. 225.

[37] P. Brunner, "Zur Lehre vom Gottesdienst," in *Leiturgia*, I (1954); cp. also the critical account of Manfred Mezger, *Probleme evangelischer Liturgik*, in *Arbeit und Besinnung*, 1954 pp. 162 ff., and the connected polemic: Albrecht Peters, *Noch einmal: Probleme evangelischer Liturgik, mit einem Nachwort von Manfred Metzger*, 1954, pp. 306 ff.

[38] P. Brunner, *op. cit.*, p. 111.   [39] *Op. cit.*, p. 112.

[40] *Op. cit.*, p. 113.

true spiritual application of the idea? In this event, too, the Spirit inheres in the Word. But in the service of the Word stands doctrine." [41] We notice—not without some anxiety— that the connexion of Word and Spirit is taken to apply not only to the performance of divine worship but also to the doctrine *of* divine worship, and wonder whether the fathers of the Confession of Augsburg were not better advised at this point when they made do in Arts. V and VII with the Gospel and the Holy Spirit and were careful not to formulate such a "doctrine," for which there is no basis in Scripture.

The basic requirement for all divine worship is: "God must be able to say with reference to what happens there that it is acceptable to Him. The worship of God is connected with the good pleasure of God. What is well-pleasing to God must be contained in His word and commandment. God has not in vain made known what He requires of us men. Whatever in divine worship is in conflict with this His revealed will can never be pleasing to Him. Only such worship pleases God, and therefore deserves the name which in its performance shows obedience to God's declaration of His will and plan, God's giving of tokens, and God's ordinances." [42] We wonder whether this is intended to mean anything other than what we said of the necessity for divine worship to be focussed in the ἀκοή, or what the Confession of Augsburg says: "*satis est consentire de doctrina evangelii et de administratione sacramentorum,*" in the sense "that there the Gospel is preached profitably to souls in the light of a pure understanding and the sacraments are administered according to the Word of God." Brunner probably does not primarily mean anything else, for he goes on to say that thus "everything that takes place in this act of worship is open to the light of actualised revelation which is attested and mediated to us by the mouth of Prophets and Apostles." [43] But clearly he intends to go *further* than this when he formulates his task "as a dogmatic task in the strictest sense of the word." [44] Let us notice carefully that in the fulfilment of this task it is not yet a question of the performance of divine worship, but only of a dogmatically correct doctrine of divine worship. "Our task becomes dogmatic as a result

[41] *Ibid.* [42] *Op. cit.*, p. 113.
[43] *Op. cit.*, p. 113. [44] *Op. cit.*, p. 114.

2A

of the fact that the answer to the question asked depends unconditionally on the actualised event of revelation. Only in this connexion with the Word of revelation by which the ordinance of God is disclosed to us, does a doctrine of divine worship become possible." [45]   In this respect he does not explicitly define what he means by "dogmatic," but the word is intended to suggest that we make the "doctrine of divine worship depend unconditionally on the actualised event of revelation"; and in so far as we do that "it must be orientated wholly by the living Word of God." [46]

This means that the formation of such doctrine is only possible in a concrete historical sphere, in the "concretely manifested Church of Jesus Christ, where the actualised revelation is known, admitted, attested, and expressed in the confessional word which reflects it. The nexus with the realised revelation only becomes a concrete reality where, at the same time, it includes a nexus with the present living witness to that revelation. Dogmatic teaching such as is our appointed task can therefore only be worked out in that sphere where the agreement about Gospel proclamation and adminis-tration of the sacraments according to the revelation finds effective practical expression." [47]   This means then that not only is the right performance of worship with its Gospel preaching dependent on a concrete churchly sphere, thus for instance on the Church of the *Konkordien* formula with its dogmatic decisions, but also that only in that Church can a dogmatically correct doctrine of worship be formulated. On this point Brunner thinks: "The association of dogmatic teaching with the concrete historical sphere where the Church of Jesus Christ is manifested is thus only for a detached spectator a matter of 'confessionalism'." And he shows this very simply and apodeictically: "On the contrary, for him who is a true participant, there are essentially only two possibilities in assessing truly dogmatic teaching: he will either hear therein a voice which belongs to the one holy Apostolic Church of Jesus Christ, or a heresy." [48]   But we would not call confessionalism (since Brunner has himself given us this catchword) the mere fact that such decisions are made with regard to dogmatic statements, even though in

---

[45] *Ibid.*   [46] *Ibid.*   [47] *Op. cit.*, p. 114.   [48] *Ibid.*

so doing we were not likely to be as tedious, and even though
in the concrete instance we felt it necessary to enquire first
whether there is in fact or ought to be such a thing as a "truly
dogmatic view about divine worship," of which Brunner has
by no means convinced us. We might, at a pinch, concede
also that this decision is not to be made about the hearing of
Gospel proclamation, as we would prefer to say, but in regard
to the "assessment of a truly dogmatic teaching"—if it is
really a question of such, for then the latter would have to be
reabsorbed in preaching. How far this must be the case in
regard to Brunner's dogmatic teaching about divine worship
is of course not clear to us, even though he says that these
dogmatic statements "are to express, at the same time, what
takes place in the concrete act of divine worship." [49] Even so,
they appear to us to be statements *about* divine worship; and
no one will compel us to link decisions of such scope with the
assessment of them, as Brunner wishes to do. But we would
describe it as "confessionalism," and strictly reject it, if in
practice dogmatic teaching could no longer be critically
appraised by Scripture, as we showed to be the case in regard
to the *Konkordien* formula. In this sense Brunner certainly
seems to us to be a confessionalist, with his "dogma consonant
with revelation," [50] We cannot accept what he says in his
doctrine of preaching [51] about "the substantial identity of the
Apostolic word and what is truly intended by dogma," nor
can we approve the unquestioning attitude with which he
couples together "Scripture and Scriptural confession." [52]
But since Brunner gives no real basis for dogma, and merely
mentions together "Scripture and confession" without going
into the question of their relationship, we cannot discuss the
matter with him. From our point of view, it is merely important to notice that Brunner goes considerably beyond what
we found doubtful in the *Konkordien* formula when he applies
his conception of dogma not only to preaching in Church
worship, but also to the doctrine of Church worship, and
"whether specific doctrinal opinions about Church worship
are still within the *consensus doctrinae*." [53] In any case he has
left far behind the "*satis est*" of the Confession of Augsburg,

[49] *Op. cit.*, p. 115.   [50] *Ibid.*   [51] *Op. cit.*, pp. 196 ff.
[52] *Op. cit.*, pp. 197 ff.   [53] *Op. cit.*, p. 114.

Art. VIII, by making the doctrine of worship and its true performance a part of the "*consentire de doctrina*," and thus also has completed the transformation of divine worship into a "school of pure doctrine."

(k) The Exegetical verification of the dogma concerning Holy Scripture

Thus this dangerous line of development, which as far as Catholicism is concerned we have seen begin with Tertullian and end with the Vatican decision to the effect that the promulgation of doctrine by the Roman Bishop speaking *ex cathedra* is infallible and irreformable, culminates similarly for the Evangelical Church with the decision that the doctrinal decrees of the *Konkordien* formula must be valid "*ad omnem posteritatem*." Such a principle would be impossible from the point of view of the Reformed Churches. Rather, in most of their older confessions, the express reservation is made at the same time that the confession is valid until modified in the light of a better understanding of the Scriptures.[54] Nevertheless, even for the Reformed Churches the question remains whether and in what way Scripture can in practice operate effectively as a test of dogmatic teaching; for the Biblicist procedure of Scriptural harmonisation for the purpose of doctrinal formulation is far more widely practised here than among the Lutherans,[55] and of course likewise prevents a genuine verification of doctrine by the test of Scripture.

The danger inherent in the desire to authorise the content of dogma which in Catholicism we traced from its beginnings with the apologists up to the two declarations of the Vatican Council concerning the credibility of the revelation, on the one hand, and the interdict on rationalisation of the faith, on the other, penetrated Evangelical theology, in much the same way, through the elaboration of a classical Protestant scholasticism; and here dogmatics succumbed to the danger again and again, and on similar lines, by evolving a *gnosis* of faith as the basis for a rationalist orthodoxy.[56] And to what extent

[54] Cp. K. Barth, *Wirklichkeit und Möglichkeit eines allgemeinen reformierten Glaubensbekenntnisses*, 1925, p. 314.   [55] Cp. above, p. 224.

[56] On this point, cp. esp. H. E. Weber, *Reformation, Orthodoxie, und Rationalismus*, 1940.

has Holy Scripture been able to counter this danger among Evangelicals? That is the real point with which we are concerned here.

We have seen that it could not and never can do this by means of a doctrine about Scripture assuming in some way or other the form of a *fides quae creditur*.[57] We can meet the Catholic objection to our "paper Pope" only in so far as we allow Scripture to interpret itself in a living way and allow this interpretation to be authenticated in the living event of preaching. Our whole doctrine of Scripture must in the last resort be reduced to the contingent fact of the canon as something dogmatically given. Then for *this* dogma as for all other dogmas we must accept the test of applying it as a principle of orientation to the exegesis of Scripture itself. This means that the unity of Scripture, implied as a dogmatic datum by the canonisation of Scripture, must ever anew be called in question by the exegesis of Scripture, and so the power of Scripture to interpret itself can in concrete fact mean that Scripture authenticates itself by its own self-evidencing authority. If the Evangelical Church is not prepared to rest its authority on this basis in its opposition to catholicism then it is in any event lost. It must therefore be bold enough at all times to authenticate its dogma of Scripture by the exposition of the canon of Scripture—but not the exposition of a "hermeneutical canon" as guaranteed by a "hermeneutical principle"—and by the ever-living process in which the Scriptures are proclaimed to the Church.

[57] Cp. above, p. 221.

PASSAGES FROM SCRIPTURE
CITED IN THE TEXT

ABBREVIATED TITLES USED IN CITATION
OF WORKS MENTIONED FREQUENTLY
IN THE FOOTNOTES

Anmerkungen und Fragen=H. Traub, *Anmerkungen und Fragen zur neutestamentlichen Hermeneutik und zum Problem der entmythologisierung*, 1952.

"Antwort"=F. Gogarten, "Zur Frage nach dem Ursprung des geschichtlichen Denkens: Eine Antwort an Wilhelm Kamlah," in *Ev. Th.*, 1954.

Balthasar=H. U. von Balthasar, *Karl Barth, Darstellung und Deutung seiner Theologie*, Cologne 1951.

Bed.=E. Troeltsch, *Die Bedeutung der Geschichtlichkeit Jesu für den Glauben*, Tübingen 1911.

Bek. Schr.=*Bekenntnisschrifften und Kirchenordnungen der nach Gottes Wort reformierte Kirche*, ed. W. Niesel, 1930.

Conf. Virt.=*Confessio Virtembergica: Das württembergische Bekenntnis von 1551*, ed. E. Bizer, Stuttgart 1952.

Denz.=H. Denzinger, *Enchiridion symbolorum definitionum ed declarationum de rebus fidei et morum.*

Dogmengeschichte=A. von Harnack, *Dogmengeschichte*, Freiburg 1893.

E. & K.=F. Gogarten, *Entmythologisierung und Kirche*, 1953.

Ev. Th.=*Evangelische Theologie.*

Existenzdialectik von S. K.=H. Diem, *Die Existenzdialectik von Sören Kierkegaard*, Zollikon-Zurich 1950. Eng. trans. *Kierkegaard's Dialectic of Existence*, tr. H. Knight, Edinburgh 1959.

Friedrich=G. Friedrich in Kittel, vol. iii.

Ges. Schr.=E. Troeltsch, *Gesammelte Schriften*, 1913.

Ges. Werke=*Sören Kierkegaard: Gesammelte Werke*, edd. H. Gottsched and C. Schrempf, 12 vols., Jena 1922 ff.

Jesus the Messiah=W. Manson, *Jesus the Messiah, The Synoptic Tradition of the Revelation of God in Christ, with special reference to Form-Criticism*, London 1943.

Jonas=H. Jonas, "Die hermeneutische Strucktur des Dogmas," in *Augustin und das paulinische Freiheitsproblem*, Göttingen 1930.

K.D.=K. Barth, *Die Kirchliche Dogmatik:* vols i (*Die Lehre vom Wort Gottes*).1, Munich 1932, 2, Zürich 1938; ii (*Die Lehre von Gott*).2, Zürich 1942; iii (*Die Lehre von der Schöpfung*).2, Zürich 1948; iv (*Die Lehre von der Versöhnung*).1, Zürich 1953.

Kittel=*Theologisches Worterbuch zum N.T.*, ed. G. Kittel, Stuttgart.

Kümmel=W. G. Kümmel, "Jesus und der judische Traditionsgedanke," in *Zeitschrift für die Neutestamentliche Wissenschaft*, 1933.

Lohse=E. Lohse, "Lukas als Theologe der Heilsgeschichte," in *Ev. Th.*, 1954.

372 ABBREVIATED TITLES

Lögtrup=K. E. Lögstrup, *Kierkegaards und Heideggers Existenzanalyse und ihr Verhältnis zur Verkündigung*, Berlin 1950.

"Prob."=E. Käsemann, "Probleme der Neutestamentlichen Arbeit in Deutschland," in *Die Freiheit des Evangeliums und die Ordnung der Gesellschaft*, Beiträge zur *Evangelische Theologie*, BD. XV, 1952.

Prot. Theol.=K. Barth, *Die protestantische Theologie im 19. Jahrhundert*, Zürich 1947.

Rengstorf=K. H. Rengstorf, *s.v.* διδάσκω, in Kittel, VOL. II, pp. 138 ff.

Schlier=H. Schlier, *"Kerygma* und *Sophia*, zur neutestamentlichen Grundlegung des Dogmas," in *Ev. Th.*, 1950-1.

Strathmann=H. Strathmann, in Kittel, VOL. IV, pp. 477 ff.

Th. Lit.-Z.=*Theologische Literaturzeitung.*

Theol., BD. I=H. Diem, *Theologie als Kirchliche Wissenschaft*, BD. I (*Exegese und Historie*) Munich 1952.

Theol. des N.T.=R. Bultmann, *Theologie des Neuen Testamentes*, Tübingen 1953.

Th. R.=*Theologische Rundschau.*

Verkündigung=F. Gogarten, *Die Verkündigung Jesu Christi*, 1948.

"Z. Verkündigung"=H. Traub, "Z. Verkündigung von dem verkündigungen Jesus," in *Ecclesia semper reformanda*, Munich 1952.

Zahn=T. Zahn, "Glaubensregel" in *Realencyclopaedie für protestantische Theologie und Kirche*, VOL. VI.

Z. K. G.=*Zeitschrift für Kirchengeschichte.*

Z. Th. K.=*Zeitschrift für Theologie und Kirche.*

INDEX OF NAMES